ELEMENTS OF METAPHYSICS

Professor Taylor's work has held its own for fifty years as the best comprehensive account of the main principles of metaphysics.

Starting with a section on General Notions, he goes on to study his subject under three main headings—The General Structure of Reality, The Interpretation of Nature, and the Interpretation of Life.

UNIVERSITY PAPERBACKS
U. P. 25

by the same author

PLATO: THE MAN AND HIS WORK
(also available in University Paperbacks)
PLATO: TIMAEUS AND CRITIAS

Elements of Metaphysics

A. E. TAYLOR

*Late Professor of Moral Philosophy
in the University of Edinburgh*

πατρὶς δὴ ἡμῖν ὅθενπερ ἤλθομεν καὶ πατὴρ ἐκεῖ

UNIVERSITY PAPERBACKS

METHUEN : LONDON
BARNES & NOBLE : NEW YORK

First published by Methuen & Co Ltd
in 1903 and reprinted fourteen times
First published in this series in 1961
Printed in Great Britain by
Morrison & Gibb Ltd, Edinburgh
Catalogue No 2/6775/27

*University Paperbacks are published
by* METHUEN & CO LTD
36 Essex Street, Strand, London WC2
and BARNES & NOBLE INC
105 Fifth Avenue, New York 3

TO
F. H. BRADLEY

*In heartfelt acknowledgment of all that
his example and his writings have been
to the men of my generation*

Ante Ararim Parthus bibet, aut Germania Tigrim,
Quam nostro illius labatur pectore vultus.

ELEMENTS
OF METAPHYSICS

PREFACE

IN acknowledging my indebtedness to recent writers for many of the ideas contained in the following pages, I have in the first place to express my deep and constant obligations to the various works of Mr. F. H. Bradley. My chief debt to other recent English-speaking philosophers is to Professor Royce and Professor Ward, and I am perhaps scarcely less indebted to Professor Stout. My chief obligations to Continental writers are to Avenarius and to Professor Münsterberg. I trust, however, that there is not one of the authors with whose views I have dealt in the course of my work from whom I have not learned something. At the same time I ought perhaps to say here once for all that I make no claim to represent the views of any one author or school, and I shall not be surprised if the thinkers to whom I owe most find themselves unable to endorse all that I have written.

With respect to the references given at the end of the several chapters, I may note that their aim is simply to afford the reader some preliminary guidance in the further prosecution of his studies. They make no pretence to completeness, and are by no means exclusively drawn from writers who support my own conclusions.

One or two important works of which I should have otherwise been glad to make extended use have appeared too recently for me to avail myself of them. I may mention especially the late Professor Adamson's *Lectures on the Development of Modern Philosophy*, Professor Ostwald's

Vorlesungen über Naturphilosophie, and Mr. B. Russell's *Principles of Mathematics*, vol. i.

Finally, I have to express my gratitude to my friends Professor S. Alexander and Mr. P. J. Hartog for their kindness in reading large portions of my proofs and offering many valuable corrections and suggestions.

1903

The sudden demand for a re-issue of this volume prevents my making any alterations beyond the correction of a number of misprints. Had the opportunity offered, I should have been glad, while leaving the main argument essentially as it stands, to have attempted certain improvements in details. I may mention in particular, as the most important of the changes I could have wished to make, that the treatment of the problem of infinite regress and of the Kantian antinomies would have been remodelled, and I trust improved, as a consequence of study of the works of Mr. Bertrand Russell and M. Couturat.

I should like to take this opportunity of thanking all those who have been kind enough to favour me with criticisms of the book.

St. Andrews, 1909

PREFACE TO THE SEVENTH EDITION

IT is disturbing as well as gratifying to a writer on Metaphysics that there should still be a demand for a work which he published more than twenty years ago. One cannot but be grateful for a demand which seems to prove that one's book still meets a real need, but one would have to be unusually vain not to be even more distressed than gratified. The difficulty arises from two distinct causes. In the first place, in Metaphysics as in all the other sciences, a lapse of twenty years inevitably involves a certain shifting of perspective. The fundamental questions, no doubt, remain the same from one age to another; the ultimate radically divergent answers to the metaphysical problem thus remain also in principle the same. But the point of view from which the problems are attacked varies with the age. Some of the immediate issues which were specially interesting in the years 1900–1903 have become antiquated in 1924, and new issues have been raised which could not have been contemplated when the present volume was first written. In particular, the philosophical questions suggested by the present state of the great positive sciences of physics, chemistry, and biology are, in many ways, different from those which were occupying our minds as recently as the opening of the century, and much which was then of momentary concern to the philosopher has now lost its actuality. In the second place—and this is a still more important consideration—Metaphysics, because it is an attempt to find the right intellectual attitude towards *ultimate* reality, is necessarily a more intimate and personal thing than any other human study. A good work on Metaphysics, even more than a good book on any other department of human thought, ought to be one into which the author has put the whole of himself. Now a man's self as he approaches his middle fifties ought to be different from his self in his early thirties in two ways: it should be richer and at the same time more simplified, and if his particular way of expressing himself is thinking and writing about Metaphysics, this double difference ought to make itself felt, in great and in small, throughout his treatment of his subject. It should be impossible for him to be content with any mere periodical " bringing up to date " of his earlier work.

For a goodly number of years, therefore, I have cherished the desire to rewrite the whole of the present book from start to finish. That desire I have reluctantly been driven, for the present, to relinquish, for the following reasons. The part of the book which deals with problems directly suggested by the positive sciences could only be made what it ought to be by one who is thoroughly at home with the issues raised by the scientific work of such men as, to mention only one or two prominent names, Rutherford, Planck, Niels Bohr, Weyl, Van t'Hoff, Mendel. But most of this work is so recent in date that it is quite impossible for those of us whose general education was got in the last decades of the nineteenth century ever to feel ourselves altogether at home with even the leading ideas which underlie it. What matters still more is that though one would be only too glad to bring whatever one may have gained either in richness or in simplification of personality during more than twenty years of life to bear on the whole substance of one's earlier work, the thing can only be done by an intense concentration and meditation impossible to a man who is still immersed in the business of active teaching. To do it by halves, patching

PREFACE TO THE SEVENTH EDITION

one's original book here and there with the results of still unfinished reflection, is to incur the grave danger of correcting a detected error in one direction by a graver error in the other.

I am therefore deeply indebted to the courtesy of my publishers for the opportunity of making in this *Preface* one or two remarks indicative of the points of principal importance on which, if I were now writing this book for the first time, I should like to lay more emphasis than I actually did twenty and odd years ago. If the volume is read in the light of these remarks, it will still, no doubt, contain a great deal of error, as any work on Metaphysics must, but it will at least express a view of reality which is, whatever its defects, as near the truth as I feel myself able to get.

The one thing of all others I have had it long on my conscience to say, is that I have always wished my book to be understood in a definitely theistic, indeed, in a definitely Christian sense. I have never disguised it from myself that when I speak of the " Absolute " I mean by the word precisely that simple, absolutely transcendent, source of all things which the great Christian scholastics call God. I would add that when, following the tradition of my own teachers, I speak of the " creatures " as " appearances " of the Absolute, I mean by this precisely what St. Thomas, for example, meant by the doctrine that they have being by " participation." I fear I may at times have fallen by inadvertence into statements which, if pressed, would suggest what is known as a doctrine of " immanentism." If I have done so, it has been by an oversight, and of every such slip I can now only say *indictum volo*. When the book was written I could not anticipate such developments as the " philosophies " of Croce and Gentile. Had they been actual for the English reader in 1903, I think it probable that, to avoid misunderstandings, I should have avoided such an expression as "appearances" altogether, and spoken frankly of "creatures." Even as it was, the protest against Monism as a name for the type of theory advocated in these pages was intended to express dissent from every "immanentist" philosophy of the ἓν καὶ πᾶν type. Even the name "Idealism" it will be noted, was only retained as a protest against all those forms of *outré* Realism which represent mind as something which merely happens to be included among the constituents of the "universe," but might, for all we can see, have been absent without making any difference to the rest. The use of the name was intended to affirm, what I would still affirm equally strongly, the principle that the *infinitus intellectus Dei* is the absolute *prius* of the whole world of "Nature." A Thomist, if I should have any such among my readers, will readily see that I conceive of the relation of that *intellectus* to our own on Augustinian rather than on Thomist lines, but he will also see that the Idealism I defend has nothing of importance in common with that which he regards it as his duty to combat. On all these ultimate issues I would now desire that my utterances may be judged in the light of the maturer exposition of what I feel to be at bottom the same view by Professor Bernadino Varisco in his two great works, *I Massimi Problemi* and *Conosci Te Stesso*,[1] and that my one-sidedness and deficiencies may be corrected by the aid of Professor James Ward's noble series of volumes, *Naturalism and Agnosticism, The Realm of Ends, Psychological Principles*. In view of the misapprehensions, as I must think them, to which many of Mr. Bradley's statements of his views have given rise, I wish to say that my sense of all I owe to him, even when I feel constrained to differ from him, is, if anything, deeper now than it was in 1903.

If the book were now to be written for the first time,

---

[1] English versions, *The Great Problems* and *Know Thyself*. London: George Allen.

PREFACE TO THE SEVENTH EDITION

I should, of course, have to take serious account of the kind of " logical pluralism " so ably advocated by Dr. G. E. Moore, and—in one of his many phases—by Mr. Bertrand Russell. As it is, I may perhaps be allowed to refer here to what I have written briefly about this type of philosophy in Hastings' *Encyclopaedia of Religion and Ethics*, vol. xii. (art. THEISM). Of the wilder varieties of " new realism " which have made some stir in the last fifteen or twenty years I do not suppose I should have thought it necessary to say anything at all.

Were it possible for me, as I do not think it is, profitably to rewrite the division of the book which deals with " Cosmology," I should, of course, have to take some account of the latest theories of physicists, chemists, and biologists about the structure of bodies and the determining factors in organic evolution, but I do not believe that the result would be any very fundamental modification in the main principles which I have defended. I may perhaps say that of recent works on such subjects, those which I should have more particularly tried to assimilate would have been Dr. A. N. Whitehead's two books, *The Principles of Natural Knowledge* and the *Concept of Nature*, and M. Meyerson's impressive volumes on *L'Explication dans les Sciences* (Paris, 1921). I would take this opportunity of directing my readers to all three. With all its defects, I trust the reissuing of my book may be, in the words of my old school motto, *ad gloriam Dei Optimi Maximi, in usum ecclesiae et reipublicae.*

ST. ANDREWS
February 1924

CONTENTS

BOOK I

GENERAL NOTIONS

CHAPTER I

THE PROBLEM OF THE METAPHYSICIAN

§ 1. The generality and simplicity of the metaphysical problem make it difficult to define the study. § 2. Problem is suggested by the presence of contradictions in ordinary experience. § 3. By making a distinction between reality and appearance the sciences remove some of these contradictions, but themselves lead to further difficulties of the same sort; hence the need for systematic inquiry into the meaning of the distinction between the real and the apparent, and the general character of reality as such. § 4. Metaphysics, as an inquiry into the ultimate meaning of "reality," is akin to poetry and religion, but differs from them in its scientific character, from the mathematical and experimental sciences in its method, from common scepticism in the critical nature of its methods as well as in its positive purpose. § 5. The study is difficult (*a*) because of the generality of its problems, (*b*) and because we cannot employ diagrams or physical experiments. § 6. The objection that Metaphysics is an impossibility may be shown in all its forms to rest upon self-contradictory assumptions of a metaphysical kind. § 7. The minor objections that, if possible, the science is superfluous, or at least stationary, may be met with equal ease. § 8. Metaphysics is partly akin to the mystical tendency, but differs from mysticism in virtue of its positive interest in the world of appearances, as well as by its scientific method. § 9. It agrees with logic in the generality of its scope, but differs in being concerned with the real, whereas logic is primarily concerned with the inferrible. § 10. The problems of the so-called *Theory of Knowledge* are really metaphysical   1

CHAPTER II

THE METAPHYSICAL CRITERION AND THE METAPHYSICAL METHOD

§ 1. In the principle that "Reality is not self-contradictory" we have a universal and certain criterion of reality which is not merely negative, but implies the positive assertion that reality is a consistent system. § 2. The validity of this criterion is not affected by the suggestion that it may be merely a *Logical* Law; § 3. Nor by the raising of doubt whether all our knowledge is not merely "relative," a doubt which is itself meaningless. § 4. As to the material of the system, it is experience or immediate psychical fact. § 5. It must be actual experience, not mere "possibilities" of experience; but actual experience must not be identified with "sensation." § 6. Nor must we assume that experience consists of subjects *and* their states; nor again, that it is a mere succession of "states of consciousness." § 7. The *differentia* of matter of experience is its *immediacy*, *i.e.* its combination in a single whole of the two aspects of *existence* and *content*. § 8. This union of existence and content is broken up in reflective knowledge or thought, but may be restored at a higher level. § 9. Experience further always appears to be implicitly complex in respect of its content. § 10. An adequate apprehension of reality would only be possible in the form of a complete or "pure" experience, at once all-inclusive, systematic, and direct. The problem of Metaphysics is to acertain what would be the general or formal character of such an experience, and how far the various provinces of our human experience and knowledge approximate to it. The knowledge Metaphysics can give us of the ultimate nature of reality as it would be present in a complete experience, though imperfect, is final as far as it goes. § 11. As to the method of Metaphysics, it must be *analytical*, *critical*, *non-empirical*, and *non-inductive*. It may also be called *a priori* if we carefully avoid confusing the *a priori* with the psychologically primitive. Why our method cannot be the Hegelian Dialectic 18

CHAPTER III

THE SUB-DIVISIONS OF METAPHYSICS

§ 1. The traditional sub-division of Metaphysics into *Ontology*, *Cosmology*, *Rational Psychology*, common to all the great modern constructive systems. § 2. Precise sense in which we adopt these divisions for the purposes of our own treatment of the subject. § 3. Relation of *Cosmology* and *Rational Psychology* to the empirical sciences . . 42

BOOK II

ONTOLOGY—THE GENERAL STRUCTURE OF REALITY

CHAPTER I

REALITY AND EXPERIENCE

§ 1. In a sense "reality" for each of us means that of which he must take account if his special purposes are to find fulfilment. § 2. But ultimately the world must possess a structure of which *all* purposes, each in its own way, must take account. This is the "Ultimate Reality" or "Absolute" of Metaphysics. In Metaphysics we regard it from the special standpoint of the scientific intellect. There are other legitimate attitudes towards it, *e.g.*, that of practical religion. § 3. The inseparability of reality from immediate experience involves the recognition of it as teleological and as uniquely individual. § 4. The experience within which all reality falls cannot be my own, nor yet the "collective" experience of the aggregate of conscious beings. It must be an individual experience which apprehends the totality of existence as the harmonious embodiment of a single "purpose." The nearest analogue our own life presents to such a type of experience is to be found in the satisfied insight of personal

CONTENTS

love. § 5. The experience of such an "Absolute" must not be thought of as a mere reduplication of our own, or of the scientific hypotheses by which we co-ordinate facts for the purposes of inference. § 6. Our conception is closely connected with that of Berkeley, from which it differs by the stress it lays on the purposive and selective aspect of experience. § 7. Realism, both of the Agnostic and of the Dogmatic type, is incompatible with the meaning we have been led to attach to "reality." But Agnosticism is justified in insisting on the limitations of our knowledge of Reality, and Dogmatic Realism in rejecting the identification of Reality with experience as a merely cognitive function of finite percipients. § 8. Subjectivism, according to which all that I know is states of my own "consciousness," is irreconcilable with the admitted facts of life, and arises from the psychological fallacy of "introjection" . . . 50

CHAPTER II

THE SYSTEMATIC UNITY OF REALITY

§ 1 The problem whether Reality is ultimately One or Many is inevitably suggested to us by the diverse aspects of our own direct experience of the world. The different theories may be classed, according to their solution of this problem, as Monistic, Pluralistic, and Monadistic. § 2. Pluralism starts from the presumed fact of the mutual independence of human selves, and teaches that this independence of each other belongs to all real beings. But (*a*) the independence with which experience presents us is never complete, nor the unity of the "selves" perfect. (*b*) The theory is inconsistent with the systematic character of all reality as presupposed in both knowledge and action. § 3. Monadism again makes the systematic unity of the real either an illusion or an inexplicable accident. § 4. Reality, because systematic, must be the expression of a single principle in and through a multiplicity. The unity and multiplicity must both be real, and each must necessarily involve the other. § 5. If both are to be equally real, the whole system must be a single experience, and its constituents must also be experiences. A perfect systematic whole can be neither an aggregate, nor a mechanical whole of parts, nor an organism. The whole must exist for the parts, and they for it. § 6. This may also be expressed by saying that Reality is a subject which is the unity of subordinate subjects, or an individual of which the constituents are lesser individuals. § 7. The nearest familiar analogue to such a systematic whole would be the relation between our whole "self" and the partial mental systems or lesser "selves." § 8. The nearest historic parallel to this view is to be found in Spinoza's theory of the relation of the human mind to the "infinite intellect of God". . 84

CHAPTER III

REALITY AND ITS APPEARANCES—THE DEGREES OF REALITY

§ 1. Reality being a single systematic whole, the nature of its constituent elements is only finally intelligible in the light of the whole system. Hence each of its "appearances," if considered as a whole in itself, must be more or less contradictory. § 2. But some "appearances" exhibit the structure of the whole more adequately than others, and have therefore a higher degree of reality. § 3. This conception of degree of reality may be illustrated by comparison with the successive orders of infinites and infinitesimals in Mathematics. It would be the task of a complete Philosophy to assign the contents of the world to their proper place in the series of "orders" of reality. § 4. In general any subordinate whole is real in proportion as it is a self-contained whole. And it is a self-contained whole in proportion as it is (*a*) comprehensive, (*b*) systematic; that is, a thing is real just so far as it is truly individual. § 5. The two criteria of individuality, though ultimately coincident, tend in particular cases to fall apart for our insight, owing to the limitation of human knowledge. § 6. Ultimately only the whole system of experience is completely individual, all other individuality is approximate. § 7. In other words, the whole system of experience is an infinite individual, all subordinate individuality is finite. Comparison of this position with the doctrines of Leibnitz. § 8. Recapitulatory statement of the relation of Reality to its Appearances 104

CHAPTER IV

THE WORLD OF THINGS—(1) SUBSTANCE, QUALITY, AND RELATION

§ 1. The natural or pre-scientific view of the world regards it as a plurality of "things," each possessing *qualities*, standing in *relation* to others, and interacting with them. § 2. Hence arise four problems: those of the Unity of the Thing, of Substance and Quality, of Relation, of Causality. § 3. No simple answer can be given to the question, *What is one thing?* The Unity of the Thing is one of teleological structure, and this is a matter of degree, and also largely of our own subjective point of view. § 4. *Substance and Quality*. The identification of the substance of things with their primary qualities, though useful in physical science, is metaphysically unjustifiable. § 5. Substance as an "unknowable substratum of qualities" adds nothing to our understanding of their connection. § 6. The thing cannot be a mere collection of qualities without internal unity. § 7. The conception of a thing as the law or mode of relation of its states useful but metaphysically unsatisfactory. Ultimately the many can be contained in the one only by "representation"; the unity in things must be that of an individual experience. § 8. *Relation*. We can neither reduce qualities to relations nor relations to qualities. § 9. Again, the attempt to conceive Reality as qualities in relation leads to the indefinite regress. § 10. We cannot escape this difficulty by taking all relations as "external." And Professor Royce's vindication of the indefinite regress seems to depend on the uncriticised application of the inadequate category of whole and part to ultimate Reality. The union of the one and the many in concrete experience is ultra-relational. SUPPLEMENTARY NOTE: Dr. Stout's reply to Mr. Bradley . . 120

CHAPTER V

THE WORLD OF THINGS—(2) CHANGE AND CAUSALITY

§ 1. The conception of things as interacting leads to the two problems of Change and Causality. The paradoxical character of change due to the fact that only what is permanent can change. § 2. Change is succession within an identity; this identity, like that of Substance, must be teleological, *i.e.* must be an identity of plan or end pervading the process of change. § 3. Thus all change falls under the logical

CONTENTS

category of **Ground and Consequence**, which becomes in its application to succession in time the Principle of Sufficient Reason. § 4. *Causality.* Cause—in the modern popular and scientific sense—means the ground of a change when taken to be completely contained in preceding changes. That every change has its complete ground in preceding changes is neither an axiom nor an empirically ascertained truth, but a postulate suggested by our practical needs. § 5. In the last resort the postulate cannot be true; the dependence between events cannot be one-sided. The real justification for our use of the postulate is its practical success. § 6. Origin of the conception of Cause anthropomorphic. § 7. Puzzles about Causation. (1) *Continuity.* Causation must be continuous, and yet in a continuous process there can be no distinction of cause from effect. Cause must be and yet cannot be *prior* in time to effect. § 8. (2) *The indefinite regress* in causation. § 9. (3) *Plurality of Causes.* Plurality of Causes is ultimately a logical contradiction, but in any form in which the causal postulate is of practical use it must recognise plurality. § 10. The "necessity" of the causal relation psychological and subjective. § 11. Immanent and Transeunt Causality: Consistent Pluralism must deny transeunt Causation; but cannot do so successfully. § 12. Both transeunt and immanent Causality are ultimately appearance 158

BOOK III

COSMOLOGY—THE INTERPRETATION OF NATURE

CHAPTER I

INTRODUCTORY

§ 1. Distinction between the experimental sciences and a Philosophy of Nature and Mind. The former concerned with the description, the latter with the interpretation of facts. § 2. Cosmology is the critical examination of the special characteristics of the physical order. Its main problems are: (1) The problem of the nature of Material Existence; (2) problem of the justification of the concept of the Mechanical Uniformity of Nature; (3) problems of Space and Time; (4) problem of the Significance of Evolution; (5) problem of the Place of descriptive Physical Science in the system of Human Knowledge 191

CHAPTER II

THE PROBLEM OF MATTER

§ 1. The physical order, because dependent for its perceived qualities on the sense-organs of the percipient, must be the appearance of a more ultimate reality which is non-physical. § 2. Berkeley's criticism is fatal to the identification of this reality with "material substance." The logical consequence of Berkeley's doctrine that the *esse* of sensible things is *percipi*, would be the subjectivist view that the physical order is *only* a complex of presentations. § 3. But this is clearly not the case with that part of the physical order which consists of the bodies of my fellow-men. These have an existence, as centres of feeling, over and above their existence as presentations to my senses. § 4. As the bodies of my fellows are connected in one system with the rest of the physical order, that order as a whole must have the same kind of reality which belongs to them. It must be the presentation to our sense of a system or complex of systems of experiencing subjects; the apparent absence of life and purpose from inorganic nature must be due to our inability to enter into a direct communion of interest with its members. § 5. Some consequences of this view . . . 198

CHAPTER III

THE MEANING OF LAW

§ 1. The popular conception of the physical order as exhibiting a rigid mechanical conformity to general *laws*, conflicts with our metaphysical interpretation. § 2. Our interpretation would, however, admit of the establishment of averages or approximately realised uniformities by the statistical method, which deals with occurrence *en bloc* to the neglect of their individual detail. § 3. "Uniformity" in nature is neither an axiom nor an empirically verifiable fact, but a postulate. A consideration of the methods actually employed for the establishment of such uniformities or "laws" of nature shows that we have no guarantee that actual concrete cases exhibit *exact* conformity to law. § 4. Uniformity is a *postulate* arising from our need of practical rules for the control of nature. It need not for this purpose be exact, and in point of fact our scientific formulæ are only exact so long as they remain abstract and hypothetical. They do not enable us to determine the actual course of an individual process with certainty. § 5. The concept of the physical order as *mechanical* is the abstract expression of the postulate, and is therefore essential to the empirical sciences which deal with the physical order. § 6. Consideration of the character of genuine machines suggests that the mechanical only exists as a subordinate aspect of processes which, in their full nature, are intelligent and purposive 216

CHAPTER IV

SPACE AND TIME

§ 1. Are time and space ultimately real or only phenomenal? § 2. The space and time of *perception* are limited, sensibly continuous, and consist of a quantitative element together with a *qualitative* character dependent on relation to the *here* and *now* of immediate individual feeling. § 3. *Conceptual* space and time are created from the perceptual data by a combined process of synthesis, analysis, and abstraction. § 4. They are unlimited, infinitely divisible, and there is valid positive ground for regarding them as mathematically continuous. Thus they form infinite continuous series of positions. They involve abstraction from all reference to the *here* and *now* of immediate feeling, and are thus homogeneous, *i.e.* the positions in them are indistinguishable. They are also commonly taken to be unities. § 5. Perceptual space and time cannot be ultimately real, because they involve reference to the *here* and *now* of a finite experience; conceptual space and time cannot be ultimately real, because they contain no principle of internal distinction, and are thus not individual. § 6. The attempt to take space and time as real leads to the difficulty about qualities and relations, and so to the indefinite regress. § 7. Space and time contain no principle of unity; there may be many space and time orders

CONTENTS

in the Absolute which have no spatial or temporal connection with each other. § 8. The antinomies of the infinite divisibility and extent of space and time arise from the indefinite regress involved in the scheme of qualities and relations, and are insoluble so long as the space and time construction is taken for Reality. § 9. The space and time order is an imperfect phenomenal manifestation of the logical relation between the inner purposive lives of finite individuals. Time is an inevitable aspect of finite experience. *How* space and time are transcended in the Absolute experience we cannot say . . . 241

CHAPTER V

SOME CONDITIONS OF EVOLUTION

§ 1. The concept of *evolution* an attempt to interpret natural processes in terms of individual growth. § 2. Evolution means change culminating in an end which is the result of the process and is qualitatively new. The concept is thus teleological. § 3. Evolution, being teleological, is essentially either progress or degeneration. If it is more than illusion, there must be real *ends* in the physical order. And ends can only be real as subjective interests of sentient beings which are actualised by the process of change. § 4. Thus all evolution must take place within an *individual* subject. § 5. Further, the subject of evolution must be a *finite* individual. All attempts to make "evolution" a property of the whole of Reality lead to the infinite regress. § 6. The distinction between progressive evolution and degeneration has an "objective" basis in the metaphysical distinction between higher and lower degrees of individuality. § 7. In the evolutionary process, old individuals disappear and fresh ones originate. Hence evolution is incompatible with the view that Reality consists of a plurality of ultimately independent finite individuals . 265

CHAPTER VI

THE LOGICAL CHARACTER OF DESCRIPTIVE SCIENCE

§ 1. Scientific *description* may be contrasted with philosophical or teleological *interpretation*, but the contrast is not absolute. § 2. The primary end of all scientific description is intercommunication with a view to active co-operation. Hence all such description is necessarily restricted to objects capable of being experienced in the same way by a plurality of individuals. § 3. A second end of scientific description is the *economising* of intellectual labour by the creation of *general* rules for dealing with typical situations in the environment. In the course of evolution this object becomes partially independent of the former. § 4. From the interest in formulating *general* rules arise the three fundamental postulates of physical science, the postulates of *Uniformity*, *Mechanical Law*, and *Causal Determination*. § 5. The mechanical view of physical Nature determined by these three postulates is systematically carried out only in the abstract science of *Mechanics*; hence the logical completion of the descriptive process would mean the reduction of all descriptive science to Mechanics. That the chemical, biological, and psychological sciences contain elements which cannot be reduced to mechanical terms, is due to the fact that their descriptions are inspired by æsthetic and historical as well as by primarily "scientific" interests. § 6. The analysis of such leading concepts of mechanical Physics as the Conservation of Mass and of Energy shows them to have only *relative* validity 279

BOOK IV

RATIONAL PSYCHOLOGY—THE INTERPRETATION OF LIFE

CHAPTER I

THE LOGICAL CHARACTER OF PSYCHOLOGICAL SCIENCE

§ 1. The various sciences which deal with the interpretation of human life all avail themselves of the fundamental categories of Psychology. Hence we must ask how the concepts of Psychology are related to actual experience. § 2. Psychology is a body of abstract descriptive formulæ, not a direct transcript of the individual processes of real life. It presupposes the previous construction of the physical order. § 3. The psychological conception of conscious life as a succession of "mental states" or "images" is a transformation of actual experience devised primarily to account for the experience of other subjects, and subsequently extended to my own. The transformation is effected by the hypothesis of "introjection." §§ 4, 5. The logical justification of the psychological transformation of facts is twofold. The psychological scheme serves partly to fill up the gaps in our theories of physiological Mechanism, and also, in respect of the teleological categories of Psychology, to describe the course of human conduct in a form capable of ethical and historical appreciation. Psychology may legitimately employ both mechanical and teleological categories. § 6. The objections sometimes brought against the possibility of (*a*) psychological, (*b*) teleological description are untenable 294

CHAPTER II

THE PROBLEM OF SOUL AND BODY

§ 1. The problem of psychophysical connection has to do with the correlation of scientific abstractions, not of given facts of experience. § 2. The "consciousness" of Psychology is thus not the same thing as the finite individual subject of experience, and Reality must not be said to consist of "minds" in the psychologist's sense. Again, we must not assume *a priori* that there can be only *one* working hypothesis of psychophysical connection. § 3. The possible hypotheses may be reduced to three, Epiphenomenalism, Parallelism, and Interaction. § 4. *Epiphenomenalism* is legitimate as a methodological principle in Physiology; it is untenable as a basis for Psychology because it implies the reduction of psychical facts to mechanical law. § 5. *Parallelism*. The arguments for Parallelism as necessarily valid to Psychophysics because of its congruity with the postulates of mechanical Physics, are fallacious. We cannot assume that Psychology must necessarily conform to these postulates. § 6. As a working hypothesis Parallelism is available for many purposes, but breaks down when we attempt to apply it to the case of the initiation of fresh purposive reactions. A teleological and a mechanical series cannot ultimately be "parallel." § 7. We are thus thrown back on the hypothesis of *Interaction* as the only one which affords a consistent scheme for the correlation of Physiology and Psychology. We have, however, to remember that what the hypothesis correlates is scientific symbols, not actual facts. The actuality represented by both sets of symbols is the same thing, though the psychological symbolism affords a wider and more adequate representation of it than the physiological . . . 313

CHAPTER III

THE PLACE OF THE "SELF" IN REALITY

§ 1. The "self" is (1) a teleological concept, (2) implies a contrasted not-self (where this contrast is absent from an experience there is no genuine sense of self); (3) but the limits which divide self and not-self are not fixed but fluctuating. The not-self is not a merely external limit, but consists of discordant elements within the individual, which are extruded from it by a mental construction. (4) The self is a product of development, and has its being in the time-series. (5) The self is never given complete in a moment of actual experience, but is an ideal construction; probably self-hood implies some degree of *intellectual* development. § 2. The Absolute or Infinite Individual, being free from all internal discord, can have no not-self, and therefore cannot properly be called a self. § 3. Still less can it be a person. § 4. In a *society* of selves we have a more genuinely self-determined individual than in the single self. Hence it would be nearer the truth to think of the Absolute as a Society, though no finite whole adequately expresses the Absolute's full nature. We must remember, however, (*a*) that probably the individuals in the Absolute are not all in *direct* relation, and (*b*) that in thinking of it as a Society we are not denying its real individuality. § 5. The self is not in its own nature imperishable; as to the particular problem of its continuance after death, no decision can be arrived at on grounds of Metaphysics. Neither the negative presumption drawn from our inability to understand the conditions of continuance, nor the lack of empirical evidence, is conclusive; on the other hand, there is not sufficient metaphysical reason for taking immortality as certain **334**

CHAPTER IV

THE PROBLEM OF MORAL FREEDOM

§ 1. The metaphysical problem of free will has been historically created by extra-ethical difficulties, especially by theological considerations in the early Christian era, and by the influence of mechanical scientific conceptions in the modern world. §§ 2, 3. The analysis of our moral experience shows that true "freedom" means teleological determination. Hence to be "free" and to "will" are ultimately the same thing. Freedom or "self-determination" is genuine but limited, and is capable of variations of degree. § 4. *Determinism* and *Indeterminism* both arise from the false assumption that the mechanical postulate of *causal* determination by antecedents is an ultimate fact. The question then arises whether mental events are an exception to the supposed principle. § 5. *Determinism*. The determinist arguments stated. § 6. They rest partly upon the false assumption that mechanical determination is the one and only principle of rational connection between facts; § 7. Partly upon fallacious theories of the actual procedure of the mental sciences. Fallacious nature of the argument that complete knowledge of character and circumstances would enable us to predict human conduct. The assumed data are such as, from their own nature, could not be known *before the event*. § 8. *Indeterminism*. The psychical facts to which the indeterminist appeals do not warrant his conclusion, which is, moreover, metaphysically absurd, as involving the denial of rational connection. § 9. Both doctrines agree in the initial error of confounding teleological unity with causal determination **359**

CHAPTER V

SOME METAPHYSICAL IMPLICATIONS OF ETHICS AND RELIGION

§ 1. If Reality is a harmonious system, it must somehow make provision for the gratification of our ethical, religious, and æsthetic interests. § 2. But we cannot assume that ethical and religious postulates are necessarily *true* in the forms in which our practical interests lead us to make them. § 3. Thus, while morality would become impossible unless on the whole there is coincidence between virtue and happiness, and unless social progress is a genuine fact, "perfect virtue," "perfect happiness," "infinite progress" are logically self-contradictory concepts. § 4. But this does not impair the practical usefulness of our ethical ideals. § 5. In religion we conceive of the ideal of perfection as already existing in individual form. Hence ultimately no part of the temporal order can be an adequate object of religious devotion. § 6. This leads to the *Problem of Evil*. "God" cannot be a finite being within the Absolute, because, if so, God must contain evil and imperfection as part of His nature, and is thus *not* the already existing realisation of the ideal. § 7. This difficulty disappears when we identify "God" with the Absolute, because in the Absolute evil can be seen to be mere illusory appearance. It may, however, be true that religious feeling, to be practically efficient, may need to imagine its object in an ultimately incorrect anthropomorphic form. § 8. The existence, within the Absolute, of finite "divine" personalities, can neither be affirmed nor denied on grounds of general Metaphysics. § 9. Proofs of the "being of God." The principle of the "ontological" and "cosmological" proofs can be defended against the criticism of Hume and Kant only if we identify God with the Absolute. The "physicotheological proof" could only establish the reality of finite superhuman intelligences, and its force depends purely upon empirical considerations of evidence 381

CHAPTER VI

CONCLUSION

§ 1. Can our Absolute Experience be properly called the "union of Thought and Will"? The Absolute is certainly the final realisation of our intellectual and our practical ideals. But (1) it includes aspects, such as, *e.g.*, æsthetic feeling, pleasure, and pain, which are neither Thought nor Will. (2) And it cannot possess either Thought or Will *as such*. Both Thought and Will, in their own nature, presuppose a Reality which transcends *mere* Thought and *mere* Will. § 2. Our conclusion may in a sense be said to involve an element of Agnosticism, and again of Mysticism. But it is only agnostic in holding that we do not know the precise nature of the Absolute Experience. It implies no distrust of the validity of knowledge, so far as it goes, and bases its apparently agnostic result on the witness of knowledge itself. Similarly, it is mystical in transcending, not in refusing to recognise, the constructions of understanding and will. § 3. Metaphysics adds nothing to our information, and yields no fresh springs of action. It is finally only justified by the persistency of the impulse to speculate on the nature of things as a whole 408

INDEX 417

ELEMENTS OF METAPHYSICS

BOOK I

GENERAL NOTIONS

CHAPTER I

THE PROBLEM OF THE METAPHYSICIAN

§ 1. The generality and simplicity of the metaphysical problem make it difficult to define the study. § 2. Problem is suggested by the presence of contradictions in ordinary experience. § 3. By making a distinction between reality and appearance the sciences remove some of these contradictions, but themselves lead to further difficulties of the same sort; hence the need for systematic inquiry into the meaning of the distinction between the real and the apparent, and the general character of reality as such. § 4. Metaphysics, as an inquiry into the ultimate meaning of "reality," is akin to poetry and religion, but differs from them in its scientific character, from the mathematical and experimental sciences in its method, from common scepticism in the critical nature of its methods as well as in its positive purpose. § 5. The study is difficult (*a*) because of the generality of its problems, (*b*) and because we cannot employ diagrams or physical experiments. § 6. The objection that Metaphysics is an impossibility may be shown in all its forms to rest upon self-contradictory assumptions of a metaphysical kind. § 7. The minor objections that, if possible, the science is superfluous, or at least stationary, may be met with equal ease. § 8. Metaphysics is partly akin to the mystical tendency, but differs from mysticism in virtue of its positive interest in the world of appearances, as well as by its scientific method. § 9. It agrees with logic in the generality of its scope, but differs in being concerned with the real, whereas logic is primarily concerned with the inferrible. § 10. The problems of the so-called *Theory of Knowledge* are really metaphysical.

§ 1. IT is always difficult, in treating of any branch of knowledge, to put before the beginner a correct preliminary notion of the nature and scope of the study to which he is to be introduced, but the difficulty is exceptionally great in the case of the body of investigations traditionally known as Metaphysics.[1] The questions which the science seeks to answer are, indeed, in principle of the simplest and most familiar kind, but it is their very simplicity and familiarity

[1] The name simply means "what comes after Physics," and probably owes its origin to the fact that early editors of Aristotle placed his writings on ultimate philosophical questions immediately after his physical treatises.

which constitute the chief difficulty of the subject. We are naturally slow to admit that there is anything we do not understand in terms and ideas which we are constantly using, not only in the special sciences, but in our non-systematised everyday thought and language about the course of the world. Hence, when the metaphysician begins to ask troublesome questions about the meaning and validity of these common and familiar notions, ordinary practical men, and even intelligent students of the special sciences, are apt to complain that he is wasting his time by raising idle and uncalled-for difficulties about the self-evident. Consequently the writer on Metaphysics is almost inevitably compelled to begin by rebutting the natural and current prejudice which regards his science as non-existent and its problems as illusory. The full vindication of metaphysical inquiry from this charge of futility can only be furnished by such a systematic examination of the actual problems of the study as will be attempted, in outline, in the succeeding chapters of this work. All that can be done in an Introduction is to present such a general description of the kind of questions to be subsequently discussed, and their relation to the more special problems of the various sciences, as may incline the reader to give an impartial hearing to what is to follow.

§ 2. The course of our ordinary experience, as well as our education in the rudiments of the sciences, has made us all familiar with the distinction between what really *is* or *exists* and what merely *appears* to be. There is no opposition more thoroughly enshrined in the language and literature of civilised races than the contrast of *seeming* with *reality*, of *substance* with *show*. We come upon it alike in our study of the processes of nature and our experience of human character and purpose. Thus we contrast the seeming stability of the earth with its real motion, the seeming continuity and sameness of a lump of solid matter with the real discontinuity and variety of its chemical constituents, the seeming friendliness of the hypocritical self-seeker with his real indifference to our welfare. In all these cases the motive which leads us to make the distinction is the same, namely, the necessity to escape from the admission of a contradiction in experience. So long as our various direct perceptions are not felt to conflict with one another, we readily accept them all as equally real and valid, and no question arises as to their relative truth or falsehood. Were all our perceptions of this kind, there would be no need for the correction, by subsequent reflection, of our first immediate impressions about the nature of ourselves and the world; error would be a term of no meaning for us, and science would have no existence. But when two immediate perceptions, both apparently equally authenticated by our senses, stand in direct conflict with one another,[1] we cannot, without doing violence to the fundamental law of rational thinking, regard both as equally and in the same sense true. Unless we abandon once for all the attempt to reconcile the course of our experience with the demand of our intellect for consistency in thinking, we are driven to make a momentous distinction. We have to recognise that things are not always what they seem to be; what appears to us is, sometimes at any rate, not real, and what really is does not always appear. Of our two conflicting perceptions, only one at best can be a correct representation of the real course of things; one of them at least, and possibly both, must be mere seeming or appearance, and we are thus cast upon the problem which every science tries, in its own sphere and its own way, to solve: what part of our conceptions about the world gives us reality and what part only appearance?[2] It is because of the importance of these puzzles of immediate perception as stimulating to such scientific reflection that Plato and Aristotle called philosophy the child of Wonder, and it is because the processes of change present them in a peculiarly striking form that the problem of change has always been a central one in Metaphysics.

§ 3. The attempt to harmonise by reflection the contradictions which beset immediate perception in all its forms is one which is not confined to a single science; the common task of all sciences is to say what, in some special department and for special purposes, must be taken as reality and what as mere appearance, and, by degrading the contradictory to the level of appearance, to satisfy the instinctive demand of our intellect for coherency and consistency of thought. But the development of scientific reflection itself in its turn, while it solves some of our difficulties, is constantly giving

---

[1] For an example of these puzzles, compare the passage (*Republic*, 524) where Plato refers to cases in which an apparent contradiction in our sensations is corrected by *counting*.

[2] Of course we must not assume that "*every* appearance is *only* appearance," or that "nothing is both reality and appearance." This is just the uncritical kind of preconception which it is the business of Metaphysics to test. Whether "every appearance is only appearance" is a point we shall have to discuss later.

rise to fresh perplexities of a higher order. Our scientific principles themselves frequently seem to present us with contradictions of a peculiarly distressing kind. Thus we find ourselves forced in some of our geometrical reasonings to treat a curve as absolutely continuous, in others to regard it as made up of a number of points. Or, again, we are alternately compelled to regard the particles of matter as inert and only capable of being moved by impact from without, and yet again as endowed with indwelling "central forces." Both the opposing views, in such a case, clearly cannot be ultimately true, and we are therefore compelled either to give up the effort to think consistently, or to face the question, Is either view ultimately true, and if so, which? Again, the principles of one branch of study may appear to contradict those of another. For instance, the absolute determination of every movement by a series of antecedent movements which we assume as a principle in our mechanical science, appears, at least, to conflict with the freedom of human choice and reality of human purpose which are fundamental facts for the moralist and the historian; and we have thus once more to ask, which of the two, mechanical necessity or intelligent freedom, is the reality and which the mere appearance? Finally, the results of our scientific reflection sometimes seem to be in violent disagreement with our deepest and most characteristic aspirations and purposes, and we cannot avoid the question, which of the two have the better title to credit as witnesses to the inmost nature of reality?

In all these cases of perplexity there are, short of the refusal to think about our difficulties at all, only two courses open to us. We may answer the question at haphazard and as it suits our momentary caprice, or we may try to answer it on an intelligible principle. If we choose the second course, then clearly before we formulate our principle we must undertake a systematic and impartial inquiry as to what we really mean by the familiar distinction between "seems" and "is," that is to say, a scientific inquiry into the general characteristics by which reality or real being is distinguished from mere appearance, not in some one special sphere of study, but universally. Now, such an inquiry into the general character of reality, as opposed to more or less unreal appearance, is precisely what is meant by Metaphysics. Metaphysics sets itself, more systematically and universally than any other science, to ask what, after all, is meant by being *real*, and to what degree our various scientific and non-scientific theories about the world are in harmony with the universal characteristics of real existence. Hence Metaphysics has been called "an attempt to become aware of and to doubt all preconceptions"; and again, "an unusually resolute effort to think consistently." As we cannot, so long as we allow ourselves to think at all, avoid asking these questions as to what "is" and what only "seems," it is clear that the attempt to dispense with metaphysical speculation altogether would be futile. We have really no choice whether we shall form metaphysical hypotheses or not, only the choice whether we shall do so consciously and in accord with some intelligible principle, or unconsciously and at random.

§ 4. Our preliminary account of the general character of the metaphysician's problem will enable us to distinguish Metaphysics from some other closely related forms of human thought, and to give it at least a provisional place in the general scheme of knowledge. (*a*) Clearly, Metaphysics, as an inquiry into the meaning of reality, will have some affinity with religion as well as with imaginative literature, both of which aim at getting behind mere appearances and interpreting the reality which lies beneath them. In one important respect its relation to both is closer than that of any other department of knowledge,—inasmuch as it, like them, is directly concerned with *ultimate* reality, whereas the special sciences deal each with some one particular aspect of things, and avowedly leave all ultimate questions on one side. Where it differs from both is in its spirit and method. Unlike religion and imaginative literature, Metaphysics deals with the ultimate problems of existence in a purely scientific spirit; its object is *intellectual* satisfaction, and its method is not one of appeal to immediate intuition or unanalysed feeling, but of the critical and systematic analysis of our conceptions. Thus it clearly belongs, in virtue of its spirit and method, to the realm of science. (*b*) Yet it differs widely in method from the other types of science with which most of us are more familiar. It differs from the mathematical sciences in being non-quantitative and non-numerical in its methods. For we cannot employ the numerical and quantitative methods of Mathematics except on things and processes which admit of measurement, or, at least, of enumeration, and it is for Metaphysics itself, in the course of its investigations, to decide whether what is ultimately real, or any part of it, is numerical or quantitative, and if so, in what sense. It differs, again, from the experimental sciences in that, like Logic and Ethics, it does nothing to increase the stock of our knowledge of particular facts or events, but merely discusses the way in which facts or events are to be interpreted if we wish to think consistently. Its question is not what in detail we must regard as the reality of any special set of processes, but what are the *general* conditions to which all reality, as such, conforms. (Just in the same way, it will be remembered, Logic does not discuss the worth of the evidence for particular scientific theories, but the general conditions to which evidence must conform if it is to prove its conclusion.) Hence Aristotle correctly called Metaphysics a science of being *quà* being, ὄντα ᾗ ὄντα, (as opposed, for instance, to Mathematics, which only studies existence in so far as it is quantitative or numerical).

Again, as an attempt to discover and get rid of baseless preconceptions about reality, Metaphysics may, in a sense, be said to be "sceptical." But it differs profoundly from vulgar scepticism both in its method and in its moral purpose. The method of vulgar scepticism is *dogmatic*,—it takes it for granted without inquiry that two perceptions or two speculative principles which conflict with one another must be equally false. Because such contradictions can be detected in all fields of knowledge and speculation, the sceptic dogmatically assumes that there is no means of getting behind these contradictory appearances to a coherent reality. For the metaphysician, on the contrary, the assumption that the puzzles of experience are insoluble and the contradictions in our knowledge irreconcilable is itself just one of those preconceptions which it is the business of his study to investigate and test. Until after critical examination, he refuses to pronounce which of the conflicting views is true, or, supposing both false, whether one may not be nearer the truth than the other. If he does not assume that truth can be got and reality known by our human faculties, he does at any rate assume that it is worth our while to make the attempt, and that nothing but the issue can decide as to its chances of success. Again, the metaphysician differs from the sceptic in respect of moral purpose. Both in a sense preach the duty of a "suspense of judgment" in the face of ultimate problems. The difference is that the sceptic treats "suspense," and the accompanying mental indolence, as an end in itself; the metaphysician regards it as a mere preliminary to his final object, the attainment of determinate truth.

§ 5. We can now see some of the reasons which make

THE PROBLEM OF THE METAPHYSICIAN

the science of Metaphysics a peculiarly difficult branch of study. It is difficult, in the first place, from the very simplicity and generality of its problems. There is a general conviction that every science, if it is to be anything more than a body of disputes about mere words, must deal with some definite subject-matter, and it is not easy to say precisely *what* is the subject dealt with by the metaphysician. In a certain sense this difficulty can only be met by admitting it; it is true, as we have already seen, that Metaphysics deals in some way with everything; thus it is quite right to say that you cannot specify any particular class of objects as its exclusive subject-matter. This must not, however, be understood to mean that Metaphysics is another name for the whole body of the sciences. What it does mean is that precisely because the distinction between the real and the apparent affects every department of our knowledge and enters into every one of the special sciences, the general problem as to the meaning of this distinction and the principle on which it rests cannot be dealt with by any one special science, but must form the subject of an independent inquiry. The parallel with Logic may perhaps help to make this point clearer. It is just because the principles of reasoning and the rules of evidence are, in the last resort, the same for all the sciences, that they have to be made themselves the subject of a separate investigation. Logic, like Metaphysics, deals with everything, not in the sense of being another name for the whole of our knowledge, but in the sense that it, unlike the special sciences, attacks a problem which confronts us in every exercise of our thought. The question of the difference between the two sciences will be discussed in a later section of this chapter.

There are two other minor sources of difficulty, arising out of the universality of the metaphysical problem, which ought perhaps to be mentioned, as they present a serious obstacle to the study of Metaphysics by minds of a certain stamp. In Metaphysics we have no such helps to the imagination as the figures and diagrams which are so useful in many branches of Mathematics; and again, we are, by the nature of the problem, entirely cut off from the aid of physical experiment. All our results have to be reached by the unassisted efforts of thought in the strictest sense of the word, that is, by the rigid and systematic mental analysis of conceptions. Thus Metaphysics stands alone among the sciences, or alone with Logic, in the demand it makes on the student's capacity for sheer hard continuous thought.

This may help to explain why men who are capable of excellent work in the domain of mathematical or experimental science sometimes prove incompetent in Metaphysics; and again, why eminent metaphysical ability does not always make its possessor a sound judge of the results and methods of the other sciences.

§ 6. It is now time to consider one or two objections which are very commonly urged against the prosecution of metaphysical studies. It is often asserted, either that (1) such a science is, in its very nature, an impossibility; or (2) that, if possible, it is useless and superfluous, since the other sciences together with the body of our practical experience give us all the truth we need; or, again, (3) that at any rate the science is essentially unprogressive, and that all that can be said about its problems has been said long ago. Now, if any of these popular objections are really sound, it must clearly be a waste of time to study Metaphysics, and we are therefore bound to discuss their force before we proceed any further.

(1) To the objection that a science of Metaphysics is, from the nature of the case, impossible, it would be in principle correct to reply that, as the proverb says, "You never can tell till you try," and that few, if any, of those who urge this objection most loudly have ever seriously made the trial. If any one thinks the task not worth his while, he is not called on to attempt it; but his opinion gives him no special claim to sit in judgment on those who think differently of the matter. Still, the anti-metaphysical prejudice is so common, and appears in so many different forms, that it is necessary to exhibit its groundlessness rather more in detail.

(*a*) It is sometimes maintained that Metaphysics is an impossibility because the metaphysician's problems, in their own nature, admit of no solution. To a meaningless question, of course, there can be no intelligible answer, and it is occasionally asserted, and often insinuated, that the questions of Metaphysics are of this kind. But to call the metaphysician's question a senseless one is as much as to say that there is no meaning in the distinction, which we are all constantly making, between the real and the apparent. If there is any meaning at all in the distinction, it is clearly a necessary as well as a proper question precisely by what marks the one may be distinguished from the other. Our right to raise this question can in fairness only be challenged by an opponent who is prepared to maintain that the contradictions which lead us to make the distinction may themselves be the ultimate truth about things. Now, whether this view is defensible or not, it is clearly not one which we have the right to assume without examination as self-evident; it is itself a metaphysical theory of first principles, and would have to be defended, if at all, by an elaborate metaphysical analysis of the meaning of the concepts "truth" and "reality." Again, the objection, if valid, would tell as much against experimental and mathematical science as against Metaphysics. If the self-contradictory can be true, there is no rational ground for preferring a coherent scientific theory of the world to the wildest dreams of superstition or insanity. Thus we have no escape from the following dilemma. Either there is no rational foundation at all for the distinction between reality and appearance, and then all science is an illusion, or there is a rational foundation for it, and then we are logically bound to inquire into the principle of the distinction, and thus to face the problems of Metaphysics.[1]

(*b*) What is essentially the same objection is sometimes put in the following form. Metaphysics, it is said, can have no place in the scheme of human knowledge, because all intelligible questions which we can ask about reality must fall within the province of one or other of the "sciences." There are no facts with which some one or other of the sciences does not deal, and there is therefore no room for a series of "metaphysical" inquiries over and above those inquiries which constitute the various sciences. Where there are facts to investigate and intelligible questions to be put, we are, it is contended, in the domain of "science"; where there are none, there can be no knowledge. Plausible as this argument can be made to appear, it is easy to see that it is fallacious. From the point of view of pure Logic it manifestly contains a flagrant fallacy of *petitio principii*. For it simply assumes that there is no "science," in the most universal acceptation of the term—*i.e.* no body of reasoned truth—besides those experimental sciences which have for their object the accumulation and systematisation of facts, and this is the very point at issue between the metaphysician and his critics. What the metaphysician asserts is not that there are facts with which the various special branches of experimental science cannot deal, but that there are questions which can be and ought to be raised about the facts with which they do deal other than those which experimental inquiry can solve. Leaving it entirely to the special sciences to tell us what in particular are the true

[1] Cf. F. H. Bradley, *Appearance and Reality*, pp. 1-4.

facts about any given part of the world's course, he contends that we still have to ask the more general question, what we mean by "real" and "fact," and how in general the "real" is to be distinguished from the unreal. To denounce the raising of this question as an attempt to exclude certain events and processes from the "province of science," is simply to misrepresent the issue at stake. Incidentally it may be added, the objection reveals a serious misunderstanding of the true principle of distinction between different sciences. The various sciences differ primarily, not as dealing with different *parts* of the world of reality, but as dealing with the whole of it so far as it can be brought under different *aspects*. They are different, not because they deal with different sets of facts, but because they look at the facts from different points of view. Thus it would be quite wrong to suppose that the difference between, *e.g.*, Physics, Physiology, and Psychology, is primarily that each studies a different group of facts. The facts studied may in great part be the same; it is the point of view from which they are regarded by which each of the three sciences is distinguished from the others. Thus every voluntary movement may be looked at either as a link in a series of displacements of mass-particles (Physics), as a combination of muscular contractions initiated from a centre in the cortex of the brain (Physiology), or as a step to the satisfaction of a felt want (Psychology). So Metaphysics does not profess to deal with a certain group of facts lying outside the province of the "sciences," but to deal with the same facts which form that province from a point of view which is not that of the experimental sciences. Its claim to do so can only be overthrown by proving what the criticism we are considering assumes, that there is no intelligible way of looking at the facts besides that of experimental science.

(*c*) More commonly still the intrinsic intelligibility of the metaphysician's problem is admitted, but our power to solve it denied. There may be, it is said, realities which are more than mere appearance, but at any rate with our human faculties we can know nothing of them. All our knowledge is strictly limited to appearances, or, as they are often called, *phenomena*.[1] What lies behind them is completely inaccess-

[1] I may be pardoned for reminding the reader who may be new to our subject, that "facts" and "processes" are only properly called *phenomena* when it is intended to imply that as they stand they are *not* genuine realities but only the partially misleading appearance of reality which is non-phenomenal or ultra-phenomenal. (We shall do well to avoid the pretentious error of calling the ultra-phenomenal, *as such*, "*noumenal*.")

ible to us, and it is loss of time to speculate about its nature. We must therefore content ourselves with the discovery of general laws or uniformities of the interconnection of phenomena, and dismiss the problem of their real ground as insoluble. This doctrine, technically known as Phenomenalism, enjoys at the present time a widespread popularity, which is historically very largely due to an imperfect assimilation of the negative element in the philosophy of Kant. Its merits as a philosophical theory we may leave for later consideration; at present we are only concerned with it as the alleged ground of objection against the possibility of a science of Metaphysics. As such it has really no cogency whatever. Not only do the supporters of the doctrine constantly contradict their own cardinal assumption (as, for instance, when they combine with the assertion that we can know nothing about ultimate reality, such assertions as that it is a certain and ultimate truth that all "phenomena" are connected by general laws, or that "the course of nature is, without exception, uniform"), but the assumption itself is self-contradictory. The very statement that "we know only phenomena" has no meaning unless we know at least enough about ultimate realities to be sure that they are unknowable. The phenomenalist is committed to the recognition of at least one proposition as an absolute and ultimate truth, namely, the proposition, "I know that whatever I know is mere appearance." And this proposition itself, whatever we may think of its value as a contribution to Philosophy, is a positive theory as to first principles the truth or falsity of which is a proper subject for metaphysical investigation. Thus the arguments by which it has been sought to demonstrate the impossibility of Metaphysics themselves afford unimpeachable evidence of the necessity for the scientific examination of the metaphysical problem.[1]

§ 7. With the other two anti-metaphysical contentions referred to at the beginning of the last section we may deal much more briefly. (2) To the objector who maintains that Metaphysics, if possible, still is useless, because the sciences and the practical experience of life between them already supply us with a coherent theory of the world, devoid of contradictions, we may reply: (a) The fact is doubtful. For, whatever may be said by the popularisers of science when they are engaged in composing metaphysical theories for the multitude, the best representatives of every special branch

[1] *Appearance and Reality*, chap. 12, p. 129 (ed. 1).

of mathematical and experimental science seem absolutely agreed that ultimate questions as to first principles are outside the scope of their sciences. The scope of every science, they are careful to remind us, is defined by certain initial assumptions, and what does not fall under those assumptions must be treated by the science in question as non-existent. Thus Mathematics is in principle restricted to dealing with the problems of number and quantity; whether there are realities which are in their own nature non-numerical and non-quantitative[1] or not, the mathematician, as mathematician, is not called upon to pronounce; if there are such realities, his science is by its initial assumptions debarred from knowing anything of them. So again with Physics; even if reduced to pure Kinematics, it deals only with displacements involving the dimensions of length and time, and has no means of ascertaining whether or not these dimensions are exhibited by all realities. The notion that the various sciences of themselves supply us with a body of information about ultimate reality is thus, for good reasons, rejected by their soundest exponents, who indeed are usually so impressed with the opposite conviction as to be prejudiced in favour of the belief that the ultimately real is unknowable. (*b*) Again, as we have already seen, the results of physical science, and the beliefs and aspirations which arise in the course of practical experience and take shape in the teachings of poetry and religion, often appear to be in sharp antagonism. "Science" frequently seems to point in one direction, our deepest ethical and religious experience in another. We cannot avoid asking whether the contradiction is only apparent or, supposing it real, what degree of authority belongs to each of the conflicting influences. And, apart from a serious study of Metaphysics, this question cannot be answered. (*c*) Even on the most favourable supposition, that there is no such contradiction, but that science and practical experience together afford a single ultimately coherent theory of the world, it is only after we have ascertained the general characteristics of ultimate reality, and satisfied ourselves by careful analysis that reality, as conceived in our sciences, possesses those characteristics, that we have the right to pronounce our theory finally true. If Metaphysics should turn out in the end to present no fresh view as to the nature of the real, but only to confirm an old one, we should still, as meta-

---

[1] As, for instance, all mental states are, according to certain psychologists, non-quantitative.

THE PROBLEM OF THE METAPHYSICIAN

physicians, have the advantage of knowing where we were previously only entitled to conjecture.

(3) The charge of unprogressiveness often brought against our science is easily disproved by careful study of the History of Philosophy. The problems of the metaphysician are no doubt, in a sense, always the same; but this is equally true of the problems of any other science. The methods by which the problems are attacked and the adequacy of the solutions they receive vary, from age to age, in close correspondence with the general development of science. Every great metaphysical conception has exercised its influence on the general history of science, and, in return, every important movement in science has affected the development of Metaphysics. Thus the revived interest in mechanical science, and the great progress made in that branch of knowledge which is so characteristic of the seventeenth century, more than anything else determined the philosophical method and results of Descartes; the Metaphysics of Leibnitz were profoundly affected by such scientific influences as the invention of the calculus, the recognition of the importance of *vis viva* in dynamics, the contemporary discoveries of Leuwenhoeck in embryology; while, to come to our own time, the metaphysical speculation of the last half-century has constantly been revolving round the two great scientific ideas of the conservation of energy and the origin of species by gradual differentiation. The metaphysician could not if he would, and would not if he could, escape the duty of estimating the bearing of the great scientific theories of his time upon our ultimate conceptions of the nature of the world as a whole. Every fundamental advance in science thus calls for a restatement and reconsideration of the old metaphysical problems in the light of the new discovery.[1]

§ 8. This introductory chapter is perhaps the proper place for a word on the relation of Metaphysics to the widely diffused mental tendency known as Mysticism.[2] Inasmuch as the fundamental aim of the mystic is to penetrate behind the veil of appearance to some ultimate and abiding reality, there is manifestly a close community of purpose between him and the metaphysician. But their diversity of method is no less marked than their partial community of purpose.

---

[1] The student will find Höffding's *History of Modern Philosophy* (English translation in 2 vols., Macmillan) particularly valuable for the way in which the author brings out the intimate historical connection between the development of Metaphysics and the general progress of science.

[2] For further discussion the reader may be referred to Royce, *The World and the Individual*, First Series, Lects. 2 and 4. See also *infra*, Bk. IV. chap. 6, § 2.

Once in touch with his reality, wherever he may find it, the mere mystic has no longer any interest in the world of appearance. Appearance as such is for him merely the untrue and ultimately non-existent, and the peculiar emotion which he derives from his contemplation of the real depends for its special quality on an ever-present sense of the contrast between the abiding being of the reality and the non-entity of the appearances. Thus the merely mystical attitude towards appearance is purely negative. The metaphysician, on the contrary, has only half completed his task when he has, by whatever method, ascertained the general character of the real as opposed to the merely apparent. It still remains for him to re-examine the realm of appearance itself in the light of his theory of reality, to ascertain the relative truth which partial and imperfect conceptions of the world's nature contain, and to arrange the various appearances in the order of their varying approximation to truth. He must show not only what are the marks of reality, and why certain things which are popularly accepted as real must, for Philosophy be degraded to the rank of appearance, but also how far each appearance succeeds in revealing the character of the reality which is its ground. Equally marked is the difference between the mystic's and the metaphysician's attitude towards ultimate reality itself. The mystic's object is primarily emotional rather than intellectual. What he wants is a feeling of satisfaction which he can only get from immediate contact with something taken to be finally and abidingly real. Hence, when he comes to put his emotions into words, he is always prone to use the language of vague imaginative symbolism, the only language suitable to suggest feelings which, because immediate and unanalysed, cannot be the subject of logical description in general terms. For the metaphysician, whose object is the attainment of intellectual consistency, such a method of symbolism is radically unsuitable.

A symbol is always a source of danger to the intellect. If you employ it for what you already understand, and might, if you chose, describe in scientific language, it is a mere substitution of the obscure for the clear. If you use it, as the mystic commonly does, for what you do not understand, its apparent precision, by blinding you to the vagueness of its interpretation, is positively mischievous. Hence, though some of the greatest metaphysicians, such as Plotinus and Spinoza, and to a certain extent Hegel, have been personally mystics, their philosophical method has invariably been scientific and rationalistic. At the same time, it is probably true that, apart from the mystic's need for the satisfaction of emotion by the contemplation of the eternal and abiding, the intellect would be prone to exercise itself in less arid and more attractive fields than those of abstract Metaphysics. The philosopher seeks, in the end, the same goal as the mystic; his peculiarity is that he is so constituted as to reach his goal only by the route of intellectual speculation.

§ 9. We have compared Metaphysics more than once with Logic in respect of the universality of its scope and the analytical character of its methods. It remains briefly to indicate the difference between the two sciences. There is, indeed, a theory, famous in the history of Philosophy, and not even yet quite obsolete, according to which no distinction can be drawn. Hegel held that the successive steps by which the human mind gradually passes from less adequate to more adequate, and ultimately to a fully adequate, conception of the nature of reality necessarily correspond, step for step, with the stages of a process by which the reality itself is manifested with ever-increasing adequacy in an ascending order of phenomena. Hence in his system the discussion of the general characteristics of reality and the general forms of inference constitutes a single department of Philosophy under the name of *Logic*. Our motive in dissenting from this view cannot be made fully intelligible at the present stage of our inquiry, but we may at least follow Lotze in giving a preliminary reason for the separation of the two sciences. Logic is clearly in a sense a more general inquiry than Metaphysics. For in Logic we are concerned with the universal conditions under which thinking, or, to speak more accurately, inference, is possible. Now these conditions may be fulfilled by a combination of propositions which are materially false. The same relations which give rise to an inference materially true from true premisses may yield a false inference where the premisses are materially false. Valid reasoning thus does not always lead to true conclusions. Hence we may say that, whereas Metaphysics deals exclusively with the characteristics of reality, Logic deals with the characteristics of the validly inferrible, whether real or unreal. The distinction thus established, however, though real as far as it goes, is not necessarily absolute. For it may very well be that in the end the conditions upon which the possibility of inference depends are identical with or consequent upon the structure of reality. Even the fact that, under certain conditions, we can imagine an unreal state of things and then proceed to reason validly as to the results which would follow if this imaginary state were actual, may itself be a consequence of the actual nature of things. And, as a matter of fact, logicians have always found it impossible to inquire very deeply into the foundations and first principles of their own science without being led to face fundamental issues of Metaphysics. The distinction between the two studies must thus, according to the well-known simile of Bacon, be compared rather with a vein in a continuous block of marble than with an actual line of cleavage. Still it is at least so far effectual, that while many metaphysical questions have no direct bearing on Logic, the details of the theory of evidence are likewise best studied as an independent branch of knowledge.

§ 10. In recent years considerable prominence has been attained by a branch of study known as *Epistemology*, or the *Theory of Knowledge*. The *Theory of Knowledge*, like Logic, is primarily concerned with the question of the conditions upon which the validity of our thinking, as a body of knowledge about reality, depends. It differs from ordinary Logic in not inquiring into the details of the various processes of proof, but confining its attention to the most general and ultimate conditions under which valid thinking is possible, and discussing these general principles more thoroughly and systematically than common Logic usually does. Since the conditions under which truth is obtainable depend, in the last resort, on the character of that reality which knowledge apprehends, it is clear that the problems of the *Theory of Knowledge*, so far as they do not come under the scope of ordinary Logic (the theory of the estimation of evidence), are metaphysical in their nature. As actually treated by the writers who give this name to their discussions, the study appears to consist of a mixture of Metaphysics and Logic, the metaphysical element predominating. There is perhaps no serious harm in our giving, if we choose, the name *Epistemology* or *Theory of Knowledge* to our discussions of ultimate principles, but the older title Metaphysics seems on the whole preferable for two reasons. The discussion of the implications of knowledge is only one part of the metaphysician's task. The truly real is not only the knowable, it is also that which, if we can obtain it, realises our aspirations and satisfies our emotions. Hence the theory of the real must deal with the ultimate implications of practical conduct and æsthetic feeling as well as those of knowledge. The Good and the Beautiful, no less than the True, are the objects of our study.

Again, if the name *Theory of Knowledge* is understood, as it sometimes has been, to suggest that it is possible to study the nature and capabilities of the knowing faculty apart from the study of the contents of knowledge, it becomes a source of positive and dangerous mistake. The capabilities and limitations of the knowing faculty can only be ascertained by inquiring into the truth of its knowledge, regarded as an apprehension of reality; there is no possible way of severing the faculty, as it were, by abstraction from the results of its exercise, and examining its structure, as we might that of a mechanical appliance, before investigating the value of its achievements. The instrument can only be studied in its work, and we have to judge of its possibilities by the nature of its products. It is therefore advisable to indicate, by our choice of a name for our subject, that the theory of Knowing is necessarily also a theory of Being.

Consult further :—F. H. Bradley, *Appearance and Reality*, Introduction; L. T. Hobhouse, *The Theory of Knowledge*, Introduction; H. Lotze, *Metaphysic*, Introduction (Eng. trans., vol. i. pp. 1-30).

CHAPTER II

THE METAPHYSICAL CRITERION AND THE METAPHYSICAL METHOD

§ 1. In the principle that "Reality is not self-contradictory" we have a universal and certain criterion of reality which is not merely negative, but implies the positive assertion that reality is a consistent system. § 2. The validity of this criterion is not affected by the suggestion that it may be merely a *Logical* Law. § 3. Nor by the raising of doubt whether all our knowledge is not merely "relative," a doubt which is itself meaningless. § 4. As to the material of the system, it is experience or immediate psychical fact. § 5. It must be actual experience, not mere "possibilities" of experience; but actual experience must not be identified with "sensation." § 6. Nor must we assume that experience consists of subjects *and* their states; nor, again, that it is a mere succession of "states of consciousness." § 7. The *differentia* of matter of experience is its *immediacy*, *i.e.* its combination in a single whole of the two aspects of *existence* and *content*. § 8. This union of existence and content is broken up in reflective knowledge or thought, but may be restored at a higher level. § 9. Experience further always appears to be implicitly complex in respect of its content. § 10. An adequate apprehension of reality would only be possible in the form of a complete or "pure" experience, at once all-inclusive, systematic, and direct. The problem of Metaphysics is to ascertain what would be the general or formal character of such an experience, and how far the various provinces of our human experience and knowledge approximate to it. The knowledge Metaphysics can give us of the ultimate nature of reality as it would be present in a complete experience, though imperfect, is final as far as it goes. § 11. As to the method of Metaphysics, it must be *analytical, critical, non-empirical,* and *non-inductive*. It may also be called *a priori* if we carefully avoid confusing the *a priori* with the psychologically primitive. Why our method cannot be the Hegelian Dialectic.

§ 1. IF we are, in the end, to attach any definite intelligible meaning to the distinction between things as they really are and things as they merely appear to be, we must clearly have some universal criterion or test by which the distinction may be made. This criterion must be, in the first place, infallible; that is, must be such that we cannot doubt its validity without falling into a contradiction in our thought; and, in the next, it must be a characteristic belonging to all reality, as such, and to nothing else. Thus our criterion must, in the technical language of Logic, be the predicate of an exclusive proposition of which reality is the subject; we must be able to say, "Only the real possesses the quality or mark X." The argument of our last chapter should already have suggested that we have such a criterion in the principle that "what is real is not self-contradictory, and what is self-contradictory is not real." Freedom from contradiction is a characteristic which belongs to everything that is real and ultimately to nothing else, and we may therefore use it as our test or criterion of reality. For, as we have seen in the last chapter, it is precisely our inability, without doing violence to the fundamental structure of our intellect, to accept the self-contradictory as real which first leads to the drawing of a distinction between the real and the merely apparent; on the other hand, where we find no contradiction in thought or experience, we have no valid ground for doubting that the contents of our experience and thinking are truly real. In every application, even the most simple and rudimentary, of the distinction between what really is and what only seems, we are proceeding upon the assumption that, if things as we find them are self-contradictory, we are not yet in possession of the truth about them; while, on the other hand, we may legitimately treat the results of our thinking and experience as fully true until they are shown to involve contradiction. Thus, in setting up the proposition "What is real is never self-contradictory" as a universal criterion, we are only putting into explicit form, and proposing to apply universally, a principle involved in all rational reflection on the course of things. Audacious as the attempt to make such a general statement about the whole universe of being appears, it is an audacity to which we are fully committed from the first moment of our refusing to accept both sides of a contradiction as true.

The principle that "Reality is not self-contradictory" at first sight might appear to be merely negative; we might object that it only tells us what reality is *not*, and still leaves us quite in the dark as to what it *is*. This would, however, be a serious misconception. As we learn from modern scientific Logic, no true and significant negative judgment is merely negative; all significant negation is really exclusion resting upon a positive basis. I can never, that is, truly declare that *A is not B*, except on the strength of some piece of positive knowledge which is inconsistent with, or excludes, the possibility of A being B.[1] My own ignorance or

---

[1] See Bosanquet, *Essentials of Logic*, Lect. 8. As an illustration we may take an extreme case: "The Jabberwock was not killed yesterday." What is the ground of this denial? At first sight it appears to be merely negative, "there are no such things as Jabberwocks to kill." But before I can say

failure to find sufficient ground for the assertion *A is B* is never of itself logical warrant for the judgment *A is not B* ; that *A is not B* I can never truly assert, except on the ground of some other truth which would be contradicted if A were affirmed to be B. Hence to say " Reality is not self-contradictory " is as much as to say that we have true and certain knowledge that reality is positively self-consistent or coherent; that is to say that, whatever else it may be, it is at least a systematic whole of some kind or other. How much further our knowledge about reality goes, what kind of a whole we can certainly know it to be, it will be the business of succeeding portions of this work to discuss; but even at the present stage of the inquiry we can confidently say that unless the distinction between the real and the apparent is purely meaningless, it is positively certain that Reality,[1] or the universe, is a self-consistent systematic whole.

§ 2. Our declaration that the principle of the self-consistency of the real affords a certain and infallible criterion of reality, may probably provoke a sceptical doubt which is of such importance that we must give it full consideration before making any further advance. I state the difficulty in what appears to me its most reasonable and telling form. "Your alleged criterion," it will be said, "is simply the logical Law of Contradiction expressed in a novel and misleading way. Now, the Law of Contradiction, like all purely logical laws, is concerned not with real things, but exclusively with the concepts by which we think of them. When the logician lays it down as a fundamental truth of his science that *A cannot be both B and not B*, his A and B stand not for things "in the real world to which our thoughts have reference," but for concepts which we frame about the things. His law is thus purely what he calls it, a Law of Thought; he says, and says truly, " you cannot, at the

---

"there are no such things as Jabberwocks" with confidence, I must have enough positive information about the structure and habits of animals to be aware that the qualities ascribed to the Jabberwock conflict with the laws of animal life. Or, if I deny the existence of Jabberwocks simply on the ground that I have never come across a specimen, this involves a positive judgment as to the relation between the animal world and the part of it I have examined, such as, "if there were Jabberwocks, I should have come across one"; or, "my acquaintance with the varieties of animals is sufficiently exhaustive to afford ground for a valid generalisation." The fact that symbolic Logic finds it *convenient* to treat the universal affirmative as a double negative must not mislead us as to its actual priority in thought.

[1] To meet the kind of criticism which finds it humorous to jest at the expense of those who "take consolation from spelling Reality with a big R," may I once for all say that when I spell Reality thus it is simply as a convenient way of distinguishing the ultimately from the merely relatively real?

same time, and in the same sense, *think* both that A is B, and that it is not B"; as to whether such a state of things, though unthinkable to us, may be real "as a fact," he makes no assertion. You take this law of our thinking, silently assume that it is also a law of the things about which we think, and go on to set it up as an infallible criterion of their reality. Your procedure is thus illegitimate, and your pretended criterion a thing of nought."[1]

Our reply to this common sceptical objection will incidentally throw an interesting light on what was said in the last chapter of the close connection between the problems of Logic and those of Metaphysics. In the first place, we may at least meet the sceptic with an effective *tu quoque*. It is you yourself, we may say, who are most open to the charge of illegitimate assumption. Your whole contention rests upon the assumption, for which you offer no justification, that because the Law of Contradiction is admittedly a law of thought, it is therefore *only* a law of thought; if you wish us to accept such a momentous conclusion, you ought at least to offer us something in the nature of a reason for it. Nor shall we stop here; we shall go on to argue that the sceptic's interpretation of the Law of Contradiction rests on a positive confusion. By a Law of Thought may be meant either (*a*) a *psychological* law, a true general statement as to the way in which we actually do think, or (*b*) a *logical* law, a true general statement as to the conditions under which our thinking is valid; the plausibility of the sceptical argument arises from an unconscious confusion between these two very different senses of the term. Now, in the first place, it seems doubtful whether the principle of contradiction is even true, if it is put forward as a psychological law. It would be, at least, very hard to say whether a human being is capable or not of holding at once and with equal conviction the truth of two contradictory propositions. Certainly it is not uncommon to meet persons who do fervently profess equal belief in propositions which *we* can see to be inconsistent; on the other hand, they are usually themselves unaware of the inconsistency. Whether, in all cases, they would, if made aware of the inconsistency, revise their belief, is a question which it is easier to ask than to answer. But it is at any rate certain that the logician does not intend his Law of Contradiction to be taken as a psycho-

---

[1] We shall meet this same difficulty again later on as the principle of the famous Kantian objection to the "ontological proof" of God's existence. *Infra*, Bk. IV. chap. 5, § 8.

logical proposition as to what I can or cannot succeed in believing. He means it to be understood in a purely logical sense, as a statement about the conditions under which any thought is valid. What he says is not that I cannot at once think that A is B and that it is not B, but that, if I think so, my thinking cannot be *true*. Now, to think truly about things is to think in accord with their real nature, to think of them as they really are, not as they merely appear to an imperfect apprehension to be; hence to say that non-contradiction is a fundamental condition of true thinking is as much as to say that it is a fundamental characteristic of real existence. Just because the Law of Contradiction is a logical law, it cannot be *only* a logical law, but must be a metaphysical law as well. If the sceptic is to retain his sceptical position, he must include Logic along with Metaphysics in the compass of his doubts, as the thorough-going sceptics of antiquity had the courage to do.

§ 3. But now suppose the sceptic takes this line. All our truth, he may say, is only relatively truth, and even the fundamental conditions of true thought are only valid *relatively* and for us. What right have you to assume their *absolute* validity, and to argue from it to the real constitution of things? Now, what does such a doubt mean, and is it rational? The answer to this question follows easily from what we have already learnt about the logical character of denial. Doubt, which is tentative denial, like negation, which is completed denial, logically presupposes positive knowledge of some kind or other. It is never rational to doubt the truth of a specific proposition except on the strength of your possession of positive truth with which the suggested judgment appears to be in conflict. This is, of course, obvious in cases where we hesitate to accept a statement as true on the ground that we do not see how to reconcile it with another specific statement already known, or believed, to be true. It is less obvious, but equally clear on reflection, in the cases where we suspend our judgment on the plea of insufficient evidence. Apart from positive knowledge, however defective, as to the kind and amount of evidence which *would*, if forthcoming, be sufficient to prove the proposition, expressions of doubt and of belief are equally impertinent; unless I know, to some extent at least, what evidence is wanted, how indeed am I to judge whether the evidence produced is sufficient or not?[1] Thus we see

---

[1] Take a concrete example. A theory as to the early religious history of the Hebrews, let us say, is put forward upon grounds derived from Semitic philology.

that the paradox of Mr. Bradley, that rational doubt itself logically implies infallibility in respect of some part of our knowledge, is no more than the simple truth. We see also that the doubt whether the ultimate presuppositions of valid thinking may not be merely "relatively" valid, has no meaning. If the sceptic's doubt whether Reality is ultimately the self-consistent system that it must be if any of our thinking can be true is to lay any claim to rationality, it must take the form of the assertion, "I positively know something about the nature of Reality which makes it reasonable to think that Reality is incoherent," or "Self-consistency is inconsistent with what I positively know of the nature of Reality." Thus the sceptic is forced, not merely to lay claim to absolute and certain knowledge, but to use the test of consistency itself for the purpose of disproving or questioning its own validity. Our criterion of Reality, then, has been proved infallible by the surest of methods; we have shown that its truth has to be assumed in the very process of calling it in question.

§ 4. Reality, then, in spite of the sceptic's objections, is truly known to be a connected and self-consistent, or internally coherent, system; can we with equal confidence say anything of the data of which the system is composed? Reflection should convince us that we can at least say as much as this: all the materials or data of reality consist of *experience*, experience being provisionally taken to mean psychical matter of fact, what is given in immediate feeling. In other words, whatever forms part of presentation, will, or emotion, must in some sense and to some degree possess reality and be a part of the material of which reality, as a systematic whole, is composed; whatever does not include, as part of its nature, this indissoluble relation to immediate feeling, and therefore does not enter into the presentation, will, and emotion of which psychical life is composed, is not real. The real is experience, and nothing but experience, and experience consists of "psychical matter of fact."[1]

Proof of this proposition can only be given in the same way as of any other ultimate truth, by making trial of it;

Though unacquainted with Semitic philology in particular, I may be able to form some sort of estimate of the cogency of the professed reasoning if I already have an adequate acquaintance with the use and value of philological evidence in parallel cases, say, in the study of Greek antiquities. But if I have no positive acquaintance at all with the use of philology in antiquarian research, it would be the merest impertinence for me to offer any opinion whatever.

[1] What follows must be regarded as a mere outline which awaits subsequent filling up by the more concrete results of Bk II. chap. 1

if you doubt it you may be challenged to perform the experiment of thinking of anything whatever, no matter what, as real, and then explaining what you mean by its reality. Thus suppose you say " I can think of A as real," A being anything in the universe; now think, as you always can, of an imaginary or unreal A, and then try to state the difference between the A which is thought of as real and the A which is thought of as merely imaginary. As Kant proved, in the famous case of the real and the imagined hundred dollars, the difference does not lie in any of the qualities or properties of the two A's; the qualities of the imagined hundred dollars are precisely the same as those of the real sum, only that they are "imaginary." Like the real dollars, the imagined dollars are thought of as possessing such and such a size, shape, and weight; stamped with such and such an effigy and inscription; containing such and such a proportion of silver to alloy; having such and such a purchasing power in the present condition of the market, and so forth. The only difference is that the real dollars are, or under specified and known conditions may be, the objects of direct perception, while the imaginary ones, because imaginary, cannot be given in direct perception. You cannot see or handle them; you can only imagine yourself doing so. It is in this connection with immediate psychical fact that the reality of the real coins lies. So with any other instance of the same experiment. Show me, we might say, anything which you regard as real,—no matter what it is, a stone wall, an æsthetic effect, a moral virtue,—and I will ask you to think of an unreal and imaginary counterpart of that same thing, and will undertake to prove to you that what makes the difference between the reality and the imagination is always that the real thing is indissolubly connected with the psychical life of a sentient subject, and, as so connected, is psychical matter of fact.

§ 5. Two points should be carefully noted if we wish to avoid serious misapprehension. It might be objected, by a disciple of Kant or of Mill, that a thing may be real without ever being given as actual psychical fact in immediate apprehension, so long as its nature is such that it *would* be psychical fact under known and specified conditions. Many, if not most, of the objects of scientific knowledge, it may be said, are of this kind; they have never entered, possibly never will enter, into the contents of any man's direct apprehension, yet we rightly call them real, in the sense that they would be apprehended under certain known conditions. Thus I have never seen, and do not expect that any one ever will see, the centre of the earth, or, to take a still stronger case, no one has ever seen his own brain. Yet I call the centre of the earth or my own brain real, in the sense that *if* I could, without ceasing to live, penetrate to a certain depth below the soil, I *should* find the centre of the earth; *if* an opening were made in my skull, and a suitable arrangement of mirrors devised, I *should* see the reflection of my own brain. A comet may be rushing through unpeopled space entirely unbeheld; yet it does not cease for all that to be real, for *if* I were there I *should* see it, and so forth. Hence the Kantian will tell us that reality is constituted by relation to *possible* experience; the follower of Mill, that it means "a permanent *possibility* of sensation."

Now, there is, of course, an element of truth in these arguments. It is true that what immediately enters into the course of my own direct perception is but a fragment of the full reality of the universe. It is true, again, that there is much which in its own nature is capable of being perceived by human beings, but will, as far as we can judge, never be perceived, owing to the physical impossibility of placing ourselves under the conditions requisite for perception; there are other things which could only be perceived if some modification could be effected in the structure of our perceptive organs. And it may therefore be quite sufficient for the purposes of some sciences to define these unperceived realities as "possibilities of sensation," processes which we do not perceive but might perceive under known or knowable conditions. But the definition, it will be seen, is a purely negative one; it takes note of the fact that we do not actually perceive certain things, without telling us anything positive as to their nature. In Metaphysics, where we are concerned to discover the very meaning of reality, we cannot avoid asking whether such a purely negative account of the reality of the greater part of the universe is finally satisfactory. And we can easily see that it is not. For what do we mean when we talk of the "possible"? Not simply "that which is not actual," for this includes the merely imaginary and the demonstrably impossible. The events of next week, the constitution of Utopia, and the squaring of the circle are all alike in not being actual. Shall we say, then, that the possible differs from the imaginary in being what would, under known conditions, be actual? But again, we may make correct inferences as to what would be actual under conditions suspected, or even known, to be merely imaginary, and no one will maintain that such consequences are realities.

If I were at the South Pole I should see the Polar ice, and it is therefore real, you say, though no one actually sees it; but if wishes were horses, beggars would ride, yet you do not say that the riding of beggars is real. Considerations of this kind lead us to modify our first definition of the "possible" which is to be also real. We are driven to say that, in the case of the unperceived real thing, all the conditions of perception except the presence of a percipient with suitable perceptive organs, *really exist*. Thus the ice at the South Pole really exists, because the only unfulfilled condition for its perception is the presence at the Pole of a being with sense-organs of a certain type. But once more, what do we mean by the distinction between conditions of perception which are imaginary and conditions which really exist? We come back once more to our original experiment, and once more, try as we will, we shall find that by the real condition as distinguished from the imaginary we can mean nothing but a state of things which is, in the last resort, guaranteed by the evidence of immediate apprehension. If we take the term "actual" to denote that which is thus indissoluble from immediate apprehension, or is psychical matter of fact, we may sum up our result by saying we have found that the real is also actual, or that there is no reality which is not at the same time an actuality. We shall thus be standing on the same ground as the modern logicians who tell us that there is no possibility outside actual existence, and that statements about the possible, when they have any meaning at all, are always an indirect way of imparting information about actualities.[1] Thus "There really exists ice at the South Pole, though no human eye beholds it," if it is to mean anything, must mean *either* that the ice itself, as we should perceive it if we were there, or that certain unknown conditions which, combined with the presence of a human spectator, would yield the perception of the ice, actually exist as part of the contents of an experience which is not our own.[2]

The second point to which we must be careful to attend may be dismissed more briefly. In defining experience as "immediate feeling" or "the content of immediate feeling" or "apprehension,"[3] we must not be understood to mean

---

[1] For the modern logical doctrine of possibility consult Bradley, *Principles of Logic*, 192-201; Bosanquet, *Logic*, i. chap. 9.

[2] This is—apart from non-essential theological accretions—the principle of Berkeley's argument for the existence of God (*Principles of Human Knowledge*, §§ 146, 147).

[3] I should explain that I use "feeling" and "apprehension" indifferently for

that it is in particular *sensation*. Sensation is only one feature of immediate feeling or apprehension, a feature which we only distinguish from others by means of a laborious psychological analysis. A pleasure or pain, an emotion of any kind, the satisfaction of a craving while actually present, are felt or apprehended no less immediately than a sense-perception. I am aware of the difference between actually feeling pleasure or pain, actually being moved by love or anger, actually getting the satisfaction of a want, and merely thinking of these processes, in precisely the same way in which I am aware of the difference between actually seeing a blue expanse and merely thinking of seeing it. A real emotion or wish differs from an imagined one precisely as a real sensation differs from an imaginary sensation. How exactly the difference is to be described is a question, and unfortunately at present an unduly neglected question, for Psychology; for our present purpose we must be content to indicate it as one which can be experienced at will by any reader who will take the trouble to compare an actual state of mind with the mere thought of the same state. Of the epistemological or metaphysical interpretation of the distinction more will be said in the course of the next few paragraphs. As an instance of its applicability to other aspects of mind than the purely sensational, we may take Kant's own example of the hundred dollars. The real hundred dollars may be distinguished from the imaginary, if we please, by the fact that they can be actually touched and seen; but we might equally make the distinction turn on the fact that the real coins will enable us to satisfy our desires, while the imaginary will not.[1]

§ 6. In the present state of philosophical opinion, the proposition that "whatever is real consists of experience," or again, "of psychical matter of fact," is in danger not so much of being rejected, as of being accepted in a fundamentally false sense. If we are to avoid the danger of such misunderstanding, we must be careful to insist that our principle does not assert that *mere* actuality is a complete and sufficient account of the nature of reality. When we say that there is nothing real outside the world of psychical fact, we are not saying that reality is *merely* psychical fact as such. What we do say is that, however much more it may be, it is at least that.

immediate and non-reflective awareness of any psychical content. The exclusive restriction of the term to awareness of pleasure and pain seems to me to rest on a serious mistake in psychology, and I therefore avoid it.

[1] In fact, we shall see in Bk. II. chap. I that in virtue of its unity with immediate *feeling*, all experience is essentially connected with purpose.

How much more we can say of reality, beyond the bare statement that it is made up of experiences or psychical matters of fact, it is the task of our metaphysical science to determine; at present our problem, though given to us in its general elements, still awaits solution. In particular, we must take care not to fall into the error of so-called "Subjective Idealism." We must not say that reality consists of "*the states of consciousness of sentient subjects*," or of "*subjects, and their states*." We must not falsify our data as metaphysicians by starting with the assumption that the psychical facts of which reality is made up are directly experienced as "states" or "modifications" of "subjects" which are their possessors. Such a theory would in fact contradict itself, for the "subject" or "I," who am by the hypothesis the owner of the "states," is never itself given as a "state of consciousness." Hence Hume was perfectly correct when he argued from the principle that nothing exists but states of consciousness, to the conclusion that the thinker or "subject," not being himself a state of consciousness, is an illusion. Yet, on the other hand, if there is no thinker or subject to "own" the passing states, they are not properly "states" or "modifications" of anything. Apart from this explicit contradiction in the formulation of the theory that all things are "states of consciousness," we must also object that the theory itself is not a statement of the data of experience, but a hypothesis about their connection. The division of experience into the self or the subject on the one side and its states on the other is not given in our immediate apprehension, but made in the progress of reflection on the contents of apprehension. Sensible things and their properties never appear to us in our direct apprehension of them to be states or modifications of ourselves; that they really are this and nothing more is simply one hypothesis among others which we devise to meet certain difficulties in our thought. Reality comes to us from the first in the guise of pieces of psychical fact; we feel certain, again, that these pieces must somehow form part of a coherent whole or system. We try to understand and account for this systematic character of the real on the supposition that the matters of fact of which it consists are connected with one another through the permanent character of the "subjects" to which they belong as temporary "states" or "modifications." But this special interpretation of the way in which the facts of experience form a system is no part of our initial postulate as to the general nature of the real; it is simply one among other theories of the concrete character of the universe, and it is for Metaphysics itself to test its merits.

Similarly, we should be making an unwarranted addition to our initial postulate about Reality if we identified it with the doctrine of Hume and his followers, according to whom what really exists is *merely* a series of "impressions and ideas" connected by certain psychological laws of succession, any profounder structural unity of experience being dismissed as a "fiction of the mind." The secret of the fallacy here lies in the *petitio principii* committed by the introduction of the word "merely" into our statement. From the identification of reality with psychical facts which somehow form a systematic unity, it does not in the least follow that the *only* unity possessed by the facts is that of conformity to a certain law or laws of sequence. *That* all reality consists of psychical facts, and *that* these facts must form a system, we are, as we have already seen, entitled to assert as a fundamental metaphysical principle which cannot be doubted without falling into contradiction; *how* they do so we have yet to discover, if we can.

The merits of the Humian solution of the problem will come before us for consideration at a later stage; the impossibility of assuming it without inquiry as a principle, may perhaps be brought home to the mind of the reader by a simple illustration. Take the case of any æsthetic whole, such as, for instance, the play of *Hamlet*. The play of *Hamlet* consists, for the student who reads it in his closet, of a succession of printed words. These words form the whole material of the play; it is composed of them all and of nothing else. Again, the words which are the material of the play are connected by the grammatical and euphonic laws which regulate the construction of English sentences, and the metrical laws of English dramatic versification. Thus it would be a true description of the play, as far as it goes, to say that it is a series of words put together in accordance with grammatical and metrical laws. It would, however, be positively false to say that *Hamlet* is nothing more than such a succession of words; its character as a work of art depends entirely on the fact that it possesses, as a whole, a further unity of structure and aim, that the words and sentences which are its material embody an internally coherent representation of human character and purpose. Apart from this inner unity of meaning, mere uniformity of grammatical and metrical construction would not of themselves constitute a work of art. It will be one object of our later discussions to show that what is thus obviously true of an æsthetic whole is universally true of every genuine system or totality.

§ 7. The data or material of reality, then, are facts of experience, and nothing but facts of experience.[1] And experience, we have said, means for our purposes *immediate* feeling or apprehension. What *immediacy* means, as we have already seen, we cannot further explain in psychological terms, except by saying that it is what distinguishes an actual mental state from the mere thought of that state. The reason why, in Psychology, we have to be content with such an account is manifest. To characterise immediate feeling further, we should have to identify the *qualities* by which it is universally marked off from what is not immediate. We should, in fact, have to describe it in general terms, and before we can do this we must cease to feel or apprehend directly, and go on to reflect upon and analyse the contents of our apprehension. What our psychological description depicts is never the experience as it actually was while we were having it, but the experience as it appears from the point of view of subsequent reflection, interpreted in the light of all sorts of conscious or unconscious hypotheses about its conditions and its constituents. Thus our psychological descriptions depend for their very possibility upon the recognition of distinctions which are not present, as such, in the experience itself as directly presented to us but created by later reflection about it. From the point of view of Metaphysics, however, it is possible to specify one universal characteristic of immediate feeling, which is of the utmost importance for our theories of reality and of knowledge. When we reflect upon any psychical fact whatever, we may distinguish within it two very different aspects. There is, in the first place, the fact that it *does* happen, that it is a genuine psychical occurrence,—the existence or *that*, as we may call it, of the piece of psychical fact in question; and there is also the peculiar character or quality which gives *this* mental occurrence its unique nature as distinguished from any other which might conceivably have been presented in its stead,—the content or *what* of the psychical

---

[1] I take "fact" as equivalent to "what is directly apprehended in a single moment of consciousness." In a previous work (*The Problem of Conduct*, chap. 1) I used the word in a different sense for "the contents of a *true* description of experience." This employment of the word, however, seems at variance with established philosophical usage, and I therefore abandon it as likely to lead to misapprehension.

fact. Thus a simple colour-sensation, say that of green, has its *that*,—it is actually present, and is thus distinguished from a merely remembered or anticipated sensation; it has also its *what*,—the peculiar quality by which it is distinguished, for example, from a sensation of blue. So again with an imagined sensation; it is actually imagined, the imagining of it is an actual occurrence with its particular place in the course of the occurrences which together make up my mental life; and again, it is the imagination of some content with qualities of its own by which it is distinguished from any other content.

The most striking illustration of the presence of these distinguishable aspects in all psychical occurrences is, of course, afforded by the case of error or illusion, the essence of which is the false apprehension of the *what*. Thus, when an ignorant villager sees a ghost, or a hypochondriac is tormented by "imaginary" symptoms of disease, the ghost or the malady is not simply non-existent; something is actually seen or felt, but the error consists in a mistake as to the nature of what is seen or felt. Now, the peculiarity by which direct and immediate apprehension is distinguished, for the metaphysician, from subsequent reflection about the contents of apprehension, is that in immediate apprehension itself we are not conscious of the distinction between these two aspects of psychical fact. The immediately experienced is always a *this-what* or process-content[1] in which the distinction of the *this* from the *what* does not enter into consciousness. In any act of reflection, on the other hand, the *what* is explicitly distinguished from the *that*, and then ascribed to it as something which can be truly said about it. The judgment or proposition, which is the characteristic form in which the result of reflection finds its expression, consists, in its most rudimentary shape, of the embodiment of this distinction in the separation of predicate from subject, and the subsequent affirmation of the first about the second. The work of thought or knowledge in making our world more intelligible to us essentially consists in the progressive analysis of a content or *what*, considered in abstraction from the *this* to which it belongs. The *this* may, as in the singular judgment or the particular judgment of perception, actually appear in our propositions as the subject to which the *what* is explicitly ascribed; or again, as in the true universals of

---

[1] Of course, the apprehended "content" may itself be a "process," as is the case in all instances of the apprehension of *change;* but the apprehended process is always distinguishable from the process of apprehension.

science, both the predicate and the ostensible subject of the proposition may belong to the content analysed, and the *this*, or directly apprehended reality of which the content forms an attribute, may not appear in the proposition at all. This is why the true universal judgment has long been seen by logicians to be essentially hypothetical, and why, again, thought or knowledge always appears to the common-sense man to be dealing with realities which have previously been given independently of the "work of the mind." He is only wrong in this view because he forgets that what is given in this way is merely the *that* or existence of the world of real being, not its *what* or content in its true character as ultimately ascertained by scientific thought.[1]

§ 8. The fundamental characteristic of experience, then, for the metaphysician, is its immediacy: the fact that in experience as such the existence and the content of what is apprehended are not mentally separated. This immediacy may be due, as in the case of mere uninterpreted sensation, to the absence of reflective analysis of the given into its constituent aspects or elements. But it may also be due, as we shall have opportunities to see more fully later on, to the fusion at a higher level into a single directly apprehended whole of results originally won by the process of abstraction and reflection. There is an immediacy of experience which is below mediate reflective knowledge. but there is also a higher immediacy which is above it. To explain and justify this statement will be the work of subsequent chapters; for the present we may be content to illustrate it by a simple example. A work of art with an intricate internal structure, such, for instance, as a musical composition or a chess problem, as directly presented to the artistically uncultivated man, is little more than a mere succession of immediately given data in which the aspects of existence and content are as yet hardly separated; it has no significance or meaning, but merely *is*. As education in the perception of artistic form proceeds, the separation becomes at first more and more prominent. Each subordinate part of the structure now acquires a meaning or significance in virtue of its place in the whole, and this meaning is at first something over and above the directly presented character of the part, something which has to be grasped by reflective analysis and comparison of part with part. The individual part has now, through analysis of its content, come to mean or stand for

---

[1] We shall see in Bk. II. chap. I that the "that" of an experience implies relation to a unique individual interest or purpose.

something outside itself, namely, its relation to all the other parts. But with the completion of our æsthetic education the immediacy thus destroyed is once more restored. To the fully trained perception the meaning of the composition or the problem, its structure as an artistic whole, is no longer something which has to be pieced together and inferred by reflective comparison: it is now directly apprehended as a structural unity. The composition has a meaning, and thus the results of the intermediate stage of reflection and comparison are not lost, but taken up into the completed experience. But the meaning is no longer external to the existence of the composition; it is what it means, and it means what it is.[1] We may subsequently see that what is thus strikingly illustrated by the case of artistic perception holds good, to a greater or less degree, of all advance in the understanding of reality. It is perhaps the fundamental philosophical defect of what is popularly called Mysticism that it ignores this difference between a higher and a lower immediacy, and thus attempts to restore the direct contact with felt reality which scientific reflection inevitably loosens by simply undoing the work of analytic thought and reverting to the standpoint of mere uninterpreted feeling.[2]

§ 9. We may perhaps specify one further characteristic which seems, at least, to belong to every datum of immediate experience. Every experience seems to be implicitly complex, that is, its aspect of *content* appears never to be absolutely simple, but always to contain a plurality of aspects, which, as directly felt, are not distinct, but are at the same time distinguishable as soon as we begin by reflection to describe and analyse it. From the nature of the case this complexity cannot be directly ascertained by inspection, for the inspection itself presupposes that we are dealing with the experience not as immediately felt, but as already sufficiently analysed and reflected upon to be described in general terms. Indirectly, however, our result seems to be established by the consideration that, as soon as we reflect upon the given at all, we find these distinguishable aspects within its content, and that, unless they were there implicitly from the first, it

---

[1] Of course this is only partly true. As we shall see in the sequel, to "be what it means and mean what it is" is an ideal never *fully* realised in the structure of any finite piece of reality, precisely because the finite, as its name implies, is never a completely systematic whole.

[2] On the psychological processes by which meaning is acquired, see Stout, *Manual of Psychology*,[3] bk. i. chap. 3; and on the apprehension of form, the same author's *Analytic Psychology*, bk. i. chap. 3. Much interesting discussion of the difference between "external" and "internal" meaning will be found in Royce, *The World and the Individual*, First Series.

is hard to see how the mere process of reflection could have given birth to them. Thus, for instance, in even the most rudimentary experience there would appear to be something answering to the distinction between the presentational quality of a sensation and its accompanying tone of pleasure or pain. It is difficult, again, not to think that in any sentient experience there must be some difference between elements which correspond to more or less stable conditions of the sentient organism itself ("organic sensation") and those which correspond to relatively novel and infrequent features of the environment. Some philosophers would indeed be prepared to go further, and to maintain that a more or less explicit consciousness of distinction between self and not-self, or again between subject and object, is logically involved in the very possibility of an experience. The question, as a psychological one, need not be raised here; it must, however, be carefully remarked that whatever view we may adopt as to the number and character of the aspects which analysis reveals within the contents of the simplest experience, those aspects, as directly apprehended, originally constitute an unanalysed whole. Our various subsequent analyses all presuppose theories as to the ultimate *what* of experience which it is the business of Metaphysics to test.

§ 10. Our foregoing discussion of the metaphysical criterion will suggest a fairly definite ideal of what a completely adequate apprehension of the whole of reality would be. A completely adequate apprehension of reality would be one which contained all reality and nothing but reality, and thus involved no element whatever of deceptive appearance. As such it would, in the first place, be all-embracing; it would include in itself every datum of direct experience, and, since nothing but data of experience, or, as we have also called them, matters of psychical fact, are the materials of reality, it would contain nothing else. In the second place, it would contain all its data without contradiction or discrepancy as part of a single system with a harmonious internal structure of its own. For wherever there is discrepancy, as we have already seen, there is imperfect and therefore partially false appearance. And, in the third place, such an all-embracing harmonious apprehension of the whole data of experience would clearly transcend that separation of existence from content which is temporarily effected by our own efforts to restate *our* experience in a consistent form. It would, because complete in itself, involve at a higher level that immediacy which, at a lower level, we know as characteristic of feeling. It would thus experience the whole of real existence directly as a system with internal consistency and structure, but without any reference to anything beyond itself. As we said of the artistic whole, so we may say of the whole of existence as it might be apprehended by a completed insight, it would be what it meant, and mean what it was. To such an ideally complete experience of reality as a single system, by way of marking its exclusively experiential nature, we may give the name, introduced into Philosophy by Avenarius, of a " pure " experience, that is, an experience which is in all its parts experience and nothing else. Of course, in adopting the name, we are not necessarily identifying ourselves with the further views of Avenarius as to what in particular the structure of such an experience would be.

Our own human experience clearly falls far short of such an ideal, and that for two reasons. To begin with, our experience is incomplete in respect of its data: there is much in reality which never directly enters into the structure of our experience at all. Of much of what falls within the scope of our knowledge we can only say, in a general way, how it would appear to ourselves supposing certain conditions of its perceptibility to be realised, and even these conditions are usually only most imperfectly known. What the actual matters of psychical fact corresponding to these conditions and to the appearance which they would determine for us are, we are totally unable to say. Again, there may well be much in the real world which never, even in this indirect way, enters into the structure of human knowledge at all. Hence our human experience and the intellectual constructions by which we seek to interpret it have always the character of being piecemeal and fragmentary. Perfect apprehension of systematic reality as a whole would be able to deduce from any one fact in the universe the nature of every other fact. Or rather, as the whole would be presented at once in its entirety, there would be no need for the deduction; every fact would be directly seen as linked with every other by the directly intuited nature of the system to which all facts belong. But in our imperfect human apprehension of the world our facts appear to be largely given us in isolation and independence of one another as bare " casual conjunctions " or " collocations," and the hypotheses by which we seek to weld them into a system, however largely determined by the character of our data, never quite get rid of an element of arbitrary " free " construction. They are never fully necessitated as to their entirety by the nature of the facts they serve to connect. Hence we can never be certain that our hypothetical constructions themselves are true in the sense of consisting of statements of what for a completed experience would be matters of fact. Our ideal is to connect our presented facts by constructions in which each link is itself matter of fact, or experience, in the sense that it would under known conditions form the content of a direct apprehension. But it is an ideal which, owing to the fragmentary character of our own experience, we are never able adequately to realise. In all our sciences we are constantly compelled to use hypothetical constructions, which often are, and for all we know always may be, merely "symbolic," in the sense that, though useful in the co-ordination of experienced data, they could never themselves become objects of direct experience, because they conflict either with the general nature of experience as such, or with the special nature of the particular experiences in which they would have to be presented. Our scientific hypotheses thus present a close analogy with the uninterpretable stages in the application of an algebraical calculus to a numerical or geometrical subject-matter. Their usefulness in enabling us to co-ordinate and predict facts of direct experience need no more guarantee their own reality, than the usefulness of such a calculus guarantees our ability to find an intelligible interpretation for all the symbolic operations it involves.[1] In a pure or completed experience, at once all-comprehending and systematic, where existence and content, fact and construction, were no longer separated, there could of course be no place for such ultimately uninterpretable symbolism.

Our fundamental metaphysical problem, then, is that of discovering, if we can, the general or formal characteristics of such a complete or "pure" experience, *i.e.* those characteristics which belong to it simply in virtue of its all-containing and completely systematic nature. Further, it would be the work of a completed Metaphysic to ascertain which among the universal characteristics of our own human

[1] For some good observations on the fallacy of assuming that mathematical symbolism must always be interpretable, see B. Russell, *Foundations of Geometry*, p. 45–46; or Whitehead, *Universal Algebra*, vol. i. p. 10 ff. For a further elaboration of the argument of the foregoing section I may refer to my *Problem of Conduct*, pp. 14–21. I need hardly warn the reader against confusing a "symbolic" concept in my sense of the word, *i.e.* one which cannot be fully interpreted in terms of direct experience, with a "symbolic" idea in Mr. Spencer's sense, *i.e.* one which is not, psychologically, a copy of the presentations for which it stands. Our use of the word is, of course, purely logical, and has nothing to do with the psychological character of mental images, but only with their meaning.

experience of the world are such as must belong to any coherent experience in virtue of its nature, and are thus identifiable with the formal characteristics of a "pure" experience. Also, our science would have to decide what features of human experience, among those which do not possess this character, approximate most nearly to it, and would thus require least modification in order to enable them to take their place in an absolutely complete and harmonious experience of reality. If we could completely carry out our programme, we should, in the first place, have a general conception of what in outline the constitution of experienced reality as a systematic whole is; and, in the second, we should be able to arrange the various concepts and categories by which we seek, alike in everyday thinking and in the various sciences, to interpret the world of our experience, in an ascending order of degrees of truth and reality, according to the extent to which they would require to be modified before they could become adequate to express the nature of a systematic experienced reality. The knowledge conveyed by such a science would, of course, not be itself the pure or all-embracing experience of Reality, but merely mediate knowledge about the general nature of such an experience, and would therefore, so far, be like all mere knowledge about an object, abstract and imperfect. It would still refer to something beyond itself, and thus have a meaning other than its own existence. But, unlike all other knowledge, our metaphysical knowledge of the formal character of an all-inclusive experienced whole would be *final*, in the sense that no addition of fresh knowledge could modify it in principle. Fresh knowledge, which in all other cases involves at least the possibility of a transformation of existing theories, would here do no more than fill in and make more concrete our conception of the system of Reality, without affecting our insight into its general structure.

We may perhaps illustrate this conception of a knowledge which, though imperfect, is yet final, by an instance borrowed from elementary Mathematics. We know absolutely and precisely, *e.g.*, what the symbol π stands for. π is completely determined for us by the definition that it is the ratio of the circumference of a circle to its diameter. And again, we can define unequivocally both the terms, circumference and diameter of the circle, which we have employed in our definition of π. Thus our knowledge of the meaning of the symbol is clearly final; no fresh accretion to our knowledge will make any modification in it. At the same time, our knowledge of π, though final, is imperfect. For the quantity π is incommensurable, and thus we can never precisely evaluate it. All we can do is to assign its value correctly within any desired degree of approximation. Again, while no approximation gives an absolutely correct value for the quantity, one approximation is, of course, closer than another. Because no approximation is more than approximately the truth, it by no means follows that all are equally wide of the mark. Similarly, it may well be that, though we can say with finality what the general nature of experience and experienced Reality as a systematic whole is, yet, when we come to ask after the character of the system in detail, we have to depend on sciences which are merely approximate in their results; it will not follow, as is sometimes assumed, that the categories of one science do not present us with a nearer approximation to the absolute truth than those of another.[1]

§ 11. We may end this chapter with some general reflections on the *method* required for such a science of Metaphysics as we have described in the preceding paragraphs. The true character of any scientific method can, of course, only be discovered by the actual use of it; a preliminary disquisition on the nature of a method not previously exhibited in actual use is apt to be at best sterile, and at worst a positive source of prejudices which may subsequently seriously hamper the process of investigation. Still, there are certain general characteristics of the method imposed on us by our conception of the problems to be solved which may conveniently be pointed out at this stage of our inquiry. Our method will, in the first place, clearly be *analytical* and *critical* in its character. We analyse experience with a view to discovering its implications, and we analyse our various scientific and unscientific theories of the contents of the world-system for the same purpose. Also, once having determined what are the formal characteristics of an all-embracing, systematic whole of experienced fact, we criticise our various concepts and theories by reference to these characteristics as an ultimate standard of reality and truth. Negatively, we may add that our method is *non-empirical*, and also *non-inductive*, in the same sense in which pure Mathematics, for instance, may be called non-inductive. It is non-empirical inasmuch as we are called upon to analyse all our data and criticise all our pre-conceived theories. We are not allowed to accept any fact without analysis, or any

---

[1] Compare my *Problem of Conduct*, pp. 22–39.

concept without criticism, as an unchallenged datum upon which we may build without preliminary justification. Hence our method is non-empirical. Also, as our analysis is concerned entirely with the internal character and self-consistency of the data analysed, it is, like the reasonings of pure Mathematics, independent of external confirmation outside the analysed data themselves, and is therefore non-inductive.[1] In precisely the same sense our method and its results may be called, if we please, *a priori;* that is to say, we proceed entirely by internal analysis of certain data, and are, alike in procedure and result, independent of experience outside the experience we are concerned with analysing. We can, of course, add that our method is *constructive*, that is, if successfully carried out it would culminate in an intellectual attitude towards the world which, as an intellectual attitude, we did not possess before entering on our study of Metaphysics; but as construction, in this sense, is characteristic of all scientific method, it does not seem necessary to specify it as a peculiarity of metaphysical procedure in particular.

Historically, our conception of metaphysical method as fundamentally analytical and directed to the detection and removal of internal contradictions in the categories of ordinary thought, is perhaps nearer to the view of Herbart than to that of any other great philosopher of the past. In our insistence upon the non-empirical and, in a sense, *a priori* character of Metaphysics, we are again, of course, largely in agreement with the position of Kant. There is, however, a most important difference between our own and the Kantian conception of the *a priori* upon which it is essential to insist. A-priority, as we have used the term, stands merely for a peculiarity of the *method* of Metaphysics; by an *a priori* method we understood one which is confined to the internal analysis of a datum and independent of external reference to outside facts. With Kant the *a priori* is a name for certain forms of perception and thought which, because revealed by analysis as present in every experience, are supposed to be given *independently of all experience* whatsoever, and so come to be identified by him as "the work of the mind," in opposition to the empirical factor in experience, which is held to be the product of an external system of "things-in-themselves." Hence Kant's whole discussion of the *a priori* is vitiated by

[1] The fundamental peculiarity of "inductive" procedure, in fact, is that, while its object is the internal analysis of its data, which, if completed, would permit of a universal conclusion being drawn from the single case, it is never able to effect the analysis, and is driven to reinforce it by external comparison with "similar" cases.

a constant confusion between what is metaphysically *necessary* (*i.e.* implied in the existence of knowledge) and what is psychologically *primitive*. This confusion, perplexing enough in Kant, reaches a climax in the works of writers like Mr. Spencer, who appear to think that the whole question of the presence of a non-empirical factor in knowledge can be decided by an appeal to genetic Psychology. It is clear that, from our point of view, the identification of the *a priori* with the "work of the mind" would involve a metaphysical theory as to the constitution of experience which we are not entitled to adopt without proof.[1]

A word ought perhaps to be said about our attitude towards the "dialectical" method as employed by Hegel and his followers. It was Hegel's conviction that the whole series of concepts or categories by which the mind attempts to grasp the nature of experienced Reality as a whole, from the most rudimentary to the most adequate, can be exhibited in a fixed order which arises from the very nature of thought itself. We begin, he held, by the affirmation of some rude and one-sided conception of the character of what is; the very imperfection of our concept then forces us on to affirm its opposite as equally true. But the opposite, in its turn, is no less one-sided and inadequate to express the full character of concrete reality. Hence we are driven to negate our first negation by affirming a concept which includes both the original affirmation and its opposite as subordinate aspects. The same process repeats itself again at a higher stage with our new category, and thus we gradually pass by a series of successive triads of categories, each consisting of the three stages of affirmation, negation, and negation of the negation, from the beginning of an intellectual interpretation of the world of experience, the thought of it as mere "Being," not further defined, to the apprehension of it as the "Absolute Idea," or concrete system of spiritual experience. It was the task of abstract Metaphysics (called by Hegel, Logic) to exhibit the successive stages of this process as a systematic orderly advance, in which the nature of each stage is determined by its place in the whole. As Hegel also held that this "dialectic" process is somehow not confined to the "subjective" or private intelligence of the student of Philosophy, but also realised in the structure of the "objective" universe, it followed that its successive stages could be

---

[1] On the confusion between the metaphysical and psychological standpoint in Kant's own treatment of the *a priori*, see B. Russell, *Foundations of Geometry*, pp. 1-4, and Adamson, *Development of Modern Philosophy*, bk. i. pp. 244-247.

detected in physical nature and in History in the same order in which they occur in "Logic," and many of Hegel's best-known works are devoted to exhibiting the facts of Physics, Ethics, Religion, and History in the light of this doctrine. The subsequent advances of the various sciences have so completely proved the arbitrariness and untrustworthiness of the results obtained by these "deductions," that some of the best exponents of the Hegelian type of Philosophy are now agreed to abandon the claim of the Dialectic to be more than a systematisation of the stages through which the individual mind must pass in its advance towards a finally satisfactory conception of Reality. But even within these limits its pretensions are probably exaggerated. No satisfactory proof can be produced that, even in abstract Metaphysics, the succession of categories must be precisely that adopted by Hegel. There are some categories of the first importance, *e.g.*, that of *order* in Mathematics, which hardly get any recognition at all in his system, and others, such as those of "Mechanism" and "Chemism," which play a prominent part, are obviously largely dependent for their position upon the actual development of the various sciences in Hegel's own time. Hence the method seems unsuitable for the original attainment of philosophical truth. At best it might serve, as Lotze has remarked, as a convenient method for the arrangement of truth already obtained by other means, and even for this purpose it seems clear that the succession of categories actually adopted by Hegel would require constant modification to adapt the general scheme to later developments of the various special sciences.

Consult further :—F. H. Bradley, *Appearance and Reality*, chaps. 13, 14; B. Bosanquet, *Essentials of Logic*, Lect. 2; Shadworth Hodgson, *Metaphysic of Experience*, bk. i. chap. 1; J. S. Mackenzie, *Outlines of Metaphysics*, bk. i. chaps. 2 and 4. And for criticism of the Hegelian dialectic: J. E. M'Taggart. *Studies in Hegelian Dialectic*, chaps. 1-3; J. B. Baillie, *The Origin and Significance of Hegel's Logic*, chaps. 8-12, especially chap. 12; and also Adamson, *Development of Modern Philosophy*, bk. i. pp. 271 ff.

CHAPTER III

THE SUB-DIVISIONS OF METAPHYSICS

§ 1. The traditional sub-division of Metaphysics into *Ontology*, *Cosmology*, *Rational Psychology*, common to all the great modern constructive systems. § 2. Precise sense in which we adopt these divisions for the purposes of our own treatment of the subject. § 3. Relation of *Cosmology* and *Rational Psychology* to the empirical sciences.

§ 1. ENGLISH philosophers, who have usually been imbued with a wholesome distrust of deliberate system-making, have commonly paid comparatively little attention to the question of the number and character of the sub-divisions of metaphysical philosophy. They have been content to raise the questions which interested them in the order of their occurrence to their own minds, and have gladly left it to the systematic historians of Philosophy, who have rarely been Englishmen, to discuss the proper arrangement of the parts of the subject. Continental thinkers, who are naturally more prone to conscious systematisation, have bestowed more thought on the problem of method and order, with the result that each great independent philosopher has tended to make his own special arrangement of the parts of his subject. The different arrangements, however, seem all to agree in conforming to a general type, which was most clearly exhibited by the otherwise rather arid Wolffian dogmatism of the eighteenth century. All the constructive systems (those, *e.g.*, of Hegel, Herbart, Lotze,) feel the necessity of giving the first place to a general discussion of the most universal characteristics which we find ourselves constrained to ascribe in thought to any reality which is to be an intelligible and coherent system and not a mere chaos. This division of the subject is commonly known by the title it bears alike in the Wolffian Metaphysic and the systems of Herbart and Lotze, as *Ontology*,[1] or the general doctrine of Being; with Hegel

[1] The name is ultimately derived from Aristotle's definition of "First Philosophy"—which along with Mathematics and Physics constitutes, according to his system, the whole of Theoretical Science—as the knowledge of ὄντα ᾗ ὄντα, *i.e.* of the general character of the real *as* real, as distinguished from the knowledge

it constitutes, as a whole, the contents of the science of *Logic*, as distinguished from the other two great departments of speculative thought, the Philosophies of *Nature* and *Mind*; and its most formal and general parts, again, compose, within the Hegelian Logic itself, the special first section entitled "Doctrine of Being."

Further, every system of metaphysical philosophy is bound to deal with more special problems, which readily fall into two principal classes. It has to consider the meaning and validity of the most universal conceptions of which we seek to understand the nature of the individual objects which make up the experienced physical world, "extension," "succession," "space," "time," "number," "magnitude," "motion," "change," "quality," and the more complex categories of "matter," "force," "causality," "interaction," "thinghood," and so forth. Again, Metaphysics has to deal with the meaning and validity of the universal predicates by which we seek to interpret the nature of the experiencing mind itself, and its relation both to other minds and to the objects of the physical world, "the soul," "the self," "the subject," "self-consciousness," "ethical purpose," and so forth. Hence it has been customary to recognise a second and third part of Metaphysics, dealing respectively with the most general characteristics of external Nature and of conscious Mind. These sections of the subject are commonly known as *Cosmology* and *Rational Psychology*. In Hegel's system they appear in a double form: in their most abstract generality they constitute the "Doctrine of Essence," and the "Doctrine of the Notion" in the Hegelian *Logic*; in their more concrete detail they form the second and third parts of his complete system or "Encyclopædia" of the philosophical sciences, the previously mentioned Philosophies of *Nature* and *Mind*.

In the pre-Kantian eighteenth century it was not unusual to add yet a fourth division to Metaphysics, *Rational Theology*, the doctrine of the existence and attributes of God, so far as they can be deduced from general philosophical principles apart from the appeal to specific revelation. Kant's onslaught on the whole Wolffian scheme in the "Dialectic of Pure Reason," while profoundly modifying for the future the view taken by metaphysicians of Cosmology and Rational Psychology, proved annihilating so far as eighteenth-century Deism and its philosophical offspring, Rational Theology,

of the mathematician and the physicist, who only deal with the real in so far as it exhibits number and magnitude, and sensible change respectively.

were concerned, and that sub-division may fairly be said to have disappeared from subsequent philosophical systems.[1]

§ 2. There are good and obvious reasons why we should adhere, in the form of our inquiry, to the main outlines of this traditional scheme. It is true that it is largely a question of simple convenience what order we adopt in a systematic metaphysical investigation. A genuinely philosophical survey of the general character of knowledge and experience would exhibit so complete a systematic unity, that you might start from any point in it and reach the same results, much as you may go round a circle equally well from any point of the periphery. But for the beginner, at any rate, it is advantageous to start with the general question what we mean by Being or Reality, and what character is to be ascribed to the whole of Being as such, before attacking the problem of the particular kind of Being which belongs to the various "realities" of common life and the special sciences. Thus we have to discuss in the first part of our programme such questions as the relation of Being in general to experience, the sense in which Being may be said to be inseparable from, and yet again to transcend, experience; the problem of the existence of different kinds or degrees of Being; the question whether Being is ultimately one or many; the relation between Real Being and its appearances. All these problems correspond with reasonable closeness to the contents of what was traditionally known as Ontology.

It is only when we have reached some definite conclusion on these most fundamental questions that we shall be in a position to deal with the more special problems suggested by the various departments of science and common life; hence we shall do well to acquiesce in the arrangement by which Ontology was made to precede the other divisions of the subject. Again, in dealing with the more complex special problems of Metaphysics, it is natural to recognise a distinction corresponding to the separation of Cosmology from Rational Psychology. Common language shows that for most of the purposes of human thought and action the contents of the world of experience tend to fall into the two groups of mere things and things which are sentient and purposive—Physical Nature on the one hand, and Minds or Spirits on the other. We must, of course, be careful not to

---

[1] Less effective in immediate results, but no less thorough and acute than the Kantian "Critique of Speculative Theology," were Hume's posthumous *Dialogues on Natural Religion*, a work which has hardly received its full meed of consideration from the professional historians of Philosophy.

THE SUB-DIVISIONS OF METAPHYSICS 45

confuse this division of the objects of experience with the distinction between an experienced object as such and the subject of experience. We are to start, in our critical investigation, not with the artificial point of view of Psychology, which sets the "subject" of presentations over-against the presentations considered as conveying information about "objects of knowledge," but with the standpoint of practical life, in which the individual agent is opposed to an environment itself consisting largely of similar individual agents. It is not "Nature" on the one side and a "perceiving mind" on the other, but an environment composed partly of physical things, partly of other human and animal minds, that furnishes the antithesis on which the distinction of Cosmology from Rational Psychology is founded. There is no confusion against which we shall need to be more on our guard than this fallacious identification of Mind or Spirit with the abstract subject of psychological states, and of the "environment" of the individual with Physical Nature. Of course, it is true that we necessarily interpret the inner life of other minds in terms of our own incommunicably individual experience, but it is equally true that our own direct experience of ourselves is throughout determined by interaction with other agents of the same type as ourselves. It is a pure delusion to suppose that we begin by finding ourselves in a world of mere physical things to some of which we afterwards come by an after-thought, based on "analogy," to ascribe "consciousness" akin to our own. Hence, to avoid possible misunderstandings, it would be better to drop the traditional appellations "Cosmology" and "Rational Psychology," and to call the divisions of applied Metaphysics, as Hegel does, the *Philosophy* of *Nature* and of *Spirit* or *Mind* respectively.[1]

[1] The fallacy of the assumption that our environment is directly given in experience as merely physical is best brought out by Avenarius in his masterly little work *Der Menschliche Weltbegriff*, which should be familiar to all students of Philosophy who are able to read German. The purely English reader will find many fruitful suggestions in Ward, *Naturalism and Agnosticism*, pt. iv., "Refutation of Dualism." Much confusion is caused in philosophical discussion by the unscholarly use of the epistemological term "object" (which properly signifies "object of *cognition*") instead of the more familiar "thing" to denote the constituent elements of our environment as it is actually experienced in practical life. In strictness the elements of the environment are "objects" only for an imaginary consciousness which is thought of as merely cognisant of presented fact, a point which Prof. Münsterberg has emphasised. For practical life the essential character of the environment is not merely that it is "presented," but that it interacts with our own purposive activity; it thus consists not of "objects," but of "things."

In including the minds of our fellows among the things which constitute our environment, we must not commit the mistake of supposing "minds" as factors

In recognising this sub-division of applied Metaphysics into two sections, dealing respectively with Physical Nature and with Mind or Spirit, we do not mean to suggest that there is an absolute disparity between these two classes of things. It is, of course, a matter for philosophical criticism itself to decide whether this difference may not in the end turn out to be merely apparent. This will clearly be the case if either minds can be shown, as the materialist holds, to be simply a peculiar class of highly complex physical things, or physical things to be, as the idealist contends, really minds of an unfamiliar and non-human type. It is sufficient for us that the difference, whether ultimate or not, is marked enough to give rise to distinct classes of problems, which have to be treated separately and on their own merits. We may feel convinced on general philosophical grounds that minds and physical things are ultimately existences of the same general type, whether we conceive that type after the fashion of the materialist or of the idealist, but this conviction does not in the least affect the fact that the special metaphysical problems suggested by our experience of physical things are largely different from those which are forced on us by our interest in the minds of our fellows. In the one connection we have, for instance, to discuss the questions connected with such categories as those of uniform spatial extension, uniform obedience to general law, the constitution of a whole which is an aggregate of parts; in the other, those connected with the meaning and value of ethical, artistic, and religious aspiration, the concept of moral freedom, the nature of personal identity. Even the categories which seem at first sight most readily applicable both to physical things and to minds, such as those of quality and number, lead to special difficulties in the two contrasted cases. This consideration seems to justify us in separating the metaphysics of Mind from the metaphysics of Nature, and the

in immediate experience to be "incorporeal realities," or "complexes of states of consciousness." The distinction between mind and body, and the concept of mind as "within the body," or again as a "function" of the body, are psychological hypotheses which only arise in the course of subsequent reflective analysis of experience. Of the worth of these hypotheses we shall have to speak later. At present it is enough to note that for direct experience a "mind" means simply a thing with individual purpose. What for my direct experience distinguishes my fellow-man from a stock or stone, is not the presence within him of an incorporeal "soul" or "consciousness," but the fact that I must take account of his individual purposes and adapt myself to them if I wish to achieve my own. Here again the reader of German will do well to consult Prof. Münsterberg (*Grundzüge der Psychologie*, vol. i. chaps. 1–3). See also a paper on "Mind and Nature" by the present writer in *International Journal of Ethics* for October 1902.

superior difficulty of many of the problems which belong to the former is a further reason for following the traditional order of the two sub-divisions, and placing Rational Psychology after Cosmology. In so far as the problems of Rational Theology can be separated from those of general Ontology, the proper place for them seems to be that section of Rational Psychology which deals with the meaning and worth of our religious experiences.

§ 3. It remains, in concluding the present chapter, to utter a word of caution as to the relation between the two divisions of applied Metaphysics and the body of the empirical sciences. It is perhaps hardly necessary to warn the student that Rational Cosmology and Psychology would become worse than useless if conceived of as furnishing in any sense a substitute for the experimental study of the physical, psychological, and social sciences. They are essentially departments of Metaphysics, and for that very reason are incapable of adding a single fact to the sum of our knowledge of ascertained fact. No doubt the discredit into which Metaphysics—except in the form of tacit and unconscious assumption—has fallen among students of positive science, is largely due to the unfortunate presumption with which Schelling, and to a less degree Hegel, attempted to put metaphysical discussion in the place of the experimental investigation of the facts of nature and of mind. At the present day this mistake is less likely to be committed; the danger is rather that applied Metaphysics may be declared purely valueless because it is incapable of adding to our store of facts. The truth is, that it has a real value, but a value of a different kind from that which has sometimes been ascribed to it. It is concerned not with the accumulation of facts, but with the interpretation of previously ascertained facts, looked at broadly and as a whole. When the facts of physical Nature and of Mind and the special laws of their connection have been discovered and systematised by the most adequate methods of experiment, observation, and mathematical calculation at our disposal, the question still remains, how we are to conceive of the whole realm of such facts consistently with the general conditions of logical and coherent thought. If we choose to define positive science as the systematic establishment of the special laws of connection between facts, we may say that over and above the *scientific* problem of the systematisation of facts there is the further *philosophical* problem of their interpretation. This latter problem does not cease to be legitimate because it has been illegitimately confounded by certain thinkers with the former.

Or we may put the case in another way. The whole process of scientific systematisation involves certain assumptions as to the ultimate nature of the facts which are systematised. Thus the very performance of an experiment for the purpose of verifying a suggested hypothesis involves the assumption that the facts with which the hypothesis is concerned conform to general laws, and that these laws are such as to be capable of formulation by human intelligence. If "nature" is not in some sense "uniform," the conclusive force of a successful experiment is logically *nil*. Hence the necessity for an inquiry into the character of the presuppositions involved in scientific procedure, and the amount of justification which can be found for them. For practical purposes, no doubt, the presuppositions of inductive science are sufficiently justified by its actual successes. But the question for us as metaphysicians, as we have already seen, is that not of their usefulness but of their truth.

It may be said that the inquiry ought in any case to be left to the special student of the physical and psychological sciences themselves. This, however, would involve serious neglect of the great principle of division of labour. It is true, of course, that, other things being equal, the better stored the mind of the philosopher with scientific facts, the sounder will be his judgment on the interpretation and implications of the whole body of facts. But, at the same time, the gifts which make a successful experimentalist and investigator of facts are not altogether the same which are required for the philosophical analysis of the implications of facts, nor are both always conjoined in the same man. There is no reason, on the one hand, why the able experimenter should be compelled to desist from the discovery of facts of nature until he can solve the philosophical problems presented by the very existence of a world of physical facts, nor, on the other, why the thinker endowed by nature with powers of philosophical analysis should be forbidden to exercise them until he has mastered all the facts which are known by the specialists. What the philosopher needs to know, as the starting-point for his investigation, is not the specialist's facts as such, but the general principles which the specialist uses for their discovery and correlation. His study is a "science of sciences," not in the sense that it is a sort of universal encyclopædia of instructive and entertaining knowledge, but in the more modest sense of being

THE SUB-DIVISIONS OF METAPHYSICS

a systematised reflection upon the concepts and methods with which the sciences, and the less methodical thought of everyday practical life work, and an attempt to try them by the standard of ultimate coherence and intelligibility.

Note.—If we retain *Psychology*, as is done, *e.g.*, by Lotze, as the title of our Metaphysic of Mind, we ought in consistency to give the word a greatly extended sense. The facts which the Metaphysic of Mind attempt to interpret, comprise not only those of Psychology in the stricter sense (the abstract study of the laws of mental process), but those of all the various sciences which deal with the concrete manifestation of mind in human life (Ethics, Æsthetics, Sociology, the study of Religion, etc.). This is one reason for preferring the Hegelian designation " Philosophy of Mind " to the traditional one of *Rational Psychology*. The associations of the word Philosophy in English are, however, so vague that the adoption of the Hegelian title might perhaps be understood as identifying this division of Metaphysics with the whole content of the mental sciences. But for the unfamiliarity of the expression, I should recommend some such phrase as Metaphysics of Human Society as the most adequate description of this branch of our science.

BOOK II

ONTOLOGY—THE GENERAL STRUCTURE OF REALITY

CHAPTER I

REALITY AND EXPERIENCE

§ 1. In a sense "reality" for each of us means that of which he must take account if his special purposes are to find fulfilment. § 2. But ultimately the world must possess a structure of which *all* purposes, each in its own way, must take account. This is the "Ultimate Reality" or "Absolute" of Metaphysics. In Metaphysics we regard it from the special standpoint of the scientific intellect. There are other legitimate attitudes towards it, *e.g.*, that of practical religion. § 3. The inseparability of reality from immediate experience involves the recognition of it as teleological and as uniquely individual. § 4. The experience within which all reality falls cannot be my own, nor yet the "collective" experience of the aggregate of conscious beings. It must be an individual experience which apprehends the totality of existence as the harmonious embodiment of a single "purpose." The nearest analogue our own life presents to such a type of experience is to be found in the satisfied insight of personal love. § 5. The experience of such an "Absolute" must not be thought of as a mere reduplication of our own, or of the scientific hypotheses by which we co-ordinate facts for the purposes of inference. § 6. Our conception is closely connected with that of Berkeley, from which it differs by the stress it lays on the purposive and selective aspect of experience. § 7. Realism, both of the Agnostic and of the Dogmatic type, is incompatible with the meaning we have been led to attach to "Reality." But Agnosticism is justified in insisting on the limitations of our knowledge of Reality, and Dogmatic Realism in rejecting the identification of Reality with experience as a merely cognitive function of finite percipients. § 8. Subjectivism, according to which all that I know is states of my own "consciousness," is irreconcilable with the admitted facts of life, and arises from the psychological fallacy of "introjection."

§ 1. IN the preceding book we have seen that the very nature of the metaphysical problem predetermines the general character of the answer we are to give to it. What our intellect can accept as finally real, we saw, must be indissolubly one with actual experience, and it must be an internally coherent system. In the present book we have to discuss more in detail the structure which must belong to any reality possessing these general characteristics. The present chapter, then, will be devoted to an examination of the implications of the experiential character of real Being; in the next, we shall deal with the nature of its unity as a single system.

We may perhaps most conveniently begin our discussion with a re-definition of some of our principal terms. We have hitherto spoken of the object of metaphysical knowledge indifferently as "Being," "What is," "What truly exists," and as "Reality," "the ultimately real." So far as it is possible to draw a distinction between these two sets of names for the same thing, we may say that each series lays special stress on a somewhat different aspect of our object. When we say that a thing "is" or "has Being," we seem primarily to mean that it is an *object* for the knowing consciousness, that it has its place in the system of objects which coherent thought recognises. When we call the same object "real" or a "reality," we lay the emphasis rather on the consideration that it is something of which we categorically *must* take account, whether we like it or not, if some purpose of our own is to get its fulfilment.[1] Thus again the "non-existent" primarily means that which finds no place in the scheme of objects contemplated by consistent scientific thought; the "unreal," that with which we have not, for any human purpose, to reckon.

This is what is often expressed by saying that reality means what is independent of our own will, what exercises resistance, what constrains or compels our recognition, whether we like it or not. Philosophers have pointed out that this way of putting the case is only half the truth. The "stubborn" facts or realities which, as we commonly say, force us to recognise them, only do so in consequence of the presence in us of definite interests and purposes which we cannot effect without adapting ourselves to the situation expressed by our statement of the "facts." What lies entirely outside my interests and plans gets no kind of recognition from me; it is "unreal" for me precisely because I have no need to take account of it as a factor to be reckoned with in the pursuit of my special ends. Thus, so long as we use the term in a relative sense and with reference to the

[1] See, in particular, Royce, *The World and the Individual*, Second Series, Lecture 1, for a telling elaboration of this thought. I should note that I do not myself use the term "existence," as is sometimes done, with special restriction to the sense of presence as a sensible event at a particular point of space and time. When so used, it is, of course, much narrower in scope than the term "Being."

special ends of this or that particular agent, there may be as many different orders of "reality" as there are special purposes, and what is "real" for the agent inspired by one purpose may be unreal for his fellows whose purposes are different. Thus, for example, to an English Christian living at home in England the rules of "caste" in India are usually for all practical purposes unreal; he has no need to take their existence into account as a condition of the successful prosecution of any of his aims and interests; for him they have no more significance than the rules of legal procedure adopted in Wonderland. But for the historian of Indian society, the native Hindu Christian, and the devout worshipper of Shiva, the rules of caste are a true reality. Not one of the three can execute *his* special purposes without taking them into account and allowing them to operate in determining his way of proceeding to his goal. Again, the kind of reality which the rules of caste possess for each of our three men is different, in accord with the differences in their characteristic purposes. For the historian, they are real as a system of ideas which have influenced and do influence the conduct of the society of which he is writing the history, in such a way that without understanding them he cannot get a clear insight into the social structure of Hinduism. To the native Christian, they are real as a standing source of difficulty and a standing temptation to be false to his highest ideals of conduct. To the Shivaite, they are real as the divinely appointed means to bodily and spiritual purification from the evil that is in the world.

§ 2. So far, then, it might seem that "reality" is a purely relative term, and that our previous choice of ultimate freedom from contradiction as our standard of reality was an arbitrary one, due to the mere accident that *our* special purpose in sitting down to study Metaphysics is to think consistently. Of course, it might be said, whatever game you choose to play at, the rules of that particular game must be your supreme reality, so long as you are engaged in it. But it depends on your own choice what game you will play and how long you will keep at it. There is no game at which we all, irrespective of personal choice, have to play, and there is therefore no such thing as an ultimate reality which we must all recognise as such; there are only the special realities which correspond to our special individual purposes. You have no right to set up the particular rules of the game of scientific thought as a reality unconditionally demanding recognition from those who do not choose to play that particular game.[1]

Such an argument would, however, be beside the point. It is true that the special nature of the facts which any one of us recognises as real depends on the special nature of his individual purposes. And it is true that, precisely because we are, to some extent, genuine individuals, no two men's abiding purposes are identically the same. It is therefore true, so far as it goes, that Reality wears a different and an individual aspect for each of us. But it is emphatically not true that there is no identical character at all about the purposes and interests of different individuals. The very recognition of the fact that any one individual purpose or interest can only get expression by accommodating itself to a definite set of conditions, which constitute the reality corresponding to that purpose, carries with it the implication that the world is ultimately a system and not a chaos, or, in other words, that there is ultimately a certain constitution of things which, under one aspect or another, is of moment for all individuals, and must be taken into account by every kind of purpose that is to get fulfilment. If the world is systematic at all,—and unless it is so there is no place in it for definite purpose of any kind, —it must finally have a structure of such a kind that any purpose which ignores it will be defeated. All coherent pursuit of purpose, of whatever type, must therefore in the end rest on the recognition of some characteristics of the world-order which are unconditionally and absolutely to be taken into account by all individual agents, no matter what the special nature of their particular purposes. This is all that is meant when it is said that the reality investigated by Metaphysics is absolute, or when the object of metaphysical study is spoken of as the Absolute.

We may, in fact, conveniently define the Absolute as that structure of the world-system which any and every internally consistent purpose must recognise as the condition of its own fulfilment. To deny the existence of an Absolute, thus defined, is in principle to reduce the world and life to a mere chaos. It is important, however, to bear in mind that in Metaphysics, though we are certainly concerned with the ultimate or absolute Reality, we are concerned with it from a special point of view. Our special purpose is to *know*, or to think coherently, about the conditions which all

[1] Compare the brilliant but not altogether convincing argument of Professor James, in *The Will to Believe*.

intelligent purpose has to recognise. Now this attitude of scientific investigation is clearly not the only one which we can take up towards the ultimately real. We may, for instance, seek to gain emotional harmony and peace of mind by yielding up the conduct of our practical life to the unquestioned guidance of what we directly feel to be the deepest and most abiding elements in the structure of the universe. This is the well-known attitude of practical religion. *Primâ facie*, while it seems to be just as permissible as the purely scientific attitude of the seeker after truth, the perennial "conflict of religion and science" is sufficient to show that the two are not identical. How they are related is a problem which we shall have, in outline, to consider towards the end of our inquiry; at present it is enough for our purpose to recognise them as divergent but *primâ facie* equally justified attitudes towards what must in the end be thought of as the same ultimate reality. As Mr. Bradley well says, there is no sin which is metaphysically less justifiable than the metaphysician's own besetting sin of treating his special way of regarding the "Absolute" as the only legitimate one.

§ 3. To return to our detailed investigation of the connection between Reality as now defined for the metaphysician, and Experience. We can now see more completely than before why it is only in *immediate* experience that reality is to be found. Our reason for identifying reality with immediate experience has nothing to do with the theory according to which "sensations," being the product of a something "without the mind," are supposed to carry with them a direct certificate of the independent existence of their "external" cause. For we have seen : (1) that immediacy means simply indissoluble union with a whole of feeling, and that this immediacy belongs to every mental state as actually lived through; (2) that the dependence of sensations in particular on an "external" cause, is in no sense an immediate datum of experience, but a reflective hypothesis which, like all such hypotheses, demands examination and justification before it can be pronounced legitimate ; (3) that it is a philosophical blunder to identify the real with the merely "independent" of ourselves. What is merely independent, as we have now seen, would for us be the merely unreal. Presence in immediate experience is a universal character of all that is real, because it is only in so far as anything is thus presented in immediate unity with the concrete life of feeling that it can be given as a condition or fact of which an individual interest must take account, on pain of not reaching accomplishment. Actual life, as we have already learned, is always a concrete unity of feeling in which the two distinguishable aspects of a psychical fact, its existence and its content, the that and the what, though distinguishable, are inseparable. Scientific reflection on the given we found to be always abstract, in the sense that its very essence is the mental separation of the content from the process. By such separation we mediately get to know the character of the separated content better, but our knowledge, with all its fulness, still remains abstract; it is still knowledge referring to and about an object outside itself. It is only when, as a result of the reflective process, we find fresh meaning in the individual process-content on its recurrence that we return once more to the concrete actuality of real existence.

Now, we may express this same result in another and an even more significant way. To say that reality is essentially one with immediate feeling, is only another way of saying that the real is essentially that which is of significance for the attainment of purpose. For feeling is essentially teleological, as we may see even in the case of simple pleasure and pain. Amid all the confusion and complexity of the psychological problems which can be raised about these most simple forms of feeling, one thing seems clear, that pleasure is essentially connected with unimpeded, pain with impeded, discharge of nervous activity. Pleasure seems to be inseparable from successful, pain from thwarted or baffled, tendency.[1] And if we consider not so much the abstractions "pleasure in general," "pain in general," as a specific pleasure or pain, or again a complex emotional

---

[1] See the whole treatment of questions of feeling in Dr. Stout's *Manual of Psychology*. I do not, of course, mean that "consciousness of activity" successful or thwarted as a fact precedes and conditions pleasure-pain. On the contrary, it is a familiar fact of experience that we often learn what our purposes are for the first time by the pain which attends their defeat. *E.g.*, a man may first realise that he is, and has been, in love by his pain at his mistress's preference of a rival suitor. And nothing seems more certain than that many pleasures are quite independent of "actual conation," as Plato long ago recognised.

I must take this opportunity to guard once for all against some plausible misconceptions. (*a*) When I speak of feeling as "purposive" or "teleological," I do not mean to make what, to my own mind, would be the monstrous assumption, that it necessarily presupposes *conscious* anticipation of its guiding end or purpose. All that I mean is that the processes of conscious life are as a matter of fact only intelligible with reference to the results in which they culminate and which they serve to maintain; or again, that they all involve the kind of continuity of interest which belong to attention. (*b*) If attentive interest is not necessarily actual conation, actual conscious effort, still less is it necessarily actual *will*. For me, as for Mr. Bradley (see his article in *Mind* for October 1902), where there is no ideal anticipation of the result of a process there is neither actual desire nor actual will. And since I cannot see that all attention implies ideal antici-

state, the case seems even clearer. Only a being whose behaviour is consciously or unconsciously determined by ends or purposes seems capable of finding existence, according as those purposes are advanced or hindered, pleasant or painful, glad or wretched, good or bad. Hence our original decision that reality is to be found in what is immediately experienced, as opposed to what is severed by subsequent reflective analysis from its union with feeling, and our later statement that that is real of which we are constrained to take account for the fulfilment of our purposes, fully coincide.

This point may perhaps be made clearer by a concrete example. Suppose that some purpose of more or less importance requires my immediate presence in the next town. Then the various routes by which I may reach that town become at once circumstances of which I have to take note and to which I must adapt my conduct, if my important purpose is not to be frustrated. It may be that there are alternative routes, or it may be that there is only one. In any case, and this is fundamental for us, the number of alternatives which my purpose leaves open to me will be strictly limited. I can, as a matter of mere mathematical possibility, go from A to B in an indefinite number of ways. If I have to make the journey in actual fact on a given day, and with existing means of transit, the theoretical infinity of possible ways is speedily reduced to, at the outside, two or three. For simplicity's sake we will consider the case in which there happens to be only one available way. This one available way is "real" to me, as contrasted with the infinity of mathematically possible routes, precisely because the execution of my purpose restricts me to it and no other. The mathematically possible infinity of routes remain unreal just because they are thought of as all alike mere possibilities; no actual purpose limits me to some one or some definite number out of the infinity, and compels me to adapt myself to their peculiarities or fail of my end. They

pation, I certainly could not agree with Prof. Royce that ultimate Reality is simply the "internal meaning of an *idea*."

My own meaning will be made clearer by reference to the illustration given at the beginning of this note. A man first realises that he has been in love because he feels pained at a rival's success. So far as this is so, I should say, there has been no actual conation, and *a fortiori*, no actual will or desire. But—and this is my point—he would not feel the pain unless the success of the rival thwarted the successful issue of a specific psychophysical tendency of an essentially forward-reaching or teleological kind. The failure may for the first time make him aware of the presence of the tendency, but it must previously have been there as a condition of its own failure.

are "imaginary" or "merely possible" just for want of specific relation to an experience which is the expression of a definite purpose.

This illustration may lead us on to a further point of the utmost importance, for it illustrates the principle that the real as opposed to the merely "possible" or "merely thought of" is always individual. There was an indefinite number of mathematically conceivable ways from A to B; there was only one, or at least a precisely determinate number, by which I could fulfil a concrete individual purpose. (Thus, if I have to make the journey to B in a given time, I *must* take the route followed by the railway.) So universally it is a current common-place that while thought is general, the reality about which we think and of which we predicate the results of our thought is always individual. Now, what is the source or principle of this individuality of the real as opposed to the generality of the merely conceivable? It is precisely that connection of reality with actual purpose of which we have spoken. The results of thought are general because for the purposes of scientific thinking we isolate the *what* of experience from its *that;* we consider the character of what is presented to us apart from the unique purpose expressed in the experience in which it comes to us. In other words, the problems of scientific thought are all of the form, "How must our general purpose to make our thought and action coherent be carried out under such and such typical conditions?" never of the form, "Of what must I take account for the execution of this one definite purpose?" The reason for this difference is at once apparent. In making "this definite purpose" a topic for reflection, I have *ipso facto* abstracted its what from its that and converted it into a mere instance or example of a certain type. It was only while it remained this purpose as actually immanent in and determining the immediate experience of actual life that it was a completely determinate unique *this;* as reflected on it becomes a type of an indefinite number of similar possibilities.

Now, it is necessary here to observe very carefully that it is from the unique individuality of the purpose expressed in an actual experience that the objects or facts of immediate experience derive the individuality in virtue of which we contrast them with the generalities or abstract possibilities of science. It is the more necessary to dwell explicitly on this point, because there is a common but erroneous doctrine that the individuality of actual existence is derived from its occupying a particular place in the space and time orders. Scientific truth is general, it is often said, because it refers alike to all places and times; actual " fact " is individual because it is what is *here* and *now*. But we should be able to see that such an account directly inverts the real order of logical dependence. Mere position in space and time can never be a true " principle of individuation," for the simple reason that one point in space and one moment in time, considered apart from the things and events which fill them, are, at any rate for our perception,[1] indistinguishable from all other points and moments. It is, on the other hand, precisely by their correlation with unique stages in lives which are the embodiment of unique and individual purpose, that places and times and the things and events which occupy them become for us themselves unique and individual. *Here*, for me, means where I now am, and *now*, this unique and determinate stage in the execution of the purposes which, by their uniqueness, make me unique in the world. Thus we seem to have reached the significant conclusion that to say " Reality is experience " involves the further propositions, " Reality is through and through purposive " and " Reality is uniquely individual."

§ 4. We have already seen that to identify reality with experience does not mean identifying it with my own experience just as it comes to me in actual life, still less with my own experience as I mentally reconstruct it in the light of some conscious or unconscious philosophical theory. My own experience, in fact, is very far from satisfying the conditions of completeness and harmony which we found in our last book to be essential to a " pure " or perfect experience. Its defectiveness is principally manifested in three ways. (1) As we have already seen, its contents are always fragmentary. It never contains more than the poorest fragment of the whole wealth of existence. The purposes or interests which make up my conscious life are narrowly limited. The major portion of the facts of the universe, *i.e.* of the conditions of which note has to be taken by its inhabitants if their aims are to be fulfilled, lie outside the range of my individual interests—at least, of those which I ever become explicitly aware. Hence, being without significance for my individual purposes, they do not directly

---

[1] This qualification has to be added to avoid prejudging the very difficult question whether " position " itself is " relative " or " absolute." Fortunately our argument is independent of the determination of the problem. Even if there should be differences between points as " absolute " as the difference between red and blue, our contention would retain its force.

enter into my special experience. I either know nothing of them at all, or know of them only indirectly and through the testimony of others for whose lives they have real and direct significance. And these others again are, in virtue of the individual interests which differentiate them from me, only partially cognisant of the same factual reality as I am.

(2) Again, my insight even into my own aims and interests is of a very limited kind. For one thing, it is only a fragment of them which is ever given in the form of what is immediately felt in an actual moment of experience. I have largely to interpret the actually felt by theoretical intellectual constructions which reach, in the form of memory, into the past, and, in the form of anticipation, into the future. And both these types of intellectual construction, though indispensable, are notoriously vitiated by fallacies. For another, even with the fullest aid of such intellectual construction, I never succeed in completely grasping the whole meaning of my life as the embodiment of a single coherent purpose. Many of my purposes never rise sufficiently into clear consciousness to be distinctly realised, and those that do often wear the appearance of having no systematic connection with one another. Small wonder, then, that the realities or "facts" of which I learn to take note for the execution of my aims more often than not appear to belong to a chaos rather than to the orderly system which we cannot help believing the world to be, could we see it as it truly is.

(3) Finally, I have the gravest grounds for the conviction that even of the realities of which I do take note I never perceive more than just those aspects which attract my attention just because they happen to be significant for my special interests. What startling experiences teach us in the case of our fellow-men may be true everywhere, namely, that everything that is has an infinity of sides to it, over and above those of which we become aware because of their special importance for our own purposes; there may be an infinite wealth of character in the most familiar things, to which we are blind only because, so to speak, it has no "economic value" for the human market. For all these reasons we are absolutely forbidden to identify our own limited experience with the experience of which we have said, that to be real is to be bound up with it, and to be bound up with it is to be real. Neither, again, can we identify this experience with the "collective experience" of the aggregate of human or other finite sentient beings in the universe. This is

obvious for more reasons than one. To begin with, "collective experience," if it has any meaning at all, is a contradictory expression. For experience, as we have seen, is essentially characterised by unique individuality of aim and interest; in this sense at least, a true experience must be that of an individual subject, and no collection or aggregate can be an individual subject. The so-called "collective experience" is not one experience at all, but simply an indefinite multiplicity of experience, thrown together under a single designation. And even if we could get over this difficulty, there remains a still more formidable one. The various experiences of finite individuals are all, we have said, fragmentary and more or less incoherent. You cannot, therefore, get an experience which is all-comprehensive and all-harmonious by adding them together. If their defect were merely their fragmentariness, it would be conceivable that, given an outside observer who could see all the fragments at once, they might constitute a whole by merely supplementing one another's deficiencies. But our finite experiences are not only fragmentary, but also largely contradictory and internally chaotic. We may indeed believe that the contradictions are only apparent, and that *if* we could become fully conscious of our own inmost aims and purposes we should at the same moment be aware of all Reality as a harmonious system; but we never do, and we shall see later that just because of our finitude we never can, attain this completed insight into the significance of our own lives. Hence the experience for which all reality is present as a harmonious whole cannot be any mere duplicate of the partial and imperfect experiences which we possess.

We thus seem driven to assert the necessary existence of a superhuman experience to which the whole universe of being is directly present as a complete and harmonious system. For "reality" has been seen to have no meaning apart from presence in a sentient experience or whole of feeling, while it has also been seen infinitely to transcend all that can be given as directly present to any limited experience. If this conclusion is sound, our "Absolute" can now be said to be a conscious life which embraces the totality of existence, all at once, and in a perfect systematic unity, as the contents of its experience. Such a conception clearly has its difficulties; how such an all-containing experience must be thought to be related to the realm of physical nature, and again to our own finite experiences, are problems which we shall have to take up in our two succeeding books. We shall find them far from simple, and it is as well for us from the first to face the possibility that our knowledge of the character of the absolute experience may prove to be very limited and very tentative. That it *is* we seem compelled to assert by the very effort to give a coherent meaning to our notion of reality, but of *what* it is we may have to confess ourselves largely ignorant.

But we may at least go so far as this, at the present stage of our argument. However different an all-containing coherent experience may be in its detailed structure from our own piecemeal and largely incoherent experience, if it is to be experience at all, it must apprehend its contents in the general way which is characteristic of direct experience as such. It must take note or be aware of them, and it must—if it is to be a direct experience at all—be aware of them as exhibiting a structural unity which is the embodiment of a consistent plan or purpose. We have to think of it as containing in a systematic unity not only all the "facts" of which our various experiences have to take note, but all the purposes which they express. Hence it is natural for us, when we attempt to form some approximate concept of such an ultimate experience in terms of our own conscious life, to conceive it as the union of perfected knowledge in an indivisible whole with supreme will. We must, however, remember that, for such an experience, precisely because of its all-comprising character, the *what* and the *that* are inseparable. Hence its knowledge must be of the nature of direct insight into the individual structure of the world of fact, not of generalisation about possibilities, and its will must have the form of a purpose which, unlike our own, is always consciously expressed with perfect harmony and completeness in the "facts" of which it is aware.[1] Hence knowledge and will, involving as they do for us discrepancy between the what and the that of experience, are not wholly satisfactory terms by which to characterise the life of the Absolute.[2] The most adequate analogue to such a life will probably be found in the combination of direct insight with satisfied feeling which we experience in the relation of

[1] For otherwise the facts which lay outside the purposes or interests of the Absolute would be "foreign" facts "given" from without and not in systematic harmony with its experience as a whole. The complete systematic unity of all facts would thus fall outside what was to be, *ex hypothesi*, an all-containing experience. *Q.E.A.*

[2] For further reflections upon the unsatisfactoriness of such a conception of the Absolute as the "union of Thought and Will," see Bk. IV. chap. 6, § 1, where it is shown that knowledge and will alike, as actual knowledge and actual will, belong only to finite beings.

intimate and intelligent love between persons. The insight of love may be called "knowledge," but it is knowledge of a quite other type than the hypothetical universals of science. I know my friend, not as one case of this or that general class about which certain propositions in Physiology, Psychology, or Ethics can be made, but as—for me at least—a unique individual centre of personal interest. Again, in my relations with my friend, so far as they remain those of satisfied love, my individual interests find their fullest embodiment. But the will to love is not first there in an unsatisfied form, and the embodiment afterwards added as the result of a process through means to an end. The purpose and its embodiment are throughout present together in an unbroken unity, and where this is not so, true mutual friendship does not as yet exist.[1] After some such general fashion we shall best represent to ourselves the kind of consciousness which we must attribute to an all-embracing world-experience. Only, we must bear in mind that, owing to the fragmentariness of our own lives, the identity of purpose on which human friendship rests can never be close and intimate enough to be an adequate representative of the ultimate unity of all experience in the Absolute.[2]

§ 5. It may be well to add a word of caution against a plausible fallacy here. If there is such an Absolute Experience as we have demanded, all the realities that we know as the contents of our environment must be present to it, and present to it as they really are in their completeness. But we must be careful not to suppose that "our" environment, as it appears to an experience which apprehends it as it really is, is a mere replica or reduplication of the way in which it appears to us. For example, I must not assume that what I perceive as a physical thing, made up of separable parts external to one another and apparently combined in a

---

[1] *I.e.* if *will* be taken strictly to mean an actual volition, love and a "will to love" cannot co-exist; if we take will improperly to mean a "standing" interest or purpose, the case is different.

[2] The student of the history of Philosophy will be reminded of the grounds on which Spinoza objects to ascribe "intellect" and "will" in the proper sense of the terms to his God, as well as of the "knowledge of the third or intuitive kind" and the "infinite intellectual love" of God for Himself which are so prominent in the fifth part of the *Ethics*. Similar considerations have sometimes led to a preference for the term "organic" rather than "purposive or "teleological," as expressive of the ultimate unity of experience. The word "organic," however, might suggest biological conceptions of growth, dependence on an external environment, etc., which would be out of place. But the student may compare with what has been said of the "purposive" character of individuality Spinoza's conception of the being of a thing as a *conatus in suo esse perseverandi*.

mechanical way into a whole which is a mere collection or aggregate of parts, is necessarily apprehended by the Absolute Experience as an aggregate of similar or corresponding parts. The thing as it appears to my limited insight may be no less different from the thing as apprehended in its true nature by such an experience, than your body, as it exists for my perception from your body as you apprehend it in organic sensation. In particular, we must not assume that things exist for the Absolute Experience in the form into which we analyse them for the purpose of general scientific theory, for instance, that physical things are for it assemblages of atoms or individual minds successions of "mental states." In fact, without anticipating the results of succeeding books, we may safely say at once that this would be in principle impossible. For all scientific analysis is in its very nature general and hypothetical. It deals solely with types and abstract possibilities, never with the actual constitution of individual things. But all real existence is individual.

To put the same thing in a different way, scientific theory deals always with those features of the *what* of things of which we take note because of their significance for our human purposes. And in dealing with these features of things, it seeks to establish general laws of linkage between them of which we may avail ourselves, for the practical purpose of realising our various human interests. This practical motive, though often not apparent, implicitly controls our whole scientific procedure from first to last. Hence the one test of a scientific hypothesis is its success in enabling us to infer one set of facts from another set. Whether the intermediate links by which we pass from the one set to the other have any counterpart in the world of real experience or are mere creations of theory, like the "uninterpretable" symbols in a mathematical calculus, is from this point of view a matter of indifference. All we require of our hypothesis is that when you start with facts capable of experimental verification, the application of it shall lead to other facts capable of experimental verification. For this reason we may justifiably conclude that to any experience which is aware of things in their concrete individuality they must present aspects which are not represented in our scientific hypotheses, and again cannot appear to it as the precise counterpart of the schemes according to which we quite legitimately reconstruct them for the purpose of scientific investigation. We shall need to bear this in mind in future when we come to discuss the real character of what appears to us as the world of physical nature.[1]

§ 6. The conclusion we have reached so far is largely identical with that of the anti-materialistic argument of Berkeley's well-known *Principles of Human Knowledge* and *Three Dialogues between Hylas and Philonous*. But there is one important difference between the two results which will lead to momentous consequences. Berkeley's argument against the independent existence of unperceived matter proceeds throughout on the principle that to be means to be present in an experience, and his exhibition of the contradictions into which the denial of this principle leads the supporter of scientific materialism remains the classic demonstration of the truth of the opposing or "idealistic" view. But it is to be noted that he works throughout with an inadequate conception of "experience" and "presence in experience." He treats experience as equivalent to mere passive "awareness" of a quality presented to perception. To experience with him means simply to be conscious of a presented quality; experience is treated as having, in psychological terminology, a merely presentational character. Hence he is led to infer that the things with which experience confronts us are nothing more than complexes of presented qualities, or, as he phrases it, that their whole being consists in being perceived.

The full extent of the paradox which this identification of the *esse* of material things with *percipi* involves, will be more apparent when we come to deal in our next book with the problem of matter. At present I merely wish to call attention to one of its many aspects. On the theory that experience is purely passive and presentational, consisting merely in the reception of certain sensations, the question at once arises, What determines what in particular the sensations we at any given moment receive shall be? On the Berkeleian view, their order must be determined altogether from without by a principle foreign to the experience which, he assumes, has nothing to do but to cognise the qualities put before it. Hence he is led to appeal to the agency of God, whom he supposes directly and immediately to cause perceptions to succeed one another in my experience in a certain definite order. Now, apart from further difficulties of

---

[1] For a full examination of the relation between reality and scientific symbolism, consult Ward, *Naturalism and Agnosticism*, part I. The more clearly it is realised that scientific hypotheses are essentially a system of mathematical symbolism, the more impossible it becomes to suppose that they deal directly with the concrete nature of things.

detail, this doctrine at once leads to the result that the attitude of God to the world of things is totally different from that of us who experience it. Experience is to me a purely passive receptivity of presentations; God's relation to the presented objects, on the other hand, is one of active production. There is no common element in these fundamentally contrasted relations; hence it is really a paralogism when Berkeley allows himself to bring God under the same categories which he applies to the interpretation of human experience, and to attribute to Him a consciousness of the things which have been declared to be only the presentations His agency raises in the human mind.[1]

Berkeley is, in fact, inconsistently combining two conflicting lines of thought. He argues, on the one hand, that since there must be some reason for the order in which presentations succeed one another in my mental life, that reason is to be found in a source independent of myself. This source he identifies with God, but, as far as the argument goes, it might equally well have been found, as by Locke, in the original constitution of matter; all that the argument requires is that it shall be placed in something outside the succession of presentations themselves. On the other hand, he also argues that since the existence of the physical world means simply the fact of its being presented to consciousness, when its contents cease to be present to my consciousness they must be present to that of God. And here again the objection might be suggested, that if presence to my own experience, while it lasts, is an adequate account of the *esse* of a thing, it does not appear why I should recognise the reality of any other experience. If I am to hold that disappearance from my experience does not destroy the reality of anything, I must logically also hold that its being, while I perceive it, is not exhausted by *my* awareness of it. Its *esse* cannot be merely *percipi*.

The complete solution of Berkeley's difficulty would be premature at this point of our discussion. But we may at once point out its principal source. It arises from his failure to take adequate account of the purposive aspect of experi-

---

[1] In *Principles of Human Knowledge*, §§ 70–75, Berkeley indeed seems on the very verge of denying that God Himself "perceives" the "ideas" which by His action He excites in us. But at § 139 we find that a "spirit" means "that which perceives ideas, and wills and reasons about them," and in the third Dialogue it is expressly stated that sensible things are "perceived by God" [Works, Edit. in Bohn's Libraries, vol. i. p. 368]. In fact, from the psychological standpoint of Berkeleian sensationalism, to deny God's possession of "ideas" (*i.e.* sense-contents) would have been tantamount to denying His spirituality.

ence. Experience, as we have seen, is not mere awareness of a succession of presented objects, it is awareness of a succession determined by a controlling interest or purpose. The order of my experiences is not something simply given me from without, it is controlled and determined by subjective interest from within. Berkeley, in fact, omits selective attention from his psychological estimate of the contents of the human mind. He forgets that it is the interests for which I take note of facts that in the main determine which facts I shall take note of, an oversight which is the more remarkable, since he expressly lays stress on "activity" as the distinguishing property of "spirits."[1] When we make good the omission by emphasising the teleological aspect of experience, we see at once that the radical disparity between the relation of the supreme and the subordinate mind to the world of facts disappears. I do not simply receive my presented facts passively in an order determined for me from without by the supreme mind; in virtue of my power of selective attention, on a limited scale, and very imperfectly, I recreate the order of their succession for myself.

Again, recognition of the teleological aspect of all experience goes far to remove the dissatisfaction which we may reasonably feel with the other half of Berkeley's argument. When I conceive of the "facts" of experience as merely objects presented to my apprehension, there seems no sufficient reason for holding that they exist except as so presented. But the moment I think of the succession of presented facts as itself determined by the subjective interests expressed in selective attention, the case becomes different. The very expression "selective attention" itself carries with it a reminder that the facts which respond to my interests are but a selection out of a larger whole. And my practical experience of the way in which my own most clearly defined and conscious purposes depend for their fulfilment upon connection with the interests and purposes of a wider social whole possessed of an organic unity, should help me to understand how the totality of interests and purposes determining the selective attention of different percipients can form, as we have held that it must, the harmonious and systematic unity of the absolute experience. The fuller working out of this line of thought must be left for later

---

[1] Unfortunately Berkeley, like so many philosophers, thought of "activity" as primarily an external relation between a "cause" and the material on which it "works." This is probably why he failed to realise the "active" character of the perceptual process.

chapters, but it is hardly too much to say that the teleological character which experience possesses in virtue of its unity with feeling is the key to the idealistic interpretation of the universe.[1]

Idealism, *i.e.* the doctrine that all reality is mental, as we shall have repeated opportunities of learning, becomes unintelligible when mental life is conceived of as a mere awareness of "given" presentations.

§ 7. We may now, before attempting to carry out in detail our general view of what is involved in being real, enumerate one or two philosophical doctrines about the nature of real existence which our conclusion as to the connection of reality with experience justifies us in setting aside. And, first of all, we can at once see that our previous result, if sound, proves fatal to all forms of what is commonly known as *Realism*. By Realism is meant the doctrine that the fundamental character of that which really is, as distinguished from that which is only imagined to be, is to be found in its independence of all relation to the experience of a subject. What exists at all, the realist holds, exists equally whether it is experienced or not. Neither the fact of its existence nor the kind of existence it possesses depends in any way upon its presence to an experience. Before it was experienced at all it had just the same kind of being that it has now you are experiencing it, and it will still be the same when it has passed out of experience. In a word, the circumstance that a mind—whether yours or mine or God's is indifferent to the argument—is aware of it as one of the constituents of its experience, makes no difference to the reality of the real thing; experience is what is technically called a relation of one-sided dependence. That there may be experience at all, and that it may have this or that char-

---

[1] The reader will do well to compare with the whole of the foregoing section the treatment of perception as essentially teleological in Dr. Stout's *Manual of Psychology*,[3] bk. iii. pt. 1, chap. 2.

I need hardly observe that recognition of the fundamental significance of purpose and selection for mental life does not of itself entail the adoption of "voluntarist" views in Psychology. What is fundamental for real mental life may perfectly well admit of analysis into hypothetical simpler elements for the purpose of the psychologist. Thus the admission that all mental life is teleological and selective need not involve the adoption of such metaphysical theories of activity as are adversely criticised by Mr. Bradley in his *Appearance and Reality*, chap. 7, or the introduction of a peculiar "consciousness of activity" as an unanalysable datum into Psychology. The antithesis between the actualities of life and the data of Psychology maintained by Prof. Münsterberg in his *Psychology and Life*, and *Grundzüge der Psychologie*, if untenable in the extreme form in which he states it, is important as a corrective of the opposite tendency to treat as ultimate for psychological analysis whatever is of supreme importance for life.

acter, there must be real things of determinate character, but that there may be real things, it is not necessary that there should be experience. This is, in brief, the essence of the realist contention, and any philosophy which accepts it as valid is in its spirit a realist philosophy.

As to the number and nature of the supposed independent real things, very different views may be held and have been held by different representatives of Realism. Thus some realists have maintained the existence of a single ultimate reality, others of an indefinite plurality of independent "reals." Parmenides, with his doctrine that the real world is a single uniform unchanging material sphere, is an instance in the ancient, and Mr. Herbert Spencer, with his Unknowable, an instance in the modern world of a realist of the former or "monistic" type. The ancient atomists, and in more recent times Leibnitz with his infinite plurality of independent and disconnected monads, and Herbart with his world of simple "reals," afford the best known instances of a doctrine of pluralistic Realism. So again, the most diverse theories have been propounded as to the nature of the "reals." Ancient and modern atomists have thought of them as material, and this is perhaps the form of realistic doctrine which appeals most readily to the ordinary imagination. But though a materialistic metaphysician is necessarily a realist, a realist need not be a materialist. Herbart thought of the independent "reals" as qualitatively simple beings of a nature not capable of further definition, Leibnitz as minds, while Agnostic philosophers of the type of Spencer conceive their ultimate reality as a sort of neutral *tertium quid*, neither mental nor material. The only point on which all the theories agree is that the reality of that which they recognise as true Being consists in its not depending for its existence or its character on relation to an experience. The differences of detail as to the number and nature of independent "reals," though of great importance for our complete estimate of an individual realist's philosophical position, do not affect our general verdict on the tenability of the first principle of Realism.

The one point of divergence among realists which may be considered as of more than secondary importance for our present purpose, is the difference between what we may call Agnostic and Dogmatic Realism. Agnostic Realism, while asserting the ultimate dependence of our experience upon a reality which exists independently of experience, denies that we can have any knowledge of the nature of this independent reality. The independent reality by which all experience is conditioned is, on this view, an Unknowable or Thing-in-itself,[1] of which we are only logically entitled to say *that* it certainly is, but that we do not in the least know *what* it is. The doctrine of Agnostic Realism has probably never been carried out by any thinker with rigid consistency, but it forms a leading feature of the philosophy of Kant as expounded in his First Critique, and through Kant has passed into English thought as the foundation of the systems of Sir William Hamilton and Mr. Herbert Spencer.[2]

Dogmatic Realism, of which Leibnitz and, at a later date, Herbart are the most important representatives in modern philosophy, on the contrary, while maintaining that real being is independent of experience, at the same time holds that it is possible to have positive knowledge not only of its existence but of its nature. In principle, both these forms of Realism have been already excluded by the argument of Book I. chap. 2, § 4. The supreme importance of the principle on which the argument rests may perhaps warrant us in once more briefly recurring to it. Our reasoning, it will be remembered, took the form of a challenge. Produce any instance you please, we said to the realist, whom we had not then learned to know by that name, of what you personally regard as reality, and we will undertake to show that it derives its reality for you from the very fact that it is not ultimately separable from the experience of a subject. A thing is real for you, and not merely imaginary, precisely because in some aspect of its character it enters into and affects your own experience. Or, what is the same thing in other words, it is real for you because it affects favourably or otherwise some subjective interest of your own. To be sure, the thing as it enters into your experience, as it affects your own subjective interests, is not the thing as it is in its fulness ; it only touches your life through some one of its many sides. And this may lead you to argue that the real thing is the unexperienced "condition" of a modification of your

---

[1] Thing-*in-itself*, *i.e.* not affected by the—according to this doctrine—extraneous conditions imposed upon it by relation to an experiencing mind.

[2] The inconsistencies of both Kant and Spencer will illustrate the reluctance of the human mind to acquiesce in a genuine Agnosticism. In the *Critique of Pure Reason* itself Kant so far contradicts himself as to treat the Thing-in-itself as the cause of sensation, though it is a fundamental doctrine of his system that the concept of causal relation can only be legitimately applied to connect facts inside experience ; and in a later work, the *Critique of Judgment*, he tentatively suggests its identity with Will. Of Mr. Spencer it has been truly said (I believe by Mr. F. C. S. Schiller in *Riddles of the Sphinx*) that in the course of his ten volumes of Synthetic Philosophy he speaks much more positively about the nature of the Unknowable than dogmatic theology ventures to speak about the nature of God.

experience. But then we had again to ask what you mean by saying that facts which you do not experience are real as "conditions" of what you do experience. And we saw that the only meaning we could attach to the reality of the "condition" was presence to an experience which transcends your own.

To this general argument we may add two corollaries or supplementary considerations, which, without introducing anything fresh, may help to make its full force more apparent.

(1) The argument, as originally presented, was concerned directly with the *that* of reality, the mere fact of its existence. But we may also state it, if we please, from the side of the *what*, the nature possessed by the real. You cannot affirm any doctrine about the real existence of anything without at the same time implying a doctrine about its nature. Even if you say "Reality is unknowable," you are attributing something beyond mere independence of experience to your reality; you are asserting that what is thus independent possesses the further positive quality of transcending cognition. Now what, in logic, must be your ground for attributing this rather than any other quality to your independent reality? It can only be the fact or supposed fact—which is indeed regularly appealed to by the Agnostic as the foundation of his belief—that our experiences themselves are all found to be self-contradictory. There is no ground for taking the unknowability of Reality to be true unless you mean by it a character which belongs not to something which stands outside all experience, but to experience itself. The same contention applies to any other predicate which the realist affirms as true of his ultimate reality.

(2) Again, we may with effect present our argument in a negative form. Try, we may say, to think of the utterly unreal, and see how you will have to conceive it. Can you think of sheer unreality otherwise than as that of which no mind is ever aware, of which no purpose has ever to take account as a condition of its fulfilment? But to think of it thus is to attribute to it, as its definition, precisely that independence in which the realist finds the mark of ultimate reality. And if "independence" constitutes unreality, presence to and union with experience must be what constitutes reality.

Yet, however fatal this line of argument may be to the principle of the realistic contention, we ought not to be satisfied with such a mere general refutation. We must try to see what is the element of truth in the realistic views to which they owe the plausibility they have always possessed for minds of a certain type. In Philosophy we are never really rid of an error until we have learned how it arises and what modicum of truth it contains.

(1) *Agnostic Realism.* We may begin with Agnosticism, with which we ought now to have no serious difficulty. Agnostic Realism, as we have seen, is in principle a doubly self-contradictory theory. For it combines in one breath the irreconcilable declarations that the reality of things is unknowable and that it knows it to be so.[1] Further, as we have just said, it makes alleged contradictions which only exist in and for experience, its sole ground for affirming that something, of which we can only specify that it is *outside* all experience, transcends cognition. To have grasped these two points is to have disposed of Agnosticism as a metaphysical theory.

Yet with all its defects Agnosticism still enshrines one piece of truth which the metaphysician is peculiarly prone to forget. Of all men the metaphysician, just because his special interest is to know something final and certain about Reality, is the most apt to exaggerate the amount of his certain knowledge. It is well to be reminded that the certainty with which we may say that Reality is experience is compatible with a very imperfect and limited theoretical insight into experience itself. In actual life this is a far from unfamiliar fact; the literature of common sense is full of observations to the effect that we never really know our own hearts, that the most difficult task of the sage is to understand himself, and so forth,—complaints which all turn on the point that even our own limited direct experience of our own meanings and purposes goes far beyond what we can at any moment express in the form of reflective knowledge. Yet it is easy, when we come to deal in Metaphysics with the nature of ultimate Reality, to forget this, and to suppose that the certainty with which we can say that the ultimately Real is an experience justifies us in wholesale dogmatising about the special character of that experience. As a protest against such exaggerated estimates of the extent of our theoretical knowledge of the nature of Reality, Agnosticism thus con-

---

[1] The sceptics of antiquity, who were more alive to this contradiction than most of our modern Agnostics, tried to evade the difficulty by saying that they maintained the unknowability of things not as a demonstrated certainty, but as a "probable opinion." But this distinction is itself illogical, for unless some propositions are certain there is no ground for considering any one proposition more probable than another. *E.g.*, if I know that a die with six faces has four pips on each of two faces, and five pips on only one, I can logically say "it is probable that with this die four will be thrown oftener than five." If I am totally uncertain what number of pips is marked on the various faces, I cannot regard one throw as more probable than another.

tains a germ of genuine and important truth, and arises from a justifiable reaction against the undue emphasising of the merely intellectual side of our experience, of which we have already seen, and shall hereafter still more fully see, ground to complain as a besetting weakness of the metaphysically minded.

(2) *Dogmatic Realism*, that is, Realism with admittedly knowable independent "reals," is a much more workable doctrine, and in one of its forms, that of the so-called "naïve realism" which supposes the world of experienced things with all its perceived qualities to exist independently of any relation to an experiencing subject in precisely the same form in which we experience it, fairly represents the ordinary views of unphilosophical "common-sense" men. Nothing seems more obvious to "common sense" than that my perception of a thing does not bring it out of nothing into existence, and again does not create for it new qualities which it had not before. It is because the thing is already there, and has already such and such a nature, says "common sense," that I perceive it as I do. Therefore the whole world of perceived things must exist independently in the same form in which they are perceived, as a condition of my perception of them.

When this view comes to be worked out as a philosophical theory, it usually undergoes some transformation. The fact of illusion, and the experimentally ascertained subjective differences between individual percipients,[1] or between different states of the same percipient, make it hard for the realist who wishes to be scientific to maintain that *all* the perceived qualities of experienced things are equally independent of the experiencing subject. Reflection usually substitutes for the "naïve" realism of everyday life, a theory of "scientific" realism according to which the existence and some of the known properties of the experienced world are independent of the experiencing subject, while others are regarded as mere secondary effects arising from the action of an independent reality on the subject's consciousness. With the further differences between the various types of scientific realism, according to the special properties which are held to belong to things independently of the percipient subject, we are not at present concerned.[2]

[1] *E.g.*, peculiarities of the individual's colour-spectrum, total and partial colour-blindness, variations in sensibility to musical pitch, etc., etc.
[2] The best known and most popular version of the theory is that of Locke and of a great deal of our popular science, according to which the "primary" qualities of matter, *i.e.* those which have to be treated as fundamental in the physical sciences, are independently real, while the rest are mere effects produced

It is, of course, clear that our general argument against the existence of any reality except as in an experience tells just as much against "naïve" realism and its more reflective outgrowth "scientific" realism as against Agnosticism. But the very plausibility and wide diffusion of realistic views of this type make it all the more necessary to reinforce our contention by showing what the truth Realism contains is, and just where it diverges from truth into fallacy. Nor is it specially difficult to do this. The important elements of truth contained in Realism seem to be in the main two. (1) It is certain that a thing may be real without being consciously present as a distinguishable aspect in *my* experience. Things do not begin to exist when I begin to be aware of them, or cease to exist when I cease to be aware of them. And again, the fact that I make mistakes and am subject to illusion shows that the qualities of things are not necessarily in reality what I take them to be. (2) Further, as is shown by the fact of my imperfect understanding of my own feelings and purposes, something may actually be an integral part of my own life as an experiencing subject without my clearly and consciously recognising it as such when I reflect on the contents of my experience.

But precisely how much do these two considerations prove? All that is established by the first is the point on which we have already insisted, that it is not *my* experience which constitutes Reality; and all that is established by the second, that experience, as we have already repeatedly seen, is not merely cognitive. But the admission of both these positions brings us not one step nearer the conclusion which the realist draws from them, that real existence is independent of all experience. Because it is easy to show that the reality of a thing does not depend on its being explicitly recognised by any one finite percipient or any aggregate of finite percipients, and again, that there is more in any experience of finite percipients than those percipients know, the realist thinks he may infer that there are realities which would still be real though they entered into no experience at all. But there is really no logical connection whatever between the premisses of this inference and the conclusion which is drawn from them.

This may be made clearer by a couple of examples.

---

by their action on our sense-organs. The more thorough-going metaphysical doctrines of realists like Leibnitz and Herbart, being much further removed from the "naïve realism" of unreflective common sense, have never enjoyed the same currency.

Take, to begin with, the case of the mental life of my fellow human beings. And, to state the case in the form in which it appears most favourable to the realist conclusion, let us imagine an Alexander Selkirk stranded on a barren rock in the midst of the ocean. The hopes and fears of our Selkirk are independent of my knowledge of them just as completely and in just the same sense in which the existence and conformation of the rock on which he is stranded are so. I and all other inhabitants of the earth may be just as ignorant of Selkirk's existence and of what is passing in his mind as we are of the existence and geological structure of his rock. And again, what Selkirk explicitly cognises of his own inner life may bear as small a proportion to the whole as what he explicitly cognises of the properties of his rock to the whole nature of the rock. Yet all this in no wise shows that Selkirk's hopes and fears and the rest of his mental life are not experience or have a reality "independent of experience." Hopes and fears which are not experience, not psychical matter of fact, would indeed be a contradiction in set terms. And what the argument fails to prove of Selkirk's mental life, it fails, for the same reason, to prove of Selkirk's rock.

We may pass from the case of the mental life of a fellow-man to the case of unperceived physical reality. A recent realist philosopher, Mr. L. T. Hobhouse, has brought forward as a clear instance of an independent physical reality, the case of a railway train just emerging from a tunnel. I do not perceive the train, he says, until it issues from the tunnel, but it was just as real while it was running through the tunnel. Its reality is therefore independent of the question whether it is perceived or not. But, in the first place, the argument requires that the train shall be empty; it must be a runaway train without driver, guard, or passengers, if the conditions presumed in the premisses are to be fulfilled. And, in the second place, we may retort that even an empty runaway train must have been despatched from somewhere by somebody. It must stand in some relation to the general scheme of purposes and interests expressed in our system of railway traffic, and it is precisely this connection, with a scheme of purposes and interests, which makes the runaway train a reality and not a mere fiction of an ingenious philosopher's imagination. If Mr. Hobhouse's argument proves the independent reality of the train in the tunnel, it ought equally to prove, and does equally prove, the independent existence of Selkirk's fluctuations from hope to despair and back again on his isolated rock. And precisely because it proves both conclusions equally, the sort of independence it establishes cannot be independence of experience. Like all realist arguments, it turns on the identification of experience with the cognitive aspect of experience, an identification too often suggested by the language of the "idealists" themselves.[1]

§ 8. The persistent vitality of Realism is due to its protest against the fallacies of an opposing theory which has of late especially found favour with some distinguished students of natural science, and which we may conveniently call Subjectivism.[2] Realism, as we saw, started from the true premisses, that there are real facts of which my experience does not make me explicitly aware, and that my cognition even of my own experience is incomplete, and argued to the false conclusion that there are therefore realities independent of any experience. Subjectivism reasons in the opposite way. It asserts truly that there is no reality outside experience, and then falsely concludes that I can know of no reality except my own cognitive states. Its favourite formula are expressions such as, "We know only the modifications of our own consciousness," "All we know is our own perceptions," "Nothing exists but states of consciousness." These formulæ are not all obviously identical in meaning, but the exponents of Subjectivism seem to use them without any conscious distinction, and we shall probably do the theory no injustice if we criticise it on the assumption that the expressions are meant to be of identical signification.

Now it is clear that the logical consequences of the subjectivist doctrine are so subversive of all the practical assumptions upon which daily life is based, that they should require the most stringent proof before we give our assent to them. If Subjectivism is true, it follows immediately that not merely the "whole choir of heaven and furniture of earth," but the

[1] Compare Ward, *Naturalism and Agnosticism*, vol. ii. p. 178 ff., and Royce, *World and Individual*, First Series, Lect. 3. Prof. Royce's treatment of Realism, though interesting and suggestive, is perhaps a little too much of a "short and easy way" with the antagonist to be quite convincing. Mr. Hobhouse's anti-idealistic argument (*Theory of Knowledge*, 517-539) seems to me only to hold good against the "Subjectivism" discussed in our next section, but the reader will do well to examine it thoroughly for himself.

[2] We might also suitably call it Presentationism, if the name were not already appropriated in a different sense as distinctive of certain psychological theories. The English reader will find a confused but typical exposition of Subjectivism in the opening chapters of Prof. Karl Pearson's *Grammar of Science*. Subjectivist writers usually call themselves "idealists," and regard themselves as disciples of Berkeley and Hume. Berkeley was, however, a subjectivist, if at all, only in respect to the physical world, while Hume's conclusions are purely sceptical. The reader of Prof. Pearson must carefully observe that the "descriptive" theory of physical science has no special connection with Subjectivism, and is, in fact, held by philosophers like Profs. Ward and Royce, who are not subjectivists.

whole of humanity, so far as I have any knowledge of its existence, is a mere subjective affection of my own "consciousness," or, as the scientific subjectivist usually, for some not very obvious reason, prefers to say, of my own brain. Every argument which the subjectivist can produce to show that "things" are, for my knowledge at any rate, "modifications of my own consciousness," applies to the case of my fellow-men with as much force as to the case of the inorganic world. The logical inference from the subjectivist's premisses, an inference which he is rarely or never willing to draw, would be that he is himself the sole real being in a world of phantoms, not one of which can with any certainty be said to correspond to a real object. And conversely, any valid ground for recognising the existence of my fellow-men as more than "states of my own consciousness," must equally afford ground for admitting the reality, in the same general sense, of the rest of the world of things familiar to us from the experiences of everyday life.[1] For if any one of the things composing the world of practical life has a reality which is not dependent upon its presence to my particular experience, then there is the same reason for believing that every other such thing has a like reality, unless there happen to be special grounds for regarding the perception to which it is present as an hallucination.

We must not, however, simply dismiss the subjectivist theory in this summary way. We must examine the doctrine in detail sufficiently to discover where the fallacy comes in, how it arises, and what modicum of sound philosophic insight it may possibly contain. To take these three points in logical order—

(*a*) The current arguments for Subjectivism are often so stated as to confuse together two quite distinct positions. When it is said that what we perceive is "our own subjective states," the meaning intended may be either that there is, at least so far as I am able to know, no real existence in the universe except that of my "states of consciousness"; or again, that there are such realities, but that the *properties* which I perceive do not belong to them in their own nature but are only subjective effects of their action upon my "conscious-

---

[1] On the existence of my fellow-men as the one real proof of the objective existence of the physical world, see Royce, *Studies in Good and Evil*, essay on "Nature, Consciousness, and Self-Consciousness," and "Mind and Nature," by the present writer, in *International Journal of Ethics* for October 1902. In the latter essay I have, I think, sufficiently exposed the flimsy reasoning by which subjectivists attempt to justify belief in the existence of other human beings from the subjectivist point of view.

ness," or, if you prefer to speak in physiological language upon my nervous system. Now, many of the arguments commonly urged by the subjectivist would at most only prove the second conclusion, in which the subjectivist agrees to a large extent with the scientific realist. Thus it is an *ignoratio elenchi* to reason as if the facts of hallucination, illusion, and discrepancy between the reports of different percipients or different sense-organs of the same percipient gave any support to the special doctrine of Subjectivism. These facts, which, as we have seen, are equally appealed to by scientific realists, prove no more than that we do not always perceive the world of things as it is, and as it must be thought of if we would think truly,—in other words, that there is such a thing as error.

Now the problem " How is it possible for us to think or perceive falsely?" is, as the student of Greek philosophy knows, both difficult and important. But the existence of error in no way shows that the things which I perceive are "states of my own consciousness"; on the contrary, error is harder to explain on the subjectivist theory than on any other. For if what I perceive has some kind of existence distinct from the mere fact of my perceiving it, there is at least a possibility of understanding how the reality and my perception of it may be discrepant; but if the existence of a thing is only another name for the fact that I perceive it, it seems impossible that I should perceive anything except as it is. On the subjectivist theory, as Plato showed in the *Theaetetus*, every percipient being ought, at every moment of his existence, to be infallible.

We may confine our attention, then, to the grounds which the subjectivist alleges for the former conclusion, that nothing can be known to exist except my own "states of consciousness," and may dismiss the whole problem of erroneous perception as irrelevant to the question. Now the general argument for Subjectivism, however differently it may be stated by different writers, consists, in principle, of a single allegation. It is alleged as a fact in the Psychology of cognition, that things are immediately perceived by us as modifications of our own sensibility, or " states of our own consciousness," and that it is therefore impossible to get behind this ultimate condition of all perception. Against this psychological doctrine we have to urge (1) that it is in flagrant contradiction with the certain facts of actual life; and (2) that, as a doctrine in Psychology, it is demonstrably false.

(1) There are certain realities, admitted by the subjectivist himself, which are manifestly *not* "states of my consciousness," and of which I yet, as the subjectivist himself admits, have a genuine though imperfect knowledge ; such realities are, *e.g.*, the ends and purposes of my fellow-men, and again many of my own ends and purposes. It is allowed on all hands that I can know not only the fact of the existence of other men, but also, to some extent at least, the character of their various purposes and interests. This is involved, for instance, in the simple fact that when I read a letter it is normally possible for me to understand the writer's meaning. It is equally involved in the fact that I can know the truth of any ordinary historical matter of fact, *e.g.*, the date of the great fire of London. Neither the date of the fire of London nor the meaning of my correspondent's sentences is a "state of my consciousness" in any intelligible sense of the words, yet both are typical instances of the kind of facts of which our ordinary knowledge of the world of everyday life and practice wholly consists. And what is true of facts relating to the deeds and purposes of others is equally true of my own deeds and purposes. The facts which make up my own life cannot, without violence to language, be reduced to "states of my consciousness." For instance, I may know that I have a certain temperament or disposition, *e.g.*, that I am irascible by temperament or of a sentimental disposition ; but though my knowing these truths about myself may in a sense be called a state of my consciousness, the truths themselves cannot be called "states of my consciousness" without a serious logical fallacy of equivocal middle term.

(2) This will be made clearer by a consideration of the psychological principle invoked by the subjectivist. What the subjectivist means when he says that in perception I am aware only of the states, or subjective modifications, of my own consciousness, is that the object of which each perceptive state is aware is simply itself as a perceptive state ; the perception perceives itself and nothing else. *E.g.*, when I say I see red, what I am really aware of is that I am in a state of perceiving red ; when I say I hear a noise, what I am aware of is that I am in a state of hearing a noise, and so universally. Now this is so far from being a truth, that it is absolutely and demonstrably false. We may, in fact, definitely lay it down that the one thing of which no one, except the introspective psychologist, is ever aware is his own perceptive state in the act of perceiving, and that, even in the case of the psychologist who sets himself purposely to study his own

states, no perceptive state ever perceives itself. What I am aware of when I look at a red surface is not "myself-as-perceiving-red," but the splash of red colour itself. When I see a man, I do not perceive "myself-as-seeing-a-man," but I perceive the other man. So when I take a resolution to act in a certain way or realise that I am in a certain mood, what I am directly aware of is not "myself-as-forming-the-resolution" or "myself-as-in-the-mood," but the resolution or the mood. Even when, as an introspective psychologist, I sit down to study the formation of resolutions or the peculiarities of emotional moods by reflection on my own experience, the state in which I study the formation of a resolution or the nature of a mood is not itself the state of resolving or of experiencing the mood in question. We cannot too strongly insist that, if by "self-consciousness" is meant a cognitive state which is its own object, *there is no such thing, and it is a psychological impossibility that there should be any such thing, as self-consciousness. No cognitive state ever has itself for its own object. Every cognitive state has for its object something other than itself.*[1]

Even where I make an assertion about my subjective condition, as when I say "I know I am very angry," the state of knowing about my feeling is as distinct from the feeling itself as the state of knowing that I see red is from the red colour that I see. What the subjectivist does is to confuse the two. Because the act of knowing is itself a state of the knowing subject, and because in some cases the knowledge may again have reference to some other state of the same subject, he infers that what I know at any moment is my own subjective condition in the act of knowing. In other

[1] The self-knowledge which is a fact in real life, as distinguished from the fictitious self-consciousness of some psychologists, is quite a different thing and involves two distinct acts of cognition: (1) the awareness of certain objects of cognition, and (2) the recognition of those objects as in some way qualifying my "self." And the "self" which I recognise as thus qualified is again no immediate datum of experience, but a largely hypothetical intellectual construction, as we shall have opportunity to see later on.

This is perhaps the place to add the further remark, that if we would be rigidly accurate in psychological terminology, we ought to banish the very expression "consciousness" or "state of consciousness" from our language. What are really given in experience are attentive processes with a certain common character. We abstract this character and give it the name of "consciousness," and then fall into the blunder of calling the concrete processes "states" or "modifications" of this abstraction, just as in dealing with physical things we first make abstraction of their common properties, under the name of "matter," and then talk as if the things themselves were "forms" of "matter." *Properly speaking, there are physical things and there are minds, but there are no such things in the actual world as "matter" and "consciousness,"* and we do well to avoid using the words where we can help it.

and more technical words, he confuses the cognitive act or state with its own object. To what absurd results this confusion would lead him, if he were logical in the inferences he makes from it, we have already seen. We can now see that psychologically the confusion is a double one. (1) The subjectivist confuses experience with mere awareness of a presented content. He ignores the presence of the true "subjective" factor of selective attention throughout experience, and is thus led to forget that all experiences imply an element which is *in* the experiencing mind but not *presented to it*. (2) And in confining his attention to the presentational aspect of experience, he goes on to confound the presented content with the fact of its presentation. As against this second confusion it is essential to a true theory of knowledge to emphasise three points of distinction between the presented content or object of a cognitive state and the state itself, considered as a process in the history of an experiencing subject. (1) The cognitive state is never its own object, it *refers* to or *cognises* an object distinct from its own existence as a psychical occurrence. This is the truth which Realism distorts into the doctrine that the object of knowledge must have a reality "independent of" experience. (2) The object of knowledge is never created by the occurrence of the psychical state in which a particular percipient becomes aware of its existence. This is just as true of so-called "merely ideal" objects as of physical things. The properties of the natural logarithms or of the circular functions in trigonometry are just as independent of my knowledge of them as the qualities of the trees and animals I should see if I turned from my writing desk and looked out at the window. (3) The object of knowledge has always a character of which only a fragment is ever presented to my perception or reflection in any cognitive state. Every cognitive state *refers to* or *stands for* a great deal more than it directly means to me.

(3) The origin of the subjectivist fallacy, as has been brilliantly shown by Avenarius,[1] is to be found in the "intrasubjective intercourse" of a plurality of percipients capable of communicating their experience to each other. So long as I am dealing solely with myself as an experiencing being and my relation to my own environment, there is no possibility of a subjectivist interpretation. In my own direct experience I have to do neither with

[1] See *Der Menschliche Weltbegriff*, pp. 21–62; and, for the merely English reader, Ward, *Naturalism and Agnosticism*, vol. ii. p. 168 ff.

"mental states" nor with mere "objects of cognition," but with *things* which in various ways by their interference assist or hinder the accomplishment of my various purposes, and of which I have therefore to take note, so as to adapt my ways of reaching my ends to their ways of behaviour. Hence the "natural" view of the world, for a single experiencing being, would be that of "naïve realism," to which the things forming my environment are real in precisely the same sense in which I am real myself. But as soon as I have to take account of the experiences of other percipients, there arises an inevitable fallacy which leads to philosophical consequences of the gravest kind. Starting with the assumption that the things I perceive are the real things, I feel a difficulty as to how the same things can be perceived by the other percipients around me. *E.g.*, if the sun I see is the real sun, what about the sun seen by some one else? Instead of finding the true explanation, that all the percipients are in relation to a common environment which is independent of its presence to any one percipient's experience, I very naturally fall into the mistake of thinking the things perceived by other men to be "ideas" or "percepts" of the real things perceived by me. These perceptual copies of the real things I, for obvious reasons, locate somewhere "in" the organisms of my fellow-percipients. Then I go on to interpret my own experience in terms of the theory I originally devised to meet the case of my fellow-men, and infer that what I myself perceive is a set of "percepts" or "ideas" produced "in" my organism by a reality "outside" all experience. And it is then an easy step to the final conclusion that, inasmuch as all known and knowable things are mere "ideas in some one's head," nothing else exists. Subjectivism is thus the last step in the development of the fallacy which begins with what Avenarius calls "introjection." Just as we learned that the existence of our fellow-men is the cardinal fact of experience which affords the most immediate refutation of the subjectivist theory, so the original source of the subjectivist fallacy is failure to recognise their experience as being on the same level of reality as our own.

(4) We need not say much on the element of truth which Subjectivism preserves in a distorted form. We have seen that, as against Realism, Subjectivism is right in maintaining the indissoluble unity of real being with experience, though it twists this truth into an absurdity by first identifying experience with my own limited and imperfect experience

and then giving a false psychological interpretation of the nature of that experience itself. How a reality can be independent of presentation in *my* experience and yet be in its very nature dependent upon experience for its existence and character, has already been sufficiently illustrated. But we may perhaps say that even in the identification of experience with my own experience there is an underlying substratum of genuine philosophic truth. For, as we have more than once insisted, there is manifestly a great deal more in my own experience than what is at any time present as the object of conscious cognition. Or, as Mr. Bradley is fond of putting it, there is always more *in* my mind than *before* it. I am never fully aware at any moment even of the full nature of my own purposes and feelings. This is why the deceitfulness of my own heart has become a common-place of religious self-examination as well as of worldly wisdom.

Again, every increase of insight into our own real feelings and purposes involves increased insight into the feelings and purposes of the other feeling beings with whom we stand in the various relations of social intercourse.[1] Hence it might fairly be contended that fully to know your own meaning, fully to understand what you want, would imply complete insight into the structure of the whole world of reality,—in fact, that self-knowledge and knowledge of the universe must ultimately be the same thing. The systematic unity of the whole world of experience may be so complete that there is nothing in it anywhere which does not correspond to some element in the experience of every one of its members. Each member may, like the monads of Leibnitz, represent the whole system though at very different levels of coherency and from very different points of view. But such a conception, though it would concede to Subjectivism that whatever forms a part of the system of real being somehow falls within my individual experience, would take as the foundation of its assertion that very distinction between what is implicitly present *in* my experience and what is explicitly *before* it which Subjectivism consistently ignores. Whether the doctrine as thus re-stated can be affirmed as more than a fascinating possibility, we shall be better able to judge when we have discussed in our next chapter the systematic unity of Reality.

[1] This is true even in what seems at first sight the exceptional case of advance in mere theoretical insight. The more clearly you realise the character of the problems which your own intellectual pursuits lead up to and the nature of their solution, the clearer becomes your insight into the problems and purposes of other workers in the same field.

Consult further :—F. H. Bradley, *Appearance and Reality*, chaps. 13, 14; T. Case, *Physical Realism*, pt. 1; L. T. Hobhouse, *The Theory of Knowledge*, pt. 3, chap. 3, *The Conception of External Reality;* H. Lotze, *Metaphysic*, bk. i. chap. 7 (pp. 207–231 of vol. i. in Eng. trans.); J. S. Mackenzie, *Outlines of Metaphysics*, bk. i. chap. 3, *Theories of Metaphysics;* J. Royce, *The World and the Individual*, First Series (Lecture on the First Conception of Being).

CHAPTER II

THE SYSTEMATIC UNITY OF REALITY

§ 1. The problem whether Reality is ultimately One or Many is inevitably suggested to us by the diverse aspects of our own direct experience of the world. The different theories may be classed, according to their solution of this problem, as Monistic, Pluralistic, and Monadistic. § 2. Pluralism starts from the presumed fact of the mutual independence of human selves, and teaches that this independence of each other belongs to all real beings. But (a) the independence with which experience presents us is never complete, nor the unity of the "selves" perfect. (b) The theory is inconsistent with the systematic character of all reality as presupposed in both knowledge and action. § 3. Monadism again makes the systematic unity of the real either an illusion or an inexplicable accident. § 4. Reality, because systematic, must be the expression of a single principle in and through a multiplicity. The unity and multiplicity must both be real, and each must necessarily involve the other. § 5. If both are to be equally real, the whole system must be a single experience, and its constituents must also be experiences. A perfect systematic whole can be neither an aggregate, nor a mechanical whole of parts, nor an organism. The whole must exist for the parts, and they for it. § 6. This may also be expressed by saying that Reality is a subject which is the unity of subordinate subjects, or an individual of which the constituents are lesser individuals. § 7. The nearest familiar analogue to such a systematic whole would be the relation between our whole "self" and the partial mental systems or lesser "selves." § 8. The nearest historic parallel to this view is to be found in Spinoza's theory of the relation of the human mind to the "infinite intellect of God."

§ 1. THE problem of the One and the Many is as old as Philosophy itself, and inevitably arises from the earliest and simplest attempts to think in a consistent way about the nature of the world in which we play our part. On the one hand, our experience, in the piecemeal shape in which it first appears as we begin to reflect on it, seems to exhibit an indefinite plurality of more or less independent things, each pursuing its own course and behaving in its own way, and connected at best with only a few of the other members of our environment. There is, for instance, no obvious connection between one man's career and those of most of his contemporaries, to say nothing of the innumerable host of his predecessors and successors in the race of life. And, similarly, the behaviour of one inanimate thing seems at first sight to be unaffected by that of most of the other things around it. The world seems to us at times to be made up of an indefinite multiplicity of beings who merely happen to be actors on the same stage, but have, in the majority of cases, no influence upon each other's parts.

Yet, on the other hand, there are equally strong *primâ facie* reasons for regarding the world as a single unity. Every addition to our theoretical insight into the structure of things adds to our recognition of the intimate connection between things and processes which previously seemed merely disconnected. Physical science, as it grows, learns more and more to look upon nature as a realm of interconnected events where no one fact is ultimately entirely independent of any other fact; political experience and social science alike reveal the intimate interdependence of human lives and purposes. And, over and above the ascertained empirical facts which point to the ultimate unity of the world, there is another potent influence which we might call the "instinctive" basis for the belief in unity. However discontinuous my environment may appear, it is never a mere disconnected multiplicity. The very circumstance that it is throughout *my* environment, and thus relative to the ends by which my attention is determined, gives it to a certain degree the character of a coherent system. At the lowest level of philosophic reflection, we cannot permanently fail to apprehend our world as in principle one, precisely because it is *our* world, and we ourselves are all in some degree beings of steady systematic purpose, not mere bundles of disconnected and conflicting impulses. While yet again, it is the very limitation of our own interests and our lack of clear insight into their full import which leads us at other times to find apparent disconnected multiplicity and lack of cohesion in our world.

The problem of Philosophy in dealing with these rival aspects of the world of experience then becomes that of deciding whether either of them can be adopted as the truth in isolation from the other. Or if neither is the whole truth, we must ask ourselves in what way the world can be at once One and Many, how the characters of systematic unity and of indefinite variety can be consistently thought of as belonging to the same Reality. Is Reality, we have to ask, One or is it Many, and if it is both, how are the unity and multiplicity connected?

The answers which different philosophical systems have given to this question may conveniently be classified under three general denominations. There are (1) the *Monistic* views, which lay the principal stress upon the unity of the real, and tend to treat the aspect of plurality and variety as illusory, or at least as of secondary importance; (2) the various forms of *Pluralism*, according to which the variety and multiplicity of real beings is the primary fact, and their systematic unity either an illusion, or at any rate a subordinate aspect of their nature; (3) *Monadism*, which aims at harmonising the positions of the monist and pluralist, by treating the world as a multiplicity of really independent things or "monads," which are somehow combined from without into a system. From this last point of view the plurality and the systematic unity are alike real and alike important for the understanding of the world, but are of different origin, the plurality being inherent in the things themselves, the unity external to them and coming from a foreign source. Within each of the three main types of theory there is, of course, room for the greatest divergence of view as to the special nature of the real. A monistic system may be purely materialistic, like that of Parmenides, who taught that the world is a single homogeneous solid sphere, or idealistic like that, *e.g.*, of Schopenhauer; or again, it may treat mind and "matter" as "aspects" of a common reality. A pluralist or monadist, again, may conceive of each of his independent real things as a physical atom, as a soul of any degree of organisation, or even, in the fashion of some contemporary thought, as a person.

With regard to the relation between this classification of philosophical theories and that of the last chapter, I may just observe that, while a monist is not necessarily an idealist, a consistent pluralist or monadist ought logically to be a realist. For the mutual independence of the various real things cannot exist without involving in itself their independence of experience. If A and B are two completely independent things, then the existence and character of A must be independent of presence to the experience of B, and similarly A must be equally independent of presence to the experience of C, or of anything in the world but itself. And we have already seen that there is always more in the nature of any finite percipient than can be present to his own experience. Thus ultimately the existence and qualities of A must be independent of all experience, including A's own.[1] For this reason I cannot but think that the various

---

[1] This consideration obviously influenced Leibnitz. It is a much-decried doctrine in his system that every "monad," or simple real thing, perceives nothing but its own internal states; there are no "windows" through which

attempts to combine Pluralism with Idealism by maintaining that the universe consists of a number of independent "souls" or "persons," rest on confusion of thought. These doctrines appear to be essentially realist in their spirit.

§ 2. We may conveniently attempt to construct our own theory of the One and the Many by first excluding views which appear mistaken in principle, and thus gradually narrowing the issues. Among these mistaken views I am forced to reckon all forms of consistent and thorough-going Pluralism. Pluralism, so far at least as I am able to see, begins by misapprehending the facts upon which it professes to base itself, and ends by giving an interpretation of them which is essentially irrational. The fundamental fact from which Pluralism starts as an ultimate datum of all experiences is the familiar one that there are other men in the world besides myself. My world is not simply a theatre for the execution of my own aims and the satisfaction of my own wants. There are interests in it which are not mine, and to which I must adapt myself if I mean to achieve my own purposes. The world thus contains minds other than my own, and what makes them *other* is that the interests and purposes by which their lives are determined are, like my own, unique and incommunicable. Now, Pluralism bids us take the facts, as thus stated, as the model for our conception of the universe. The pattern upon which the pluralist views of Reality are constructed is that of a community consisting of a great number of selves or persons, each with its own unique interests, and each therefore at once internally simple and indivisible and exclusive of all the rest. In whatever special form the pluralist thinks of his ultimate realities, whether as physically indivisible particles, as mathematical points, or as sentient beings, it is always from the facts of human social life conceived in this ultra-individualist way that he in the last resort derives his concept of their simplicity and mutual repulsion.

But (*a*) the facts themselves are not correctly stated. The human experiences upon which the pluralist relies for his conclusion present at once too much and too little unity for the purposes of his theory. On the one hand, the selves

---

one monad can behold the states of another. It is easy to show that this doctrine leads to extremely far-fetched and fantastic hypotheses to account for the apparent communication between different monads, but not so easy to show that Pluralism can afford to dispense with it. See in particular Leibnitz's *New System of the Nature of Substances* (Works, ed. Erdmann, 124 ff. : ed. Gerhardt, iv. 477 ff. ; Eng. trans. in Latta's *Leibniz: the Monadology*, etc., p. 297 ff.), especially §§ 13-17 and *Monadology*, §§ 7-9, 51.

or persons composing society are not themselves simple, undifferentiated unities. Just as your interests and mine may often collide, so within what the pluralist assumes as the indivisible unit of my own personality there may be a similar collision. What I call my "own interests," or my own "apperceptive systems" or "trains of thought," may exhibit the same kind of incompatibility and the same sort of conflict for superiority as is found where your ideas and mine clash. Thus Ethics and Psychology are led to distinguish between my "true" self and the false selves by which it may on occasion be dominated, between my "higher" self and the "lower" selves which, in morality, have to be repressed by the higher, my "permanent" self, and the temporary interests by which it is often overpowered, to say nothing of "subliminal" consciousness and "dual" or "alternating personality." The "self" is so far from being a mere unit, that the variety and, what is more, the incompatibility of its contents is a matter of everyday experience.[1]

Pluralism may, of course, and often does, verbally admit this. The units of the pluralist, we are often told, are not mere units devoid of variety, but wholes which are the union of differences. But to concede this is to cut away the ground from under the pluralist's feet. If the variety and the mutual struggle between the elements of the self are not enough to destroy its unity, by parity of reasoning the multiplicity of selves in the world and their mutual repulsions are not enough to prove that the whole of Reality is not, in spite of its multiplicity of detail, a unity more complete than any of the partial unities to be met with in our experience. In fact, the pluralist has to meet the following dilemma. Either his units are mere units without internal variety, and then it is easy to show that they are the merest nothings, or they have internal variety of their own, and therefore simply repeat within themselves the problem they are supposed to solve.

On the other hand, just as the facts of experience show us internal struggle and repulsion within the supposed units, so they also exhibit other relations than that of mutual exclusion between the different units. Human personal interests, for instance, are never merely mutually exclusive. No society consists of individuals whose purposes and

---

[1] See for a recent treatment of this point in its bearing upon the theory of volition and moral accountability, Mr. Bradley's article on "Mental Conflict and Imputation" in *Mind* for July 1902. There is probably no part of Psychology which suffers more from an improper over-simplification of awkward facts.

interests are simply reciprocally repellent. My aims and purposes may never completely coincide with those of other members of the same community, yet they have no meaning and could get no realisation but for the fact that they are, partially at any rate, comprised in the wider whole of social interests and purposes which makes up the life of the social organisations to which I belong. As the very etymology of such words as "society" and "community" shows—to say nothing of the results of psychological inquiry into the process of learning by imitation—the conception of human selves as independent units which somehow happen to stand in merely accidental or external relations is in flagrant conflict with the most fundamental facts of our social experience. It is only by the systematic suppression of fact that personal and social life can be made to support the hypothesis of Pluralism.

(*b*) Again, even if we could accept the pluralist account of the facts, the theory which Pluralism puts forward to account for them is in the end unintelligible. What Pluralism does, consciously or unconsciously, is to separate the unity of the world from its multiplicity. The multiplicity is supposed to be grounded in the ultimate nature of the real things themselves, their unity as a system, if they really are a system, to be imposed upon them from without. We are, in fact, left to choose between two alternatives. Either the world is not a systematic whole at all, but a mere chaos of purely independent atoms, in which case the whole of our thought, with its indispensable presupposition of the systematic unity of the object of knowledge, is an illusion, or else the world really is a system, but a system, so to say, by accident. The things of which the system is composed are real as detached separate units, but by a fortunate chance they happen all to possess some common relation to an external *tertium quid* (for instance, to God), by which they are combined into a system and thus become knowable as a connected whole.

Now we cannot, if we are intellectually conscientious, rest finally content with a statement of this kind, which leaves the plurality and the systematic unity of the real world side by side as two independent unconnected facts. If the contents of the world really form a system at all, in any way whatever, that is itself one fact among others which a sound metaphysical theory must recognise, and of which it must offer some intelligible account. *E.g.*, suppose you say, with some recent pluralists, that the world consists of a number of independent persons or spirits, who nevertheless form a connected system or "moral kingdom," in virtue of the fact that they all find their moral ideal in God, the most perfect among them. You have now not one ultimate fact before you, the multiplicity of independent selves, but two, this multiplicity and the relation of each element in it to God. Unless you are going to treat this second fact as an "ultimate inexplicability," *i.e.* a fortunate accident, you are now bound to treat the systematic relation of the selves to God and through God to each other as no less a part of their ultimate nature than their distinction from each other. Their separateness and independence is thus no longer for you the ultimate truth; they are just as truly one by your account as they are many. Their union in a system is no longer an external relation foreign to their own nature, but the deepest truth about that nature itself.

I will repeat the essence of this argument in another form. Any genuine Pluralism must be resolute enough to dismiss the idea of a systematic interconnection between its independent realities as an illusion of the human mind. But in doing so it must, to be consistent, deny the possibility of their mutual knowledge of each other's states. Each real thing must be a little world to itself, shut up within the closed circle of its own internal content. And thus, supposing Pluralism to be true, and supposing myself to be one of the real things of the pluralist scheme, I should have no means of knowing it to be true. Pluralism is unable to stand the question propounded by Mr. Bradley as the test of a philosophical doctrine, "Is the truth of this theory consistent with the fact that I know it to be true?"

The persistent popularity of Pluralism in many quarters is in fact due to the intrusion into Metaphysics of other than genuinely philosophical interests. It is maintained, not on its philosophical merits as a consistent theory, but because it is believed by its adherents to safeguard certain interests of morality and religion. It gives us, we are told, a "real God" and "real moral freedom." But, apart from the question whether these claims are justified by candid examination of the doctrine,[1] we must protest against their

---

[1] As the reader will readily collect from the preceding discussion, I do not myself admit that they are justified. On the contrary, I should hold that any consistent Pluralism must issue in what, if I held it myself, I should feel compelled to describe as Atheism, and the doctrine of blind chance as the arbiter of all things. In this matter I should like to associate myself entirely with the emphatic protest of Mr. Bradley, in *Mind* for July 1902, p. 313, and with the

which belonged to them as members.[1] But an organism, like a machine, fails to exhibit the perfect systematic unity of the One and the Many of which we are in quest. In the machine the aspect of multiplicity was relatively more real than that of unity; in the fully evolved organism the unity seems more completely real than the multiplicity. For the unity is a conscious one; in some degree at least it exists for itself, and its members again for it. Whereas it must be very doubtful whether the member exists for itself, and still more doubtful whether the whole exists in any sense for the members. And though the member cannot retain its peculiar form of existence except as a member in the whole, yet in even the highest organism the unity is so far relatively independent that it is unaffected by the removal of some of the members.

Not every member is of vital significance for the life of the whole. But in a complete systematic unity, as we saw, the unity and the multiplicity of the system must be equally real and equally interdependent. This can only be the case if the whole is for its members as well as the members for the whole. And that this may be so, just as the all-embracing whole of reality must, as we have learned, be an experience, so each of its members must be itself an experience. And because the members form a single system, just as there can be nothing in the experience of any member which is not contained in the experience which is the whole, so, on the other side, there can be nothing in the whole which does not in some way affect the experience of every member. Only in this way can we conceive of a systematic Reality in which the unity and the multiplicity of the system are alike real and equally real. Such a view is, strictly speaking, hardly to be called either Pluralism or Monism. It is not Pluralism, for it does not make the unity of the system an illusion or an inexplicable accident; it is not Monism, in the current sense of the word, because it does not make the multiplicity deceptive. If a name is wanted, we might perhaps agree to call it Systematic Idealism.

§ 6. We may say, then, that Reality is a systematic Experience of which the components are likewise experiences. It would be much the same thing if we called

---

[1] As Aristotle more than once says, a human hand, for instance, is not when severed from the rest of the body a "hand" at all, except ὁμωνύμως "equivocally," any more than the "hand" of a statue is a true hand. (*I.e.* it is only a "true hand" so long as it *does the work* of a hand. Captain Cuttle's hook probably deserved the name of "hand" better than the severed member it replaced).

it a subject which is the unity of subordinate subjects. It is tempting again, at first sight, to say it is a self of selves. But the extreme ambiguity of the term "self" as used in contemporary Psychology makes it desirable to avoid an expression which is capable of the gravest misuse.[1] It is scarcely possible to say with any precision what we mean by one "self," whereas it is possible in a general way to say what we mean by one experience. An experience may be called one and the same in so far as it is the systematised expression of a single coherent purpose or interest, in so far, in fact, as it has a teleological unity. In practice it may be impossible to say precisely when this condition is fulfilled, but the slightest acquaintance with the psychological facts of the struggle between competing systems of ideas in normal, and of "dual" and "multiple" personality in abnormal, mental life is sufficient to show that the limits thus set by our definition to the single experience do not coincide with those ascribed to my "self" or "personality" in any of the shifting senses of the terms. The limits within which experience remains *one* experience according to our definition are, as the facts just alluded to show, often narrower, but again, the definition suggests that they may also be wider, than any which would currently be given to the "self."

Moreover, what we have already said as to the possibility of each "member" of our system being itself a system of lesser systems, forbids us to identify our view with any doctrine which asserts merely atomic and simple "selves" as the elements of Reality.

Another way of expressing the same thought would be to say that Reality is an Individual of which the elements are lesser individuals. The advantage of this form of expression is that it emphasises the fundamentally teleological character of the unity of the real, and also of each and all of its constituents. A thing, as we have already seen, is individual just so far as it is unique, and only that which is the embodiment of a single purpose or interest can be unique. A single whole of experience, owing its unity as a whole precisely to the completeness and harmony with which it expresses a single purpose or interest, is necessarily an individual. The all-embracing experience which constitutes Reality is thus in its inmost nature a complete individual. And the lesser experiences which form the elements or

---

[1] I shall attempt to show in a later chapter (Bk. IV. chap. 3) that, in any useful signification of the term "self," Reality is not a "self" nor yet a mere community of "selves."

material content of Reality are each, just so far as each is truly one experience, individual in the same sense as the whole. We may thus call Reality a complete or perfect individual of minor or incomplete individuals.

What the fundamental distinction between the supreme individual whole and the lesser individuals must be taken to consist in we shall discuss in our next chapter. Meanwhile we may note two points :—(1) The important thing about an individual is not its mere numerical unity, but its qualitative uniqueness. Any experience which we can pronounce to be individual must be called so, not merely because it is numerically one and not many, but because it is the consistent and harmonious embodiment of a coherent purpose Numerically considered, every such individual is necessarily many as well as one, precisely because it is a system. This applies especially to the supreme or absolute individual, the complete system of experience. It is individual primarily not because it is numerically one, but because it is the complete expression of a coherent idea or purpose. It has been the defect of too many monistic theories to overlook this, and to lay the main stress on the numerical oneness of the real.

(2) An experience individual in the sense already explained is what we mean by a "spirit." Spirit cannot be properly defined by contradistinction from a supposed non-spiritual reality, such as "matter," for such a definition would only amount to the assertion that spirit is what is not other than spirit, and would tell us nothing of the term to be defined. Nor, again, is spirit properly defined as a series of states or modifications of the abstraction "consciousness." The positive characteristic by which spiritual existence may be recognised is that in it the *what* and the *that* are combined in the unity of immediate feeling. And immediate feeling, as we have seen, is essentially teleological. Where you have a connected system of factors which can only be understood as a whole by reference to an explicit or implicit end, which constitutes their unity, you have spirit, and where you have spirit you have such a system. So that to call reality an individual of individuals is the same thing as to say that it is a spiritual system of which the elements, constituents, or terms, are in their turn spiritual systems.[1]

[1] Again, I must remind the reader that this recognition of the teleological character of mind does not in the least preclude the necessity for psychological analysis of mental states. Still less does it require us to include in our analysis a volitional element as one distinguishable aspect or component of the isolated mental state by the side of others, such as the presentational and emotional

Our doctrine may thus be seen to be fairly entitled to the name Idealism, which current usage has appropriated to the view that all existence is ultimately mental.

§ 7. Such a relation as we have asserted between the individual whole of Reality and the elements or terms within the whole is necessarily unique, and cannot be adequately illustrated from any less perfect type of systematic unity recognised by everyday or by scientific thought. In particular, we must carefully avoid the mistake of conceiving the relation of the elements to the totality in a mechanical way as that of "parts" to a "whole of parts"; or, again, in a merely biological way, as that of "members" to an organism. All such analogies lose sight of the intimate character of a union in which the elements and the totality exist not merely in and through, but also for each other.

The individual experiences which compose the supreme experience have a genuine, if an imperfect and partial, individuality of their own. They are not in it merely "ideally" or implicitly, as the points on a curve may be said to be in the periphery. And the whole, again, is a real individual, not a mere aggregate in which the parts are real but their unity merely imaginary. We may, if we like, say that it is made up of experiences or minds, but we must not say that it is a *collection* of minds. For a mere collection, as we have seen, in so far as it is a collection and nothing more, cannot be said to have any genuine individuality, precisely because it has no teleological unity of structure beyond that which we arbitrarily, and with reference to ends lying outside its own nature, impose upon it in the very act of counting its members, *i.e.* arranging them in serial order. Whether we could properly speak of the absolute whole as a *society* of minds is a further and a more difficult question. A society is much more than a mere collection: it has a purposive unity of structure which exists not merely for the sociological observer from without, but for its own members as active in assigning to each of them his own special place in relation to all the rest. How far society can be said to have such a unity *for itself* is a question which we cannot answer until we have dealt more fully with the problem of the relation between selfhood and individuality. And until we have answered it, we must

aspects. It might even be contended that a "tripartite" or three-aspect Psychology commits the mistake of counting in the whole psychical fact as one of its own components.

defer the decision as to whether the systematic individuality of the Absolute would be adequately recognised if we thought of it as a society. (See *infra*, Bk. IV. chap. 3.)

If we are to look at this stage for some analogue within our partial experience for the kind of unity of individuals in a single supreme individual which we have demanded for the system of Reality, we shall probably do best to turn to what is after all the most familiar thing in the world,—our own personal experience. If we consider the nature of any coherent purpose or "mental system," we shall find that, as the coherent embodiment of a purpose, it possesses a degree of individuality of its own. In proportion to the comprehensiveness, and again to the inner harmony or systematic structure of the interest it embodies, it constitutes a genuine self-existing individual whole of the kind which psychologists recognise as a "self." And again, in so far as my life exhibits determinate character, so far do these systematic purposes or minor "selves" form a larger system, also individual, which may be called my "total self." And both the many lesser "selves" and the larger "self" are real in the same sense of the word. Neither exists merely in or for the other; the wider or whole "self" is no mere collection or resultant or product of the more special "selves," nor are they again mere results of a theoretical process of analysis and abstraction. In so far as they are genuine systems at all, they are not mere "parts" of a whole, but each is the expression, in a concrete conscious life, of the nature of a larger whole from a special "point of view." The whole, if not equally in every part, is yet as a whole present in every part, and precisely for that reason the category of part and whole is inadequate to express their relation. Somewhat after this fashion we must conceive the structure of any individual whole of lesser individuals. Why, in spite of the analogy, it is desirable not to speak of the whole of Reality as a "Self," will be made clearer as we proceed.[1]

§ 8. The view we have formulated is perhaps more closely akin to Spinoza's conception of the relation of the human mind to the "infinite intellect of God," than to any other historically famous theory. According to Spinoza, the individual human mind is an "eternal mode of consciousness which, taken together with all other such 'modes,' makes up the infinite intellect of God." The meaning of the

---

[1] See *infra*, Bk. IV. chap. 3, where we shall find that the relation of the individual self to a social whole probably furnishes a still better, though not altogether satisfactory, illustration of our principle.

epithet "eternal" we cannot, of course, enter into until we have discussed the relation of the time-process to experience. The rest of the definition pretty clearly coincides in its general sense with the view we have tried to expound of the nature of the relation between the supreme experience and its constituent experiences. For the "modes" of Spinoza are definitely thought of as genuinely individual manifestations of the nature of his ultimate reality, "substance" or "God." Their individuality and their infinite multiplicity is no result of illusion or illegitimate abstraction. And, on the other hand, "substance" itself is genuinely individual; it is no mere abstract name for the common properties of a number of ultimately independent things.

Most of the adverse criticism which Spinozism has met with, as far at least as regards its doctrine of the nature of the human mind, seems to be based on misapprehension about the first of these points. From his use of the numerical category of whole and part to express the relation between substance and its modes, Spinoza has incorrectly been taken to be denying the fact of the genuine individuality of the finite experience, and therefore to be declaring the very existence of the finite to be mere baseless illusion. With his doctrine as thus misinterpreted, ours has, of course, no similarity. Nothing is explained away by calling it "illusion"; the "illusory" fact is there in spite of the hard names you choose to bestow on it, and demands explanation no less than any other fact. Our theory aims not at dismissing finite individuality as illusion, but at ascertaining what it means, what are its limits, and how it stands related to the complete individual whole of experience which Spinoza calls the *infinitus intellectus Dei*.[1]

The mention of Spinoza will no doubt suggest to the reader the famous doctrine, which has played so large a part in the subsequent development of philosophical Monism, of the double "aspects" or "attributes" of Reality. It is from Spinoza that modern Monism has learned the view that the mental and physical orders are related as two parallel but distinct manifestations of a common underlying reality, so that to every member of one order there corresponds a determinate member of the other. The two are thus everywhere inseparable and everywhere irreducible "parallel" expressions of a nature which is neither mental

---

[1] For Spinoza's doctrine see especially *Ethics*, I. 15, 25; II. 11, 40; III. 6–9; V. 22, 23, with the explanations of any good exposition of his system, such as that of Pollock or Joachim.

nor physical. On this fundamental point our theory, as will have been seen already, completely parts company with Spinozism. That the nature of one and the same common whole should be *equally* manifested in two entirely irreducible forms, is a patent impossibility. Either the unity of the whole or the absolute disparateness of its twin manifestations must be surrendered if we are to think consistently. Hence we cannot avoid asking in which of the two series the assumed common nature is more adequately expressed. According as we answer this question we shall find ourselves led in the end either to thorough-going Materialism or to thorough-going Idealism. For our own part, the perception that Reality is experience and nothing else has already committed us to the view that both of the seemingly disparate series must in the end be mental. Thus our doctrine may be said to be much what Spinoza's would be if the attribute of "extension" were removed from his scheme, and the whole of Reality identified with the "infinite intellect of God."[1]

Consult further:—B. Bosanquet, *Essentials of Logic*, lect. 2; *Logic*, vol. ii. chap. 7; F. H. Bradley, *Appearance and Reality*, chaps. 13, 14, 20; L. T. Hobhouse, *Theory of Knowledge*, pt. 3, chap. 6, "Reality as a System"; H. Lotze, *Metaphysic*, bk. i. chap. 6 (Eng. trans., vol. i. pp. 163–191); J. S. Mackenzie, *Outlines of Metaphysic*, bk. i. chaps. 2, 3; bk. iii. chap. 6; J. E. M'Taggart, *Studies in Hegelian Cosmology*, chap. 2.

[1] See further on the "Parallelistic" doctrine, Bk. IV. chap. 2.

CHAPTER III

REALITY AND ITS APPEARANCES—THE DEGREES OF REALITY

§ 1. Reality being a single systematic whole, the nature of its constituent elements is only finally intelligible in the light of the whole system. Hence each of its "appearances," if considered as a whole in itself, must be more or less contradictory. § 2. But some "appearances" exhibit the structure of the whole more adequately than others, and have therefore a higher degree of reality. § 3. This conception of degree of reality may be illustrated by comparison with the successive orders of infinites and infinitesimals in Mathematics. It would be the task of a complete Philosophy to assign the contents of the world to their proper place in the series of "orders" of reality. § 4. In general any subordinate whole is real in proportion as it is a self-contained whole. And it is a self-contained whole in proportion as it is (*a*) comprehensive, (*b*) systematic; that is, a thing is real just so far as it is truly individual. § 5. The two criteria of individuality, though ultimately coincident, tend in particular cases to fall apart for our insight, owing to the limitation of human knowledge. § 6. Ultimately only the whole system of experience is completely individual, all other individuality is approximate. § 7. In other words, the whole system of experience is an infinite individual, all subordinate individuality is finite. Comparison of this position with the doctrines of Leibnitz. § 8. Recapitulatory statement of the relation of Reality to its Appearances.

§ 1. REALITY, we have seen, is to be thought of as a systematic whole forming a single individual experience, which is composed of elements or constituents which are in their turn individual experiences. In each of these constituents the nature of the whole system manifests itself in a special way. Each of them contributes its own peculiar content to the whole system, and as the suppression or change of any one of them would alter the character of the whole, so it is the nature of the whole which determines the character of each of its constituents. In this way the whole and its constituent members are in complete interpenetration and form a perfect systematic unity. In the happy phrase of Leibnitz, we may say that each of the partial experiences reflects the whole system from its own peculiar "point of view." If we call the completed system, as it is for itself, Reality *par excellence*, we may appropriately speak of the partial experiences in which its nature is diversely manifested as its Appearances. We must remember, however, that to call them appearances is not to stamp them as illusory or unreal. They will only be illusory or unreal when we forget that they are one and all partial aspects or manifestations of a whole of which none of them adequately exhausts the contents.

When we forget this and treat any partial experience as though it were the complete and adequate expression of the whole nature of Reality,—in other words, when we try to apply to existence or the universe as a whole conceptions which are only valid for special aspects of existence,—we shall inevitably find ourselves led to contradictory and absurd results. Each partial aspect of a total system can only be ultimately understood by reference to the whole to which it belongs, and hence any attempt to treat the part in abstraction as itself a self-contained whole,—or, in other words, to treat the concepts with which we have to work in dealing with some special aspect of the world of experience as ultimately valid in their application to the whole system,— is bound to issue in contradiction. Again, just because our knowledge of the structure of the system as a whole is so imperfect as it is, our insight into the structure of its constituents is also necessarily limited. Hence it will commonly happen that, even within the limits of their applicability, the special concepts of our various sciences are not, when thought out, free from internal contradiction. For instance, we are led to absurd results when we try, as Materialism does, to interpret the whole system of experience in terms of the concepts used in the purely physical sciences; and again, even in their restricted use as physical categories, these concepts seem incapable of being so defined as to involve no element of contradiction.

In both these senses all Appearance implies an element of contradiction; only for an insight which could take in at once the whole system of existence would its details be completely coherent and harmonious. But this does not alter the fact that, so far as our insight into any part of the whole and its connection with other parts is self-consistent, it does convey genuine, though imperfect, knowledge of the whole. Though our detailed insight into the structure of the whole may never reach the ideal of perfect self-consistency, yet it may approximate to that ideal in different degrees, at different stages, or with reference to different aspects. And the closer the approximation the less the modification which our knowledge would require to bring it into complete harmony with itself, and the greater therefore the element of truth about Reality which it contains.

In particular, we must carefully avoid falling into the mistake of thinking of the Reality and the world of its appearances as though they formed two distinct realms. In a systematic unity, we must remember, the whole can exist only in so far as it expresses its nature in the system of its parts, and again the parts can have no being except as the whole expresses itself through them. To the degree to which this condition is departed from by any of the types of system familiar to us, those systems fall short of being perfectly systematic. Reality, then, being a systematic whole, can have no being apart from its appearance, though neither any of them taken singly, nor yet the sum of them thought of collectively,[1] can exhaust its contents. And though no appearance is the whole of Reality, in none of them all does the whole Reality fail to manifest itself as a whole. The whole is truly, as a whole, present in each and every part, while yet no part is the whole.[2]

We may once more illustrate by an appeal to our own direct experience. Consider the way in which we set to work to execute any systematic scheme or purpose, *e.g.*, the mastery of a particular science or a particular business. We have in such a case a central aim or purpose, which in the process of execution spreads out into a connected system of subordinate ideas and interests welded into one by the reference to a common end which pervades the whole. The supreme or central aim is only realised in the successive realisation of the subordinate stages; at the same time, while it is what sustains all the members of the system, it has no existence apart from them, though it is identical neither with any one of them nor yet with their sum collectively considered.

§ 2. If our conviction that Reality is a single systematic unity pervading and manifesting itself in lesser systematic unities is correct, we shall expect to find that some of the lesser systematic unities with which we have to deal in practical life and in the various sciences exhibit more of the

---

[1] Not the sum of them, because the systematic whole of Reality is not a sum but a single experience. To identify it with the *sum* of its appearances would be the same error which occurs in Ethics as the identification of happiness (a qualitative whole) with the sum of pleasures (a quantitative collection).

[2] The reader will find it instructive to observe how Prof. Sidgwick unconsciously assumes that the distinction between Reality and Appearance means a distinction between two more or less independent "worlds" or "things" (*Philosophy: its Scope and Relations*, Lectures 1 and 4), and thus deprives his own criticism of the antithesis of all validity as against a view like our own.

full character of the whole to which they belong than others. The "points of view" from which each minor system reflects the whole, though all true, need not be all equally true. Though the whole, in a genuine system, must be present as a whole in every part, it need not be equally present in all; it may well *not* be "*as* full, *as* perfect in a hair as heart." To take a concrete example, a cluster of mass-particles, a machine, a living organism, and a human mind engaged in the conscious systematic pursuit of truth, are all to some degree or other systematic unities, and all to some degree, therefore, repeat the structure of the universal whole to which they all belong. But it does not follow that all manifest the structure of that whole with equal adequacy and fulness. Indeed, any philosophy which admits development as a genuine feature of the world-process must maintain that they do not, that the nature of the whole system of Reality is exhibited with infinitely greater adequacy and clearness in the working of the conscious mind than in the changes of configuration of the system of mass-particles or even the vital processes of the physical organism.

In practical life, too, one of our most ineradicable convictions is that there are degrees of worth which coincide with degrees of the adequacy with which partial systems exhibit the nature of the larger wholes to which they belong. For instance, among the different mental systems which may be called my partial "selves," there are some which I call "truer" than others, on the ground that they more fully reveal my whole character as an individual human being. My whole character undoubtedly appears in and determines all the subordinate systems which make up my mental life. Each of them *is* the whole character in a special aspect, or as reacting upon a special system of suggestions, but some of them contain the whole in a more developed and explicit form than others. I am in one sense myself wherever I may be and whatever I may be doing, and yet I am "more myself" in health than in sickness, in the free pursuit of self-chosen studies than in the forced discharge of uncongenial tasks imposed on me by the necessity of earning an income.

We ought, then, to be prepared to find the same state of things universally in the relation of Reality to its Appearances. In a world where "higher" and "lower," "more" and "less" true have a meaning, some of the lesser systems in which the nature of the whole is expressed must be fuller and more adequate representations of that nature than others. This is as much as to say that it would require comparatively little transformation of some of the partial systems recognised by our knowledge to show how the common nature of the whole system of Reality is expressed in them; in other cases the amount of transformation required to show how the whole repeats itself in the part would be much more extensive. To take a single instance, if our preceding analysis of the general nature of Reality is sound, we can see much more clearly how that nature reappears in the structure of a human mind than how it is exhibited in what we call a physical thing, and we may therefore say the human mind expresses the fundamental character of the whole system much more fully and adequately than physical nature, as it exists for our apprehension. More briefly, the same thought may be expressed by saying that Reality has degrees, and that the forms of Appearance in which its common nature is most fully and clearly manifested have the highest degrees of reality.

§ 3. This conception of Reality as capable of degrees may at first seem paradoxical. How can anything, it will be asked, be more or less "real" than anything else? Must not anything either be entirely real or not real at all? But the same difficulty might be raised about the recognition of degree in other cases where its validity is now universally admitted. Thus to some minds it has appeared that there can be no degrees of the infinite or the infinitesimal; all infinites, and again all zeros, have been declared to be manifestly equal. Yet it hardly seems possible to escape the conclusion that the concept of successive orders of infinitely great, and again of infinitely small, magnitudes is not only intelligible but absolutely necessary if our thought on quantitative subjects is to be consistent. (When the sides of a rectangle, for instance, become infinitely great or infinitely small relatively to whatever is our standard of comparison, it still remains a rectangle, and its area therefore is still determined by the product of its sides, and is therefore infinitely great or small, as the case may be, in relation not only to our original standard but to the sides themselves.[1]) What is in one sense not a matter of degree, may yet in another not only admit but positively require the distinction of degrees of more and less. And this is precisely the case with Reality as it

---

[1] So, again, a velocity which is already infinitesimal may receive an acceleration which is infinitesimal in relation to the velocity itself. The reader's own studies will no doubt furnish him with numerous other illustrations of the same kind.

manifests itself in its various appearances. In the sense that it is the same single experience-system which appears as a whole and in its whole nature in every one of the subordinate experience-systems, they are all alike real, and each is as indispensable as every other to the existence of the whole. In the sense that the whole is more explicitly present in one than in another, there is an infinity of possible degrees of reality and unreality. We should be justified in borrowing a term from mathematical science to mark this double relation of the appearances to their Reality, and speaking of them as successive orders of Reality. And we might then say that it is one of the principal problems of a complete Philosophy to ascertain and arrange in their proper sequence, as far as the limitations of our knowledge permit, the orders of Reality.

§ 4. Such a task as this could only be carried out by an intelligence equally at home in metaphysical analysis and in the results of the special sciences, and would form the proper work of applied Metaphysics. In a discussion of general metaphysical principles it is sufficient to indicate the general nature of the criteria by which the degree of reality exhibited by any special partial system must be determined. Now, this general nature has been already made fairly clear by the foregoing inquiry into the unity of Reality. Reality, we have seen, is one in the sense of being an individual self-contained whole of experience. And its individuality means that it is the systematic embodiment of a single coherent structure in a plurality of elements or parts, which depend for their whole character upon the fact that they are the embodiment of precisely this structure. If this is so, we may say that degrees of reality mean the same thing as degrees of individuality, and that a thing is real precisely to the same extent to which it is truly individual.

A thing, that is, no matter of what kind, is really what it appears to be, just in so far as the thing, as it appears for our knowledge, is itself a self-contained and therefore unique systematic whole. Or, in other words, just in so far as what we recognise as one thing shows itself, in the face of philosophical criticism and analysis, to be a self-contained systematic whole, so far are we truly apprehending that thing as a manifestation of the fundamental character of Reality, of seeing it as it really is, and so far does our knowledge give us genuine Reality. On the other hand, just so far as what at first seemed a self-contained whole is discovered by subsequent analysis not to be so, so far have we failed to see the facts in their true place in the single whole of Reality, and so far is our knowledge affected with error and unreality. Or, again, the more truly anything is a self-contained individual whole, the higher its place in the scale of Reality.

When we ask what are the marks by which one thing may be shown to be more of a true individual whole than another, we shall find that they may be reduced to two, both of which we can easily see to be in principle the same, though, owing to the limitations of our insight, they do not always appear to coincide in a given case. One thing is *ceteris paribus* more truly an individual whole than another: (1) when the wealth of detailed content it embraces is greater; (2) when the completeness of the unity with which it embraces that detail is greater. Or, the degree of individuality possessed by any system depends: (1) on its *comprehensiveness;* (2) on its *internal systematisation*. The more a thing includes of existence and the more harmoniously it includes it, the more individual it is.

It is manifest, of course, that these two characteristics of a systematic whole are mutually interdependent. For, precisely because all Reality is ultimately a single coherent system, the more there is outside any partial system the greater must be the dependence of its constituents for their character upon their connection with reality outside, and the less capable must the system be of complete explanation from within itself. The more the partial system embraces, the less will its constituents be determined by relation to anything outside itself, and the more completely will its organisation be explicable by reference to its own internal principle of structure. That is, the greater the comprehensiveness of the system, the completer in general will be its internal coherence. And, conversely, the more completely the working of the whole system in its details is explicable from within as the expression of a single principle of internal structure, the less must be the dependence of its contents on any external reality; and therefore, seeing that *all* reality is ultimately interconnected, the less must be the extent of what lies outside the system in question. That is, the greater the internal unity, the greater in general the comprehensiveness of the system. Thus ultimately the two criteria of individuality coincide.

§ 5. In practice, however, it constantly happens, as a consequence of the fragmentary way in which our experiences come to us, that comprehensiveness and thorough-going systematic unity seem to be opposed to one another. Thus we can see, as a general principle, that the systematic organisation of knowledge depends upon its extent. The wider our knowledge, the greater on the whole the degree to which it exhibits organic structure; the systematisation of science and its extension ultimately go together. Yet at any one moment in the development of knowledge the recognition of fresh truths may necessitate a temporary introduction of disorganisation and discrepancy among the accepted principles of science. Thus in the history of geometry the recognised principles of the science were temporarily disorganised by the admission of incommensurable magnitudes which was forced upon the early Greek mathematicians by the discovery that the side and diagonal of a square have no common measure, and the discrepancy was only removed when it became possible to revise the principles of the theory of numbers itself. So again at the present day there is a real danger that premature anxiety to give the study of Psychology precise systematic character by an exact definition of its subject and its relation to the various physical and mental sciences, may stand in the way of the extension of our knowledge of the facts of psychical life. We have often to purchase an important extension of knowledge at the cost of temporary confusion of principles, and to be content to wait for the future readjustment of facts to principles in the course of subsequent progress.

So in our moral life we judge one man's character more individual than another's, either on the ground of the superior breadth of his interests, or of the superior consistency with which his interests are wrought into a self-consistent whole. The man of many interests has so far a truer individuality than the man of few, and again the man of steady purpose than the man whose energies are dissipated in seemingly conflicting pursuits. But the two criteria do not always, for our insight, coincide. An increase in variety and breadth of interests may be accompanied by a diminution in coherency of aim, and a gain in coherency of aim appears often to be bought by concentration upon a few special objects. And we should find it hard or impossible to decide, where the two aspects of individuality appear to fall thus apart, whether the man of many interests and relatively dissipated energies, or the man of few interests and intense concentration upon them, exhibits the higher individuality. For what looked like self-dissipation in the pursuit of disconnected objects might really be the systematic pursuit of a consistent purpose too wide to be clearly apprehended in its unity either by contemporary observers or by the actor himself, yet apparent enough to the reflective historian reading the significance of a life by its whole effect upon society, and what seemed at the time the single object of the man of one idea might similarly be found in the light of the sequel to be the hasty combination of radically inconsistent aims.[1]

Such reflections, however, only show that our limited insight is insufficient to assign to every appearance with certainty its own place in the ordered system of appearances through which the single Reality expresses itself. They do not touch our general position, that where comprehensiveness and harmony *can* be seen to go together, we are justified in using them as the measure of the individuality and therefore of the reality of the partial system in which we discover them. It is on such grounds, for instance, that we may safely pronounce that an organism, which is the living unity of its members, is more individual and therefore a higher reality that a mere aggregate of pre-existing units, in which the nature of the parts is wholly or mainly independent of the structure of the whole; and again, that a mind consciously and systematically pursuing a coherent self-chosen system of ends is more individual, and therefore again a higher reality, than an organism reacting according to the temporary character of its environment or its momentary internal condition in ways which form no systematic execution of a connected scheme of ends. And it is clear that, if only on this ground, we should have to say that we are nearer the truth in thinking of the individual whole of complete Reality as an organism than in thinking of it as an aggregate, and nearer the truth still in thinking of it as a mind. Similarly in our judgments upon our own lives and character. So far as one life possesses more breadth and again more conscious unity of aim than another, so far it is more truly individual, and therefore a more adequate type of complete reality. Just so far as I am individual, I am truly real. And just so far as I fall short of systematic individuality, whether from the poverty of my interests or their mutual incompatibility, the appearance of unity in my life is illusory, and I must be pronounced an unreal appearance.

At this point we may observe our metaphysical criterion of reality coincides with our ethical criterion of moral worth. For in morality too we esteem one life worthier than

---

[1] See for illustrations of the impossibility of carrying out a single principle in our actual judgments of particular cases, Mr. Bradley's already quoted article in *Mind* for July 1902.

another, either for the superior comprehensiveness of its ideals or for the thoroughness with which they are wrought into a harmonious whole of coherent purpose. The better man is either the man of the wider ideal, or again the man of completer and purer self-devotion to his ideal. And thus for Morality the measure of our worth, as for Metaphysics the measure of our reality, lies in our individuality. And for Morality no less than for Metaphysics individuality is pre-eminently a thing of degrees. In both cases, again, the same difficulty besets us as soon as we attempt to use our criterion for application to particular cases. Its two aspects fall apart; it is not always the more comprehensive ideal which is served with the higher fidelity of purpose. And so our actual moral judgments on the worth of particular men, like our metaphysical judgments on the order of reality to which particular things belong, are often necessarily uncertain and fluctuating. We rate one man morally high for the comprehensive rationality of his ideals, though he suffers from a lack of concentrated energy, another for the steady and earnest purpose with which he follows what we perhaps deplore as a contracted ideal.

§ 6. One more point of supreme importance concerning the relation of the lesser individuals to the perfect individual which is the absolute whole of Reality. Now that we have learned what is meant by degrees of individuality, we can see that there can, in the last resort, be only one perfect and complete individual, the whole of Reality itself, and that the subordinate individuals can never be wholly and entirely individual in themselves. For to be a complete individual would be, as we have seen, to be a whole system absolutely self-contained and explicable solely by reference to internal structure. Whatever requires, for the full understanding of its systematic character, reference to existence outside itself, we have seen, must also, so long as it is considered apart from the rest of existence, be internally wanting in complete systematic harmony, and thus must fall doubly short of the ideal of individuality.

And precisely because the whole of experience is a single system, no lesser system within the whole is entirely explicable in terms of its own internal structure. For a full understanding of the nature of the lesser system, and of the way in which it manifests a common character through the variety of its elements, you have always, in the last resort, to go outside the system itself, and take into account its relation to the rest of the whole system of existence.

And for that very reason no subordinate individual, considered in itself, is a completely coherent self-determined whole. For a limited knowledge like our own, which has in the main to deal with subordinate systems as we find them, and without that complete understanding of the whole structure of Reality which would enable us to see their precise place in the whole, the subordinate systems themselves, when closely scanned by a resolute philosophical analysis, will inevitably exhibit some degree of discrepancy and want of systematic unity.

Consider, for instance, such a system as is formed by the life-work of a man of marked "individuality." On the whole, the life of such a man may fairly be said to be the systematic working out of a consistent scheme of purposes. But this is, after all, only approximately the truth. It is not the case that the nature of the central or dominant purpose of the scheme is of itself enough to determine the nature and order of the successive stages by which it finds expression. We have to take into account factors in the man's "heredity," and again in his social and physical environment which form no part of the nature of his central dominant ideal and yet influence the manner of its fulfilment. We are thus thrown back for our full understanding of the "individual" system in question upon circumstances which are, so far as that system is concerned, "accidental," *i.e.* which are equally with itself part of the whole system of experienced fact, without our being able to see *how* it and they form a wider coherent whole. The subordinate individual, because incapable of explication solely from within, is in the end only approximately "individual," and we therefore fall into contradictions whenever we isolate it from the rest of Reality and treat it as absolutely individual and self-contained.

In dealing with subordinate wholes, we always, if we go far enough, come to a point where we have to recognise their dependence upon a realm of external fact which *our* knowledge fails to see in its systematic relation with them, and has therefore to treat as accidental or as an ultimate "collocation." This is why, as has already been said, full knowledge of our own aims and interests as a genuine systematic whole would coincide with complete insight into the structure of the whole universe. We may invert the sentiment of a hackneyed verse, and say with equal truth that until you know what God and man is, you cannot really know what the "flower in the crannied wall" is. This is as much as to say that every appearance must involve some element of contradiction for our philosophical analysis precisely because we cannot in the end see fully *how* any appearance is related to the whole of Reality. But we must carefully remember that if appearances, taken by themselves, are contradictory, this is not because they are appearances, but because, as so taken, they are all to some extent *mere* appearance. The conclusion of the whole matter is, that the individuality of anything less than the ultimate whole of being is a matter of degree and approximation. We shall be equally in error if we assume that because no subordinate system is fully individual, some are not more individual and therefore more real than others or if we declare that, because whatever is real at all must be in its degree individual, therefore every element of Reality is completely real in its isolation. The first error is that of a one-sided Monism, the second that of an equally one-sided Pluralism.

Once more we may note a point of coincidence between our general metaphysical theory of individuality and our personal experience as moral agents. In so far as each of us is truly an individual, his aims and ends form a system with an internal unity pervading its structure, and therefore capable of progressive realisation as a system. Yet again, because each of us is less than the whole of Reality, or, what is the same thing, because the systematic unity of our inner life is never complete, and our totality of interests relations, and aspirations never a completely self-contained ordered whole, our ideals will always be found to contain aspects which will not fully harmonise, elements which fall outside such a unity of structure as it is possible to effect within the limit of our single personality. And thus all our victories contain an inseparable element of defeat. The defeated aspects of the self may no doubt, and in general do, in proportion to the degree of our individuality, belong to the " lower " and relatively more " untrue " self, yet they are elements in the whole self, and their suppression is a genuine if necessary self-suppression. There is a sense in which an aspect of failure is an inevitable feature in the life of every subordinate and therefore imperfect individual. Human life, even in the millennium, as we rightly feel, would not be human life if the note of sadness were altogether absent from it. Only in the single experience of the absolute whole can the discordant notes be finally resolved into a faultless harmony.

§ 7. Technically, we may mark the distinction between complete and approximate individuality by saying that the absolute whole is an infinite individual, whereas all lesser wholes are but finite individuals. And here it is important to note carefully the true meaning of these often much-abused terms. The infinite must not be confounded with the indefinite or unfinished. Its fundamental property is not the merely negative one of having no end or "last term," but the positive one of having an internal structure which is the harmonious and complete expression of a single self-consistent principle. The finite, again, is finite not primarily merely because it has a "last term," *i.e* because there is something else outside it, but because its "last term" is arbitrarily determined, *i.e.* determined by something other than the principles of its internal structure. In other words, the essential defect of the finite is that it is not solely determined by its own structural principle.

We can see this even in the simple case of the familiar "infinite series" of arithmetic and algebra. Such a series as $1, \frac{1}{2}, \frac{1}{4} \ldots$ is "infinite" not merely because you never come to the last term, but because its character is determined from *within*, solely by the principle according to which each term is derived from the one before it; that the series has no end is a simple consequence of this positive property of self-determination. But suppose I take n terms of this series and no more, where n is a specified number, the resulting series is now *finite*, not primarily because there are more terms of the same kind outside it, but because the number of terms to be taken is not prescribed by the law of formation of the series, but fixed with reference to some object independent of the principle of the series itself. In other words, only the infinite is in the full sense of the words a completely self-determined whole. The finite is the imperfect, not primarily because there is something outside it, but because its contents are not solely prescribed by the principle of structure which they embody. I, for instance, am a finite being, not principally or merely because there are other men in the world, but because my ideas and purposes are not a fully coherent systematic whole in themselves.[1]

The view we have taken of individuality and the dis-

---

[1] For a fuller exposition of the conception of infinity here adopted I may refer the reader to the famous essay of Dedekind, *Was sind und was sollen die Zahlen*, especially pp. 17–20. The English reader will find an account of Dedekind's work, with an acute discussion of its metaphysical significance, in Royce, *The World and the Individual*, First Series, Supplementary Essay. It does not seem necessary for the purpose of this chapter to specify the points in which I find myself unable to follow Professor Royce in his use of the theory. See *infra*, chap. 4, § 10.

tinction between finite and infinite individuality is closely akin to some of the most fundamental ideas in the philosophy of Leibnitz. It was the doctrine of Leibnitz that each of his monads "represented" the nature of the whole system of existence, *i.e.* repeated the structure of the whole in its own special structure, from a particular "point of view." According to the fulness and clearness of the "representation," *i.e.* the adequacy with which the structure of the monad repeated the structure of the whole system, the monads were classed as higher or lower in the scale of existence. The clearer a monad's representation of the whole within itself, the greater the monad's "activity"; the more confused the representation, the greater its "passivity." It followed that, inasmuch as no created monad fully exhibits the systematic structure of the whole of Reality within itself, every one contains some element of "passivity," and that to be "passive" primarily means not to be affected by extraneous influences, but to contain internal "confusion."

Thus the "activity" of Leibnitz exactly corresponds to what we have called individuality, and his "passivity" to that want of complete internal systematisation which we have found inseparable from finite existence. The immense significance of this definition of activity and passivity in terms of internal systematisation will be more apparent when we come, in our concluding book, to discuss the meaning of human freedom, and its connection with determination and "causality." For the present it is enough to note that our own doctrine is substantially that of Leibnitz freed from the inconsistency which is introduced into it by the monadistic assumption of the complete independence of the various finite individuals. It is, of course, impossible to unite, as Leibnitz tried to do, the two thoughts. Either there is ultimately only one independent individual, the infinite individual whole, or there is no meaning in speaking of higher and lower degrees of individuality. Leibnitz's inconsistency on this point seems due entirely to his desire to maintain the absolute individuality of the particular human "soul," a desire which is explained, partly at least, by his anxiety not to come into collision, as Spinoza and others had done, with the official theology of the period.

§ 8. The definition of infinite and finite individuality completes the general outline of our conception of Reality as a whole, and its relation to its constituent elements. Recapitulating that doctrine, we may now say that the real is a single all-embracing whole of experience or psychical matter of fact, determined entirely from within by a principle of internal structure, and therefore completely individual. Because the matter of the system is in all its parts experience, the principle of its structure must be teleological in character.[1] That is, the system must be the embodiment, in a harmonious unity of conscious feeling, of a consistent interest or mental attitude. As such we may call it the realisation indifferently of a purpose or idea, and we may speak of the absolute experience as the completed expression of an absolute knowledge or an absolute will.

But if we do so, we must bear in mind that there can be here no question of a thought which works upon and reconstructs into systematic harmony a body of data originally supplied to it in a relatively unintelligible and disconnected form from some foreign source, or of a volition which gradually translates into reality an end or purpose originally present to it as an unrealised idea. The processes of thought and volition can clearly have no place in an experience for which the what and the that are never disjoined; as we shall by and by see more fully, they involve existence in time, and existence in time can belong only to the finite and imperfect. Hence it is best, in the interest of intellectual clarity and candour, to avoid the use of such expressions as knowledge and will in speaking of the absolute experience; at best they are in large part metaphorical, and at worst potent weapons of intellectual dishonesty.[2] The constituents of the system, again, are lesser experience systems of the same general type, in each of which the nature of the whole manifests itself, though to different degrees. They are thus all finite individuals of varying degrees of individuality. The more comprehensive and the more internally unified by an immanent principle of teleological structure such a system, the more fully individual it is, and the more adequately does it reveal the structure of the all-pervading whole. This is the intellectual justification for our instinctive belief that what is for our human experience highest and best is ultim-

---

[1] It would not be hard to show that in the end all systematic structure is teleological. For all such structure in the last resort is a form of order, and depends on the possibility of saying "here this is first, that is second." And wherever we predicate order we are asserting the embodiment in detail of some dominant purpose.

[2] In fact, it is clear that if we speak of "idea" or "volition" in connection with the absolute individual, we cannot mean *actual* "ideas" or *actual* "volitions." We must be using the psychological terms improperly in something of the same sense in which we speak of a man's "guiding ideas" or "settled will" to denote what clearly, whatever it may be, is *not* actual ideational or volitional process. See further, Bk. IV. chap. 6, § 1.

ately in the constitution of the universe most completely real.

Consult further:—F. H. Bradley, *Appearance and Reality* chap. 24, "Degrees of Truth and Reality"; Plato, *Republic*, vi. 509 ff., with the commentary in R. L. Nettleship's *Lectures on Plato's Republic*, or Bosanquet's *Companion to the Republic*.

CHAPTER IV

THE WORLD OF THINGS—(1) SUBSTANCE, QUALITY, AND RELATION

§ 1. The natural or pre-scientific view of the world regards it as a plurality of "things," each possessing *qualities*, standing *in relation* to others, and interacting with them. § 2. Hence arise four problems: those of the Unity of the Thing, of Substance and Quality, of Relation, of Causality. § 3. No simple answer can be given to the question, *What is one thing?* The Unity of the Thing is one of teleological structure, and this is a matter of degree, and also largely of our own subjective point of view. § 4. *Substance and Quality*. The identification of the substance of things with their primary qualities, though useful in physical science, is metaphysically unjustifiable. § 5. Substance as an "unknowable substratum of qualities" adds nothing to our understanding of their connection. § 6. The thing cannot be a mere collection of qualities without internal unity. § 7. The conception of a thing as the law or mode of relation of its states useful but metaphysically unsatisfactory. Ultimately the many can be contained in the one only by "representation"; the unity in things must be that of an individual experience. § 8. *Relation*. We can neither reduce qualities to relations nor relations to qualities. § 9. Again, the attempt to conceive Reality as qualities in relation leads to the indefinite regress. § 10. We cannot escape this difficulty by taking all relations as "external." And Professor Royce's vindication of the indefinite regress seems to depend on the uncriticised application of the inadequate category of whole and part to ultimate Reality. The union of the one and the many in concrete experience is ultra-relational. SUPPLEMENTARY NOTE: Dr. Stout's reply to Mr. Bradley.

§ 1. WHEN we turn from the inquiry into the structure of Reality as it must be conceived by a consistent Philosophy, to consider the aspect in which it appears to ordinary non-philosophical thought, the systematic unity which has demanded our attention in the two preceding chapters seems to be replaced by a bewildering and almost incalculable variety. According to the naïve pre-scientific theory of existence to which the experiences of practical life naturally give rise, and which serves as the point of departure for all the more scientific and systematic theories of the physicist, the psychologist, and the metaphysician, the world is composed of a multitude of apparently independent things, partly animated, like ourselves, partly inanimate. Each of these things, while in some sense a unit, is thought of as possessing an indefinite multiplicity of *qualities* or *properties*, as capable of standing in a variety of *relations* to other things, and as *acting* upon other things and *being influenced* by them in a variety of ways.

In all these respects, it should be observed, the naïvely realistic thought of the pre-scientific mind treats what from a more developed point of view would be distinguished as mental and physical existences alike. Human persons, like the other things of which my environment is composed, are thought of as being at once units and the possessors of diverse properties, as capable of a variety of relations to one another and to other things, and as interacting with each other and the rest of the environment. The recognition of the psychical as an order distinct from the physical, with its momentous consequences for general metaphysical theory, belongs to a later and much more sophisticated stage of intellectual development. Also, it must be noted, for the naïvely realistic intelligence, I am myself thought of as simply one object or thing in an environment of things of a similar nature, and my relations to that environment are conceived as being of the same type as the relations between its various component parts. I too am, for my own thought, so long as it remains at this primitive level, simply a thing with numerous properties, in various relations to other things, and interacting with them in diverse ways.[1]

We have called this exceedingly primitive way of conceiving the nature of existence "pre-scientific," on the ground that both in the mental development of the individual and in that of a community of individuals it precedes even the most tentative conscious efforts to organise thought about the world into a coherent whole. All scientific and philosophical constructions may be regarded as so many artificial modifications of this earlier point of view, instituted and carried out for the purpose of rendering it more coherent and systematic. At the same time, our use of the epithet "pre-scientific" must not be allowed to mislead. The "pre-scientific" view may and does co-exist in the same mind with the various modifications of it which arise in the effort to think consistently. We are all of us habitually "naïve realists" in respect of those aspects of the world of experience which lie outside the limits of our personal scientific studies; and even as regards those aspects of existence in respect of which our theoretical views may be of a much more developed type, we habitually relapse into the "pre-scientific" attitude when our immediate object is practical[2]

[1] See the admirable account of the "natural conception" of the world in the first chapter of Avenarius, *Der Menschliche Weltbegriff*.
[2] May I say here once for all, that when I oppose *practice* to intellectual speculation, I must be understood to mean by practice the alteration by myself of some datum of given existence. The activity of thought is thus for me not

success in action rather than logical consistency in thinking. For the purposes of everyday life, the most "advanced" man of science is content to be a naïve realist outside his laboratory.

Again, pre-scientific as the primitive attitude towards existence is, in the sense of being unaffected by the deliberate effort after system and coherency of thought, it is so far scientific as to be a real though rudimentary and unconscious product of our intellectual need for order and system of some kind in our thought about things. It is a genuine though an unconscious result of our earliest reflection on the course of experience, and thus a true thought-construction, not a passive reproduction of a merely "given" material. It performs in rudimentary fashion, and without explicit purpose, the same task of systematising experience which the various scientific and philosophical theories of the more developed mind undertake more elaborately and with conscious intent. It is thus pre-scientific, but not properly speaking unscientific.

As the mass of ascertained fact accumulates and reflection upon it becomes more systematic and deliberate, our primitive conception of the systematic nature of the real inevitably proves unsatisfactory for two reasons. New facts are discovered which we cannot fit into the old scheme without modification of its structure, and, again, the concepts in terms of which the scheme was originally constructed prove on examination to be themselves obscure and ambiguous in their meaning. There is thus a double motive perpetually operative in bringing about reconstruction of the original scheme. To the various sciences it falls in the main to devise such alteration of the old schematism as is necessary for the inclusion of fresh facts; it is the special province of metaphysical criticism to examine the various terms both of the original scheme and its subsequent modifications, with a view to determining how far they form an ultimately intelligible and coherent system.

§ 2. When we scrutinise the original "pre-scientific" theory of the world from this point of view, we shall find that its four leading features give rise to four metaphysical problems of great generality and considerable difficulty. The conception of the world as made up of a multiplicity of things, each of which is one, gives rise to the problem of the unity of the thing; the plurality of the qualities, and again

practical, precisely because the "truths" which I know or contemplate are not *quâ* truths given existences operated upon and altered by the act of thinking.

of the relations ascribed to the single thing, gives rise to the problems of *Substance* and *Quality* and of *Relation;* the belief in the interaction between different things finally gives rise to the exceptionally important and difficult problem of *Causality*. The four problems are not altogether disconnected; in particular, it is hard to discuss the sense in which a thing can be spoken of as "one," without at the same time raising the question how the "one" thing stands to its many properties, and again discussing the general meaning of relation. And the problem of Causality may be raised in so general a form as to include the other three. Still, for the sake of having a definite order of discussion, it will be well to take them as far as may be separately, and to proceed from the simpler to the more complex. When we have indicated in outline our solution of these problems, we shall have to ask what is the general conception of a thing which our results establish, and whether and on what grounds we are warranted in believing in the actual existence of things answering to our conception. The present chapter will be devoted to the examination of the first three problems; in the succeeding chapter we shall discuss the meaning of Causality, and indicate our general conclusion as to the existence of "things." With this result our survey of the general structure of Reality will be completed, and we shall then proceed in our third and fourth books to examine the most important of the special problems suggested by the existence of physical nature and conscious mind respectively.

§ 3. *The Unity of the Thing.*—The problem we have to face is as follows: in what sense do we call any thing "one thing," and what gives it its character as a unity? It is obvious that we may attack this question from either of two rather different points of view. We may ask either, why do we mark off just this portion of our environment from all the rest as a single thing among many things; or, again, how is the oneness which we predicate of any part of the environment so marked off compatible with the multiplicity of its properties? The question we propose to deal with in this section is the former of the two just propounded; the latter shall be dealt with next as the problem of substance and its qualities. What, then, do we mean by the unity which we ascribe to whatever we recognise as one thing among a multiplicity of others? We have, in a way, implicitly answered this question already by the result arrived at in our discussion of the character of the elements or constituents of the system of Reality. But whereas, in our former investigation, we started from the general notion of Reality as a systematic whole of experience, and went on to ask what character is imposed on the elements of such a system by their presence in it as its elements, we have now to raise the same question from the other side; starting with our everyday recognition of our environment as divided into things, we have to ask how far these things possess the character which must belong to the genuinely individual members of an individual whole of subordinate individuals.

For the purpose of the inquiry we must begin by taking the term thing in the same wide and ambiguous sense in which everyday thought and discourse use it. We must reckon among the things which are the topic of discussion, human persons, animals, plants, greater and smaller inorganic masses, in a word, whatever the most matter-of-fact commonsense thinking recognises as possessed of a character in virtue of which it can as a whole determine the course of experience at a given moment. The character or aspect in virtue of which such a whole determines the course of experience in this one special way rather than another, is by this definition excluded from our conception of a thing; it is not the thing itself but its quality or property or relation to some other thing, and forms the subject of our second and third problems. Thus we may say of a thing, in the sense in which we are using the term, that it is what has existence as a whole here and now in the series of experiences, though in saying so we must be careful to bear in mind that the here and now of the thing's existence are not indivisible points of space or time, but continuous stretches of extension and duration. Now, when we ask in what sense such a thing is one, and why we mark off the limits which separate the one thing from the other things just where we do, it at once becomes apparent that the oneness is a matter of degree. We seem at first sight able with comparatively little difficulty to decide that the organism of a human being or of one of the higher animals is one thing; when we come to deal with the lower organisms which consist of loosely aggregated colonies of largely independently functioning cells, we begin to feel more diffidence in pronouncing what is one organism, though we still think we can say what is one cell. So, in dealing with inanimate masses, while we might be ready to say without much misgiving that a machine of our own construction is one, we should find it much harder to decide whether what we perceive as a mere inorganic mass is one or many, and harder still to give reasons for our decision in a particular case. And even in the cases where our decision is most unhesitatingly pronounced, subsequent reflection will show that the matter may not be so obvious as it seems. For instance, a pair of separated Siamese twins would undoubtedly be generally held to be two organisms and not one; but whether they were one or two before the severance is a question we should find it easier to ask than to answer.

When we try to detect some common principle in our various judgments as to whether a thing is one thing or several, the following results seem to emerge:—(1) A thing is clearly not made *one*, as is sometimes assumed, by the possession of an unbroken contour or an uninterrupted temporal existence. The succession of my mental states may make up one mental life, and again my organism from the cradle to the grave may be pronounced in some sense one, though no one can prove that there are no gaps in their temporal existence. Again, even if we leave out of account the corpuscular theories of body according to which every thing that looks to us like a spatially continuous whole with an unbroken contour is really composed of discrete particles with interstices between them, it is abundantly clear that common sense regards as one thing the parts of a system which works as a connected whole, quite independently of the existence or non-existence of immediate contact between them.

(2) Again, the unity of the one thing does not depend upon identity of material, whatever that phrase may mean. My organism still remains one thing, though its material is constantly changing by the loss of some elements and the acquisition of others.

(3) On the positive side, it is clear that the unity we attribute to one thing is that of teleological structure. A thing is one or many according to the point of view from which you look at it, *i.e.* according to the idea or purpose in the light of which you study it. That is one thing which functions as one, in other words, which is the systematic embodiment of a coherent scheme of structure. Thus, when we are considering the whole of an organism as subservient to the realisation of a unique individual aim or interest, the organism is necessarily judged to be one, because in respect of that interest it behaves as a whole; when we are studying the specific mode of reaction of a particular nerve, for instance, the same organism just as naturally appears to us a multiplicity of distinct but interconnected things. Similarly, a system of material particles appears one thing to us so long as our interest in the system is directed to those

ways in which it behaves as one, *e.g.*, the exchanges of energy between it and other systems external to it. Generally we may say that whatever is called one is called so because it is the systematic expression of a single aim or interest. A thing, in fact, is one just in so far as it has the character we ascribed, in our last chapter, to a finite individual. Its unity is never *merely* numerical, but always qualitative, the unity of coherent structure.

Even in our rough-and-ready way of treating continuity of contour as evidence of oneness in inanimate and apparently structureless masses, we may detect the influence of this principle. We judge the sensibly continuous mass to be one rather than many things, because in many obvious respects it functions as one (*e.g.*, in respect of its weight, the simultaneous displacement of its parts in rotation or translation through space). Also, no doubt, our judgment is influenced by the analogy of our own bodies, which are sensibly continuous. We project in imagination into the sensibly continuous inanimate mass the same kind of teleological unity which we find in our own mental life. The sensibly discontinuous, on the other hand (*e.g.*, two inorganic masses separated by an apparently empty interval), is judged to be many things rather than one, because, in imagination, we project such an inner mental life into each of the discontinuous parts.

If all this is so, it would follow that the line of demarcation between one thing and another can never be drawn with hard and fast precision. For if one thing ultimately means one individual, the embodiment of a unique self-consistent idea, the only thing which is fully and absolutely one will be the infinite individual Reality itself. The extent to which any lesser portion of the whole can be pronounced one thing will depend on the extent to which it exhibits self-contained systematic individuality, and thus will be a matter of degree. The highest kind of finite unity we can conceive will be that of a life which is the conscious progressive realisation of coherent purpose. Such a life is one not merely for the outside observer who detects its underlying unity of aim, but for itself. Its oneness may thus be said to be both objective and subjective. Thus the more completely our own inner life is the systematic expression of consistent purpose, the greater the right with which we may regard ourselves as being each truly " one thing " and as such truly individual. But when we remember how far what any one of us calls " his " inner life is from exhibiting such complete internal coherency of structure, we shall realise that even in the highest case the unity is still a matter of degree.

This is still more palpably the case with the lower forms of organic life. Not to speak of the well-known puzzles which arise when we seek to determine whether a creature which is a colony of largely independent cells is one animal or many, our difficulties begin as soon as we have to deal with any type of life below the most fully self-conscious. We can say, to some extent, that a human character is one so long as it is the conscious expression of systematic purpose, but it is less easy to say in what sense we call an animal's conscious life one. The absence of anything like systematic unity of aim and interest from the life of animal impulse makes it appear, at least at first sight, more reasonable to speak of it as a bundle or collection of distinct impulses and instincts rather than as one.[1] If, in spite of this, we still habitually speak and think of the particular higher animal as *one* rather than many, the reason no doubt is that we tacitly ascribe to it something like the conscious unity of interest which we find in our own mental life, though with a diminished clearness.

When we come to the inanimate world, it seems to become purely a matter of our own subjective interest what we shall call one thing and what we shall call many. That is one which may be regarded as acting as one whole in respect of its bearing upon any interest of ours; that many which, in respect of our interests, does not behave as a whole. Thus, except where we are dealing with forms of life to which we can with more or less plausibility ascribe some degree of conscious unity of aim and interest, there seems no valid reason for drawing the line between different things in one place rather than in another, except reasons of convenience. It is important to bear this in mind in applying our idealistic theory of existence to the case of the inanimate world. If the foundations of the idealistic theory are sound, every real existence must be a finite individual experience of some order of individuality, and this must of course hold good of that part of existence which appears to us as the inanimate world. The inanimate world must be— as we shall see more fully in the succeeding book—a system of individual experiences, which appears to us lifeless and purposeless merely because the kind of life it possesses is too far removed from our own for us to recognise it. But

---

[1] Such a view of the mental life of the animal seems to have been actually held, for instance, by the late Professor T. H. Green. Yet see Green, Works, ii. 217.

we must most carefully observe that the line of demarcation between the different individual experiences which constitute the reality of that world need not in the least coincide everywhere with the line which we, for purposes of our own, draw between different things.

§ 4. *The Problem of Substance and Quality.*—More important, in the history of metaphysical theory, has been the other aspect of the problem of the unity of things. What we call one *thing* is said, in spite of its unity, to have many *qualities*. It is, *e.g.*, at once round, white, shiny, and hard, or at once green, soft, and rough. Now, what do we understand by the *it* to which these numerous attributes are alike ascribed, and how does it possess them? To use the traditional technical names, what is the *substance* to which the several qualities belong or in which they inhere, and what is the manner of their *inherence*? The full difficulty of this problem may be most easily exhibited by considering the ways in which popular thought commonly tries to solve it.

(1) One of the commonest and most obvious solutions is to identify the "substance" which has the qualities (or, to use the more general scholastic expression, the *accidents*) with some one group of the thing's properties which we regard as specially important or permanent. The "substance" is then taken to be just this group of "primary" qualities, and is said to have or possess the less permanent "secondary qualities." For obvious reasons, the "primary" qualities have in modern Philosophy usually been identified, as by Galileo, Descartes, and Locke, with those mathematical properties of body which are of fundamental importance for the science of mechanical Physics.[1] And usually, though not always, the way in which the substance, as thus defined, *has* the secondary qualities, has been further explained by saying that these latter are subjective changes in our sensibility produced by the action of the primary qualities upon our various sense-organs. Neither of these special views is, however, necessarily involved in the identification of the substance of things with their fundamental qualities. The essential principle of the theory consists simply in the recognition of some groups of qualities as of primary im-

---

[1] Strictly speaking, the "solidity" or "impenetrability" of the ultimate particles of matter, which is with Locke and Newton one of the most prominent "primary" qualities, is not a "mathematical" property, but it still owes its inclusion in the list to the conviction of these philosophers that it is, like extension and form, fundamentally important for mathematical Physics. The explanation of the "secondary" qualities as *subjective* appears to go back to Democritus.

portance, and the identification of the one "substance" which has the many properties with this group.

Now, it would be impertinent for us to raise any objection to the use of such a theory as a working hypothesis in the physical sciences, so long as it does in those sciences the work for which it is required. The object of the physical sciences as a body is simply to enable us to describe and calculate the course of events in nature with the highest degree of accuracy and the least complicated set of formulæ. If this end is most successfully attained by treating a certain group of the properties of sensible things as of primary importance and all the rest as mere derivatives of them, this fact of itself affords sufficient justification for the scientific use of the distinction. For the special objects of physical science any group of properties which thus lends itself to the purposes of description and calculation is of primary importance. But it is no less true that its importance for physical purposes does not afford the least ground for regarding it as equally valuable as a solution of the metaphysical problem of the meaning of substance. For instance, one reason why the mathematical properties of body are of such supreme importance for Physics is that in respect of them bodies can be treated as differing not in kind but only in number. This is why they are of such inestimable service as the basis of our calculations as to the behaviour of things. But it might very well be that the true nature of things is most fully manifested just in those points in which they are different in kind; from the standpoint of the metaphysician, a view of non-human nature, however serviceable, which rests entirely upon the aspects in which things are most alike, may be as superficial as the statistical sociologist's view of human nature. The true being of a concrete thing may be as inadequately expressed by its mathematical properties as the true character of an individual man by a list of anthropometrical results.[1]

In point of fact, we can readily see that the distinction between "primary" and "secondary" qualities, when propounded as an answer to the problem about substance, leaves us just where we were before. For (1) we ascribe the primary qualities to the "substance" of the thing in just the same fashion as the secondary. The thing *is* of such and such a configuration, *is* of such and such a mass, *is* solid, etc.; just as it *is* rough, or heavy, or green. Or, again, it *has* configuration, mass, solidity; just as it *has* weight,

[1] See the further elaboration of this analogy in Bk. III. chap. 3, § 2 ff.

taste, colour. Hence the old problem breaks out again with respect to the primary qualities themselves, however the list of them may be constructed. Again we have to ask, what is the *it* which possesses shape, mass, velocity, etc.?

(2) Moreover, the theory fails to explain the nature of that "possession" of the secondary qualities which it ascribes to the group of primary qualities. In what way, we ask, do the primary qualities have or possess the secondary? The only serious attempt to answer this question seems to be that of the numerous philosophers (Descartes, Galileo, Locke, etc.) who treat the secondary qualities as "subjective" effects of the primary qualities upon our sense-organs. Now, this familiar solution of the problem seems deficient in logic. For the one solid argument which has been advanced in favour of the subjectivity of secondary qualities seems to be the contention that they cannot be perceived without sense-organs of a special type. Colours, it is said, exist only for an eye, sounds for an ear, taste for a tongue, and so forth. And differences of structure or temporary condition in the sense-organ lead to the perception of different secondary qualities, as when, to take the stock examples, everything looks yellow to the jaundiced eye, the same water feels warm to one hand and cold to the other, and so forth.

But these considerations seem just as applicable to the supposed "primary" as to the "secondary" qualities of things. Geometrical form, for instance, is imperceptible apart from sight or touch; motion, again, and consequently change of configuration, and similarly mass, which is a ratio of accelerations, require either sight or touch for their perception. Of course, we can think of motions and masses which we are not actually perceiving, just as we can think of an absent colour or smell, and in both cases we can in reasoning about motions or masses or colours or smells abstract altogether from the presence of a percipient. But this does not affect the fact that the mathematical qualities of body are just as dependent for perception upon the presence of a percipient with suitable sense-organs as anything else. Configurations, extensions, and motions which no one perceives by sight or touch or any other sense are exactly in the same case as a colour which no one sees or a sound which no one hears. The argument from the indispensability of a perceiving organ ought logically to tell just as much in the one case as the other.[1]

---

[1] Professor Sidgwick's defence of the Lockian view (*Philosophy: its Scope and Relations*, p. 63 ff.) seems to me to ignore the point at issue, namely, that in

Again, and this is a point of the first importance, experience never gives us the "primary quality" by itself. What we get in actual experience is always the conjunction of primary and secondary qualities in a concrete perception. Thus we never perceive extension apart from some special visual or tactual filling of the "secondary" kind. The extended has always some quality of colour, or texture, or resistance. An extension which is totally devoid of colour, tactual quality, and everything which belongs to the so-called sensible, non-mathematical, or "secondary" properties of body, is an unreal abstraction, got by leaving out an aspect which in actual experience appears inseparable from it, and therefore presumably illegitimate. Illegitimate, that is, when offered as an account of the fundamental reality of body, however useful for the special purposes of natural science. Thus the attempt to take the so-called primary qualities as the unitary "substance" which has or "possesses" the secondary qualities, and to dispose of these latter as "subjective," leads to no satisfactory result. The former, too, must be merely qualities possessed by a more ultimate substance.

§ 5. Hence it constantly happens that the same writers who treat substance as identical with the primary qualities of things, alternate this view with another according to which substance is an unknowable unit of which we can say no more than that it, whatever it may be, is what is presupposed in all propositions about the behaviour of things as the "unknown substratum" of their various qualities. According to this view, the many qualities of the thing in some inexplicable manner "flow" either from the nature of its own unknown substratum or substance, or from the relations in which this substratum stands with that of other things.[1] Our knowledge is then held to be confined to these consequences of the unknown ultimate character of real things; we are ignorant, it is said, of the substance both of physical and of mental existence, we know only its attributes or manifestations. Or it is otherwise phrased thus: we do not know what things really are, we know only their effects on one another and on

---

any sense in which "secondary" qualities get their meaning from the content of sensation, primary qualities do the same. The whole point is that the sensation is not merely (as process) the *occasion* of our cognition of, *e.g.*, hardness or softness, but also (as content) furnishes the very meaning of "hard" or "soft." Cf. with what follows, *Appearance and Reality*, chap. 1.

[1] The former alternative is that of scholasticism; in modern science the latter has been more or less consciously adopted by those thinkers who retain the notion of substances. The various qualities are on this view consequences of the relations in which each substance stands (*a*) to other interacting substances, and (*b*) in particular to the unknown substratum of our "consciousness."

our own senses. This is, for instance, the view represented by those portions of Locke's Essay in which emphasis is laid upon our inability in the last resort to know the true substance of things.

Now, such a general doctrine as this is manifestly open to grave objections. (1) If we are serious in maintaining the unknowable character of the substratum of a thing's qualities, it is hard to see how the assertion of its existence can be any addition to our knowledge of the thing. To say that we are entirely ignorant of the nature of this substratum only amounts to saying in other words, that we have really no idea how the many qualities can be qualities of a single thing. If this is so, it does not appear what we gain by talking of the single thing at all as the owner or possessor of its qualities. It would, we might think, be better to abandon the confessedly unintelligible notion of a single substratum in which the qualities "inhere," and say that the thing, for our intellect, is simply the many qualities themselves. How this view would have to be reconciled with the tacit assumption of the thing's unity as a substance, which underlies all the judgments in which its attributes are predicated of it, we shall have to discuss more fully in the next section.

(2) A still more serious difficulty remains behind. Not only is an "unknowable substratum of qualities" a superfluous luxury in metaphysical theory, but the nature of the supposed relation between such a substratum and the attributes which "flow" from it is unintelligible. We can understand neither what a substance or substratum totally devoid of qualities could possibly be, nor yet how the various qualities of the world of things presented to our experience could "flow" as secondary consequences from one or more such substrata. We cannot conceive how things could first "be" without this being of theirs possessing any definite character, and then subsequently, in virtue of their relations among themselves, give rise to their qualities or characteristic modes of being. Nothing can be at all without being in some determinate way, and this "being in some determinate way" is precisely what we mean by the qualities of a thing. A thing cannot be without behaving in special ways towards its environment, and these special ways of behaving are the thing's qualities. We cannot, therefore, divorce the being or *that* of a thing from its determinate mode of being or *what*, and regard the latter as something which supervenes on or is derived from the former, or the former as something which can exist without and apart from the latter. Things are not

first there and afterwards in some mysterious way clothed with qualities; their qualities are simply their special way of being there. As Lotze well puts it, all such attempts to formulate a theory of the way in which the *what* of things flows from a mere *that*, are attempts to answer the absurd question how Being is made.[1] The notion that things have a *that* or substance prior to their *what* or quality, and consisting simply in "being" which is not this or that determinate mode of being, is thus unmeaning as well as superfluous.

§ 6. Accordingly the whole notion of a substantial unity in things behind the multiplicity of their states or qualities has been regarded with disfavour by many students of positive science. The qualities being all that interests us in things, and the notion of an indeterminate substratum contradictory, we ought, it is argued, to identify the thing and the series of its states and qualities without more ado. From this point of view the thing ceases to be an unknown somewhat, which in some mysterious way *has* properties; it becomes the properties themselves thought of as a collection. It is no longer the unperceived *this* which *has* warmth, redness, etc., it is the warmth, the redness, and the rest of the sensible qualities taken collectively. For phenomenalist Metaphysics, as for associationist Psychology, the thing is a "bundle of attributes" and nothing more.

When we ask how, if a "thing" is merely the series or sum of its attributes, and possesses no underlying unity to which the attributes belong, the whole of our ordinary language about things comes to be constructed on the contrary assumption, how it is that we always talk and think as if every "bundle" of attributes were owned by something of which we can say that it *has* the quality, we are met by the phenomenalist with a reference to Psychology. Owing to the fact, which Phenomenalism and Associationism are content to accept as ultimate, that sensible qualities are always presented to our perception in definite groups, it is argued that the thought of any one member of such a group is enough to revive by association the thought of the other qualities which have regularly been presented simultaneously with itself or in immediate succession to it. Hence, because thus associated in our perception, the group comes naturally, though illegitimately, by one of those mental fictions of which Hume treats so fully, to be thought of as one, though it is actually a discrete multiplicity. The unity of the thing thus lies not in itself, but solely in our way of perceiving and thinking.

[1] See chaps. 1 and 2 of bk. i. of his *Metaphysic*.

A more recent version of the same doctrine, which avoids the old associationist mistake of treating perception as a merely passive reception of a given material, is that the unity of the one subject of many predicates is ultimately derived from the unity of our own acts of attention. The qualities appear to belong to "one" thing because *we* attend to them together as one in a single moment of attention. Thus the unity of substance which common sense believes itself to find in its objects has really been put into them by the perceiving mind itself. What is "given" to it is a disconnected plurality of qualities; by attending to groups of them as one it makes those groups into the attributes of a single reality. This is the essence of the doctrine of Kant, according to which the concept of "substance" is simply one form of the "synthetic unity of apperception," *i.e.* the process by which we project the unity of our own acts of attention into their objects, and thus create an orderly world for our own thought out of sensations which as they are given to us are a chaos. In principle, Kant's doctrine, though intended as a refutation of Hume's Associationism, only differs from Hume's in the stress it rightly lays on the element of subjective interest in perception; the two theories agree on the main point, that the bond which unites the many qualities of sense perception into one thing is a subjective one,—in Hume's expressive phrase, a "fiction of the mind."[1]

With the psychological aspects of this doctrine we are not directly concerned in the present inquiry. For us the problem is not by what precise steps the mind comes to "feign" a unity in its objects which is not really there, but whether this conception of a feigned or subjective unity imposed by the mind upon a number of actually disconnected qualities is itself ultimately intelligible. Thus the metaphysical issue may be narrowed down to the following question: Can we intelligibly hold that a thing is in reality simply a number of qualities, not in their own nature connected, which we arbitrarily regard for our own purposes as one?[2] In other words, can we say the thing is simply identical with its qualities considered as a mere sum or

---

[1] The reader who desires to study Kant's doctrine in detail may begin by taking up Kant's own *Prolegomena to the Study of any future Metaphysic*, which may be profitably consulted even by those who find the *Critique of Pure Reason* too diffuse and technical. The latest and cheapest translation is that included in the Open Court Publishing Co.'s series of Philosophical Classics.

[2] "Arbitrarily" because it is, as all recent psychology insists, the direction of our attention which determines *what* qualities shall be presented together, and thus become "associated."

collection, and any further unity of the kind the old Metaphysics denotes by "substance," a mental addition of our own to the facts?

Now there are two considerations—both ultimately reducible in principle to one—which seem fatal to the identification of a thing with its qualities, considered as merely discrete. (1) There can be no doubt that it is largely true to say that a given group of qualities appear to us to be the qualities of one thing because we attend to them as one. And again, attention is undoubtedly determined by, or, to put it in a better way, is an expression of, our own subjective interests. But these considerations do not in the least show that attention is purely arbitrary. If we take any group of qualities to form one thing because we attend to it as one, it is equally true that we attend to it as one because it affects our subjective purposes or interests as one. That group of qualities is "one thing" for us which functions as one in its bearing upon our subjective interests. What particular interest we consider in pronouncing such a group one, in what interest we attend to it, may be largely independent of the qualities of the group, but the fact that the group does function as one in respect to this interest is no "fiction" or creation of our own thought; it is the expression of the nature of the group itself, and is independent of "our mind" in precisely the same sense in which the existence and character of any single member of the group of qualities is independent. There is no sense in assigning the single quality to "the given," and the union of the qualities into a single group to "the work of the mind"; in one sense both are the "work of the mind," in another both are the expression of the nature of the "given."[1]

(2) Again, the insufficiency of the simple identification of the thing with its qualities considered as a mere collection, may be illustrated by considering what the group of qualities must contain. The group of qualities is obviously never present in its entirety at any moment of experience. For the majority of what we call the qualities of a thing are simply the ways in which the "thing" behaves in the presence of various other things, its modes of reaction upon

---

[1] In Psychology this comes out in the rejection by the best recent writers of the whole associationist account of the process of perception, according to which the perception of a thing as a whole was taken to mean the actual presence in sensation of one of its qualities *plus* the reinstatement by association of the "ideas" of the others. For the modern doctrine of the perception of a whole, as distinct from the mere perception of its constituent parts, consult Stout, *Analytic Psychology*, bk. i. chap. 3, or *Manual of Psychology*,[3] bk. i. chap. 3.

a number of stimuli. Now, at any moment of the "thing's" existence it is only actually reacting upon a few of the possible stimuli, and thus only exhibiting a few of its qualities. The vast majority of its qualities are at any moment what Locke calls "powers," *i.e.* ways in which it *would* behave if certain absent conditions were fulfilled. Thus the thing to which we ascribe a number of predicates as its qualities is never the actual group of predicates themselves. Grass is green, but its greenness is not a fact in the dark; the sun is capable of melting the wax, and this capacity qualifies it permanently, but it does not actually melt the wax unless the wax is there, and various other conditions are also given; a man is temperamentally choleric, but he is not actually at every moment of his existence in a passion. He is only predisposed to fly into a passion readily on the occurrence of provocation. Most of a thing's qualities thus are mere possibilities; the nature of the thing is to act in this or that way under certain definite conditions which may or may not be realised in actual existence. Thus the collection of qualities with which Phenomenalism identifies a thing has itself no real existence as a collection. The collection is just as much a "fiction of the mind" as the unity which we attribute to it. Yet the fact that the thing's qualities are mainly mere possibilities does not destroy the existence of the thing. It actually is, and is somehow qualified by these possibilities. And for that very reason its existence cannot be identified with the actual realisation of these possibilities in a group or collection of events. We might add as a further consideration, that the number of such possibilities is indefinite, including not only the ways in which the thing has behaved or will behave on the occurrence of conditions at present non-existent, but also all the ways in which it would behave on the occurrence of conditions which are *never* realised in actual existence. But the previous argument is already in itself sufficient, the moment its significance is fairly grasped, to dispose of the notion that anything can be merely identical with a group of actually existing sensible qualities. The being of the things must be sought not in the actual existence of the group of sensible qualities, but in the law or laws stating the qualities which would be exhibited in response to varying sets of conditions.[1]

---

[1] This is just as true of the so-called primary qualities of things as of any others. Thus the mass and again the kinetic energy of a conservative material system are properly names for the way in which the system will behave under

§ 7. Considerations of this kind compel us to forego the attempt to find the substance or being of a thing in the mere sequence of its different states considered as an aggregate. To make Phenomenalism workable, we are forced to say at least that the thing or substance to which the various attributes are assigned is the "*law* of its states," or again is "the *mode of relation* of its various qualities." Such a definition has obviously a great advantage over either of the two we have just rejected. It is superior to the conception of the thing as an unknown substratum of qualities, since it explicitly excludes the absurd notion of a world of things which first *are*, without being in any determinate way, and then subsequently set up determinate ways of existing among themselves. For a law, while not the same thing as the mere collection of occurrences in which it is realised, has no existence of its own apart from the series of occurrences which conform to it. Again, every law is a statement of possibilities, a formula describing the lines which the course of events will follow *if* certain conditions are operative; no law is a mere register of actually observed sequences.[1] Hence, in defining the thing as the "law of its states," we avoid the difficulty dealt with in the last paragraph, that the collection of the thing's states never actually exists as a "given" collection. Thus for ordinary practical purposes the definition is probably a satisfactory one.

Yet it should be evident that in calling the thing the "law" of its states, we merely repeat the metaphysical problem of the unity of substance without offering any solution of it. For, not to dwell on the minor difficulty that we might find it impossible to formulate a *single* law connecting *all* the ways in which one thing reacts upon others, and thus ought more properly to speak in the plural of the laws of the states, we are now left with two distinct elements or aspects of the being of the thing, namely, the successive states and the law of their succession, and how these two aspects

determinate conditions, not of modes of behaviour which are necessarily actually exhibited throughout its existence. The laws of motion, again, are statements of the same hypothetical kind about the way in which, as we believe, particles move if certain conditions are fulfilled. The doctrine according to which all events in the physical world are actual motions, rests on no more than a metaphysical blunder of a peculiarly barbarous kind. Cf. Stallo, *Concepts and Theories of Modern Physics*, chaps. 10-12.

[1] Thus, *e.g.*, so fundamental a proposition in our current mechanical science as the "first law of motion" is avowedly a statement as to what *would* be the behaviour of things under a condition which, so far as we know, is never actually realised. On the thing as the "law of its states," see Lotze, *Metaphysic*, I. 3. 32 ff. (Eng. trans., vol. i. p. 88 ff.), and L. T. Hobhouse, *The Theory of Knowledge*, pp. 545-557.

are united the theory fails to explain. We have the variety and multiplicity on the one hand in the states or qualities of the thing, its unity on the other in the form of the law connecting these states, but how the variety belongs to or is possessed by the unity we know no better than before. Thus the old problem of substance returns upon us; the many qualities must somehow be the qualities of a single thing, but precisely how are we to conceive this union of the one and the many?[1]

At this point light seems to be thrown on the puzzle by the doctrine of Leibnitz,[2] that the only way in which a unity can, without ceasing to be such, contain an indefinite multiplicity is by "representation." Experience, in fact, presents us with only one example of a unity which remains indubitably one while embracing an indefinite multiplicity of detail, namely, the structure of our experience itself. For the single experience regularly consists of a multiplicity of mental states, both "focal" and "marginal," simultaneous and successive, which are nevertheless felt as one single whole because they form the expression of a coherent purpose or interest. And this conscious unity of feeling, determined by reference to a unique interest, is the only instance to which we can point when we desire to show by an actual illustration how what is many can at the same time be one. If we can think of the thing's qualities and the law of their connection as standing to one another in the same way as the detailed series of acts embodying a subjective interest of our own, and the interest itself which by its unity confers a felt unity on the series, we can in principle comprehend how the many qualities belong to the one thing. In that case the thing will be one "substance" as the embodiment of an individual experience, determined by a unique subjective

---

[1] Mr. Hobhouse (*op. cit.*, p. 541 ff.) thinks that the solution is simply that those qualities belong to one "substance," which are apprehended together as occupying one space. As a working criterion of what we mean by one bodily thing, this account seems satisfactory, and has probably suggested itself spontaneously to most of us. But it leaves untouched the more fundamental question how the identification of a certain sight-space with a certain touch-space is effected, and what are the motives which lead to it. Mr. Hobhouse is content to take the identification as "given in adult perception," but it seems to me to emerge from his own good account of the matter that it is the still more primitive apprehension of my own body as a felt unity upon which the synthesis between sight and touch spaces is based. If so, the ultimate source of the "unity of substance" must be sought deeper than Mr. Hobhouse is willing to go for it. And *quaere*, whether his account, if accepted as ultimate, would not lead to the identification of substance with space? For the difficulties which arise when you say the substance is the space *and* its filling of qualities, see *Appearance and Reality*, chap. 2, pp. 19, 20 (1st ed.).

[2] *Monadology*, §§ 8–16, 57–62.

SUBSTANCE, QUALITY, AND RELATION 139

interest, and therefore possessing the unity of immediate feeling. Its many qualities will "belong" to it in the same sense in which the various constituents of an experience thus unified by immediate feeling are said to "belong" to the single experience they constitute. And thus our idealistic interpretation of the general nature of Reality will be found to contain the solution of the problem of Substance and Quality.

Now it is fairly clear that some such idealistic solution is already contained in germ in the pre-scientific view of the world of things. There can be little doubt that our original notion of the unity of the thing as contrasted with the multiplicity of its qualities has been obtained by "introjectively" ascribing to whatever groups of qualities act upon us as one in respect of some interest of our own, the same conscious unity of feeling which we know in ourselves and our fellows. We shall have frequent opportunities, as we proceed, of discovering the enormous extent to which the whole pre-scientific view of the world is based upon the interpretation of all existence in terms of our own. Systematic Idealism will thus gradually be found to be no more than the consistent and deliberate carrying through of that anthropomorphic interpretation of Reality which lies at the bottom of all man's attempts to make his surroundings intelligible to himself. It will follow, if our general attitude towards the problem of substance is tenable, that only what we have already defined as an individual experience can truly be called a "substance," and that such experiences are "substances," if the word is to be retained in our philosophical vocabulary, to the same degree to which they are truly individual. And thus we should be led in the end to the distinction between the one infinite substance which forms the whole of Reality and the finite and imperfect substances which are its components.

Again, we should have once more to remember that since, in general, we call that group of qualities one which acts on our interests as one, and our insight into those interests themselves is limited and confused, the boundaries assigned by us to the group of qualities we ascribe to a single substance as "its" states will be more or less arbitrary, and dependent upon the degree of our actual insight. It is possible for us to group together as states of the same thing qualities which a profounder insight would have disjoined, and *vice versâ*. And in the end, if all that is is contained in a single coherent self-determined system, it is clear that, speaking rigorously, there will ultimately be only one "substance"—the central nature or principle of the system itself—of which all subordinate aspects or parts of existence will be the attributes.

§ 8. *The Problem of Relation.*—More perplexing than the problem of Substance and its Qualities is the question to which the pre-scientific assumption that the world consists of a number of *interrelated* things gives rise. This problem of Relation becomes still more prominent when reflection upon the problem of Substance and Quality has made it manifest that what we call the qualities of things are one and all dependent upon their relations either to our perceptive organs or to other things. Put quite simply the problem is as follows: Things stand in a variety of relations to one another, and what we commonly call the qualities of each are dependent on (*a*) its modes of relation to other things, (*b*) its relation to our percipient organism. Again, the various qualities of one thing stand in relation among themselves. To begin with, they all exhibit the relations of identity and difference. They all so far possess a common nature as to be capable of being compared in respect of the special ways in which they manifest that nature, and are thus so far identical; again, they can be discriminated and distinguished, and are so far in the relation of difference. Further, the qualities of one thing are interconnected, as we have already seen, by various special laws or modes of relation, which exhibit the changes in the behaviour of the thing corresponding to changes in the surrounding circumstances.

Thus Phenomenalism, when it has banished the notion of a substantial unity in things, has to identify the world of things, as we have already seen, with qualities in relation to one another. But now the question arises, How are we to understand the conception of qualities in relation? Can we, on the one hand, reduce all qualities to relations or all relations to qualities, or, on the other, can we form an intelligible idea of the way in which a single whole or system can be formed by the union of the two? There are, of course, other questions of great though relatively secondary importance connected with the problem of relation, *e.g.*, the question as to the number of ultimately irreducible kinds of relation, but the scope of the present work will permit of nothing beyond a brief discussion of the central difficulty. We will take the various alternatives in order.

SUBSTANCE, QUALITY, AND RELATION

(1) Philosophers have often been tempted to evade the difficulty of showing how qualities *and* relations together can make up a system by suppressing one member of the antithesis altogether. Thus it has been maintained, on the one hand, that the world of real things consists entirely of simple unrelated qualities, and that what we call relations between these qualities are merely our own subjective ways of apprehending them. On the other hand, it has been suggested that there may be nothing in the real world except relations, and that what we call qualities of various kinds are nothing but forms of relation. But neither of these views seems seriously tenable.

For (*a*) reality cannot consist of *mere* relations. Every relation implies two or more terms which are related. And these terms cannot be created by the relation itself. In every relation the terms have *some* character of their own over and beyond the mere property of being terms in that relation. Thus, to take a simple example, the successive terms of the series of ordinal numbers express in themselves nothing beyond determinate position in an ordered series, but when they are applied to the actual arrangement of any content in serial order, that content is (*c*) not created by the arrangement of it in an ordered series of terms, and (*b*) is dependent for the actual order of its terms upon some positive character of its own. In other words, whenever you actually count you count something other than the names of the numbers you employ, and you count it in an order which depends on the character of the particular things counted.[1] And so generally of all relations. A question has been raised which presents considerable difficulty and cannot be discussed here, whether there are or are not merely *external* relations (*i.e.* relations which are independent of the special qualities of their terms). But even if we admit that there may be such merely external relations, which do not depend upon the nature of the terms between which they subsist, it is at least clear that there cannot be relations without *any* terms, and that the terms are not created out of nothing by the relation

---

[1] This is true even where we merely count a number of qualitatively equivalent units in order to ascertain their sum. It is their positive character of being qualitatively equivalent which makes it permissible in this case to take any one of them indifferently as first, any other as second, etc. Whenever you apply the numerical series to the arrangement in order of the qualitatively dissimilar, the nature of your material as related to the character of your special interest in it decides for you what you shall call first, second, third, etc.

between them.[1] Perhaps it might be rejoined that what I call the terms of a certain relation, though no doubt not created by that particular relation, may be themselves analysed into other relations, and those again into others *ad indefinitum*. Thus it might be said that the term A of the relation A−B may no doubt have a quality of its own which is not created by this relation. But this quality, call it A_1, is found on analysis to be resoluble into the relation C−D, and the quality C_1 of C again into the relation E−F, and so on without end. This would not, however, amount to a reduction of qualities to mere relations. For it would give us, as the unit of our scheme of things, a pair of terms or qualities in relation; and however often we repeated the process of analysis, we should still always be left with the same type of triad, two terms and a relation, as the result of analysis. Whatever its worth, this particular solution falls under our second alternative, and must be considered in connection with it.

(2) But again, it is even more manifest that we cannot reduce all reality to qualities, and dismiss the relations between them as simply *our* subjective mode of apprehension. This line of thought is capable of being worked out in two slightly different ways. We might hold that what really exists is disconnected simple qualities, each distinct from all others as red is from sweet, or loud from hot, and that the whole network of relations by which everyday and scientific thought bring these "reals" into connection is a mere intellectual scaffolding to which nothing in the real world corresponds. Something like this would be the logical outcome of the Humian doctrine that all relations are "the work of the mind," and that reality is the residuum left after we have removed from our conception of the world everything which is of our own mental fabrication. The grounds upon which this doctrine was advanced by Hume and his followers have already been destroyed by the progress of Psychology and the consequent abandonment of the old hard-and-fast distinction between sensation and mental construction. It was the belief of Hume, and apparently of Kant, that what is given in "sensation" is single uncompounded qualities, and that all relations between these psychical atoms are produced by a subsequent process of subjective synthesis. But the advance of Psychology,

---

[1] As to the possibility of relations which are in this sense external to their terms, see B. Russell, *The Philosophy of Leibniz*, p. 130, and the articles by the same writer in *Mind* for January and July 1901.

by leading to the recognition that sensation itself is a continuous process containing a multiplicity of "marginal" elements which in all sorts of ways modify the character of its central or "focal" element, has made it impossible any longer to maintain an absolute distinction between the sensory and the intellectual factor in cognition.

And apart from the illusory nature of the distinction on which the theory was based, it is sufficiently condemned for Metaphysics by its own inherent absurdity. For the fundamental presupposition of Metaphysics, as of all serious science, is that Reality is a coherent system. But, according to the view which regards relations as pure "fictions of the mind," just that element in our thought which gives it its systematic character is an unwarranted addition of our own to the real. Order and system are in fact, on this view, mere illusion. And, as has often been pointed out by the critics of Hume, it is quite inconceivable how, in a world where nothing but disconnected simple qualities exist, the illusion should ever have arisen. If even our own inner life is simply incoherent, it is quite impossible to see how we can ever have come, even by a fiction, to read system into the world of fact.

A more plausible attempt to reduce all relations to qualities proceeds on the following lines. Relations, it is said, are of subjective manufacture, but they are, for all that, not mere fictions. For every relation between two terms, say A and B, is based upon the presence in A and B of certain qualities, which are called the *fundamenta relationis* or basis of the relation. These qualities may be the same in both the terms, in which case the relation is called symmetrical; such a case is that, *e.g.*, of the equality of A and B, a relation having for its *fundamentum* the fact that A and B have both the same magnitude. Here the real fact is taken to be that A has this magnitude, and again that B has it. The subjective addition to the facts is thought to come in in the voluntary comparison of A and B in respect of this property and the consequent assertion of their equality. Or the qualities which are the foundation of the relation may be different in each of the terms, in which case the relation is technically called asymmetrical. Examples of such asymmetrical relations are, *e.g.*, A greater than B, B less than A, or again, A father to B, B son to A. Here the actual facts would be taken to be A possessed of magnitude x, B of magnitude $x-y$, A qualified by the circumstance of begetting B, B by the circumstance of being begotten by A. The subjective addition would come in, as before, when we brought A and B under one point of view by comparing them in respect of these properties.

The inherent difficulties of the reduction of relations to qualities are, however, only thinly disguised in this version of the doctrine. To argue that the establishment of judgments of relation presupposes subjective comparison of the related terms from a more or less arbitrarily chosen point of view, is metaphysically irrelevant. The whole question is as to whether the result of the process is to make things more intelligible as a systematic whole; if it is, the subjectivity of the process is no ground for discrediting the result as truth about the real. If it is not, the philosophers who insist on the subjectivity of relations should explain how we can coherently think of a systematic whole of reality in terms of quality apart from relation. This they have never been able to do, and that for obvious reasons. It is manifestly impossible to give any intelligible account of the qualities which we recognise as *fundamenta* of relations without introducing previous relations. Thus the possession of the common magnitude x may be assigned as the foundation of the relation of equality between A and B; but when we ask what is meant by predicating of A and B possession of the magnitude x, we find that we are thrown back upon a relation between A, B, and some third term S, which we take as our unit of measurement. A and B are both of magnitude x because each contains S, let us say, x times exactly. So again the fact "A begetter of B" was assigned as the *fundamentum* of the asymmetrical relation of paternity between A and B, and the same fact under another name as the *fundamentum* of the asymmetrical relation of filiation between B and A.

But now what is meant by saying that the *same* fact qualifies A and B in *different* ways? Any answer to this question plunges us back at once into a perfect network of relations. For first, that a fact x may be known to qualify A and B differently, A and B must themselves be discriminated, *i.e.* they must be compared and found different, and without relation difference is unmeaning. For ultimately two terms are different only when they also possess a common character which admits of their comparison with reference to a common standard. Thus only things which are like can be different, and the problem of the relation of their likeness to their difference is inevitably forced upon us by the very existence of the difference. And similarly, the common fact x qualifies either term in a definite way, which can be discriminated from the ways in which other facts qualify the same term, and this discrimination leads in precisely the same manner to the assertion of various relations among the different qualities of A and again of B.[1]

It is not difficult to see the common source of the difficulties which beset both the attempt to reduce all reality to qualities, and the attempt to identify it with mere relations. In actual experience our world always comes to us as at once many and one, never as merely single nor as merely discrete. If you pay exclusive regard to the aspect of unity and interconnection, you will naturally be tempted to dwell on the relations between your elements to the exclusion of the various elements themselves; if you think solely of the aspect of variety, it is equally natural to treat the elements as real and their relations as fictions. But in either case you arbitrarily concentrate your attention on a single aspect of the experienced fact taken in isolation from the other, and are thus led to results which are bound to collide with the whole facts. A true view, if possible at all, can only be got by impartial adherence to the whole of the facts.

§ 9. We are thus brought to the second of our alternatives. Can we conceive of Reality as *qualities in relation* or qualities *and* their relations? This is really, in a somewhat more developed form, the same problem as that suggested by the definition of a thing as the " law of its states." We are now to take the qualities as fixed terms with a character of their own which stand in or support further relations, and we have to ask if the view of the world thus formulated is entirely intelligible. And it speedily becomes clear that such a view is confronted by a formidable difficulty. For suppose that A and B are two qualities which stand in any relation C. (For simplicity's sake we might suppose this relation C to be, *e.g.*, that of being discriminated, and we might take as instances of A and B, say, two definitely discriminated shades of the same colour.) Then A and B, standing in the relation C, are not identical with A and B as they would be apart from this relation. (A, for instance, as qualified by contradistinction from B, is not the same thing as *mere* A not in any way affected by B, a fact which is frequently

---

[1] See the elaborate discussion of the relational scheme implied in any assertion of difference in Royce, *The World and the Individual*, Second Series, lect. 2.

brought home to us with startling force by the effects of contrast.) At the same time the relation C cannot create its own terms; A, which is qualified in some special way by its standing to B in the relation C, may also exist out of this relation, and the mere fact of our recognising it as A shows that, both in the relation C and outside it, it has a recognisable identical character. (*E.g.*, A as discriminated from B is not precisely the same thing as A before discrimination, but the difference of A from B has not been created by the act of discrimination; it must previously have been different in order to be discriminated.)

Thus we seem forced to split up the quality A, which we took as one of the terms of our relation, into two aspects, A (A_1) the quality as it was before the establishment of the relation, and A (A_2) the quality as it is after the establishment of the relation. And the two aspects thus discovered in what we took for the single quality A must again be somehow in relation to one another. Hence within A (A_1) and A (A_2) itself the same process will be repeated, and what we began by regarding as the fixed terms of the relation will turn out to be themselves systems of qualities in relation, and this process will have no limit. The classification of the contents of experience into fixed terms with relations between them, it is contended, is no solution of the problem how the experienced world can be both one and many but a mere restatement of it. "We have to take reality as many and to take it as one, and to avoid contradiction. . . . And we succeed, but succeed merely by shutting the eye which if left open would condemn us." Hence the conclusion is drawn that "a relational way of thought . . . must give appearance and not truth. It is a makeshift, a device, a mere practical compromise, most necessary but in the end most indefensible."[1]

§ 10. The foregoing reasoning, which has been condensed from the fuller exposition in Mr. F. H. Bradley's *Appearance and Reality*, demands most careful examination, as the consequence to which it leads is of supreme importance for our whole metaphysical view of the nature of ultimate Reality. If the conclusion of Mr. Bradley is sound, it is clear that our discursive thought with its scheme of predication, which is from first to last relational, can never give us adequate insight into the nature of the union of the one and the many. We shall then have to conclude that it is

---

[1] Bradley, *Appearance and Reality*, chap. 3. Compare also chap. 15, "Thought and Reality."

not in thought about Reality, but in some mode of experience, if such there is, which enables us to transcend the separation of subject from predicate, and is therefore suprarelational, that we come nearest to experiencing the real as it really is. We should thus be more or less in sympathy with the traditional Mysticism which has always made the transcending of the distinction of subject from predicate the keynote of its special way of experiencing the Divine. On the other hand, if the relational scheme of ordinary knowledge could be defended as a self-consistent way of regarding the facts, we should have the advantage of being able to construe the absolute Experience in terms of our own intellectual life much more completely than Mysticism allows.

How, then, might the interpretation of the world as a system of qualities in relation be defended against Mr. Bradley's powerful formulation of the mystic's objection, and what is the worth of the defence? Two possible lines of argument suggest themselves as sufficiently plausible to call for examination. (1) The edge of the objection would be turned, as far as it rests upon the unsatisfactoriness of the indefinite regress, if we could regard *all* relations as "external," that is, as making no difference in the qualities they relate. Now, some relations, it has been asserted, are merely external, *e.g.*, relations of position and again of *sense* in the geometrical meaning of the word (like the difference between a right-hand and a left-hand glove). Why, then, may this not ultimately be the case with all relations? But if all relations are external, we can no longer argue that the related terms must contain a further relation between themselves as the basis and themselves as the result of the first relation, and so the whole anti-relational case falls to the ground.

Such a view seems, however, to suffer from fatal deficiencies. For (*a*) it is at least hard to see how any relation can be ultimately external to its terms. For you cannot hold two terms in a relation of any sort without discriminating them; until they are at least discriminated as two they cannot be terms with a relation between them. Thus discrimination, and therefore the relation of distinction, is fundamental in all relation. But where we can distinguish there must already be in the discriminated terms some difference to afford a basis for discrimination. Only what is already different can be distinguished. And with this admission the door is once more opened for the indefinite regress.

(*b*) And even if this were not so, it seems unthinkable that *all* relations should be in the end external to their terms. If no relation in the end makes any difference to its terms, and thus has no foundation in their nature, it becomes a standing miracle how or why the terms should enter into relations to which they are all the time absolutely indifferent. The logical consequence of such a view would surely be the dismissal of all relations as pure illusion, and the reduction of real existence to a chaos of disconnected reals which we by some inexplicable intellectual perversity persist in taking for a system. The now universally recognised failure of Herbart's attempt to work out a theory of Realism on these lines seems ominous for the success of any future doctrine of the same kind.

(2) Much more subtle is the line of thought suggested by Professor Royce in the Supplementary Essay appended to his book, *The World and the Individual*, First Series. Professor Royce admits the indefinite regress as an inevitable consequence of the reduction of the world to terms in relation, but denies that it affects the soundness of the reduction. On the contrary, he regards it rather as a proof of the positive correctness of the interpretation of existence which gives rise to it. His argument, which is based upon the modern doctrine of infinite series, may be briefly summarised as follows :—It is a recognised characteristic of an infinite series (and of no others) that it can be adequately "represented" by a part of itself. That is to say, if you take any infinite series you please, you can always construct a second series such that it consists of a selection, and only of a selection, from the terms of the first series, and that every term is derived from and answers to the corresponding term of the first series according to a definite law. And this second series, as it is easy to prove, is itself infinite, and therefore capable of being itself represented adequately in a third series derived from it in the same manner as it was derived from the first, and so on indefinitely.

For instance, let the first series be the infinite series of the natural integers 1, 2, 3, 4, . . . then if, *e.g.*, we construct a second series, 1^2, 2^2, 3^2 . . . of the second powers of these integers, the terms of this second series are derived by a definite law from those of the first to which they correspond, and again they constitute a selection out of the terms of the first series. Every one of them is a term of the first series, but there are also terms of the first series which are not repeated in the second. Again, if we make a third series from the second in the same way as the second was made from the first, by taking the terms $(1^2)^2, (2^2)^2, (3^2)^2$, and so on, the terms of this third series fulfil the same conditions; they correspond according to a fixed law with the terms of the second, and are also themselves a selection from those terms. And thus we may go on without end to construct successive infinite series each of which "adequately represents" the preceding one. And we are led into this indefinite regress by the very attempt to carry out consistently a single definite principle of correspondence between our original infinite series and its first derivative. In constructing the first derived series in our illustration $1^2, 2^3, 3^2 \ldots$ we necessarily also construct the series $(1^2)^2, (2^2)^2, (3^2)^2, \ldots$ and the other successive derivatives. Therefore Prof. Royce claims that any consistent attempt to make an orderly arrangement of the terms of an infinite whole *must* lead to the indefinite repetition of itself. Hence that each term of every relation on analysis turns out itself to consist of terms in relation, is no valid objection to the soundness of our principle of interpretation, but a necessary consequence of the infinity of Reality.[1] Any consistent attempt to exhibit an infinite whole as an orderly system of terms *must* lead to the indefinite regress.

Now it strikes one at once that Professor Royce's conclusion is in danger of proving too much. You certainly do not show a method of dealing with facts to be sound by showing that it leads to the indefinite regress. It is a common experience that the liar who tells his first lie must tell a second to back it, and a third to support the second, and so on indefinitely. And you cannot put a quart of liquor into a pint pot without first putting half the quart into half the space, and so forth *ad indefinitum*. Yet these considerations do not prove that lying or putting quarts of liquor into pint pots is a consistent way of dealing with reality. A purpose may lead in execution to the indefinite regress because it is self-contradictory and therefore self-defeating, as these familiar illustrations suggest. And this raises the question whether the purpose to arrange an infinite whole in an ordered system of terms may not lead to the indefinite regress for the same reason, namely, that the treatment of a true whole as a sequence of terms is incompatible with its real nature. It is at least worth while to

[1] The reader who desires further knowledge of the researches in the theory of Numbers upon which Prof. Royce's doctrine is based, may profitably consult Dedekind, *Was sind und was sollen die Zahlen*, and Couturat, *L'Infini Mathématique*.

ask whether Professor Royce's own treatment of the subject does not contain indications that this is actually the case.[1]

To begin with, we may note one point of some importance in reference to which Prof. Royce's language is at least ambiguous. He speaks of the indefinite succession of infinite series which arise from the single purpose of "representing" the series of natural integers adequately by a selection out of itself as if they could be actually constructed in pursuance of this purpose. But this is clearly not the case. All that you can actually do is to construct the various series *implicitly* by giving a rule for their formation. The actual construction of the series would be a typical instance of a self-defeating and therefore internally contradictory purpose, inasmuch as it would involve the actual completion of an unending process. Hence we seem forced to make a distinction which Prof. Royce has perhaps unduly neglected. If your purpose of ordering the number series on a definite plan means no more than the formulation of a rule for obtaining any required number of terms of the successive series, it can be executed, but does not involve the indefinite regress; if it means the actual completion of the process of formation of the series, it does involve the indefinite regress, but is therefore self-contradictory and cannot be realised in act. Similarly, we may say of the scheme of qualities in relation, that if it is taken for no more than a rule for the systematic arrangement and organisation of a finite material, it does not involve the completion of an infinite process, and is both workable and useful; but if presented as an account of the way in which a completed all-embracing and perfectly harmonious experience of the whole of Reality is internally organised, it involves the completion of the infinite process, and is therefore self-contradictory and finally inadequate.[2]

---

[1] Professor Royce's own illustration of the map of England executed upon a portion of the surface of the country is really a typical instance of a self-contradictory purpose. He argues that such a map, to be theoretically perfect, must contain a reduced facsimile of itself as part of the country mapped, and this again another, and so on indefinitely. But the whole force of the reasoning depends on overlooking the distinction between the surface of England as it is before the map is made, and the surface of England as altered by the presence of the map. Prof. Royce assumes that you set out to represent in the map a state of things which can in fact have no existence until after the map is made. The previous existence of the map at a certain spot is falsely taken to be one of the conditions to which the map-maker is to conform in executing it. Every one of the supposed "maps within the map" will thus involve distortion and misrepresentation of the district it proposes to map. It is as if Hamlet had chosen "Hamlet" as the subject of the "play within the play." The professor's illustration thus does less than justice to his theory.

[2] The fundamental defect in Professor Royce's reasoning seems to me to lie

This reflection may serve to lead up to another which seems to take us into the heart of the matter. The researches upon which Prof. Royce's defence of the relational scheme is based were in the first instance investigations into the significance of the number-series. As such they start with the conception of a system which is a whole of *parts* external to one another[1] as the object of inquiry. Consequently, while such investigations are of the highest philosophical importance as bringing out the implications of this concept, they are only valid as an analysis of ultimate Reality, provided that the concept of whole and part is an adequate expression of the way in which the whole Reality is present in its constituents and they in it. But if, as we ourselves urged in a previous chapter, the conception of a whole of parts is entirely inadequate to express the intimate union between the absolute experience and finite experiences,[2] the proof that the indefinite process is logically implied in the relation of whole and part does not show it to belong to the structure of ultimate Reality. Rather, we should be inclined to urge, the fact that the relational scheme leads to the indefinite process proves that the conception of whole and part upon which it is based does not truly represent the mode of union between a completed experience and its components. And therefore the attempt to interpret this union in terms of the number-series cannot stand the test of criticism.

At the same time, Professor Royce's argument in any case throws considerable light upon the problem of relation. For it shows *why* the attempt to construct the world as a system of qualities in relation leads to the indefinite regress. For a complete experience embodying at one stroke the whole of existence, such a construction would, as we have seen, because essentially incomplete, be impossible. But when *we* try to piece together the data of our fragmentary experience into a connected whole, we inevitably have to start with more or less isolated facts as fixed terms and weld them

---

in the tacit transition from the notion of an infinite *series* to that of an infinite completed *sum*. Thus he speaks of the series of prime numbers as a "whole" being present at once to the mind of God. But are the prime numbers, or any other infinite series, an actual sum at all? They are surely not proved to be so by the existence of general truths about any prime number.

[1] See, *e.g.*, Dedekind, *op. cit.*, § 2: "It frequently happens that different things *a*, *b*, *c* . . . are apprehended upon whatsoever occasion under a common point of view, mentally put together, and it is then said that they form a *system*; the things *a*, *b*, *c* . . . are named the *elements* of the system"; and § 3 (definitions of *whole* and *part*).

[2] *Ante*, Bk. II. chap. 2, § 5.

together by a relation. In doing so we unavoidably put ourselves at the point of view from which the numerical series arises; we unavoidably treat existence *as if* it were a whole of mutually external parts. And so the indefinite regress involved in the nature of the number-system inevitably parades the whole of our discursive and relational thinking about existence. But its presence is due to the inadequacy of the conception of Reality with which discursive thought has to work.

On the whole, then, it seems that Prof. Royce's investigations only make it more apparent than before that the relational scheme which discursive thought uses does not adequately express the true nature of the real, and that the mystics of all ages have been so far justified in their contention that the form of our experience which presents the truest analogy to the experience of the Absolute must be supra-relational, or, in other words, that the most real type of finite experience must be one which transcends the distinction of subject and predicate. To admit this is, however, not to admit that we are altogether ignorant how the one and the many are united in Reality. For there are many other types of human experience besides that which is dominated by the discursive and relational intellect.

In immediate simple feeling we have obviously a type of conscious experience in which distinction and relation have as yet not emerged. And I have tried in Bk. I. chap. 2 to show how in the direct intuition of an æsthetic whole by trained artistic perception we have at a higher level an experience which contains the results of an elaborate process of distinction and relation, but contains them in a way which transcends the relational form and reverts in its directness to the unity of immediate feeling. While again we have in the personal love which is one with mutual insight a form of experience that, if translated into the language of the intellect, would require for its description a whole world of relations and predicates, and is yet, as experienced, an intimate unity no relational scheme can more than faintly adumbrate. And it is worthy of consideration that religious emotion in all ages has borrowed from these forms of experience its favourite expressions for the highest modes of communion between the finite and the infinite, the "beatific vision," the "love of God," etc.

It seems indeed as if the function of the mere intellect were always that of a necessary and valuable intermediary between a lower and a higher level of immediate apprehension. It breaks up, by the relations and distinctions it introduces, the original union of the *what* and the *that* of simple feeling, and proceeds to make the *what*, which it deals with in its isolation, ever more and more complex. But the ultimate issue of the process is only reached and its ultimate aim only satisfied so far as it conducts us at a higher stage of mental development to the direct intuition of a richer and more comprehensive whole in the immediate unity of its *that* and its *what*. The besetting philosophical sin of the mere mystic is not so much his refusal to accept the work of the mere intellect as the highest and truest type of human experience, as his tendency to satisfy his demand for the fuller union of the *what* with the *that* by reverting to the lower forms of immediacy upon which intellectual reflection has not done its work, instead of pressing on to the higher in which the effect of that work is preserved though its form is transcended.

These reflections may serve to obviate the objection that to reject the relational scheme when it is offered as the ultimate truth is to deny the value and significance of the scientific work we accomplish by means of it. Though the scheme of relations cannot adequately express the mode of union between the finite and the infinite, there is no fresh addition to the system of relations into which scientific analysis translates the real world of experience that does not increase our knowledge of what the real world must contain, though it may fail to explain how it contains it. And, in conclusion, let it be remembered that it is true not only of the religious mystic's special experience of union with deity, but of all direct experience, that the relational scheme is quite inadequate to explain how it holds its double aspects, its unity and its multiplicity, its *that* and its *what*, in complete interpenetration. For no living experience is a mere whole of parts, and none, therefore, can be fully represented by a scheme based upon the concept of whole and part.[1]

---

[1] It is no answer to this view to urge that as soon as the intellect undertakes to reflect upon and describe Reality it unavoidably does so in relational terms. For it is our contention that the same intellect which uses these relational methods sees *why* they are inadequate, and to some extent at least how they are ultimately merged in a higher type of experience. Thus the systematic use of the intellect in Metaphysics itself leads to the conviction that the mere intellect is not the whole of Reality. Or, in still more paradoxical language, the highest truth for the mere intellect is the thought of Reality as an ordered system. But all such order is based in the end on the number-series with its category of whole and part, and cannot, therefore, be a perfectly adequate representation of a supra-relational Reality. Hence Truth, from its own nature, can never be quite the same thing as Reality.

Consult further:—F. H. Bradley, *Appearance and Reality*, chaps. 1–3, 15, 27; L. T. Hobhouse, *Theory of Knowledge*, pp. 172–181 (Qualities and Relations), 540–557 (Substance); H. Lotze, *Metaphysic*, bk. i. chap. 1 (The Being of Things), chap. 2 (The Quality of Things), chap. 3 (The Real and Reality); J. Royce, *The World and the Individual*, First Series, Supplementary Essay; B. Russell, "The Concept of Order" (*Mind*, January 1901), and article on "Position in Space and Time" (*Mind*, July 1901); G. F. Stout, "Alleged Self-contradictions in the Concept of Relation" (*Proceedings of the Aristotelian Society*, New Series, vol. ii. pp. 1–14, with the accompanying discussion, pp. 15–24).

SUPPLEMENTARY NOTE TO CHAPTER IV.

Dr. Stout's Reply to Mr. Bradley's Criticism of the Concept of Relation.

Since the preceding chapter was written, I have had the opportunity of studying Dr. Stout's paper in the current volume of *Proceedings of the Aristotelian Society*. I have not thought it necessary to make any alterations in the text of Chapter 4, in consequence of Dr. Stout's criticism, but I may perhaps be permitted to add the following remarks, which must not be regarded as a systematic appreciation or examination of Dr. Stout's views. The latter, as he himself pleads, cannot indeed be finally judged until he has worked out the theory of Predication for which his present paper merely prepares the way.

1. Dr. Stout begins by admitting what to my own mind is the essence of the anti-relational argument. "No relation or system of relations can ever constitute a self-subsistent and self-contained Reality. The all-inclusive universe cannot ultimately consist in (? of) a collection of interrelated terms" (*op. cit.*, p. 2). This being once conceded, I should have thought it an inevitable consequence that a "collection of interrelated terms" cannot give us the final truth about the nature of anything. For the whole idealist contention, as I understand it and have tried to sustain it in the present work, is that the structure of the whole is so repeated in any and every one of its members that what is not the truth about the whole is never the *ultimate* truth about anything.

precisely because there is ultimately nothing apart from the whole, and the whole again is nothing apart from its members. So much, I had thought, we have all learned from Hegel, and therefore Dr. Stout's dilemma that any proposition asserting relation (p. 5) must be false, unless the relational scheme, so long as it is not affirmed of the ultimate whole itself, gives us truth, does not seem to me to possess any real cogency. With Mr. Bradley himself, as quoted by Dr. Stout, I should urge that if the relational scheme is not itself internally discrepant, there remains no valid ground for disputing its applicability to the whole.

2. Dr. Stout's introduction into a "relational unity" of the third term,—*relatedness* does not seem to me to remove the difficulties inherent in our problem. And the illustration by which he supports it appears to be unsound. He argues that when my hat is on my head this state of things implies (1) the two related terms, the hat and the head, (2) a relation of *on* and *under*, (3) the fact that the terms stand in this relation—their relatedness. For (1) and (2) by themselves would be compatible with my hat being on the peg and my head bare. But surely there is here a confusion between the relation of *above* and *below*, and the very different relation of *on* and *under*. The latter relation includes, as the former does not, immediate contact as part of its meaning. If there are (1) a hat and a head, and (2) the relation *on* and *under*—in this sense—between the two, there is surely no need of a third factor to complete the concrete actuality of "hat on head." If the hat is not actually on the head, then (2), the supposed relation, is not there at all. And if (2) is there the whole fact is already there. In a word, Dr. Stout seems to me to count in the concrete fact of "thing exhibiting related aspects" as a third constituent in itself, precisely as popular Logic sometimes counts in the actual judgment, under the name of *Copula*, as one factor of itself.[1]

Then to Dr. Stout's use of his distinction between the relation and the fact of relatedness, I think it may be replied that it leaves us precisely where we were before. The hat is qualified by being *on* the head, the head by being *in* or

---

[1] Or does Dr. Stout merely mean that there may be a hat and a head, and also a relation of on and under (*e.g.*, between the *hat* and the *peg*), and yet my hat not be on my head? If this is his meaning, I reply we have not really got the *relation* and its *terms*; if the hat is not on the head, hat and head are not terms in the relation at all. I do not see why, on his own principles, Dr. Stout should not add a fourth factor to his analysis, namely, qualified*ness*, or the fact that the qualities are there, and so on indefinitely.

under the hat, and hat and head together by the relation of *on* and *under* between them. But how these various aspects of the fact are to be combined in a single consistent view we are no nearer knowing.

3. *The endless regress.* I think it will be seen from the preceding chapter that in my own view a genuine endless regress is evidence of the falsity of the conception which gives rise to it, and that I hold this on the ground that the endless regress always presupposes the self-contradictory purpose to sum an admittedly infinite series. Hence I could not concur, so far as I can see at present, in Dr. Stout's distinction between the endless regress which does and that which does not involve self-contradiction. As to his illustration of endless regress of the second kind, the infinite divisibility of space (p. 11), I should have thought that there is no actual endless regress in question until you substitute for infinite divisibility infinite actual *subdivision*, and that when you make this substitution it commits you at once to the self-contradictory completion of an unending task. (Cf. what was said above, § 10, with reference to infinite numerical series.)

4. Dr. Stout goes on to deny that there is any endless regress, self-contradictory or not, involved in the relational scheme. According to him, what connects the relation with its terms is not another relation (which would of course give rise to an endless regress), but their relatedness, which is "a common adjective both of the relation and the terms" (p. 11). I have already explained why this solution appears to me merely to repeat the problem. The relatedness, so far as I can see, is a name for the concrete fact with its double aspect of quality and relation, and I cannot understand how mere insistence upon the concrete unity of the fact makes the conjunction of its aspects more intelligible.

5. Dr. Stout further supports his contention by a theory of the nature of continuous connection which I have perhaps failed to understand. Replying in anticipation to the possible objection of an opponent, that if the "relatedness" connects the terms with their relation there must be a second link to connect the term with its relatedness, he says "there is no intermediate link and there is need for none. For the connection is continuous, and has its ground in that ultimate continuity which is presupposed by all relational unity" (p. 12, cf. pp. 2–4). And, as he has previously told us, "so far as there is continuous connection there is nothing between [*i.e.* between the connected terms], and there is therefore no relation."

SUBSTANCE, QUALITY, AND RELATION

Now there seems to me to be a contradiction latent here. Continuous connection, of course, implies distinct but connected terms which form a series. Where there are no such distinct terms there is nothing to connect. Now it is, as I understand it, part of the very nature of a continuous series that any two terms of the series have always a number of possible intermediate terms between them. And therefore, in a continuous series, there are *no* immediately adjacent terms. Dr. Stout's own illustration brings this out—

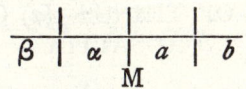

$$\beta \mid \alpha \mid a \mid b$$
$$M$$

In a diagram like the accompanying *b* and *β* are, he argues, "mediately conjoined," but *a* and *α* are "immediately co-adjacent." Surely Dr. Stout forgets here that what can be intelligibly called "co-adjacent" are not lines but points or positions on the lines. And between any point in *α* and any point in *a* there are a plurality of intermediate positions, except for the special case of the extreme left point of *a* and the extreme right point of *α*. These, of course, coalesce in the single point M, and there is therefore no connection, mediate or immediate, left in this case.[1] The illustration, I think, may serve to reveal a serious discrepancy in Dr. Stout's theory. He sees that relations presuppose a unity which is supra-relational, and which he calls "continuous," on the ground of its supra-relational character. At the same time, to save the relational scheme from condemnation as leading to the endless regress, he has to turn this supra-relational unity itself into a sort of relation by calling it an immediate connection between *adjacent* terms, and thus ascribing to it the fundamental character of a *discontinuous* series. And I cannot help regarding this procedure as unconscious evidence to the truth of the principle, that what is not the truth about the whole of Reality is not ultimately the truth about any reality.

---

[1] If you consider the *lines a* and *α*, as Dr. Stout prefers to do, I should have thought two views possible. (*a*) There are not two lines at all, but one, the "junction" at M being merely ideal. Then there remains nothing to connect and there is no relation of "immediate connection." Or (*b*), the junction may be taken as real, and then you have a perfectly ordinary case of relation, the terms being the terminated lines *a* and *α*, and the relation being one of contact at M. On every ground (*a*) seems to me the right view, but it is incompatible with the reduction of continuity to "immediate connection." Thus the source of the difficulty is that (1) immediate connection can only hold between the immediately successive terms of a discontinuous series, and yet (2) *cannot* hold between them precisely *because* they are discontinuous.

CHAPTER V

THE WORLD OF THINGS—(2) CHANGE AND CAUSALITY

§ 1. The conception of things as interacting leads to the two problems of Change and Causality. The paradoxical character of change due to the fact that only what is permanent can change. § 2. Change is succession within an identity; this identity, like that of Substance, must be teleological, *i.e.* must be an identity of plan or end pervading the process of change. § 3. Thus all change falls under the logical category of Ground and Consequence, which becomes in its application to succession in time the Principle of Sufficient Reason. § 4. *Causality*. Cause—in the modern popular and scientific sense—means the ground of a change when taken to be completely contained in preceding changes. That every change has its complete ground in preceding changes is neither an axiom nor an empirically ascertained truth, but a postulate suggested by our practical needs. § 5. In the last resort the postulate cannot be true; the dependence between events cannot be one-sided. The real justification for our use of the postulate is its practical success. § 6. Origin of the conception of Cause anthropomorphic. § 7. Puzzles about Causation. (1) *Continuity*. Causation must be continuous, and yet in a continuous process there can be no distinction of cause from effect. Cause must be and yet cannot be *prior* in time to effect. § 8. (2) *The indefinite regress* in causation. § 9. (3) *Plurality of Causes*. Plurality of Causes is ultimately a logical contradiction, but in any form in which the causal postulate is of practical use it must recognise plurality. § 10. The "necessity" of the causal relation psychological and subjective. § 11. Immanent and Transeunt Causality: Consistent Pluralism must deny transeunt Causation; but cannot do so successfully. § 12. Both transeunt and immanent Causality are ultimately appearance.

§ 1. THE fourth of the features which characterise the pre-scientific view of the world we found to be the belief that things act and are acted upon by one another. The problems to which this belief gives rise are so vast, and have been historically of such significance for Metaphysics, that they will require a separate chapter for their discussion. In the conception of the interaction of things as it exists for the naïve pre-scientific mind, we may distinguish at least two aspects. There is (1) the belief that things *change*, that within the unity of the one thing there is a succession of different states; and (2) the belief that the changes of state of various things are so inter-connected that the changes in one thing serve as occasions for definite changes in other things.

We thus have to discuss, first, the general notion of change as an inseparable aspect of the being of things, and next the concept of systematic inter-connection between the changes of state of different things.

(*a*) *Change.* The problem presented by the apparently unceasing mutability of existence is one of the earliest as well as one of the most persistent in the whole range of Philosophy. In itself it might seem that the successive presentation in time of various states is neither more nor less noteworthy a feature of the world of experience than the simultaneous presentation of a like variety, but the problem of mutability has always appealed with special force to the human imagination from its intimate connection with our personal hopes and fears, ambitions and disappointments. Tempora mutantur, *nos* et mutamur in illis; there is the secret of the persistence with which our philosophic thought has from the first revolved round this special problem. There, too, we may find a pregnant hint of the central paradox implied in all mutability—namely, that only the identical and permanent can change. It is because the self which changes with the flux of time and circumstance is still in some measure the same old self that we feel its changes to be so replete with matter for exultation and despair. Were we completely new-made with each successive change in our self, there would no longer be ground for joy in transition to the better or grief at alteration for the worse.

The thought that only what is permanent can change has affected Philosophy in different ways at different periods of its history. At the very dawn of Greek Philosophy it was the guiding principle of the Ionian physicists who sought to comprehend the apparent variety of successive phenomena as the transformations of a single bodily reality. As the difficulties inherent in such a materialistic Monism became more apparent, the felt necessity of ascribing unity of some kind to existence led Parmenides and his Eleatic successors to the extreme view that change, being impossible in a permanent homogeneous bodily reality, must be a mere illusion of our deceptive senses. While yet again the later Ionian physicists, and their Sicilian counterpart Empedocles, sought to reconcile the apparent mutability of things with the criticism of Parmenides by the theory that what appears to the senses as qualitative change is in reality the mere regrouping in space of qualitatively unalterable "elements" or "atoms"—μεῖξις διάλλαξίς τε μιγέντων.

At a more developed stage of Hellenic thought, the necessity of taking some account of the mutability as well as of the permanence of existence impelled Plato to draw the momentous distinction between two worlds or orders of being—the real, with its eternal unvarying self-identity, and the merely apparent, where all is change, confusion, and instability. In spite of Plato's manifest failure to make it intelligible how these two orders, the eternal and the temporal, are ultimately connected, this distinction in one form or another has continued ever since to haunt all subsequent metaphysical construction. Even our modern scientific Materialism, with its loudly avowed scorn for all merely metaphysical questions, shows by its constant endeavour to reduce all material existence to a succession of changes in a homogeneous medium, both the persistence with which the intellect demands a permanent background for change, and the difficulty of finding logical satisfaction for the demand.

Yet there have not been wanting attempts to get rid of the paradox by denying its truth. As the Eleatics sought to escape it by reducing change itself to a baseless illusion, so some at least of the disciples of Heracleitus seem to have evaded it by refusing to admit any permanent identity in the changeable, and they have not been entirely without imitators in the modern world. Incessant change without underlying unity has had its defenders in the history of Metaphysics, though they have not been numerous, and we must therefore briefly consider what can be urged for and against such a concept. Apart from the general difficulty of seeing how what changes can at the same time be permanently identical with itself, the only special argument in favour of the doctrine that only incessant change is real seems to be the appeal to direct experience. In any actual experience, it is contended, however contracted its limits, we are always presented with the fact of change and transition; we never apprehend an absolutely unchanging content. Even where the object before us exhibits no succession, self-examination will always detect at least alternating tension and relaxation of attention with the accompanying fluctuations of bodily sensation.

Now there can, of course, be no gainsaying these facts of experience, but the conclusion based on them evidently goes much further than the premisses warrant. If experience never gives us mere persistence of an unchanging content, neither does it ever give us mere change without persistence. What we actually experience always exhibits the two aspects of identity and transition together. Usually there will be, side by side with the elements which sensibly change in the course of the experience, others which remain sensibly constant throughout it. And even when, through inattention, we fail to detect these constant elements, the successive states of the changing content itself are not merely momentary; each has its own sensible duration through which it retains its character without perceptible changes. Experience thus entirely fails to substantiate the notion of mere change apart from a background of permanent identity.

The positive disproof of the notion must, however, be found in its own inherent absurdity. Change by itself, apart from a background of identity, is impossible for the reason that where there is no underlying identity there is nothing to change. All change must be change of and in some thing. A mere succession of entirely disconnected contents held together by no common permanent nature persisting in spite of the transition, would not be change at all. If I simply have before me first A and then B, A and B being absolutely devoid of any point of community, there is no sense in saying that I have apprehended a process of change. The change has been at most a change in myself as I passed from the state of perceiving A to the state of perceiving B, and this subjective transition again can only be called change on the assumption that the I who am qualified first by the perception of A and its various emotional and other accompaniments, and then by that of B and its accompaniments, am the same. And where you have not merely a change of perception but an actual perception of change, the case is even clearer. What we perceive in such a case is "A changing into B," the two successive states A and B being held together by the fact that they are successive states of some more permanent unity γ. Apart from the presence of this identical γ in both the earlier and later stages of the process, there would be no meaning in speaking of it as one of change.

§ 2. Change, then, may be defined as succession within an identity, the identity being as essential to the character of the process as the succession. In what way, then, must we think of this identity or common nature which is present throughout the whole succession of changes? It should be clear that this question—how that which changes can be permanent?—is simply our old problem of quality and substance, how the many states can belong to one thing, considered with special reference to the case of states which form a succession in time. Thus, whatever is the true nature of the unity to which the many states of one thing belong, will also be the true nature of the identity which connects the successive stages of a process of change.

Now we have already seen in what the unity to which the many states belong must be taken to consist. We found that this unity is essentially teleological; that group of states, we saw, is one thing which functions as one in regard to an end or interest, or, as we may also say, is the embodiment of coherent structure. The same is true of the process of change. The earlier and later stages of the process are differences in an identity precisely because they constitute one process. And a process is one when it is the systematic realisation of a single coherent end. To be one process means to be the systematic expression in a succession of stages of a single coherent plan or law. The succession of stages is thus welded into a unity by the singleness of the plan or law which they embody, and it is this systematic connection of each stage with all the rest which we express by saying that whatever changes possesses an underlying permanent identity of character. It would amount to precisely the same thing if we said the successive states of anything that changes form a connected system.

We must be careful here, as we were in dealing with the problem of Substance, not to be misled by taking symbolic aids to imagination for philosophical truths. Just as it is easy to imagine the "substance" of things as a sort of material substratum, it is easy to imagine the identity which pervades all changes as that of a number of pieces of matter, and to think of the changes as constituted by their motion through space. But such a representation must not be taken for anything more than an aid to imagination. It helps us to make a mental diagram, but it throws absolutely no light upon the real nature of the connection between the identity and the succession. For the same problem breaks out within each of the "self-identical" pieces of matter; we have to say what we mean by calling it one and the same throughout the series of its changing positions, and the necessity of answering this question shows us at once that the identity of a material particle throughout its motion is only one *case* of that identity pervading succession which belongs to all change, and in no sense affords any explanation of the principle it illustrates.[1] As a recent writer puts it, "it seems to be a deeply rooted infirmity of the human mind ... that it can hardly conceive activities of any sort apart from material bases, ... through habitually seeking to represent all phenomena in mechanical terms, in terms of the motion of little bits of matter, many of us have come to believe that in so doing we describe the actual events underlying phenomena."[2] This "disease of the intellect," as the same writer aptly calls it, is nowhere more insidious than where we are dealing with the problem of Change.

Change, then, involves two aspects. It is a succession of events in time, and these events are connected by a systematic unity in such a way that they form the expression of a plan or law of structure. The series of successive states which make up the history of a thing are the expression of the thing's nature or structure. To understand the thing's structure is to possess the key to the succession of its states, to know on what principle each gives way to its successor. And similarly, to have complete insight into the nature or structure of Reality as a whole would be to understand the principles according to which every transitory event in the history of the Universe, regarded as a series of events in time, is followed by its own special successor.

It is evident that, in proportion as our knowledge of any thing or system of things approaches this insight into the laws of its structure, the processes of change acquire a new character for us. They lose their appearance of paradox, and tend to become the self-evident expression of the identity which is their underlying principle. Change, once reduced to law and apprehended as the embodiment in succession of a principle we understand, is no longer change as an unintelligible mystery. We should bear this in mind when we reflect on the doctrine of Plato that the physical world must be unreal because the scene of incessant change. Such a view is only to be understood by remembering that before the invention of the mathematical methods which have enabled us with such conspicuous success to reduce physical phenomena to orderly sequence according to law, the physical world necessarily appeared to the philosopher a scene of *arbitrary* change following no recognisable principle. Change, so

---

[1] For a discussion of the same point in dealing with *energy*, see Professor Schuster, *British Association Report*, 1892, p. 631.
[2] W. M'Dougall in *Mind* for July 1902, p. 350.

far as understood in the light of its principle, has already ceased to be mere change.[1]

§ 3. *Ground and Consequence.* In the technical language of Logic, the underlying principle of any system is called its *Ground*, the detail in which the principle finds systematic expression is called its *Consequence*. Ground and Consequence are thus one and the same systematic whole, only considered from two different points of view. The Ground is the pervading common nature of the system, thought of as an identity pervading and determining the character of its detail; the Consequence is the same system, looked at from the point of view of the detail, as a plurality of differences pervaded and determined by an identical principle. The understanding of a process of change thus clearly consists in bringing it under the principle of Ground and Consequence. In so far as we are successful in detecting a principle in the apparently arbitrary succession of events, these events become for us a system with a common principle of structure for its Ground, and a plurality of successive states as its Consequence.

Change is not, however, the only instance of the principle of Ground and Consequence. These two aspects may also be found in systematic wholes which contain no element of succession in time, *e.g.*, in a body of logical deductions from a few fundamental premisses. The special peculiarity of the case of Change is that it is the principle of Ground and Consequence as applied to a material which is successive *in time*. As thus applied, the principle has received the special name of the *Principle of Sufficient Reason*, and may be formulated thus: *Nothing takes place unless there is a sufficient reason why it should occur rather than not.* It is clear that such a proposition is a mere result of the application of the conception of Reality as a systematic whole to the special case of the existence of the successive in time. It is therefore simply one case of the fundamental axiom of all knowledge, the axiom that what truly exists is a coherent whole.[2] We must of course observe that the principle does nothing to solve the perhaps insoluble problem *why* succession in time should be a feature of experience. This is a question which could only be answered if we could show that succession in time is a logical consequence of the existence of any multi-

---

[1] See the admirable remarks of Bosanquet in *Companion to Plato's Republic*, pp. 275, 276.
[2] On the category of Ground and Consequent and the principle of Sufficient Reason, consult Bosanquet, *Logic*, bk. i. chap. 6, and bk. ii. chap. 7.

plicity forming a systematic whole. Until we are able to establish this result, we have simply to accept succession as a datum of our experience. (Yet for some light upon the problem, see *infra*, Bk. III. chap. 4, § 9.)

§ 4. *Causality.* So far we have said nothing of a concept which is much more familiar in the popular treatment of the problem of Change than that of Ground and Consequence, the concept of *Cause*. In proceeding to discuss this concept, it is necessary in the first place to explain which of the numerous senses of the word we are taking for examination. There was an old scholastic distinction, which still reappears occasionally in philosophical writings, between the *Causa cognoscendi*, or reason for affirming a truth, and the *Causa existendi* or *fiendi*, the cause of the occurrence of an event. It is this latter meaning of the word "cause," the meaning which is predominant wherever the term is used in modern scientific language, that we shall have in view in the following sections.

The *Causa cognoscendi*, or logical *reason* for the affirmation of a truth, as distinguished from the psychological factors which lead a particular individual to affirm it, is clearly identical with what modern logicians call the *Ground*. A given proposition must logically be affirmed as true in the last resort, because it fills a place in a wider system of truths which no other proposition would fill. Thus, *e.g.*, a special proposition about the relation between the sides and angles of a triangle is logically necessitated, because it is an integral element in the development of a system of geometrical ideas which repose as a whole upon certain fundamental assumptions as to the character of spatial order. The original presuppositions cannot be worked out to their logical consequence in a body of internally coherent geometrical notions unless the proposition in question is included in that body. And reciprocally, the logical justification for regarding these presuppositions rather than any others as sound, lies in the fact that they yield a body of internally consistent consequences. Incidentally, we see by means of this illustration that Ground and Consequence are mutually convertible, which is what we might have inferred from the way in which we defined them as mutually complementary aspects of a single systematic whole.

What we are concerned with in the everyday and scientific treatment of Causation, is not this purely logical relation of Ground and Consequence, but something partly identical with it, partly different. The *Causa fiendi* has no significance except in connection with occurrences or events in time, and may roughly be said to correspond with what Aristotle denotes the "Source of Change"—ἀρχὴ κινήσεως or ὅθεν ἡ κίνησις—and his mediæval followers named the *Efficient* Cause. Cause, in the popular sense of the word, denotes the attempt to carry out the principle of the interconnection of events in a system along special lines by regarding every event as completely determined by conditions which are themselves previous events. Widely as the popular and the scientific uses of the term "cause" diverge in minor respects, they agree in the essential point. That every event has its cause is understood, both in everyday life and in the sciences which use the concept of causation, to mean that the occurrence and the character of every event in the time-series is completely determined by preceding events. In more technical language, causation for everyday thought and for the sciences means *one-sided dependence* of the present on the past, and the future on the present.

It is, of course, obvious that the principle of Causation as thus understood is not a necessary logical deduction from the principle of Ground and Consequence. It might be the case that all occurrences form a coherent plan or system, such that if you once grasped the principle of the system you could infer from it what precise occurrence must take place at any one moment, and yet it might be impossible to discover this principle by an examination of the course of events up to the present moment. In other words, the principle of the systematic interconnection of events might be valid, and yet the events of the present might depend on those which will succeed them in the future no less than on those which have preceded them in the past. In that case it would be impossible with absolute logical certainty to infer what will occur at a given moment from the mere examination of what has preceded, *i.e.* the principle of Causation as used in the sciences would not be logically valid.[1]

Cause, as currently understood, is thus identical not with the whole true logical ground, but with the ground so far as it can be discovered in the train of temporally antecedent circumstances, *i.e.* cause is *incomplete* ground. This point is important, as it shows that the principle of Causation is not, like the principle of Sufficient Reason, axiomatic. It is no necessary logical consequence of the knowability or

---

[1] It is no answer to this suggestion to urge that the present, being real, cannot be conditioned by the future, which is unreal. Such a rejoinder commits the metaphysical *petitio principii* of taking for granted that only the present is real. It is obvious that one might say with equal cogency that the past, being over and gone, is now unreal and therefore cannot influence the real present.

systematic character of the Real that an event should be completely determined by temporally antecedent events; for anything that is implied in the systematic character of the Real, the event may be equally dependent on subsequent occurrences. Again, the principle of Causation cannot be empirically established by an appeal to the actual course of experience. Actual experience is certainly not sufficient to show that every event is absolutely determined by its antecedent conditions; at most the success of our scientific hypotheses based upon the assumption of causality only avails to show that events may be inferred from their antecedents with sufficient accuracy to make the causal assumption practically useful.

Regarded as a universal principle of scientific procedure, the causal assumption must be pronounced to be neither an axiom nor an empirical truth but a *postulate*, in the strict sense of the word, *i.e.* an assumption which cannot be logically justified, but is made because of its practical value, and depends upon the success with which it can be applied for confirmation. In the sense that it is a postulate which experience may confirm but cannot prove, it may properly be said to be *a priori*, but it is manifestly not *a priori* in the more familiar Kantian sense of the word. That is, it is not a necessary and indispensable axiom without which systematic knowledge would be impossible. For, as we have already seen and shall see more fully in the immediate sequel, it may not be, and indeed in the last resort cannot be, true.

§ 5. This last statement will possibly appear startling to the reader who is unacquainted with the history of metaphysical investigations into Causality. But it is easy to show that it is really the expression of an obvious truth. For the causal principle, as we have just seen, is an imperfect expression of the really axiomatic principle of Sufficient Reason or Ground and Consequence. And it is readily seen that the expression it gives to that principle, because imperfect, must be partially false. What the principle of Ground and Consequence says is, that the whole of existence is a single coherent system in which every part is determined by the nature of the whole as revealed in the complete system. But if this is true, each constituent of the system can only be completely determined by its connections with all the rest. No constituent can be entirely determined by its relations to a lesser part of the whole system, in the way presupposed by the notion of one-sided causal dependence. The "cause" must, if the principle of Ground and Consequence be valid, be determined by the "effect" no less than the "effect" by the "cause." And therefore the causal postulate cannot be the whole truth.

How this fatal logical defect in the principle of Causation makes itself felt in the logic of the inductive sciences, and how logicians have sought without success to avoid it, we shall incidentally see as our discussion proceeds. At present we must be content to note that, owing to this flaw, Causation, wherever it is asserted, can only be Appearance and never complete Reality, and that no science which works with the concepts of cause and effect can give us the highest truth. Of course, the logical defects of the concept need not impair its practical usefulness. Though it can never, for the reason given already, be ultimately true that any event is absolutely determined by antecedent events, the assumption may be sufficiently near the truth to yield useful deductions as to the course of occurrences, precisely as a mathematical approximation to the value of a surd quantity may, without being the exact truth, be close enough for practical use. Also, it might well be the case that the causal postulate approximates more nearly to the truth in some spheres of investigation than in others, a consideration which is not without its bearing on the ethical problems of freedom and responsibility.

If we ask how the causal postulate, being as it must be only imperfectly true, comes to be made, the answer is obvious. The whole conception is anthropomorphic in origin, and owes its existence to our practical needs. To take the latter point first, logically there is no better reason for treating an event as determined solely by antecedents, than for treating it as solely determined by subsequent events. Yet when the latter supposition is made, as it is by all believers in omens and presages, we all agree to condemn it as superstitious. Why is this? Two reasons may be assigned. (*a*) Even granting that an event may be determined by subsequent events, yet, as *we* do not know what these events are until after their occurrence, we should have no means of inferring by *what* particular events yet to come any present event was conditioned, and thus should be thrown back upon mere unprincipled guess-work if we attempted to assign its, as yet future, conditions.

(*b*) A more important consideration is that our search for causes is ultimately derived from the search for *means* to the practical realisation of results in which we are interested.

We desire to know the conditions of occurrences primarily, in order to produce those occurrences for ourselves by setting up their conditions. It is therefore essential to us for our practical purposes to seek the conditions of an occurrence exclusively among its antecedents, and the causal postulate which asserts that the complete conditions of the event are comprised somewhere in the series of antecedent events is thus the intellectual expression of the demand made by our practical needs upon Reality. We postulate it because, unless the postulate is approximately realised, we cannot intervene with success in the course of events. We refuse, except as a pure speculation, to entertain the notion that an event may be determined by subsequent as well as by antecedent events, because that notion leads to no practical rules for operation upon our environment.

§ 6. As might be expected of a postulate so obviously originated by our practical needs, the concept of cause on examination reveals its anthropomorphic character. This is particularly obvious when we consider the concept of Causation as it figures in everyday unscientific thought. The various scientific substitutes for the popular notion of cause all exhibit traces of the endeavour to purge the conception of its more anthropomorphic elements. In the popular use of the concept this anthropomorphism comes out most strikingly in two ways. (*a*) A cause, as popularly conceived, is always a person or thing, *i.e.* something we can imagine as a whole, and into which we can mentally project a conscious life akin to our own. To the scientific mind it seems obvious that causes and effects are alike *events* and events only, but for popular thought, while the effect is always a quality or state (*e.g.*, death, fever, etc.), the cause is regularly a thing or person (the bullet, the poison, the tropical sun, etc.).

(*b*) Closely connected with this is the emphasis popular thought lays upon what it calls the *activity* of the cause. The cause is never thought of as merely preceding the effect as an "inseparable antecedent"; it is supposed to *make* the effect occur, to bring it about by an exercise of activity. According to the most coherent expositions of this type of thought, in causation one thing is always *active* in producing a change in another thing which is *passive*. The origin of this notion is sufficiently obvious. As all philosophers since Hume have recognised, the "activity" of the cause results from the ascription to it of the characteristic feeling of self-assertion and self-expansion which accompanies our own voluntary interference in the course of events. Similarly, the "passivity" of the thing in which the effect is produced is only another name for the feeling of coercion and thwarted self-assertion which arises in us when the course of nature or the behaviour of our fellows represses our voluntary execution of our designs.

Science, in its attempt to extend the concept of causal determination over the whole domain of existence, has naturally felt these anthropomorphic implications as obstacles. From the effort to expel them arises what we may call the common scientific view of causation, as ordinarily adopted for the purposes of experimental investigation and formulated in the works of inductive logicians. The concept of a thing, except as the mode of interconnection of states, being unnecessary for the sciences which aim simply at the reduction of the sequence of occurrences to order, the notion of causation as a transaction between two things is replaced in the experimental sciences by the conception of it as merely the determination of an event by antecedent events. Similarly, with the disappearance of things as the vehicles of causal processes falls the whole distinction between an active and a passive factor. As it becomes more and more apparent that the antecedent events which condition an occurrence are a complex plurality and include states of what is popularly called the thing acted upon as well as processes in the so-called agent, science substitutes for the distinction between agent and patient the concept of a system of reciprocally dependent interacting factors. These two substitutions give us the current scientific conception of a cause as the "totality of the conditions" in the presence of which an event occurs, and in the absence of any member of which it does not occur. More briefly, causation in the current scientific sense means sequence under definitely known conditions.

Indispensable as this notion of the determination of every event by a definite collection of antecedents and by nothing else is for practice, regarded as a logical formulation of the principle of the systematic unity of existence, it is open to grave objections, most of which will be found to have made themselves felt in the logic of the inductive sciences quite independently of conscious metaphysical analysis. In dealing with these difficulties, we shall find that their general effect is to place us in the following dilemma. If we wish to state the causal principle in such a way as to avoid manifest speculative falsehood, we find that it has to be modified until it becomes identical with the principle of Ground and Consequence in its most universal form, but as thus modified it is no longer of any service for the purposes of the experimental sciences. You seem driven to take it either in a form in which it is true but practically useless, or in one in which it is useful but not true. To illustrate the way in which this dilemma arises, we may examine three of the main problems which have actually been created by the scientific use of the principle,—(a) the puzzle of continuity, (b) the puzzle of the indefinite regress, (c) the puzzle of the plurality of causes.

§ 7. (a) *The Puzzle of Continuity.* Continuity is, strictly speaking, a property of certain series, and may be defined for purposes of reference much as follows. A series is continuous when any term divides the whole series unambiguously into two mutually exclusive parts which between them comprise all the terms of the series, and when every term which so divides the series is itself a term of the series. From this second condition it obviously follows that a number of intermediate terms can always be inserted between any two terms whatever of a continuous series; no term of the series has a *next* term. This is the peculiarity of the continuous with which we shall be specially concerned. Thus the series of points on a straight line is continuous because (1) any point P on the line divides it into two collections of points in such a way that every point of the one is to the left of every point of the other, and every point of the second to the right of every point of the former; and (2) every point which divides the line in this way is a point on the line. Again, the whole series of real numbers is continuous for the same reason. Every member of the number-series divides it into two classes, so that every number of one is less than every number of the other, and every number which thus divides the series is itself a term of the number-series.

But the series of *rational* real numbers is not continuous, because it can be divided into mutually exclusive classes by terms which are not themselves members of the series. (*E.g.*, $\sqrt{2}$ is not a member of the series of rational numbers, but we can exhaustively divide all rational numbers into the two mutually exclusive classes, rational numbers *less* than $\sqrt{2}$ and rational numbers *not less* than $\sqrt{2}$.)[1] From the continuity of

[1] For a fuller explanation of what is meant by continuity, consult Dedekind, *Stetigkeit und irrationale Zahlen*, specially §§ 3-5, or Lamb's *Infinitesimal Calculus*, chap. 1. Readers who have been accustomed to the treatment of continuity by the older philosophical writers should specially remark (1) that

the series of real numbers it follows that any other series which corresponds point for point with the terms of the number-series will be continuous. Now one such series is that of the successive parts of time. Every moment of time divides the whole series of moments into two mutually exclusive classes, the moments *before* itself and the moments which are *not before* itself. And whatever thus divides the time-series is itself a moment in that series. Hence from the continuity of the time-series it follows that any puzzles created by this property of continuousness will apply to the case of Causation. In what follows I shall not discuss the general problem of the continuous, a problem which requires special mathematical equipment for its efficient handling, but shall confine myself to the difficulties introduced by continuity into the scientific concept of causal relation.

We may conveniently attack the problem by taking it up in the form in which Hume bequeathed it to modern science. As any careful reader of Hume must perceive, Hume's whole doctrine of Causation is based on the assumption that the causal process is not continuous. Experience is supposed by him to come to us not in an unbroken stream, but in isolated separate pieces which we subsequently proceed to link together artificially by the notion of Causation. We are supposed to begin by observing the sequence of an event B on a previous distinct event A, and the problem of Causation thus becomes that of discovering the nature of the link by which the originally distinct A and B are connected in our scientific thought. In more technical language, Hume thought of the series of events as one in which every member has a next term, and this way of conceiving it has coloured the whole subsequent treatment of Causation by the inductive logicians who have commonly got their metaphysical doctrines from Hume.

Now, recent Psychology, in deserting the old notion of the atomic sensation for that of the "stream of consciousness," has completely destroyed the supposed empirical foundation for this Humian theory of the discontinuity of the course of events. The real problem for the inductive logician we can now see to be not to discover the link by which an originally separate A and B have got joined to-

---

continuity is properly a characteristic of *series*, and (2) that though continuity implies indefinite divisibility, the reverse is not, as was sometimes assumed by earlier writers, true. The series of rational numbers is a familiar illustration of endless divisibility *without* continuity.

gether in thought, but to find the source of the distinction we habitually draw within what comes to us as one continuous process between an earlier stage A which we call cause, and a later stage B which we call effect. We are not, however, concerned here with the psychological weakness of Hume's doctrine, but with the logical difficulty to which it gives rise.

We may state the difficulty thus: (1) Causation cannot possibly be thought of as discontinuous, *i.e.* as the sequence of one distinct event upon an assemblage of other events without gross contradiction. To think of it as discontinuous, we must conceive the *cause* A to exist first in its completeness, and then to be suddenly followed by the effect B. (That the cause A consists of a number of conditions, a, b, c . . . which themselves come into existence successively, and that A is not there until the last of these conditions has been realised, makes no difference to the principle.) Now this seems to be what is actually implied by the language of those inductive logicians who insist that in all Causation the cause must *precede* the effect. But what can such precedence mean? It can only mean that after the complete realisation of the conditions included in the cause A, there must intervene a space of empty time *before* the effect B enters on the scene. However brief and "momentary" you take this gap in the stream of events to be, the gap must be there if your language about the cause as being *before* the effect is to have any meaning. For if there is no such gap, and the entrance of B is simultaneous with the complete realisation of its conditions A, it is no longer true to say that the cause A is *before* the effect B. A does not exist as A until a, b, c . . . are all present, and as soon as they are present B is present too. And thus the relation between A and B is not that of the sequence of a later event on an earlier. They are actually *together*.

In fact, the doctrine that the cause precedes the effect rests upon the notion that the time-series is one in which each member has a next term. And this seems inconceivable. For not only can you subdivide any finite time, however small, into two mutually exclusive parts, but the point at which the division is effected is itself a moment in the time-series lying *between* the beginning and the end of the original interval. Time therefore must be continuous, and if causation is not equally continuous, we must suppose that gaps of empty time are what separate the first event, the cause, from the subsequent event, the effect. Yet *if* this could be regarded as a defensible doctrine on other grounds, it would then follow that the assemblage of events A is not the totality of conditions requisite for the occurrence of B. The "totality of conditions," *i.e.* the *cause* as previously defined, would be the events A *plus* a certain lapse of empty time.[1] And so the cause would once more turn out not to precede the effect, or we should have to suppose the end of the interval of empty time included in it as separated from the beginning of B by a second lapse, and so on indefinitely.

(2) These difficulties, in a more or less clearly apprehended form, have led many recent writers on inductive Logic to modify the definition which was still satisfactory to Mill. Cause and effect, we are now told, are not distinct events, but earlier and later stages in a continuous process. The real business of science is not to discover "laws of connection" between distinct events or "phenomena," but to invent general mathematical formulæ by the aid of which we may trace the course of continuous processes. The discovery of causes, from this point of view, is reduced to the construction of formulæ which exhibit some quantity as a function of a time-variable. Fully worked out, this view of the nature of experimental science leads to the so-called "descriptive" ideal of scientific explanation, advocated by such eminent thinkers as Kirchhoff, Mach, and Ostwald among physicists, and, with various modifications, Avenarius, Münsterberg, Royce, and James Ward among recent philosophers. According to this doctrine, the ultimate ideal of science, or at any rate of physical science, is simply the description of the course of events by the aid of the fewest and simplest general formulæ. *Why* things happen as they do, it is now said, is no proper question for science; its sole business is to enable us to calculate *how* they will happen. With the general epistemological questions raised by this doctrine we must deal later in our third and fourth books. At present we are concerned only with its bearing on the notion of Causal Relation.[2]

---

[1] There would arise further difficulties as to whether the magnitude of this lapse is a function of A, or whether it is the same in all cases of causal sequence. But until some one can be found to defend such a general theory of causal sequence it is premature to discuss difficulties of detail.

[2] For the English reader the best sources of information as to the "descriptive" theory of science are probably volume i. of Professor Ward's *Naturalism and Agnosticism;* and Mach, the *Science of Mechanics* (Eng. trans.). Students who read German may advantageously add Avenarius, *Philosophie als Denken der Welt gemäss dem Prinzip des kleinsten Kraftmasses.* Professor J. A. Stewart is surely mistaken (*Mind*, July 1902) in treating the doctrine as a discovery of "idealist" metaphysicians. Whatever may be thought of some of

The important point for our immediate purpose is that the reduction of all events to continuous processes really does away with Causation altogether, as is recognised by those adherents of the theory who openly propose to expel the word "cause" from the language of science.[1] For in a continuous process it is purely arbitrary where we shall mentally draw the dividing line which is to mark the boundary between the "earlier" and the "later" stage. What the descriptive formula, with the aid of which we trace the course of the process by giving a series of successive values to our time-variable presents, is not the "cause" of the process but the "law" of it. Instead of looking upon the later stages of the process as determined by the earlier, we are now looking upon the process as a whole as the expression in detail of a single principle. We have, in fact, abandoned the category of cause and effect for that of Ground and Consequence. We are seeking the ground of the whole process not in a set of temporally preceding events, but in its own pervading principle.

From this point of view the one-sided dependence of effect on cause, characteristic of the causal relation, disappears. Whether we shall infer the later stages of the process from the earlier, or the earlier from the later, depends simply upon our choice of positive or negative values for our time-variable. For "descriptive" science, what we suggested at first as a paradoxical possibility is the actual fact. The past is determined by the future in precisely the same sense in which the future is determined by the past, namely, that as both are stages of the same continuous process, if once you know the principle of the process you can start equally well with either and reason to the other.[2] Thus, within the limits of experimental science itself, the conception of causal relation has given way to the conception of events as logically connected into a system in virtue of their underlying ground or principle. For practical purposes experimental science has, in its application of this conception, to be guided by two postulates, neither of which can be metaphysically justified. It has to assume (*a*) that the course of events is composed of a plurality of more or less independent continuous processes, each of which has its own ground within itself, at least to such an extent as to be capable of being treated for our purpose as independent of others; (*b*) that the underlying ground or

the uses to which "idealists" put the theory, they cannot claim the credit of its invention.

[1] Cf. Mach, *op. cit.*, p. 483 ff.; Pearson, *Grammar of Science*, chap. 4.
[2] *E.g.*, eclipses can be calculated equally well for the future or the past.

grounds of all events can be adequately expressed in terms of mathematical symbolism.

As to the first of these points, our discussion of the unity of Reality convinced us that there must in the end be a single ground of all existence, and therefore the complete reason of any partial process cannot be entirely within itself. The independence of the various processes must be relative, and even the belief that it is sufficient to enable us to treat them for our own special purposes as self-contained and independent, must be a postulate prompted by our practical needs, and justified in the end by its success. The second point will engage our attention more fully in subsequent chapters. At present one remark upon it must suffice. The calculability of the laws of continuous processes depends upon our ability to reduce them to numerical and quantitative forms. Wherever we have the appearance, at any stage in a process, of a new quality, we have in fact an apparent breach of continuity, and it ceases to be in our power to exhibit the new stage of the process as a mere transformation of what was already expressed in former stages. Hence the success of natural science in reducing all sequences of events to continuous processes depends upon the assumption that we can establish equations between qualitatively different magnitudes.

Now this assumption is even more evidently than the preceding a postulate. We have to make it, if we are to calculate the course of events, but we have no guarantee that it will succeed beyond the fact of its actual success. If it fails anywhere, as we shall hereafter contend that it does in the critical case of the sequence of psychical on physical events, and *vice versâ*, two results will follow, one practical, the other speculative. The practical consequence of the failure is that in such cases we cannot apply the concept of continuous process, and have to fall back upon the cruder notion of causal sequence. Thus, in attempting to create a science of Psychophysics we cannot hope to exhibit the whole of a psychophysical process as the continuous realisation of a single principle; we must be content to establish laws of causal connection between the physical and the psychical sides of the process. The speculative consequence is that the principle of Ground and Consequence is only imperfectly represented by the conception of a continuous process, inasmuch as that conception is only applicable where qualitative differences within the consequences of a single ground can be disregarded. This hint will prepare us for subsequent criticism of the concept of continuity when we come to deal with the metaphysics of the time-process.[1]

§ 8 (*b*). *The Indefinite Regress.* The defects of the causal postulate as a principle of explanation may also be exhibited by showing the double way in which it leads to the indefinite regress. The indefinite regress in the causal series is an inevitable consequence of the structure of time, and, as we please, may be detected both outside and inside any causal relation of two events, or two stages of a continuous process. For it follows from the structure of the time-series (*a*) that there are an indefinite number of terms of the series between any two members, between which there is a finite interval, and (*b*) that there is also an indefinite number of terms before or after any given member of the series. Like the series of real numbers, the time-series, because it satisfies the definition of a continuous infinite series, can have neither a first nor a last term, nor can any member of it have a next term.[2] Applying this to the case of Causation, we may reason as follows:—

(1) The same reasons which lead us to demand a cause A for any event B, and to find that cause in an assemblage of antecedent events, require that A should be similarly determined by another assemblage of antecedent events, and that this cause of A should itself have its own antecedent cause, and so on indefinitely. Thus the causal principle, logically applied, never yields an intelligible explanation of any event. Instead of exhibiting the transition A – B as the logical expression of a coherent principle, it refers us for the explanation of this transition to a previous instance of the same kind of transition, and then to another,

---

[1] *Infra*, Bk. III. chap. 4. It will be enough to refer in passing to the curious blunder which is committed when the principle of Causality is confounded with the doctrines of the Conservation of Mass and Energy. That the principle of Causality has nothing to do with these special physical theories is manifest from the considerations: (1) That it is at least not self-evident that all causal relation is physical. Philosophers have indeed denied that one mental state directly causes another, but no one has based his denial on the assertion that there can be no causality without mass and energy. (2) The principle of Causality, as we have seen, is a postulate. If we are ever to intervene successfully in the course of events, it must be possible with at least approximate accuracy to regard events as determined by their antecedents. The doctrines of conservation of mass and energy are, on the contrary, empirical generalisations from the observed behaviour of material systems. Neither science nor practical life in the least requires them as an indispensable condition of success. In practical life they are never appealed to, and the ablest exponents of science are most ready to admit that we have no proof of their validity except so far as it can be established by actual observation. In short, they are largely *a posteriori*, while the principle of Causality is, as already explained, *a priori*. See *infra*, Bk. III. chap. 6, § 6.

[2] Neither can have a first term, because each has two opposite *senses*, positive and negative in the one case, before and after in the other.

and so forth without end. But it is impossible that what is not intelligible in one instance should become intelligible by the mere multiplication of similar unintelligibilities.

(2) Similarly if we look within the transition A–B. This transition being continuous must have its intermediate stages. A becomes B because it has already become C, and the transition A–C–B is again "explained" by showing that A became D which became C which became E which became B. And each of the stages A–D, D–C, C–E, E–B can be once more submitted to the same sort of analysis. But in all this interpolation of intermediate stages there is nothing to show the nature of the common principle in virtue of which the stages form a single process. We are, in fact, trying to do what we try to do wherever we establish a relation between terms, to answer a question by repeating it. And we decided at the end of our last chapter that this kind of repetition is never an answer to any question. How entirely it fails to answer the question we ask whenever we look for a cause is obvious. We want to know why B exists, and we are told that B exists because it is determined by the previous existence of A. But why does A exist? Because of the previous existence of C. And so ultimately the existence of everything depends on the existence of something else, and this again on the existence of still something else. If this is so, since nothing can exist until its cause has existed, and the cause again not until its cause has existed, then, as this unending series has no first term, nothing can ever come into existence at all. This inevitable introduction of the indefinite regress whenever we try to think out the causal principle to its logical consequences, has sometimes been treated as proving the inherent defectiveness of the human mind. What it proves rather is that Causality is not a proper formulation of the real principle of the unity of all experience.

A word may be said about the attempts which philosophers have made to extricate themselves from the difficulty without giving up Causality as an ultimate principle of explanation. The least philosophical method of escape is that of arbitrarily postulating a first cause with no preceding cause, which amounts to the same thing as a beginning of existence or a first moment of time. This way out of the difficulty obviously amounts to an arbitrary desertion of the causal principle at the point where it becomes inconvenient to remain faithful to it. Whatever the nature of the event you pitch upon as your "first cause," the causal principle, if logically valid at all, is just as applicable here as anywhere else

Your "first cause" must have had a previous cause, or else the whole causal scheme must be, as we have contended that it is, the illogical and imperfect perversion of a genuine principle of systematic connection, useful and indeed indispensable in practice, but quite indefensible in theory.

It would not help you out of the difficulty to distinguish between a first event and a first moment of time, by postulating a first cause with an indefinite lapse of empty time before it. For the causal principle would then require you to look for the determining conditions of the first event in the preceding lapse of empty time. But this lapse, because merely empty, cannot contain the determining conditions for any special occurrence in preference to others. This is why the conception of a beginning of the causal series in time, with an empty lapse before it, has always led to the insoluble riddle, " Why did God create the world when He did, rather than at some other point of time?"

Nor can the difficulty be escaped by taking refuge in the continuity of the stream of events. For (1) as we have seen, the recognition of events as continuous processes necessarily leads to the surrender of the causal principle as inadequate to express the real connection of facts. Causality, as a special form of the category of Ground and Consequence, must stand or fall with the view of occurrences as sequences of discontinuous events. And (2) even apart from this consideration, the appeal to continuity can at best only be worked as a rejoinder to the internal analysis of a sequence into an infinite process. When it is urged that, on the causal principle, there must be an infinite number of intermediate stages between the cause and the effect in any given case, it is possible to retort that the stages are not "really" distinct, but only distinguished by an artificial abstraction, that the process is actually one and continuous, and therefore does not involve an infinite regress, except for the logician who erroneously construes it as discontinuous. But with the external regress *in indefinitum* you cannot deal in this way. The absence of a beginning follows as necessarily from the principle of explaining the later stages of a continuous process as conditioned by the earlier, as it does when the stages are taken to be distinct events. (This is easily seen from the simple consideration that the time-variable in your formula for the successive stages of the process may have an unlimited range of possible values from $-\infty$ to $+\infty$.)

In short, whether the succession of events be taken as continuous or not, the attempt to translate the axiom that whatever happens has its ground in the nature of the whole system to which it belongs, into the doctrine that the posterior in time is completely determined by and dependent on the prior, leads straight to the infinite regress. And, as we said in our last chapter, the occurrence of the infinite regress is always a sign that there is imperfection somewhere in the thought which sets it up. For it always implies the formal contradiction of the actual summation by successive increments of an infinite series. Further considerations on this point may be deferred till we come to treat of the continuity of time.[1]

§ 9 (*c*). *The Plurality of Causes.* The indefinite regress may be shown to be inherent in Causation by a different line of argument, without appealing to the principle of the continuity of time. As the reader is doubtless aware, it was a favourite doctrine of John Stuart Mill, that whereas the same cause is always followed by the same effect—in the absence of counteracting circumstances—the same effect need not be preceded by the same cause. An effect may be "produced" on different occasions by entirely different sets of antecedents. Thus death may be due either to disease or to violence, and both the disease and the violence may have very different forms, yet the result is the same, namely, death. Heat may ensue from friction, percussion, chemical combination, and so forth. This doctrine of the Plurality of Causes is an obvious result of generalisation from the important practical consideration that different means will often lead us to the same end, so that where we cannot employ one we can often fall back on another.

Mill's critics have not failed to point out that his doctrine is based on the rather illogical combination of a concrete cause with an abstract effect. He considers the "effect" in its utmost generality simply as a state or quality, *e.g.*, "heat," "death," and rightly contends that this general state or quality may issue on different occasions from different combinations of conditions. But he fails to observe that in any concrete case this effect exists in a special form, and with special modifications corresponding to the special character of the antecedents. Death, for instance, may result from a thousand circumstances, but the total effect in each case is never mere death, but death in some one special shape. A man who is shot and a man who is drowned are both dead, but one is dead with the special symptoms of death by

[1] I suppose I need not remind my reader that when a number is spoken of as the actual sum of an infinite series (as when 2 is called the sum of the series $1+\frac{1}{2}+\frac{1}{4}+\frac{1}{8}+ \ldots$ to infinity), the word *sum* is used in a derivative and improper sense for the limiting value assumed by the sum of *n* terms as *n* increases indefinitely). See Lamb, *Infinitesimal Calculus*, p. 11.

drowning, the other with those of death by shooting. The water will kill you and a bullet will kill you, but death with a bullet-hole does not come from drowning, nor death with one's lungs filled with water from a gunshot. If you take cause and effect at the same level of concreteness, they are always strictly correlative. Any variation in the one must have a corresponding variation in the other, for circumstances which vary without affecting a result are by definition no part of its conditions.

So far Mill's critics among the inductive logicians. But we can push the argument a step further, and show that it leads logically to a dilemma. (1) There cannot really be more than one "cause" for one "effect"; yet (2) in any sense in which we can single out one "effect" from the rest of the contents of the universe, and assign it its "cause," there is *always* a possibility of the Plurality of Causes. We will consider the alternative of this dilemma separately.

(1) Cause and effect must be strictly correlative. For to say that there may be variations in the cause not followed by corresponding variations in the effect, is to say that there can be conditions which condition nothing; and to admit variation in the effect without variation in the cause, is to allow that there are occurrences which are at once, as effects, determined, and yet again are not determined, by the assemblage of their antecedents. Thus Plurality of Causes is excluded by the very conception of a cause as the totality of conditions. Following up this line of thought further, we see that it leads to a perplexing result. The "totality of conditions" is never a real totality. For there are no such things as isolated effects and causes in the world of events. The whole fact which we call an effect is never complete until we have taken into account its entire connection with everything else in the universe. And similarly, the whole assemblage of conditions includes everything which goes to make up the universe. But when we have thus widened our conception of the cause and the effect, both cause and effect have become identical with one another and with the whole contents of the universe. And thus Causation itself has disappeared as a form of interconnection between the elements of Reality in our attempt to work out its logical implications.

This is an inevitable consequence of the continuous interconnection of all Reality established by our examination of the problem of the One and the Many in Chapter II. In other words, you never have reached the full cause of any event until you have taken into account the *totality* of its conditions, *i.e.* the totality of its connections with all the rest of existence. But this totality cannot be obtained in the form presupposed by the phrase "totality of conditions" as a plurality of events. For to obtain it in this fashion would mean to sum an infinite series. But when you abandon the form of the infinite series, cause and effect alike become identical with the systematic whole of Reality.

(2) On the other hand, the *usefulness* of the causal postulate depends entirely upon our ability to establish single threads of Causality within the stream of events, *i.e.* on our ability to assign particular assemblages of events, less than the "totality," to particular subsequent events as their necessary and sufficient condition. Unless we can do this we can formulate no rules for the practical employment of means for the production of a desired result, and, as we have already seen, it is the necessity of knowing the means to our ends which is the primary, and indeed the sole, motive for the establishment of the causal postulate. Now, to effect this assignation of particular causes to particular effects, we have to make use of a distinction which is more practically necessary than theoretically defensible. We distinguish between indispensable conditions and accessory circumstances, which may or may not be present without affecting the nature of the special result in question.

Now it is clear that the making of this distinction depends upon the separation of a certain part of the "total" stream of events from the rest, and its isolation as "the special result in question." And this isolation, as we have seen, must always rest upon arbitrary abstraction. When once this arbitrary abstraction of some one part or aspect of the stream of events from its context has been made, we are compelled to recognise the existence of the context from which we have abstracted by saying that any effect may enter into or form part of a variety of different larger effects, according to the nature of the context in which it occurs. And, from the very principle of the complete correlation of condition and conditioned, it follows that what we call the special or partial effect will be preceded by varying conditions, according as it enters into different larger wholes or contexts. Thus any form of the causal postulate of which we can make effective use necessitates the recognition of that very Plurality of Causes which we have seen to be logically excluded by the conception of cause with which science works. As we contended above, any form of the principle in which it is true is useless, and any form in which it is useful is untrue.

The final result of our discussion, then, is that the causal postulate according to which events are completely determined by antecedent events leads to the belief that the stream of events is discontinuous. This belief is inherently self-contradictory, and therefore ultimately untrue. The principle of Ground and Consequence cannot therefore be adequately represented by the causal postulate, however indispensable that postulate may be in practice. Whether the conception of a continuous stream of events affords any better formulation of the principle of the systematic interconnection of all Reality, we shall be better able to judge after the discussions of our third book. If it does not, we shall have to recognise that the conception of temporal succession itself is not adequate to express the way in which the Many and the One of real existence are united, *i.e.* that time is not real, but only phenomenal.

§ 10. A word may be said here as to the nature of the "necessity" which we ascribe to the connection of cause and effect. There can be little doubt that the origin of this "necessity" must be found in our own feelings of constraint when our action is dictated from without. It is clear, however, that we have no right to ascribe this feeling of constraint to the event which is determined by its connection with the rest of the system of Reality. All that is meant in science by the "necessity" of the causal relation is that given the conditions the result follows, and not otherwise. In other words, *if* you assert the existence of the conditions, you are logically bound to assert the existence of the result. The constraint thus falls within ourselves, and is of a hypothetical kind. So long as your purpose is to think logically, you feel constraint or compulsion when, after asserting the condition, you seek for any reason to escape asserting the result. It is one of the conspicuous services of Hume to philosophy, that he for the first time brought out clearly this subjective character of the "necessity" of the causal relation, though it must be admitted that he went on to complicate his argument by an admixture of error when he sought to base the necessity of the logical inference from Ground to Consequence on the psychological principle of Association.

§ 11. Before closing our discussion of Causality, we must briefly take note of certain special difficulties by which the problem has been complicated in the systems of some eminent philosophers. A distinction has often been drawn between Transeunt and Immanent Causality. In so far as the changes of state of one thing are regarded as occasions of change of state in others, the relation has been technically called one of

Transeunt Causality; the determination of a thing's change of state by its own previous changes has, on the other hand, been named Immanent Causality. As a consequence of this distinction, grave difficulties have arisen in connection with the notion of Transeunt Causality. Such Causality, *i.e.* the determination of the changes of one thing by the changes of others, is of course an essential feature in the pre-scientific view of the world of experience as a multiplicity of interacting things.

For systematic Pluralism this conception inevitably presents insoluble difficulties. For it is impossible to reconcile the ultimate absolute independence of the various real things with the admission that the sequence of states in any one depends upon sequences of states in any of the others. If a plurality of things are ultimately independent of each other, it is manifest that each must form a complete whole, self-determined and containing the ground of its details entirely within itself. Conversely, if a thing cannot be explained by a principle of purely internal systematic connection, but requires for its complete explanation reference to an outside reality with which it stands in interconnection, its independence can be only partial. Hence Pluralism, in its more consistent forms, has always sought to deny the reality of Transeunt Causality, and to reduce all causal relations to the internal determination of the states of a thing by its own previous states. Historically, the principal devices which have been adopted for this purpose are (*a*) Occasionalism, and (*b*) the theory of a Pre-established Harmony.

(*a*) *Occasionalism.* Occasionalism has appeared in the history of Philosophy as a professed solution of the special problem of the apparent interaction between body and mind, taken as two entirely disparate and independent realities, though it is equally applicable in a wider sense to the more general problem of the apparent connection of any two independent real things. The doctrine is most closely associated with the names of the Cartesians, Arnold Geulincx and N. Malebranche, but was in part also adopted by Berkeley as a consequence of his belief in the pure passivity of non-mental things. Starting from the Cartesian conception of mind and body as two entirely independent and disparate kinds of reality, Geulincx and Malebranche were confronted by the apparent fact that mental states lead to modifications of bodily state in voluntary motion, and *vice versâ*, bodily states determine the occurrence of mental states whenever a sensation follows upon a stimulus.

The "natural view of the world" unhesitatingly accepts these cases as instances of interaction or Transeunt Causality on exactly the same level as the origination of change of state in one body by change in another, and Descartes himself had acquiesced in this interpretation. But such a view, as his successors saw, is quite incompatible with the alleged disparateness and independence of the two orders of existence, the bodily and the mental. Geulincx and Malebranche accordingly took refuge in the doctrine that the interaction is only apparent. In reality there is a complete solution of continuity wherever the series of changes in the one order terminates and that in the other begins. What really happens, they taught, is that God adapts the one series to the other. On the occurrence of the bodily stimulus, God intervenes to produce the sensation or emotion which is required to harmonise our action with our environment. Similarly, on the occurrence of a volition, God interferes to set the corresponding movement going in our bodily organism.

Thus the change in the one order is merely an occasion for the intervention of God, who is the actual cause of the corresponding change in the other. Within each order the series of changes once initiated are then supposed to be causally connected. The divine interference only comes in where the two orders come into contact. Berkeley adopted half of this doctrine without the complementary half. Inasmuch as, according to him, physical or non-mental things are mere complexes of presentations, or, in his own terminology, "ideas," and ideas are purely inert, the real cause of every sensation must be God, who thus directly intervenes to give us an indication of the further sensations we shall receive according to the action we take on the present presentation. Transeunt Causality in the reverse direction, the immediate origination of bodily movement by volition, Berkeley seems to have admitted without criticism as a self-evident fact.[1]

It will not be necessary here to discuss the half-hearted version of Occasionalism adopted by Berkeley. It is clear that the admission of direct origination of bodily change by mental cannot be consistently combined with the denial of all Transeunt Causality in the reverse direction. If all physical existence, my own body included, is nothing more than an inert complex of presentations, it is just as hard to see how

[1] For the various views here summarised, see as original sources, Geulincx, *Metaphysica Vera*, Pars Prima, 5–8; Malebranche, *Entretiens sur la Metaphysique et sur la Religion*, 7th dialogue; Berkeley, *New Theory of Vision*, pp. 147, 148; *Principles of Human Knowledge*, §§ 25–33, 51–53, 57, 150; *Second Dialogue between Hylas and Philonous*.

it can be the recipient of mentally originated change as to see how it can originate mental change. What is not in any sense active cannot be passive, for passivity is simply repressed and thwarted activity.

We confine ourselves, then, to Occasionalism of the thorough-going type. Now, against such Occasionalism there is the obvious objection that it transforms the whole course of our existence into one long succession of miracles, a point upon which Leibnitz is fond of insisting in his criticisms of Malebranche. And the doctrine is not really consistent with itself for two reasons. (1) It is clear that, according to any possible definition of Causation, the doctrine of Occasionalism involves causal interaction between God on the one hand and both the supposedly disparate orders of reality on the other. Changes in either order definitely determine the intervention of God to originate definitely determined changes in the other order. Thus God's internal determinations are at once causes and effects of changes in either order. But if, *e.g.*, a material change of state can be the cause of a determination in God, the whole basis of the denial that a change in the material order can originate change in another order of reality, is swept away. The nett result of the theory is simply to re-establish the transeunt action of the two orders on each other by means of a roundabout circuit through the mind of God.

What Geulincx and Malebranche really had in mind was the simple reflection that we cannot tell *how* a physical change can bring about a mental change, or *vice versâ*.[1] But this problem is not advanced in the least by introducing God as a third factor. How a change in the one order can bring about a determination in the mind of God, and how again God brings about the corresponding change in the other order, are simply two insoluble problems of the same kind as that they were intended to explain. After the introduction of God as third factor in the causal process, the fact still remains as before, that certain definite changes in the one order ensue upon definite changes in the other, and this is precisely the fact which is denoted by the name of Transeunt Causality.

Of course the problem would alter its character if God were conceived as another expression for the total system of Reality. The doctrine of Occasionalism would then become simply a statement of the view that no two things are really

---

[1] Geulincx expresses the principle in the following formula (*op. cit.*, pt. 1, 5): quod nescis quomodo fiat, id non facis.

independent, and that it is in virtue of their inclusion in a larger systematic whole that what we call separate things can influence each other. But, in spite of numerous passing utterances which point to this view, it is quite certain that Occasionalism was seriously intended by its authors as a solution of the problem of Causality on strictly traditional theistic lines.

(2) A second defect of the doctrine lies in the failure of its originators to extend it to *all* cases of causal relation. It is a mere prejudice when Geulincx and Malebranche allow themselves to assume that the sequence of physical change on preceding physical change, or mental change on preceding mental change, is more self-explanatory than the sequence of a mental change on a physical. In both cases we can ascertain that one state definitely follows a previous one; in neither can we answer the ultimately unmeaning question, by what machinery this sequence is brought about. For any answer must obviously consist in the interpolation of an intermediate link, and with regard to the production of this intermediate link the same question arises, and thus we come to the indefinite regress, the invariable indication that we have been asking an unmeaning question.

(*b*) *The Pre-established Harmony.* More philosophical was the attempt of Leibnitz to reconcile Pluralism with the apparent interaction of things. According to Leibnitz, every ultimately real thing or monad is a self-contained whole; it contains, therefore, in itself the ground of the sequence of its own states. Hence there can be no real origination of change in one monad by the occurrence of change in another. The life of every monad must consist purely in the development of its own internal nature. As Leibnitz phrases it, there are no windows in the monads through which states and qualities can fly from one to another. Yet some account must be taken of the apparent fact that, since the world of experience is not a chaos, the changes in one thing seem to be connected by definite law with the changes in others.

Now, according to Leibnitz, this apparent interaction can only be accounted for, if we decline to tolerate the perpetual miracle of Occasionalism, by the theory of a Pre-established Harmony between monads. If the whole of the independent monads are of such a nature that each, while actually following the law of its own development, behaves in the way required by the internal development of all the rest, then, though each is really self-contained, there will be the appearance of interaction. Leibnitz illustrates the possibility of such a harmony by the case of two clocks which keep time with each other, without either the actual regulation of the one by the other, or the maintenance of a connection between them, simply because each is properly constructed; and again, by the case of a number of musicians playing from the same music but concealed from each other's observation, who keep time and tune simply because each is playing his own score correctly.

Probably this is the most satisfactory hypothesis which can be devised for the conciliation of apparent interaction with a radical Pluralism. But its logical defects are apparent on the face of it. When we ask to what the harmony between the internal states of the several monads is ultimately due, Leibnitz hesitates between two answers. It is due, according to one account, to the choice of God, who in His wisdom saw *fit* to establish the best of all the possible worlds. But at the same time it was God's recognition of the harmony between the monads of this special world-system which led Him to give it the preference over other antecedently possible systems, and to bring it rather than any other from mere possibility into actual existence.

Now it seems clear that, if the creative activity of God is to be taken seriously, the relation of God to the system must be one of Transeunt Causality. But if Transeunt Causality is admitted in the single case of God's attitude towards the monads, it no longer seems obvious why it should be denied as regards the attitudes of the monads among themselves. For there is now at least one property of each monad of which the ground lies not in itself but in God, namely, its actual existence;[1] and the principle that every monad is the ground of all its own properties once being deserted, there remains no further reason for denying interaction. If, on the other hand, we lay stress on the view that the harmony is no mere result of an arbitrary creative act, but is a property contained in the concept of the world of monads, thought of as merely possible, why may we not equally well think of a world of interacting and interconnected and therefore not ultimately independent things as possessing equal claims to realisation? The Pluralism of Leibnitz, from which his denial of Transeunt

[1] Not that existence can intelligibly be treated as a property; on this point Kant's famous criticism of the "ontological proof" seems conclusive. But *from the point of view of Leibnitz* it must be imagined as an additional predicate, somehow added by the creative act of God to those already contained in the concept of the world as "possible."

Causality logically follows, seems to rest upon nothing better than uncriticised prejudices.[1]

§ 12. We may briefly indicate the view as to the problem of Transeunt Causality which is involved in our discussion of the causal postulate. For any purpose for which it is possible and desirable to think of the world as a plurality of things, Transeunt Causality must be maintained. For precisely because the things in the world in the end form a connected system, the complete ground of the states of a thing cannot lie in itself but only in the whole system. In any sense in which there are a plurality of things, and in which the principle of ground and consequence can be approximately represented by the causal determination of subsequent occurrences by anterior occurrences, we must be prepared to find that the states of one thing appear among the conditions of the subsequent states of other things.

But again, since the apparently separate things are not entirely independent, but are the detailed self-expression of a single system, Transeunt Causality must in the end be appearance. Inasmuch as all interconnection between things depends upon their inclusion in the single system of Reality, it may be said that, when you take the whole into account, all Causality is ultimately immanent. But again, as we have already seen, Immanent Causality is an imperfect way of expressing the systematic connection of all existence according to the principle of Ground and Consequence. Fully thought out, Immanent Causality, as the determination of one state of the whole by a preceding state, is transformed into the concept of the interconnection of the various states by the purely logical principle that they form together the detailed expression of a single coherent principle of structure. And thus all Causality is finally imperfect appearance.

A point of some interest is the following. As we have seen, only individual experiences can in the end possess the kind of relative independence and internal unity which thought seeks to express in the notion of a thing. We may add that just in the degree to which any existence has this individuality, and thus forms a self-contained whole, will its behaviour have its ground within the thing itself. Hence the more completely individual a thing is, the more will the

---

[1] For Leibnitz's doctrine consult further, *The Monadology, etc., of Leibniz*, edit. by R. Latta, Introduction, pts. 2 and 3, and translations of *Monadology, New System of the Communication of Substances*, with the *First* and *Third Explanations* of the New System. Also see the elaborate criticisms of B. Russell, *The Philosophy of Leibniz*, chap. 4 and following chapters.

conditions upon which its states depend appear when we apply the postulate of Causality, to be included in other states of the same thing. Thus the more individuality a thing has, the more fully will it appear to exhibit Immanent as distinguished from Transeunt Causality in its internal structure, that is, the less will be the modifications that structure undergoes in its intercourse with other things. If we like to denote the maintenance of unchanged internal structure against instigations to change from without by the term "empirical activity," we may express our result by saying that the more individual a thing is, the more empirically active it is.

When we come to deal with the special problems of moral and social life, we shall have to face further questions as to the connection of causal determination with moral freedom and responsibility, and again with conscious purposive action for ends. Our previous discussion will then be found to have cleared the way for these more complex questions, by removing the difficulties which arise when the causal postulate is mistaken for an axiomatic principle of the interpretation of the systematic nature of Reality.

Consult further:—B. Bosanquet, *Essentials of Logic*, pp. 164, 165; *Logic*, vol. i. p. 253 ff., vol. ii. p. 212 ff.; F. H. Bradley, *Appearance and Reality*, chaps. 5 (Motion and Change), 6 (Causation), 7 (Activity), 8 (Things); H. Lotze, *Metaphysic*, bk i. chaps. 4 (Becoming and Change), 5 (Nature of Physical Action); L. T. Hobhouse, *Theory of Knowledge*, pt. 2, chaps. 8, 15 (for discussion of " Plurality " of Causes); Karl Pearson, *Grammar of Science*, chaps. 3 and 4; B. Russell, *Philosophy of Leibniz*, chaps. 4, 11 (Pre-established Harmony); James Ward, *Naturalism and Agnosticism*, pt. 1, lectures 2–6; Hume's famous discussion of Causation (*Treatise of Human Nature*, bk. i. pt. 3, §§ 3–15) seems to me to have lost little of its value, and to be still perhaps the most important single contribution of modern Philosophy to the systematic discussion of Causality.

BOOK III

COSMOLOGY—THE INTERPRETATION OF NATURE

CHAPTER I

INTRODUCTORY

§ 1. Distinction between the experimental sciences and a Philosophy of Nature and Mind. The former concerned with the description, the latter with the interpretation, of facts. § 2. Cosmology is the critical examination of the special characteristics of the physical order. Its main problems are: (1) the problem of the nature of Material Existence; (2) problem of the justification of the concept of the Mechanical Uniformity of Nature; (3) problems of Space and Time; (4) problem of the Significance of Evolution; (5) problem of the Place of descriptive Physical Science in the System of Human Knowledge.

§ 1. IN our two remaining Books we shall have to deal with the more elementary of the problems created by the apparent existence of two orders of Reality, a physical and a psychical, which again at least seem to stand in reciprocal interaction. In the present Book we shall discuss some of the leading characteristics which everyday thought and scientific thought respectively assign to the physical order, and shall ask how these characteristics compare with those we have seen ground to ascribe to Reality, *i.e.* we shall attempt to form a theory of the place of physical existence in the whole system of Reality. In the Fourth Book we shall discuss in the same way some of the leading characteristics of the psychical order as currently conceived, and the nature of its connection with the physical order. Our treatment of these topics will necessarily be imperfect and elementary for more reasons than one: not only are the facts of which some account must be taken so numerous and complicated that they would require for their mastery something like an encyclopædic acquaintance with the whole range of the experimental sciences, physical and psychological, but their adequate interpretation, especially on the cosmological side, would demand a familiarity with the ultimate foundations of mathematical theory which is rarely possessed either by the experimentalist or by the metaphysician. The utmost we can hope to accomplish in this part of our work is to establish one or two broad results as regards general principles : any suggestions we may make as to the details of interpretation must be avowedly tentative.

We must be careful to distinguish the task of a Philosophy of Nature and a Philosophy of Mind from those of the experimental sciences which deal directly with the fact of the physical and psychical orders. The fundamental business of the latter is, as we have already seen, the discovery of descriptive formulæ by the aid of which the various processes which make up the physical and psychical orders may be depicted and calculated. The fewer and simpler these formulæ, the more they economise the labour of calculation, the more completely do the experimental sciences perform the work for which we look to them. And so long as our formulæ adequately accomplish this work of calculation, it is indifferent for the experimental sciences whether the language in which they are couched represents a "reality" or not. The "atoms," "forces," and "ethers" of our physical, the "sensations" of our psychological formulæ, might be as purely symbolic creations of our own imagination as the "imaginary quantities" of mathematics, without their unreality in any way interfering with their scientific usefulness. In the words of an eminent physicist, "the atomic theory plays a part in physics similar to that of certain auxiliary concepts in mathematics, . . . although we represent vibrations by the harmonic formula, the phenomena of cooling by exponentials, falls by squares of times, etc., no one will fancy that vibrations *in themselves* have anything to do with the circular functions, or the motion of falling bodies with squares" (Mach, *Science of Mechanics*, p. 492). When it is asserted that the usefulness of a scientific hypothesis, such as, *e.g.*, the atomic theory or the hypothesis of the existence of an etherial undulating medium, of itself proves the real existence of things corresponding to the concepts employed by the hypothesis, the same fallacy is committed as when it is contended that if an algebraical calculus is generally capable of geometrical interpretation, every step in its operations must be interpretable.

The work of the Philosophy of Nature and of Mind only begins where that of the experimental sciences leaves off.

Its data are not particular facts, as directly amassed by experiment and observation, but the hypotheses used by experimental science for the co-ordination and description of those facts. And it examines these hypotheses, not with the object of modifying their structure so as to include new facts, or to include the old facts in a simpler form, but purely for the purpose of estimating their value as an account of ultimately real existence. Whether the hypotheses are adequate as implements for the calculation of natural processes is a question which Philosophy, when it understands its place, leaves entirely to the special sciences; whether they can claim to be more than useful formulæ for calculation, *i.e.* whether they give us knowledge of ultimate Reality, is a problem which can only be dealt with by the science which systematically analyses the meaning of reality, *i.e.* by Metaphysics. We may perhaps follow the usage of some recent writers in marking this difference of object by a difference in terminology, and say that the goal of experimental science is the Description of facts, the goal of Metaphysics their Interpretation. The difference of aim is, however, not ultimate. Description of facts, when once we cease to be content with such description as will subserve the purpose of calculation and call for description of the fact as it really is, of itself becomes metaphysical interpretation.

The chief danger against which we must guard in this part of our metaphysical studies is that of expecting too much from our science. We could never, of course, hope for such a complete interpretation of facts as might be possible to omniscience. At most we can only expect to see in a general way how the physical and again how the psychical order must be thought of if our view as to the ultimate structure of Reality is sound. For an exact understanding of the way in which the details of physical and psychical existence are woven into the all-embracing pattern of the real, we must not look. And the value of even a general interpretation will of course depend largely upon our familiarity with the actual use the various sciences make of their hypotheses. With the best goodwill in the world we cannot hope to avoid all misapprehensions in dealing with the concepts of sciences with which we have no practical familiarity.

Though this general caution is at least equally applicable to the amateur excursions of the student whose mental training has been confined to some special group of experimental sciences into the field of metaphysical criticism, it would be a good rule for practice if every student of

Metaphysics would consider it part of his duty to make himself something more than an amateur in at least one branch of empirical science; probably Psychology, from its historical connection with philosophical studies, presents unique advantages for this purpose. And conversely, no specialist in experimental science should venture on ultimate metaphysical construction without at least a respectable acquaintance with the principles of Logic, an acquaintance hardly to be gained by the perusal of Jevons's *Elementary Lessons* with a supplement of Mill.

§ 2. Cosmology, then, means the critical examination of the assumptions involved in the recognition of the physical as a distinct order of existence, and of the most general hypotheses employed by popular thought and scientific reflection respectively for the description of specially physical existence. It is clear that this very recognition of a distinction between the physical and other conceivable forms of existence implies a degree of reflective analysis more advanced than that embodied in the naïve pre-scientific view with which we started in our last two chapters. In the simple conception of the world of existence as consisting of the changing states of a plurality of interacting things, there was not as yet any ground for a distinction between the psychical and the purely physical. That there really exists a widespread type of thought for which this distinction has never arisen, is put beyond doubt by the study of the psychology of the child and the savage. Both, as we know, draw no hard-and-fast line between the animated and the inanimate, and the savage, in his attempts to account for the phenomena of life, does so habitually by supposing the physical organism to be tenanted by one or more lesser organisms of the same order of existence. The "soul" he ascribes to things is simply a smaller and consequently less readily perceptible body within the body.

For civilised men this conception of all existence as being of the same order, an order which we might describe from our own more developed standpoint as at once animated and physical, has become so remote and inadequate, that we find it hard to realise how it can ever have been universally accepted as self-evident truth. Physical science, and under its guidance the current thought of civilised men, has come to draw a marked distinction between the great majority of sensible things, which it regards as purely physical, and a minority which exhibit the presence of "consciousness." Thus has arisen a theory of the division of existence into two great orders, the physical and the psychical, which so dominates our ordinary thought about the world, that all the efforts of philosophers, both spiritualist and materialist, to reduce the two orders once more to one seem powerless to make any impression on the great majority of minds.

When we ask what are the distinguishing marks of the physical order as currently conceived, the precise answer we obtain will depend on the degree of scientific attainments possessed by the person to whom our question is addressed. But in the main both current science and everyday thought, so far as it has reflected on the problem, would probably agree as to the following points. (*a*) Physical existence is purely *material* or *non-mental*, or again is *unconscious*. The exact significance of these predicates is probably rarely clear even to those who make the freest use of them. On the face of it, such epithets convey only the information that existence of the physical kind differs in some important respect from existence of a mental kind; the nature of the difference they leave obscure. Reflection, however, may throw some light on the matter.

The distinction between persons and animals on the one side and mere things on the other seems to rest in the last resort on an important practical consideration. Among the things which, according to the naïve Realism of the pre-scientific theory, form my environment, there are some which regularly behave in much the same general way in response to very different types of behaviour on my own part. There are others again which behave differently towards me according to the differences in my behaviour towards them. In other words, some things exhibit special individual purposes, dependent in various ways on the nature of my own individual purposes, others do not. Hence for practice it becomes very important to know what things can be counted on always to exhibit the same general type of behaviour, and what cannot, but require individual study before I can tell how they will respond to different purposive behaviour of my own. It is on this practical difference that the distinction of mental and conscious from purely physical and unconscious existence seems to be based. We shall probably not be far wrong in interpreting the *unconsciousness* of purely material existence to mean that it exhibits no traces of purposive individuality, or at least none that we can recognise as such. More briefly, the physical order consists of the things which do not manifest recognisable individuality.

(*b*) Closely connected with this peculiarity is a second. The physical order is made up of events which conform rigidly to certain universal *Laws*. This is an obvious consequence of its lack of purposive individuality. The elements of which it is composed, being devoid of all purposive character of their own, always behave in the same surroundings in the same regular uniform way. Hence we can formulate precise general Laws of their behaviour. Originally, no doubt, this uniformity of the physical order is thought of as a point of contrast with the irregular behaviour of purposive beings, who respond differently to the same external surroundings according as their own internal purposes vary. With the growth of Psychology as an experimental science of mental processes there inevitably arises the tendency to extend this concept of uniform conformity with general Law to the processes of the psychical order, and we are then confronted by the famous problem how to reconcile scientific law with human "freedom." The same antithesis between the apparently regular and purposeless behaviour of the elements of the physical order and the apparently irregular and purposive behaviour of the members of the psychical order is also expressed by saying that the sequence of events in the physical order is *mechanically* determined by the principle of Causality, whereas that of the psychical order is *teleological*, *i.e.* determined by reference to *end* or purpose.

(*c*) Every element of the physical order fills a position in *space* and in *time*. Hence any metaphysical problems about the nature of space and time are bound to affect our view of the nature of the physical order. Here, again, there is a point of at least possible contrast between the physical and the psychical. As the accumulation of experience makes it increasingly clearer that the bodies of my fellow-men and my own body, in so far as it is an object perceived like others by the organs of the special senses, exhibit in many respects the same conformity to certain general laws, and are composed of the same constituent parts as the rest of the sensible world, such animated bodies of purposive agents have to be included along with the rest of sensible existence in the physical order. The individual's purposive individuality has now to be thought of as residing in a distinct factor in his composition of a kind foreign to the physical order, and therefore imperceptible by the senses, *i.e.* as a *mind* or *soul* or *stream of consciousness* in the current psychological sense. Such a mind or soul or stream of consciousness is then

INTRODUCTORY

usually regarded as not filling a series of positions in space, and sometimes as not filling a series of positions in time.

(*d*) The physical order, as thus finally constituted by the introduction of the concept of an imperceptible soul or mind, now comprises all sensible existence [1] as an aggregate of events in time and space, linked together by the principle of Causality, and exhibiting conformity with general law. To this conception recent science has made an important addition in the notion of a continuous *evolution* or *development* as manifesting itself throughout the series. So that we may ultimately define the physical order as a body of events occupying position in time and space, conforming to general laws with rigid and undeviating uniformity, and exhibiting continuous evolution.[2]

From these general characteristics of the physical order, as conceived by current science and current popular thought, arise the fundamental problems of Cosmology. We have to discuss—(1) the real nature of material existence, *i.e.* the ultimate significance of the distinction between the two orders, and the possibility of reducing them to one; (2) the justification for the distinction between mechanical and teleological processes, and for the conception of the physical order as rigidly conformable to uniform law; (3) the leading difficulties of the conceptions of time and space, and their bearing on the degree of reality to be ascribed to the physical order; (4) the philosophical implications of the application of the notion of evolution or development to the events of the physical order; (5) finally, we ought perhaps to deal very briefly and in a very elementary fashion with the problem of the real position of descriptive physical science as a whole in its relation to the rest of human knowledge.

Consult further :—F. H. Bradley, *Appearance and Reality*, chap. 26 (pp. 496–497, 1st ed.); H. Lotze, *Outlines of Metaphysic*, pp. 77–79; J. S. Mackenzie, *Outlines of Metaphysics*, bk. iii. chap. 2; J. Ward, *Naturalism and Agnosticism*, lect. 1.

[1] *I.e.* existence of the *same kind* as that perceived by the senses, whether actually so perceived or not. In this sense the solid impenetrable extended atoms of Newton or Locke are "sensible" existence, inasmuch as their properties are the same in kind as certain perceptible properties of larger masses, though they are not themselves actually perceptible.

[2] Of course the evolution must be mere subjective appearance if, as is sometimes assumed, the processes of the physical order are one and all purely mechanical. But this only shows that the current concept of the physical order is not free from inconsistencies.

CHAPTER II

THE PROBLEM OF MATTER

§ 1. The physical order, because dependent for its perceived qualities on the sense-organs of the percipient, must be the appearance of a more ultimate reality which is non-physical. § 2. Berkeley's criticism is fatal to the identification of this reality with "material substance." The logical consequence of Berkeley's doctrine that the *esse* of sensible things is *percipi* would be the subjectivist view that the physical order is *only* a complex of presentations. § 3. But this is clearly not the case with that part of the physical order which consists of the bodies of my fellow-men. These have an existence, as centres of feeling, over and above their existence as presentations to my senses. § 4. As the bodies of my fellows are connected in one system with the rest of the physical order, that order as a whole must have the same kind of reality which belongs to them. It must be the presentation to our sense of a system or complex of systems of experiencing subjects; the apparent absence of life and purpose from inorganic nature must be due to our inability to enter into a direct communion of interest with its members. § 5. Some consequences of this view.

§ 1. IN the preceding chapter we have very briefly indicated the nature of the steps by which reflective thought comes to distinguish sharply between a physical and a psychical order of existence. The physical order, when the concept has been brought into its complete shape by the inclusion of my own body and all its parts, is thought of as a system comprising all the bodies in the universe, that is, all the existences which are of the same kind as those which I directly perceive by means of the special senses.[1] Now, with regard to the whole physical order thus conceived two things seem fairly obvious upon the least reflection, that it does not depend for its *existence* upon the fact of my actually perceiving it, and that it does depend upon my perception for all the *qualities* and *relations* which I find in

---

[1] This definition of the physical order approximates very closely to that adopted by Prof. Münsterberg in his *Grundzüge der Psychologie*, vol. i. pp. 65-77. Prof. Münsterberg defines a *physical* fact as one which is directly accessible to the perception of a plurality of sentient individuals, as opposed to the psychical fact which can be directly experienced only by one individual. It must be remembered, of course, that my body as directly experienced in "common sensation" and "emotional mood" belongs to the psychical order. It is only my body as perceptible by other men that is a member of the physical order.

it. Its *that* appears independent of the percipient, but its *what*, on the other hand, essentially dependent on and relative to the structure of the perceiving organ. As we have already seen, the familiar experience of the variations in perception which accompany differences in the permanent structure or temporary functioning of the organs of sense led, very early in the history of Philosophy, to the recognition of this relativity, so far as the so-called "secondary" qualities, *i.e.* those which can only be perceived by one special sense-organ, are concerned. We have also seen sufficiently (in Bk. II. chap. 4) that the same consideration holds equally good of those "primary" qualities which are perceptible by more senses than one, and have probably for that reason been so often supposed to be unaffected by this relativity to a perceiving organ.

Without wasting the reader's time by unnecessary repetition of our former reasoning, it may be worth while to point out here how this thorough-going relativity of the qualities of the physical order to a percipient organ leads directly to the indefinite regress, the apparently invariable consequence of all contradictions in Metaphysics, when we try to take those qualities as independently real. I perceive the properties of physical existence by special sense-organs, and the properties as perceived are conditioned by the structure of those organs. But each sense-organ is itself a member of the physical order, and as such is perceived by and dependent for its perceived qualities upon another organ. This second sense-organ in its turn is also a member of the physical order, and is perceived by a third, or by the first organ again. And there is no end to this mutual dependence. The physical order, as a whole, must be a "state" of my nervous system, which is itself a part of that order. We shall see more fully in our final Book, when we come to discuss the problem of Mind and Body, that this contradiction is an inevitable result of the inconsistency involved in the inclusion of my own body in the physical order, an inconsistency which is, in its turn, a necessary consequence of the hard-and-fast separation of the two orders of existence.[1]

---

[1] Cf. Bradley, *Appearance and Reality*, chap. 22, pp. 260-267 (1st ed.). The attempts which have been made to exempt "primary" qualities from this relativity do not seem to demand serious criticism. The argument in the text applies as directly to extension and shape as to colour or smell. It is not defensible to contend, as Mr. Hobhouse does, that qualities, whether primary or secondary, depend on the percipient organ only for their *perception*, not for their existence. The contention rests upon taking two aspects of experience which

Considerations of this kind have led to the general recognition that the physical order must be regarded as phenomenal, as the manifestation to sense-perception of a reality which is in its own nature inaccessible to sense-perception, and therefore, in the strictest sense of the words, not physical. When we ask, however, how this non-physical reality of which the physical order is the phenomenal manifestation to our senses, is to be thought of, we find ourselves at once plunged into the same difficulties which we have already met, in a more general form, in discussing the concept of Substance. Popular thought, and science so far as it is content to accept the notions of popular thought without criticism, have commonly fallen back on the idea of the non-phenomenal ground of the physical order as an unperceived "substratum." To this substratum it has given the name of *matter*, and has thus interpreted the physical order as the effect produced by the causal action of an unperceived matter upon our sense-organs, or rather, to speak with more precision, upon *their* unknown material substratum. Frequently, as might have been expected, the attempt has been made to identify this substratum with those of the known qualities of the physical order which appear least liable to modification with the varying states of the percipient organs, and lend themselves most readily to measurement and calculation, the so-called "primary" qualities of mechanical science. This is the standpoint adopted by Newton and, in the main, by Locke, and largely through the influence of their work still remains the most familiar to the ordinary English mind. But the inconsistencies we have already found inherent in such a conception of Substance as is here presupposed, so inevitably make themselves felt upon any serious examination, that the doctrine regularly appears in the history of thought as a mere temporary halting-place in the advance to the more radical notion of matter as the entirely unknown non-phenomenal substratum of the sensible properties of bodies.

§ 2. This latter notion is again manifestly open to all the objections previously brought against the more general concept of substance as an unknown substratum or support

are always given together, the *that* and the *what* of a sense-content, and arguing that because these two aspects of a single whole can be distinguished, therefore the one can exist in actual separation from the other. It would be quite as logical to infer by the same method and from the same premisses that there can be a perceptive state without any content, as that the contents can exist as we know them, apart from the state.

of properties. It is from these objections that Berkeley's famous criticism of the concept of matter, the most original attempt at a constructive theory of the real nature of the physical order in the history of English Philosophy, starts. Berkeley first takes the identification of material substance with the primary qualities of body, which Locke had made current in English speculation, and shows, by insisting upon the relativity of perceived quality to percipient organ, that it is untenable. Having thus driven his opponent to surrender this identification, and to define matter as the unknown substratum of the physical order, he proceeds to argue that this notion of an unknown substratum is both useless and unintelligible. It is useless, because our knowledge of the actual properties and processes of the physical order can neither be extended nor made clearer by the addition of an unknowable; it is unintelligible, because we can give no account to ourselves of the nature of the "support" supposed to be bestowed by the substratum or the properties.

Material substance being thus dismissed as an unmeaning fiction, what is left as the reality of the physical order? According to Berkeley, nothing but the actual presentations, or "ideas," in which the percipient subject is aware of the properties of bodies. A body is simply such a complex of presentations to a percipient; except as so presented it has no existence. As Berkeley is fond of putting it, the *esse* of the material thing is simply *percipi*, the fact of its being presented. But just when we expect Berkeley to accept the complete subjectivist contention that bodies are simply "states of the percipients' consciousness" and nothing more, he remembers that he has to account both for the fact that we cannot perceive what we please and where we please, but that our perceptions form an order largely independent of our own choice, and for the deep-seated conviction of the common-sense mind that things do not cease to exist when my perception of them is interrupted. To reconcile his theory with these apparently conflicting facts, he has recourse, as is the custom of philosophers and others in a difficulty, to divine assistance. The continued existence of the physical world in the intervals of perception, and its systematic character and partial independence of our volition, he explains by the hypotheses that God produces perceptions in us in a fixed order, and that God continues to be aware of the system of presentations which I call the physical world, when my perception of it is suspended. The same explanation would, of course, have to be invoked to account for the existence of physical realities which no human subject perceives.[1]

It is fairly obvious that the two halves of Berkeley's theory will not fit together into a coherent whole. If the whole *esse* of physical things is merely *percipi*, there can be no reason why I should suppose them to exist at all except in so far as and so long as they are presented to my perception. The whole hypothesis of an omnipresent divine perception which remains aware of the contents that have vanished from my own perception, thus becomes purely gratuitous. It also labours under the disadvantage of being, on Berkeley's theory, internally inconsistent. For if it is necessary to invoke the agency of God to account for the occurrence of presentations to my experience, it is not clear why we have not to suppose a second deity who causes the series of presentations in the experience of God, and so on indefinitely. On the other hand, if God's experience may be taken as uncaused, it is not clear why my own experience might not have been taken so in the first instance, and the introduction of God into the theory avoided. Thus the logical outcome of the doctrine that the *esse* of physical things is merely *percipi*, would have been either Solipsism, the doctrine according to which I have no certain knowledge of any existence except my own, everything else being a mere state or modification of myself; or the Humian scepticism, which resolves my own existence, as well as that of the external world, into a mere sequence of fleeting mental processes. Conversely, if I have adequate reason to believe that any member of the physical order whatever is more than a presentation, and has an existence in some sense independent of my perception, I have no right to declare of any member of that order, unless for special reasons, that its being consists *merely in* being perceived.

§ 3. Why, then, did Berkeley, as a matter of fact, accept neither the solipsist nor the sceptical conclusion? Why does he, after all, credit the members of the physical order with an existence independent of the fact of my perceiving them, and thus introduce a patent contradiction into his system? It is not hard to see the reasons by which he must have been influenced. The whole physical order cannot be

---

[1] See particularly the detailed statement of his contention and the elaborate examination of objections in the *Three Dialogues between Hylas and Philonous*, which form a commentary on the briefer exposition of *Principles of Human Knowledge*, §§ 1-134.

dismissed as a mere subjective illusion, because there are some members of it which undoubtedly have an existence independent of the fact of being perceived by my sense-organs. Such members are my own body and the bodies of my fellow-men.

Both my own body and those of my fellow-men, as they are perceived by the various special senses, belong to the physical order, and share its qualities. But over and above its existence as a member of the perceived physical order, my own body has further another quite different kind of existence. It is, in so far as I perceive its parts, as I do other bodily existence, by the sensations of the various special sense-organs, a complex of presentations, like everything else in the physical world. But my body is not merely an object presented to me by the organs of the special senses; it is also something which I feel as a whole in common or organic sensation, and in the changing organic thrills of my various emotional moods. This unique feeling of my body as a whole accompanies every moment of my conscious life and gives each its peculiar tone, and there seems to be no doubt that it forms the foundation of the sense of personal identity. If we recollect the essentially teleological character of feeling, we shall be inclined to say that my body as thus apprehended is nothing other than myself as a striving purposive individual, and that my experience of it is the same thing as the experience of my purposive attitudes towards my environment. It is, in fact, this experience of my body as apprehended by immediate feeling, that Psychology describes as the "subject" of the various "mental states" of which it formulates the laws. For Metaphysics, it does not seem too much to say, this double existence of my own body, as a presented object about which I have knowledge in the same way as about everything else, and as an immediately felt unity, affords the key to the whole problem of the "independent" existence of a reality beyond my own presentations. To see how this comes about, we must first consider the influence it has on our conception of one very special part of the physical order, the bodies of our fellows.

The bodies of our fellow-men are, of course, from one point of view complexes of presentations which we receive through our sense-organs; so far their *esse*, as Berkeley would have said, is *percipi*. But all practical communion with my fellows through the various institutions of society is based upon the conviction that, over and above their existence as presentation-complexes, or contents of my perceptive states, the bodies of my fellows have the same kind of existence as directly apprehended in immediate feeling which I ascribe to my own. In other words, all practical life is a mere illusion, unless my fellow-men are, like myself, centres of purposive experience. By the existence independent of my own perception which I ascribe to them, I mean precisely existence as feeling purposive beings. Hence, unless all social life is an illusion, there is at least one part of the physical order, external to myself, of which the *esse* is not mere *percipi*, but *percipere*, or rather *sentire*. If my fellow-men are more than complexes of presentations or "ideas in my head," then the subjectivist reduction of all reality to states of my "consciousness" breaks down, at least for this part of the physical order. Hence the acceptance or rejection of the subjectivist theory will ultimately depend on the nature of the evidence for the independent existence of human feelings and purposes beyond my own.

On what grounds, then, do we attribute such "independent" existence as experiencing subjects to our fellows? According to the current subjectivist explanation, we have here a conclusion based on the argument from the analogy between the structure of my own body, as presented in sense-perception, and those of others. I infer that other men have a mental life like my own, because of the visible resemblances between their physical structure and my own, and this inference receives additional support from every fresh increase in our anatomical and physiological knowledge of the human frame. But, being an argument from analogy, it can never amount to a true scientific induction, and the existence of human experience, not my own, must always remain for the subjectivist a probability and can never become a certainty.

I am convinced that this popular and superficially plausible view is radically false, and that its logical consequence, the belief that the real existence of our fellows is less certain than our own, is a grave philosophical error. That the argument from analogy is no sufficient basis for the belief in human experience beyond my own, can easily be seen from the following considerations:—(1) As ordinarily stated, the data of the supposed inference do not actually exist. For what I perceive is not, as the subjectivist assumes, three terms—my own mental life, my own anatomical structure, and the anatomy of my neighbour, but two, my own mental life and my neighbour's anatomy. If

I cannot be sure of the reality of my neighbour's experience until I have compared the anatomy and physiology of his organism with that of my own, I shall have to remain in doubt at least until science can devise a mechanism by which I can see my own nervous system. At present one of the terms on which the analogical argument is said to be based, namely, my own internal physical structure, has to be mostly taken on trust. It would be little less than the truth to invert the subjectivist's position, and say that, until science can devise means for seeing our own brains, we infer the resemblance of our own anatomy to our neighbour's from the previously known resemblance of his inner experience and ours.

(2) And even supposing this difficulty already surmounted, as it conceivably will be in the future, there is a still more serious flaw in the presumed analogical inference. If I once have good ground for the conviction that similarity of inner experience is attended by similarity of physical structure, then of course I can in any special case treat the degree of structural resemblance between one organism and another as a sufficient reason for inferring a like degree of resemblance between the corresponding inner experiences. But upon what grounds is the general principle itself based? Obviously, if my own inner experience is the only one known to me originally, I have absolutely no means of judging whether the external resemblances between my own organism and yours afford reason for crediting you with an inner experience like my own or not. If the inference by analogy is to have any force whatever in a particular case, I must already know independently that likeness of outward form and likeness of inner experience at least in some cases go together. The plausibility of the usual subjectivist account of the way in which we come to ascribe real existence to our fellows, is simply due to its tacitly ignoring this vital point.

How, then, do we actually learn the existence of feeling purposive experience outside our own? The answer is obvious. We learn it by the very same process by which we come to the clear consciousness of ourselves. It is a pure blunder in the subjectivist psychology to assume that somehow the fact of my own existence as a centre of experience is a primitive revelation. It is by the process of putting our purposes into act that we come to be aware of them as our purposes, as the meaning of our lives, the secrets of what we want of the world. And, from the very fact of our existence in a society, every step in the execution of a purpose or the satisfaction of a want involves the adjustment of our own purposive acts to those of the other members of our social whole. To realise your own ends, you have to take note of the partly coincident, partly conflicting, ends of your social fellows, precisely as you have to take note of your own. You cannot come to the knowledge of the one without coming by the same route and in the same degree to the knowledge of the other. Precisely because our lives and purposes are not self-contained, self-explaining wholes, we cannot possibly know our own meaning except in so far as we know the meaning of our immediate fellows. Self-knowledge, apart from the knowledge of myself as a being with aims and purposes conditioned by those of like beings in social relations with myself, is an empty and senseless word.

The recent psychological studies of the part which imitation plays in all learning make this result still more palpably manifest. For they reveal the fact that, to an enormous extent, it is by first repeating without conscious aim of its own the significant purposive acts of others that a child first comes to behave with conscious significance itself. It is largely by learning what others mean when they utter a word or execute a movement that the child comes to know his own meaning in using the same word or performing the same movement. Thus we may confidently say that the reality of purposive significant experience which is not my own is as directly certain as the reality of my own experience, and that the knowledge of both realities is inevitably gained together in the process of coming to clear insight into my own practical aims and interests. The inner experience of my fellows is indubitably real to the same degree as my own, because the very existence of my own purposive life is meaningless apart from the equal existence of theirs.[1]

§ 4. We may now apply the results obtained in the previous section to the general question as to the "independent" existence of the physical order. In doing so we observe two consequences of the highest importance. (1) Now that we have found that at least a part of that

[1] See the fuller exposition of this line of argument in Royce, *Studies in Good and Evil*, essay on "Nature, Consciousness and Self-Consciousness," to which I am largely indebted throughout the present chapter, and for a detailed criticism of the alleged "analogical" inference the closely related reasoning of my own essay on "Mind and Nature" in *International Journal of Ethics*, October 1902. The similar but briefer criticism in Royce, *The World and the Individual*, Second Series, lecture 4, "Physical and Social Reality," p. 170, I had not had the opportunity to study when the above was written. For the whole subject of imitation, see in particular Professor Baldwin's *Mental Development in the Child and the Race.*

order, namely, the bodies of our fellow-men, are not mere complexes of presentations in our own experience, but have a further existence as themselves experiencing subjects, and are so far "independent" of their actual presentation in our own experience, we can no longer conclude, from the dependence of the physical order for its sensible properties upon presentation to ourselves, that it has no further existence of its own. If one part of that order, which as presented stands on the same footing with the rest, and is, like it, dependent on presentation for its sensible properties, is certainly known to be more than a mere presentation-complex, the same *may* at least be true of other parts. We can no longer assert of any part of the physical order, without special proof, that its *esse* is merely *percipi*.

We may go a step further. Not only *may* other parts of the physical order possess a reality beyond the mere fact of being presented to our sense-perception, but they *must*. For (a) we have to take note, for the obtaining of our own practical ends, of the factors in our *material* environment precisely as we have to take note of the purposive behaviour not our own which forms our *social* environment. Just as our own inner life has no coherent significance except as part of a wider whole of purposive human life, so human society as a system of significant conduct directed to the attainment of ends, cannot be understood without reference to its non-human surroundings and conditions. To understand my own experience, reference must be made to the aims, ideals, beliefs, etc. of the social whole in which I am a member; and to understand these, reference has again to be made to geographical, climatic, economical, and other conditions. Thus of the physical order at large, no less than of that special part of it which consists of the bodies of my fellows, it is true to say that its existence means a great deal more than the fact of its presentation. Unperceived physical existence must be real if I am myself real, because my own inner life is unintelligible without reference to it.

(b) This conclusion is further strengthened by the evidence supplied by the various sciences, that human life forms part of a great system characterised by evolution or development. If one part of a connected historical development is more than a complex of presentations, the other stages of that development cannot possibly be mere presentation-complexes. Against any "Idealism" which is mere Subjectivism or Presentationism calling itself by a less suspicious name, it would be a sound and fair argument to contend that it reduces evolution to a dream, and must therefore be false.[1]

It cannot, then, be true of the physical order as a whole, that it has no reality beyond the fact of its presentation to my senses. Elements in it not so presented must yet have reality, inasmuch as my own inner life requires the recognition of their reality as a fundamental condition of the realisation of my own "subjective" ends. As the facts of hallucination, "suggestion," and subjective sensation show, what appears to us as an element in the physical order *may* sometimes have no reality beyond the fact of its appearance; there *may* be presented contents of which it would be true to say that their *esse* is *percipi*. But the very possibility of distinguishing such hallucinatory presentations from others as illusory, is enough to prove that this cannot be true of the whole physical order. It is precisely because physical existence in general is something more than a collective hallucination, that we are able in Psychology to recognise the occurrence of such hallucinations. As has been already observed, you are never justified in dismissing an apparent fact of the physical order as mere presentation without any further reality behind it, unless you can produce special grounds for making this inference based upon the circumstances of the special case.

(2) The second important consequence of our previous conclusion is this,—We have now seen what was really meant, in the crucial case of our fellow-men, by maintaining an existence "independent" of the fact of presentation to our sense-organs. Their "independent" existence meant existence as centres of experience, as feeling, purposive beings. The whole concept of "independent" existence was thus social in its origin. We have also seen that the grounds on which an "independent" existence must be ascribed to the rest of the physical order are essentially of the same kind as those on which we asserted the "independent" existence of our fellow-men. It appears patent, then, that "independent" existence must have the same general sense in both cases. It can and must mean the existence of centres of sentient purposive experience. If we are serious in holding that the *esse* of the physical order, like that of ourselves and our fellows, is not mere *percipi*, we must hold that it is *percipere* or

[1] For a study of the significance of the "partial independence" of the physical world on my will as a factor in producing belief in its "external reality," see Stout, *Manual of Psychology*,[3] bk. iii. pt. 2, chaps. 1–2, "The Perception of External Reality."

sentire. What appears to us in sense-perception as physical nature must be a community, or a complex of communities of sentient experiencing beings: behind the appearance the reality[1] must be of the same general type as that which we, for the same reasons, assert to be behind the appearances we call the bodies of our fellows.

This conclusion is not in the least invalidated by our own inability to say what in particular are the special types of sentient experience which correspond to that part of the physical order which lies outside the narrow circle of our own immediate human and animal congeners. Our failure to detect specific forms of sentience and purpose in what we commonly call "inorganic" nature, need mean no more than that we are here dealing with types of experience too remote from our own for detection. The apparent deadness and purposelessness of so much of nature may easily be illustrated by comparison with the apparent senselessness of a composition in a language of which we are personally ignorant. Much of nature presumably appears lifeless and purposeless to us for the same reason that the speech of a foreigner seems senseless jargon to a rustic who knows no language but his own.

It would be easy, but superfluous, to develop these ideas more in detail by the free use of imaginative conjecture. The one point of vital principle involved is that on which we have already insisted, that existence "independent" of sense-perception has only one intelligible meaning. Hence it must have this same meaning whenever we are compelled to ascribe to any part of the perceived physical order a reality which goes beyond the mere fact of its being perceived. The assertion that the physical order, though dependent for its perceived qualities upon the presence of a percipient with sense-organs of a particular type, is not dependent on any such relation for its existence, if it is to have any definite meaning at all, must mean for us that that order is phenomenal of, or is the appearance to our special human sense-organs of, a system or complex of systems of beings possessing the same general kind of sentient purposive experience as ourselves, though conceivably infinitely various in the degree of clearness with which they are aware of their own subjective aims and interests, and in the special nature of those interests.

---

[1] The doctrine of degrees of reality must be borne in mind throughout this discussion. The reality of which the physical order is phenomenal may itself be phenomenal of a higher reality.

§ 5. We may end this chapter by drawing certain conclusions which follow naturally from the acceptance of this doctrine. (1) It is clear that the result we have reached by analysis of what is implied in the "independent" existence of the physical order agrees with our previous conclusions as to the general structure of Reality. For we saw in our last Book that it seemed necessary to hold not only that Reality as a whole forms a single individual experience, but also that it is composed of members or elements which are themselves sentient experiences of varying degrees of individuality. And in our discussion of the unity of the thing we saw reason to hold that nothing but a sentient experience can be individual; thus we had already convinced ourselves that if there are things which are more than complexes of presentations arbitrarily thrown together for the convenience of human percipients in dealing with them as unities, those things must be sentient experiences on subjects of some kind. We have now inferred from the actual consideration of the physical order that it does, in point of fact, consist of things of this kind. Our result may thus be said to amount in principle to the logical application to physical existence of the previously ascertained conclusion, that only what is to some degree truly individual can be real.

It is interesting to contrast with this consequence of our metaphysical attempt to interpret the course of physical nature, the result which inevitably follows from consistent adherence to the procedure of descriptive science. The whole procedure of descriptive science depends upon our willingness to shelve, for certain purposes, the problem wherein consists the reality of the physical order, and to concentrate our interest upon the task of adequately and with the greatest possible economy of hypothesis describing the system of presented contents in which it reveals itself to our senses. For purely descriptive purposes, our sole interest in the physical order is to know according to what laws of sequence one presented content follows upon another. Hence, so long as we can establish such laws of connection between presented contents, it is for purely scientific purposes indifferent how we imagine the Reality in which the sequence of presentation has its ground. Whether we think of it as a system of finite subjects, the will of a personal Deity, a complex of primary qualities, or an unknown substratum, or whether we decline to raise any question whatever about the matter, the results are the same, so long as our sole object is to exhibit the sequence of presented sense-contents as regulated by laws which admit of calculation. Science can go its way in entire indifference to all these alternative metaphysical interpretations of the Reality which is behind the phenomenal order.

The logical consequence of this absorption in the problem of describing the phenomenal sequence of events, apart from inquiry into their ground, is that the more thoroughly the task is carried out the more completely does individuality disappear from the physical order as scientifically described. Everyday thought looks on the physical order as composed of interacting things, each of which is a unique individual; current science, with its insistence on the uniform behaviour of the different elements of the material world, inevitably dissolves this appearance of individuality. In the more familiar atomic theories, though the differences between the behaviour of the atoms of different elements are still retained as ultimate, the atoms of the same element are commonly thought of as exact replicas of each other, devoid of all individual uniqueness of behaviour. And in the attempts of contemporary science to get behind atomism, and to reduce all material existence to motions in a homogeneous medium, we see a still more radical consequence of the exclusive adoption of an attitude of description. Individuality has here disappeared entirely, except in so far as the origination of differential motion in a perfectly homogeneous medium remains an ultimate inexplicability which has to be accepted as a fact, but cannot be reconciled with the theoretical assumptions which have led to the insistence upon the homogeneity of the supposed medium.

The logical reason for this progressive elimination of individuality from scientific descriptions of the processes of the physical order should now be manifest. If all individuality is that of individual subjects of experience, it is clear that in disregarding the question of the metaphysical ground of the physical order we have already in principle excluded all that gives it individuality from our purview; the more rigorously logical our procedure in dealing exclusively with the phenomenal contents of the physical order, the less room is left for any recognition of an element of individuality within it. Our purpose to describe the phenomenal logically involves description in purely general terms. It is only when, in Metaphysics, we seek to convert description of the phenomenal into interpretation of it as the appearance to sense of a more ultimate Reality, that the principle of the individuality of all real existence can come once more to its rights.

(2) It is perhaps necessary at this point to repeat, with special reference to the interpretation of the physical order, what has already been said of all interpretation of the detail of existence by reference to its ground. We must be careful not to assume that lines of division which we find it convenient for practical or scientific purposes to draw between things, correspond to the more vital distinctions between the different individual subjects of experience which we have seen reason to regard as the more real existences of which the physical order is phenomenal. This is, *e.g.*, an error which is committed by confident theories of the animation of matter which attribute a "soul" to each chemical atom. We must remember that many of the divisions between things which we adopt in our descriptive science may be merely subjective demarcations, convenient for our own special purposes but possibly not answering to any more fundamental distinctions founded on the nature of the realities of the physical order themselves. It does not in the least follow from our view of nature as the manifestation to our senses of a system of sentient individuals, that the relations between those individuals are adequately represented by the relations between the different factors of the material world as it is constructed in our various scientific hypotheses.

Thus, *e.g.*, our own self-knowledge and knowledge of our fellows show that in some sense there is a single experience corresponding to what, for physical science, is the enormous complex of elements forming the dominant centres of the human nervous system. But apart from our direct insight into human experience, if we only knew the human nervous system as we know a part of inorganic nature, we should be quite unable to determine that this particular complex was thus connected with an individual experience. In general we have to admit that, except for that small portion of physical nature in which we can directly read purposive experience of a type specially akin to our own, we are quite unable to say with any confidence how nature is organised, and what portions of it are "organic" to an individual experience. This caution must be constantly borne in mind if we are to avoid the abuse of our general theory of the meaning of the physical order in the interests of "spiritualistic" and other superstitions. It may also serve to guard against over-hasty "Philosophies of Nature," like those of Schelling and Hegel, which start with the unproved assumption that approximation to the human external form of organisation is a trustworthy indication of the degree in which intelligent experience is present in physical nature.

(3) One more point may receive passing notice. It is clear that if physical nature is really a society or a number of societies[1] of experiencing subjects, we must admit that, from the special character of our human experience with its peculiar interests and purposes, we are normally debarred from social communion with any members of the system except those who are most akin in their special type of purposive life to ourselves. Of the vast majority of the constituents of the physical order it must always be true that, while we may be convinced, on grounds of general metaphysical theory, that they possess the character we have ascribed to them, we have no means of verifying this conclusion in specific cases by the actual direct recognition of the individual life to which they belong, and consequent establishment of actual social relations with them. Yet it does not follow that we are always absolutely debarred from such direct social relations with extra-human sentient life. The "threshold of intercommunicability" between physical nature and human intelligence may conceivably be liable to fluctuations under conditions at present almost entirely unknown. Conceivably the type of experience represented in literature by the great poets to whom the sentient purposive character of physical nature has appealed with the force of a direct revelation of truth, and known in some degree to most men in certain moods, may depend upon a psychological lowering of this threshold. It is thus at least a possibility that the poet's "communion with nature" may be more than a metaphor, and may represent some degree of a social relation as real as our more normal relations with our human fellows and the higher animals. It may be true that in the relations of man with nature, as in his relations with man, it is the identity of purpose and interest we call love which is the great remover of barriers.

(4) It should hardly be needful to point out that such a view of the meaning of nature as has been defended in this chapter is in no way opposed to, or designed to set artificial restrictions on, the unfettered development of descriptive physical science. Whatever our view of the ultimate nature

---

[1] *Societies* would be the more natural supposition. We have no reason to deny that the various types of non-human intelligence may be cut off from social intercourse with each other, as they are from intercourse with ourselves.

of the physical order, it is equally necessary on any theory for the practical control of natural processes in the service of man to formulate laws of connection between these processes. And the work of formulating those laws can only be satisfactorily done when the analysis of the physical order as a system of sense-contents is carried on with complete disregard of all metaphysical problems as to its non-phenomenal ground. It would not even be correct to say that, if our metaphysical interpretation is valid, the view of nature presented in descriptive physical science is *untrue*. For a proposition is never untrue simply because it is not the whole truth, but only when, not being the whole truth, it is mistakenly taken to be so. If we sometimes speak in Philosophy as though whatever is less than the whole truth must be untrue, that is because we mean it is untrue *for our special purposes* as metaphysicians, whose business is not to stop short of the whole truth. For purposes of another kind it may be not only true, but *the* truth.[1]

Our metaphysical interpretation of the physical order is no more incompatible with full belief in the value and validity for *their own purposes* of the results of abstract descriptive science, than the recognition of the singleness and purposiveness of a human experience with the equal recognition of the value of physiological and anatomical investigation into the functions and mechanism of the human body. Of course a man, as he really exists, is something quite different from the physiologist's or anatomist's object of study. No man is a mere walking specimen of the "human organism"; every man is really first and foremost a purposive sentient agent. But this consideration in no way affects the practical value of anatomical and physiological research into the structure of the man as he appears in another man's system of sense-presentations. What is true in this case is, of course, equally applicable in all others.

We have yet to discuss the most serious stumbling-block in the way of the idealist interpretation of nature, the apparent conformity of its processes to rigid laws of sequence, which at first sight might seem to exclude the possibility of

---

[1] That is, there are degrees of truth as well as of reality, and the two do not necessarily coincide. The degree of truth a doctrine contains cannot be determined apart from consideration of the purpose it is meant to fulfil. For the special purposes of Metaphysics, the purpose of thinking of the world in a finally consistent way, whatever is not the whole truth is untrue. But what the metaphysician regards as the lesser truth may be the higher truth relatively to other purposes than his own. Compare the doctrine of Dr. Stout's essay on "Error" in *Personal Idealism*.

their being really the acts of purposive subjects. This difficulty will form the topic of our succeeding chapter.

Consult further :—F. H. Bradley, *Appearance and Reality*, chap. 22; L. T. Hobhouse, *Theory of Knowledge*, pt. 3, chap. 3; H. Lotze, *Metaphysic*, bk. ii. chaps. 5, 6; H. Münsterberg, *Grundzuge der Psychologie*, i. pp. 65–92; K. Pearson, *Grammar of Science*, chap. 2 (The Facts of Science), 8 (Matter) [mainly written from the "phenomenalist" standpoint, but with unconscious lapses into a more materialistic view]; J. Royce, Nature, Consciousness, and Self-Consciousness" (in *Studies of Good and Evil*); *The World and the Individual*, Second Series, Lect. 4; "J. Ward, *Naturalism and Agnosticism*, Lects. 1–5, 14, 19. Of the older philosophical literature, Descartes, *Meditation* 6; Leibnitz, *Monadology* and *New System;* Locke, *Essays*, bk. iv. chap. 11; Kant's "Refutation of Idealism," in the second edition of the *Critique of Pure Reason*, in addition to the already cited works of Berkeley, will probably be found most important.

CHAPTER III

THE MEANING OF LAW

§ 1. The popular conception of the physical order as exhibiting a rigid mechanical conformity to general *laws*, conflicts with our metaphysical interpretation. § 2. Our interpretation would, however, admit of the establishment of averages or approximately realised uniformities by the statistical method, which deals with occurrence *en bloc* to the neglect of their individual detail. § 3. "Uniformity" in nature is neither an axiom nor an empirically verifiable fact, but a postulate. A consideration of the methods actually employed for the establishment of such uniformities or "laws" of nature shows that we have no guarantee that actual concrete cases exhibit *exact* conformity to law. § 4. Uniformity is a *postulate* arising from our need of practical rules for the control of nature. It need not for this purpose be exact, and in point of fact our scientific formulæ are only exact so long as they remain abstract and hypothetical. They do not enable us to determine the actual course of an individual process with certainty. § 5. The concept of the physical order as *mechanical* is the abstract expression of the postulate, and is therefore essential to the empirical sciences which deal with the physical order. § 6. Consideration of the character of genuine machines suggests that the mechanical only exists as a subordinate aspect of processes which, in their full nature, are intelligent and purposive.

§ 1. In our view of the underlying reality of the physical order, as explained in the last chapter, we have scarcely gone further, except in the explicitness of our phraseology, than we should be followed by many who profess a complete disbelief in metaphysical construction and an exclusive devotion to positive natural science. From the side of positive science we have often been reminded that no hard-and-fast line can logically be drawn between the organic and the inorganic, that we are not entitled to assume that the continuity of evolution ceases when we are no longer able to follow it with our microscopes, that we are, with the eye of scientific faith, to discern in the meanest particle of matter the "promise and potency" of all life, and so forth. All which statements seem to be confused ways of suggesting some such conception of the physical order as we have attempted to put into more precise and logical form. It is not until we come to deal with the problem indicated by the title of this chapter that our most serious difficulties begin. We have to face the objections which may be urged against our view of the physical order on the strength of the principle known in inductive Logic as the " Uniformity of Nature."

The events of the physical order, it may be urged, cannot be expressions of the more or less conscious purposes and interests of individual centres of experience, and that for a simple reason. How a purposive agent will behave is always a mystery, except to those who actually understand his purposes. It is impossible, apart from actual insight into those purposes, to infer from the mere examination of his past behaviour what his behaviour in the future will be. For the special characteristic of purposive action is its power to find new ways of response to stimulus. Hence it is that we rightly regard the power to learn by experience, that is, to acquire more and more *appropriate* reactions to stimulus, as the test of a creature's intelligence. Where there is no progressive adaptability there is no ground to assume intelligence and purpose. Hence again the impossibility of calculating beforehand with any certainty what course the behaviour of an intelligent being will take, unless you are actually aware of the purposes he is seeking to realise.

Now, except in the case of the organic world, it may be urged, we do not find progressive *adaptability* in Nature. The inorganic constituents of the physical order always react with absolute uniformity in the same way upon the same environment. Their behaviour exhibits absolutely undeviating conformity to general routine laws of sequence, and can therefore be calculated beforehand, provided that the resources of our mathematics are adequate to deal with the problems it presents, with absolute exactitude and certainty. That this routine uniformity exists in physical nature is, in fact, a fundamental principle in the logic of inductive science. Every indication of sentience and purpose is thus absent from physical nature, outside the world of living organisms; it is a realm of rigid conformity to laws of sequence. And these sequences, because absolutely without exception and incapable of modification, are purely *mechanical*, *i.e.* non-purposive and non-intelligent. Nature is, in fact, a complicated *mechanism*, in which every event follows from its conditions with undeviating *necessity*.

Views of this kind are often supposed to be logically necessitated by the principles of physical science. It is manifest that if they are sound our whole preceding interpretation of the physical order is invalidated. For this reason, as well as because of the far-reaching consequences often drawn from them as to human freedom and moral responsibility, it will be necessary to examine their foundation in some detail.

§ 2. The main problems confronting us in this examination will then be—(1) How far is calculable uniformity of sequence really incompatible with the presence of purpose and intelligence? (2) Have we any real ground for ascribing *such* uniformity to the actual sequences of physical nature? (3) if not, What is the real logical character of the principle of the so-called uniformity of nature? (4) and What amount of truth is contained in the conception of the physical order as a *mechanism?* Into the problem suggested by the popular contrast between the *necessity* of mechanical sequence and the *freedom* of purposive action, it will be needless to enter at any length. For, as we saw in dealing with the popular view of necessary causal relation, the necessity of a mechanical sequence is a purely subjective and logical one. The sequence is necessary only in the sense that *we* are constrained, so long as we adhere to the purpose of thinking logically, to affirm the consequent when we affirm the antecedent. True *necessity* is always compulsion, and therefore, so far from being opposed to purposive action, can only exist where an actual purpose is overruled or thwarted.[1] So long as we are dealing solely with phenomenal sequence in the physical order, necessity is a mere anthropomorphic name for routine undeviating uniformity of sequence.

(1) *Calculable Uniformity and Intelligent Purpose.* It is sometimes assumed that all successful *prediction* of a thing's behaviour is incompatible with the ascription of intelligence or purpose to the thing. Thus it has been argued, and continues to be argued in moral philosophy of a popular type, that if we are intelligent beings with purposes of our own, it must always be impossible for an onlooker to predict how we shall behave in circumstances which have not yet arisen. This extreme view of the incompatibility of calculability with intelligent purpose, however, manifestly rests on a double confusion. To begin with, those who assert this view com-

---

[1] Speaking strictly, all necessity would appear to arise from the presence of conflicting purposes or interests in the *same* experience. *E.g.*, the logical necessity of affirming the conclusion when the premisses are affirmed, implies (1) the presence of the general purpose to think logically; (2) the presence of some purpose or interest which, if gratified, would demand the affirmation of a result inconsistent with the previously affirmed premisses; (3) the repression of this affirmation by the dominant purpose (1). I believe that careful analysis will reveal these same elements in every genuine case of necessitation. *I.e.* the mere defeat of my purpose is not true necessitation unless it is defeated by a second interest or purpose which I also identify with myself. Thus all necessity would ultimately be self imposed. This is not without its bearing on Ethics, as we shall see.

monly make the mistake of supposing that *prediction* of the future stands somehow on a different logical level from *calculation* of the past from present data. Prediction of my future behaviour is supposed somehow to conflict with my character as a purposive being in a way in which inference as to my past behaviour does not. This is, of course, an elementary fallacy in Logic. The conditions required for the successful inference of the absent from the present are identical in the two cases, as we have already seen in dealing with the problems of Causality. Precisely the same kind of insight is requisite to judge how a given man must have behaved in a certain situation in his past history as are needed to determine how he will behave in a situation which is yet to arise. We may thus dismiss from consideration the special case of *prediction*, and confine ourselves to the general question, how far the general calculability of the course of a process is incompatible with its purposive and intelligent character.

An answer to this question is at once suggested by reflection upon our ordinary attitude towards such attempts to calculate the course of our own behaviour.[1] It is by no means every such calculation that we resent. So far from being affronted by the assumption that our conduct exhibits sufficient uniformity to admit of calculation, we expect our personal friends to have sufficient reliance on its uniformity to assume with confidence that we shall certainly do some things and refuse to do others, that we must have acted in certain ways and cannot have acted in others. "You ought to know me better than to suppose me capable of that" is between friends a tolerably keen expression of reproach, "I know I can count on you to do it," a common expression of confidence. On the other hand, we should certainly resent the assumption on the part of a comparative stranger of such a knowledge of our character as would warrant confident calculation of our conduct, and if the calculation was avowedly drawn not from personal knowledge at all, but from general propositions of Psychology or Anthropology, we should pretty certainly feel that a more than accidental success threatened our moral individuality.

Now, what is the explanation of this difference of feeling? Manifestly it must be sought in the great difference between the grounds on which the calculation is based in the two cases. In the first case we expected and welcomed the

---

[1] Compare with what follows, F. H. Bradley, *Ethical Studies*, Essay I, and *infra*, Bk. IV. chap. 4.

calculation, because we felt it to be founded upon our friend's personal acquaintance with the guiding interests and purposes of our life; it was an inference based upon insight into our *individual* character. In the other case we resented the success of the calculation, because we assumed it to be made in the absence of any such personal insight into our individual purposes and interests, on the basis of mere general propositions about human nature. We rightly feel that the regular success of calculation of this second sort is inconsistent with the ascription of any reality to our individual character. If all our actions can be calculated from general theorems in a science of human nature, without taking individual purpose into account, then the apparent efficacy of individual interests and purposes in determining the course of our history must be an empty illusion; we cannot be truly intelligent agents, seeing that we never really do anything at all.

Thus we see that it seems necessary to draw a marked distinction between two types of calculability. Calculation based on insight into individual character and purpose is so far from being inconsistent with purposiveness and intelligence, that the more coherent and systematic the purposes by which a life is controlled, the more confident does such calculation become. Calculation without such special knowledge, and based upon mere general propositions, on the other hand, cannot be regularly successful where one has to deal with the behaviour of individual purposive beings.[1]

Now, the difficulty as to our interpretation of the physical order as the presentation to our sense of a system of intelligent purposive beings, is that the successes of physical science seem at first sight to show that just this "mechanical" calculation of the course of events from observed sequence, without insight into underlying individual purpose, *is* possible when we are dealing with physical nature. For, on the one hand, we ourselves admitted that if physical nature is permeated by individual purposes, we do not know what those

[1] Our ordinary calculations as to the behaviour of our fellow-men, beyond the circle of our own intimates, seem to involve a mixture of the two types. We base our conclusions partly on conjectures drawn from the observed past acts of our fellows as to their special interests and purposes, partly on generalisations as to the purposes and interests which are most widely operative in human life. Practical men never allow themselves to forget that the conclusions thus obtained are problematical in the highest degree. The whole course of our investigation will go to show that the notion of a deductive science of human nature, by which the concrete conduct of an individual man might be inferred with certainty from physiological and psychological generalities, is a ridiculous chimera. See *infra* Bk. IV. chap. 4.

purposes in detail are; and, on the other, it is undeniable that physical science, which systematically disregards their presence, has been signally successful in the past, and may be expected to be even more successful in the future, in detecting uniformities in physical nature, and so submitting it to exact calculation. Hence it might be thought that the actual success of the empirical sciences cannot be reconciled with the principles of our metaphysical interpretation of the course of nature.

We must, however, draw a very important distinction. There is one method by which uniformities of a certain kind can be detected in the behaviour of purposive intelligent beings, without insight into the nature of their individual purposes—the method of statistical averages. Thus, though it would be quite impossible to say with certainty of any individual man that he will shoot himself or will get married, except on the strength of insight into his individual character and interests, we find by experience that it is possible to say, within a certain narrow range of error, what percentage of Englishmen will shoot themselves or will get married in the year. The percentage is, of course, rarely or never precisely realised in any one year, but the longer the period of years we take for examination, the more exactly do the deviations from the average in individual years compensate one another. The explanation is, of course, that on the whole the incentives to marriage or suicide, in a reasonably stable state of society, remain constant from year to year, so that by taking an average of several years we can eliminate results which are due to individual peculiarities of temperament and situation, and obtain something like a measure of the degree in which the general conditions of social existence impose a certain common trend or character on the interests and purposes of individuals.

Two things are at once noticeable in connection with all uniformities obtained by the method of averages. One is that the result formulated in the statistical law is always one to which the actual course of events may reasonably be expected to conform within certain limits of deviation, never one to which we have a right to expect absolute conformity. Not only is the actual number of marriages, *e.g.*, in any one year, usually slightly above or below the average percentage computed, *e.g.*, for a ten years' period, but as we compare one longer period with others, the average percentage for the longer period itself fluctuates. It is only in the "long run," that is, in the impossible case of the actual completion of an interminable series, that the computed average would be exactly realised. As every one who has to deal with averages in any form knows, precise realisation of the computed average within a finite series of cases would at once awaken suspicions of an error somewhere in our calculations. Thus the uniformities of this kind are never absolutely rigid; they are ideal limits to which the actual course of events is found to approximate within certain limits of divergence.

The second point is that the existence of such a uniformity never affords logical ground for confident affirmation as to the actual event in a particular concrete case. To revert to our illustration, just as we have no right to infer from the approximately constant percentage of marriages per year in a given society, that this precise percentage will be realised in any one special year, so we have still less right to infer that a particular member of that society will or will not marry. Nothing but insight into the character, situation, and interests of this special member of society can give me the right to judge with confidence how he will actually behave. Similarly, it is possible to say within certain limits of error how many persons over sixty years of age may be expected to die in the next twelve months, but it would be the height of logical presumption to infer that a particular man will die during the year, except on the strength of special information about his pursuits, habits, and general state of health.[1] Thus our general conclusion must be, that calculation and the establishment of uniformities is possible, without insight into individual purpose, but that the uniformities thus obtained are always variable and approximate, and afford no safe ground for inference as to special concrete cases.

§ 3. (2) *Uniformity in Physical Nature.* The existence of ascertainable uniformities in physical nature, then, will not conflict with our general interpretation of the physical order, provided that these uniformities are of the type just illustrated by reference to ordinary social statistics. On the other hand, the exact and rigid conformity of the actual course of concrete events with such uniform general "laws," would certainly be inconsistent with the presence of teleological adaptation

---

[1] It will be recollected that the approximate constancy of such social statistics has been, foolishly enough, brought forward as an alleged disproof of moral freedom. The more vulgar forms of the necessitarian argument have even been pushed to the inference that, if the number of suicides up to December 31 has been one less than the average in some given year, some one *must* kill himself before the day is out to make up the percentage. What must happen if the number has been one *more* than the average we are never told.

to ends. A reign of rigid routine conformity to general law cannot co-exist with individual purposive life. Now, it is commonly assumed, and we shall shortly see that the assumption is both necessary and justified as a practical methodological postulate, that the "reign of law" in physical nature is absolute. But are there any grounds for recognising this assumption as more than a possibly unrealised postulate made for human practical purposes? I think it is easy to show that there are none whatever, and that the conception of a nature devoid of purpose and sentience, and swayed absolutely by mechanical "laws," is simply a metaphysical nightmare of our own invention.

To begin with, it is clear that the undeviating conformity of the actual course of any concrete process to scientific "law" cannot be verified as an empirical fact by observation or experiment. For in no observation or experiment can we ever deal with the whole of any concrete actual event or process. We have always, for the purposes of our observation, to select certain of the general aspects of the process, to which we attend as the "relevant factors" or "conditions" of the result, while we disregard other aspects as "immaterial" or "accidental" circumstances. And this artificial abstraction, as we saw in discussing Causality, though indispensable for our practical purposes, is logically indefensible. Again, within the aspects selected for attention, all that experiment can establish is that the deviation from uniform law, if there is any deviation, is not sufficiently great to affect our measurements and calculations. But how far our standards of measurement are from rigid precision may be readily learned from the chapter on physical standards in any good work on the logic of the inductive sciences.[1] Our failure to detect deviation from law is absolutely worthless as evidence that no deviation has taken place.

Thus, if the absolute uniformity of natural processes is more than a practical postulate, it must be an axiom, that is, it must be implied in the very notion of those processes as elements in a systematic whole. But it should at once be clear that we have no more ground for asserting such uniformity as an axiom, than we had for treating the causal postulate as axiomatic. It is by no means implied in the concept of a systematic whole that its parts shall be connected by uniform law. For the unity of the system may be teleological, that is, the parts may be connected by the fact

---

[1] Compare Mach, *Science of Mechanics*, p. 280 ff. (Eng. trans.); Jevons, *Principles of Science*, chaps. 13, 14.

that they work together to realise the same end, to execute the same function. In that case the behaviour of any one part will depend on the demands laid upon it by the plan which the working of the system fulfils. As these demands vary from time to time, the behaviour of the part under consideration will then vary correspondingly, though to all appearance its surroundings may, for a spectator who fails to grasp the end or purpose realised by the system, be identical.[1] This is actually the case with those systematic wholes in which human insight can directly detect unity of purpose or aim. A man with definite purposes before him does not react in a uniformly identical way upon situations which, apart from their relation to his purpose, would be pronounced identical. He learns, for instance, from previous failure in the same circumstances, and so acquires the power to react on them in a way better adapted to the obtaining of his end. Or his progressive execution of his purpose, where there has been no failure, may require different conduct on the two occasions. To speak with strict logical accuracy, the situations, relatively to his special purpose, are never identical, though it may be no difference could be detected in them apart from that relation to this peculiar purpose. Relatively to the system of intelligent purposes which realises itself through the circumstances, every situation is, properly speaking, unique.

Now, if we consider the methods by which the uniformities called "laws" of nature are actually formulated, we may see ground to conclude that they may one and all be uniformities of the approximate non-exact type. In many cases, if not all, these uniformities have manifestly been obtained by statistical methods. Thus, for example, when it is said that all the atoms of a given chemical element are absolutely alike, *e.g.*, that every atom of oxygen has the atomic weight 16, there is absolutely no valid ground for regarding this uniformity as actually realised without deviation in individual cases. If the atom should prove, as it may, to be no more than a convenient device of our own, useful for computing the behaviour of sensible masses but with no real existence of its own, it is of course evident that there can be no question of the real conformity of individual cases to the law. But even if there really are indivisible bodies answering to our conception of atoms, still we have to

---

[1] Compare Lotze, *Metaphysic*, bk. i. Introduction X., chap. 3, § 33 (Eng. trans., vol. i. pp. 18, 90–93); bk. i. chap. 7, § 208 ff. (Eng. trans., vol. ii. pp. 88–91).

remember that we have no means of dealing with the individual atom directly. We infer its properties indirectly from the behaviour of the sensible masses with which we can deal more directly. Hence, at most, the statement that the atom of oxygen has a certain weight means no more than that we can for our practical purposes disregard any possible individual divergences from this value. The oxygen atoms, if they really exist, might actually fluctuate in individual atomic weight about an average; yet, so long as we cannot deal with them individually but only in bulk, these fluctuations, if only sufficiently small, would produce no appreciable effect on our results, and would therefore properly be treated in our science as non-existent. Conceivably, then, such chemical uniformities may afford no safer ground for precise statements about the weight of the individual atom, than anthropological statistics do for precise statement about the actual height, weight, or expectation of life of an individual man. And we can readily see that a non-human observer with senses incapable of perceiving the individual differences between one man and another, might be led from the apparent uniformity of behaviour exhibited by large collections of human beings to the same sort of conclusions which we are tempted to make about atoms.[1]

Similarly with other cases of apparently rigid uniformity. As any one who has worked in a laboratory knows,[2] such results are in actual practice obtained by taking the mean of a long series of particular results and treating the minor divergences from this mean as non-existent because they are negligible for all practical purposes. In other words, the apparently rigid conformity of natural processes to uniform law is an inevitable consequence of the fact that we are debarred by various limitations of a subjective kind from following the course of any process in its individual detail, and have therefore to make all our inferences from the observation and comparison of series of processes sufficiently extended for individual differences to neutralise each other. But in all this there is absolutely no warrant for the conclusion that the course of any one individual process is absolutely uniform with that of any other. There is room

---

[1] See the full exposition of this view in Ward, *Naturalism and Agnosticism*, vol. i. lecture 4, on which the present paragraph is founded. Cf. J. T. Merz, *History of European Thought*, vol. i. pp. 437-441.

[2] My remark is founded more particularly upon the methods by which quantitative uniformities are obtained in the investigations of Psychophysics. I have no direct acquaintance with first-hand experimentation in other spheres, but the method by which it is made to yield general uniformities seems to be of the same kind.

within the uniformity got by these methods of comparison for an infinite variety of individual detail, of which our scientific constructions take no account, either because our means of observation are insufficient to detect it, or because, when detected, it is of no significance for the original object of our science—practical success in interference with the course of events.

It is easy to point out some of the conditions upon which failure to detect actually existing individual deviations from uniformity may depend. Professor Royce has, in this connection, laid special stress upon one such condition, the limitation of what he calls the time-span of our attention. We are unable, as the student of Psychology knows, to attend to a process as a whole if its duration exceeds or falls short of certain narrow limits. Now, there seems no foundation in the nature of the attentive process for the special temporal limitations to which it is subject in our own experience, and we have no means of denying the possibility that there may be intelligent beings whose attention-span is much wider, or again, much more contracted, than our own. One can even conceive the possibility of a being with a power of varying the span of attention at will. Now, it is clear that if we could so vary our attention-span as to be able to take in as single wholes processes which are at present too rapid or too slow to be perceived by us in their individual detail, such a purely subjective change in the conditions of our own attention might reveal individuality and purpose where at present we see nothing but routine uniformity. In the same way, we can readily understand that a being with a much wider attention-span than our own might fail to see anything but purposeless routine in the course of human history. Supposing that we are placed in the midst of a universe of intelligent purposive action, it is clear that we can only hope to recognise the nature of that action in the case of beings who live, so to say, at the same rate as ourselves. A purposive adaptation to environment with consequent deviation from uniformity in reaction would necessarily escape our notice if it took place with the rapidity of the beat of a gnat's wing, or again, if it required centuries for its establishment.[1]

Other similar subjective conditions which would necessarily cut us off from the recognition of purposive fresh adaptations widely different from those which occur in our own life, are the limitations of our power of attending to

[1] Cf. Mr. H. G. Wells's tale, *The New Accumulator*.

more than a certain number of presentations simultaneously; and again, the restriction of our sense-perception to a few types, and the impossibility of perceiving contents belonging to those types when they fall below or above the lower and upper "thresholds" of sensibility. These considerations do not, of course, positively prove that the routine uniformity of natural processes is only subjective appearance, but they are sufficient to show that there is no valid reason for taking it to be more, and in conjunction with our previous positive argument for the sentient individuality of all real existence, they suffice to bring our general interpretation of the physical order under Mr. Bradley's canon that "What must be and can be, that *is*."

§ 4. (3) What, then, are we to make of the principle of the "Uniformity of Nature"? Any principle which does actual work in science must somehow be capable of justification, and if our interpretation of the physical order really conflicts with a fundamental scientific principle, it must contain fallacy somewhere. Fortunately, there is no real conflict. In dealing with the principle of Uniformity, we must distinguish very carefully between the sense in which it is actually required for the purposes of science and the sense which has been put upon it in the set of metaphysical doctrines popularly but illogically deduced from the actual procedure of the sciences. As we have seen already, it is impossible to affirm the principle of Uniformity as an axiom of systematic thought. It is also not capable of verification as an empirical truth. Its logical character must therefore be that of a postulate, an assumption defensible on the ground of practical usefulness, but only so far as it actually succeeds.

Now, this is precisely the place which the principle fills in the actual procedure of the sciences. We have absolutely no means of showing that the concrete course of Nature is strictly uniform, as has already been seen. But also, we have no need, for our scientific ends, that it should be uniform. All that we require is that natural processes, when dealt with in the bulk, should exhibit no divergence from uniform routine except such as we may neglect for the purposes of practical calculation and control of the course of events. The actual success of the empirical sciences shows that this demand for approximate uniformity is actually fulfilled with sufficient closeness for all our practical purposes. That it would be so fulfilled we could have had no theoretical means of divining before putting it to the actual test. In this sense the principle, like that of Causality may be said to be a postulate made *a priori* and in advance of experience. But, once more like the principle of Causality, it could not be presumed to be trustworthy unless the subsequent results of its employment vindicated it; it cannot, therefore, be *a priori* in the Kantian sense of being known to be true independent of empirical verification.[1]

This result is confirmed by consideration of the way in which the principle of uniform law is actually applied to concrete cases. Scientific laws, as we all know, are purely general and abstract. They state not what *will* happen, but what *would* happen providing that certain specified conditions and no others were operative in determining the result. In this abstract form they are, of course, statements of exact and absolute uniformities. But in this abstract form they cannot be directly applied to the calculation of the actual course of any process. To take, for instance, an example which has been used by Professor Ward.[2] We learn in Mechanics that equilibrium is maintained on the lever when the moments of the weights about the fulcrum are equal and opposite. As an abstract generalisation this is a statement of a rigid uniformity. But in order that it may be universally true, we must suppose the conditions implied in the formulation of the proposition to be fulfilled. The lever itself must be absolutely rigid, and must be weightless; it must be of absolutely uniform structure, the fulcrum must be a mathematical point, in order that friction may be excluded, and so forth. Similarly, the weights must be thought of as mere masses without any further difference of quality, and thus only capable of affecting the lever through the one property of their weight; their attachments, again, must be of ideal tenuity, or fresh complications will be introduced. But when all these conditions have been taken into account, the principle has become so abstract as to amount to the tautology that what only operates by its mass and its distance from the fulcrum will not operate by any other property.

In any actual case, the course of events will be liable to be affected by all the conditions which had to be excluded

---

[1] Compare once more the passage already quoted from Lotze, *Metaphysic*, i. 3. 33.

[2] See *Naturalism and Agnosticism*, vol. i. lecture 2, and compare the elaborate proof given by Mach, *Science of Mechanics*, pp. 9-23, that all the so-called demonstrations of the general theory of the lever are mere reductions of the more complicated to the simplest cases of a relation which ultimately depends for its recognition on nothing more cogent than the evidence of the senses.

from the abstract formulation of the principle. No actual lever will be weightless or incapable of being bent or broken; its construction will never be uniform. Actual loads, again, may influence the behaviour of a lever differently according to their bulk, their chemical composition, the nature of their attachments. At an actual fulcrum there will be some degree of friction between the lever-bar and its support, and so on. In actual fact, any or all of these circumstances may affect the behaviour of the lever bar when the loads are suspended from it. Consequently, it is quite impossible to apply the mechanical generalisation with certainty to determine the course of events in a concrete case.

What holds good in this instance holds good in all similar cases of the "laws" of nature. In so far as these laws are really exact they are all hypothetical, and deal only with the problem, What would be the course of a physical sequence, assuming its complete ground to be contained in the conditions enumerated in the enunciation of the law? That is, they all, in so far as they are absolute, are different forms of the tautological proposition, that where there is nothing to make any difference between two cases, there will be no difference. But the moment we apply our laws to the calculation of the actual course of an individual process, we have to recognise that the condition for their rigid exactness is absent; in the individual process there are always aspects not comprised in the conditions for which the law was enunciated, and nothing but actual experience can inform us whether the presence of these aspects will perceptibly affect the result in which we are interested. As applied to the study of an individual process, the principle of Uniformity is thus a postulate, like the principle of Causality, which can only be justified by its actual success.

Again, like the principle of Causality, the principle of Uniformity may be successful to different degrees, according to the special nature of the processes for which it is assumed. As the causal postulate rested on the assumption that a selection from the antecedents of an event may for practical purposes be treated as equivalent to its complete ground, so the more general postulate of Uniformity rests on the assumption that individual purpose may be left out of account in assigning the ground of a process. It does not follow that these postulates will receive the same amount of empirical justification for all departments of the physical order. There may well be certain processes in which the individual purposive character is so prominent that, even for our practical purposes, we cannot safely calculate their course without taking their end or purpose into consideration. In that case the principle of Uniformity and that of Causality would, for this part of the physical order, lose their practical value. It is a popular belief that such a failure of these practical postulates actually takes place where we come to deal with the conscious volitions of human agents. The problem is one which must be kept for fuller consideration in our next Book, but we can at present make two general statements.

(1) Such a failure of the postulates of Causality and Uniformity in application to a particular sphere would not involve a breach of the fundamental logical principle of Ground and Consequence, since, as we have seen sufficiently already, both postulates impose special restrictions on that principle for which the nature of the principle itself affords no warrant. It would thus not be an unthinkable or logically untenable position to hold that no general laws of human action can be formulated.

(2) While this extreme denial of the possibility of laws of human action is logically possible, the actual success of those sciences which deal with human behaviour in the statistical way forbids us to accept it. The success of these sciences shows that human behaviour, considered in the gross, does exhibit certain approximate uniformities. But there seems to be no means of proving that all aspects of human behaviour would show such uniformity if considered in gross in the same fashion. It is at least conceivable that some social activities would fail to exhibit approximation to an average value, no matter how extended the area and period taken as the basis of investigation. We might conceivably have to admit that there are departments of social life for which no " laws " can be formulated. If we disregard this possibility in practice, the reason is a methodological one. It is our *interest* to discover such uniformities, and therefore, as failure *may* only mean a temporary check to the success of our investigations, we properly make it a rule of method to assume that it is no more than this. We treat all sequences as capable, by proper methods, of reduction to uniformity, for the same reason that we treat all offenders as possibly reclaimable. We desire that they should be so, and we cannot prove they are not so, and we therefore behave as if we knew they were so.

A word may be said as to the nature of the practical need upon which the postulate of Uniformity is based. As we have previously seen, the allied postulate of Causality arose from the practical need of devising means for the control of natural processes. But the causal postulate alone is not enough to satisfy this need. For even if we can assume that every event is determined, sufficiently for practical purposes, by its antecedents, and thus that the knowledge of those antecedents, when obtained, is a knowledge of the means to its production, our practical command over the production of the event is not yet assured. For we can have no general confidence in our power to produce the event by employing the ascertained means, so long as it is possible that the result may on each occasion be affected by variations too minute for our detection, or for other reasons not accessible to our perception. We need to be assured that what seems the same to us is, for practical purposes, the same, and so that the employment of the *same* means may be trusted to lead to the same result. This is the condition which is expressed in an abstract form by the principle of Uniformity, which states that the course of natural processes conforms to general laws; in their actual application to the concrete processes of actual nature these laws are properly practical rules for the production of effects, and their inviolability means no more than that we may successfully treat as the same, in their bearing on the results in which we are interested, things which appear the same in relation to certain standards of comparison. As we have seen, the validity of this assumption could never have been known *a priori ;* it can only be said to be actually valid where actual use has justified it. At the same time, it is clearly a principle of method to assume the universal applicability of our practical postulates wherever it is to our interest that they should be applicable, as explained in the last paragraph. This is why we rightly assume the applicability of the postulates in spheres where the successful establishment of general uniformities has not hitherto been effected, so long as no positive reason can be shown why they should not apply. We shall find this last reflection suggestive when we come to deal with the ethical difficulties which have been felt about the application of the postulates of Uniformity and Causality to voluntary action.

It is of course clear that our reduction of Uniformity to a mere practical postulate does not introduce any element of pure "chance" into the actual order of existing things. "Chance" is a term with more than one meaning, and its ambiguity may easily lead to misapprehensions. Chance may mean (*a*) any sequence for which our actual knowledge cannot assign the ground. In this sense chance, as another name for our own mere ignorance, must of course be recognised by any theory which does not lose sight of the fact of human ignorance and fallibility.

Or again, chance may mean (*b*) a sequence of which the ground is partially understood. We may know enough of the ground of the sequence to be able to limit the possibilities to a definite number of alternatives, without knowing enough to say which alternative completely satisfies the conditions in a special case. It is in this sense that we speak of the "chances" of any one of the alternative events as capable of computation, and make the rules for their computation the object of special mathematical elaboration in the so-called "Theory of Probability."

(*c*) Finally, chance may mean "pure" chance, the existence of something for which there is no "ground" whatever, as it stands in no organic interconnection with a wider system of real existence. Chance in this last sense is, of course, absolutely excluded by our conception of the systematic unity of the real as expressed in the principle of Ground and Consequence, as an ultimate axiom of all consistent thought. Our denial of the absolute validity of the principles of Causality and Uniformity would only amount to the admission of "pure" chance into things if we accepted those principles as necessary consequences of the axiom of Ground and Consequence. If they are mere practical postulates, which present the axiom of Ground under artificial restrictions for which there is no logical justification in the axiom itself, the admission that they are not ultimately true in no way conflicts with full recognition of the thorough systematic unity of existence; it merely means that the view of the nature of that unity assumed by our practical postulates, though eminently useful, is inadequate.

We may here conveniently recapitulate our results. On metaphysical grounds, we felt compelled to regard the physical order as the manifestation to our special sensibility of a system of interconnected beings with sentient and purposive experiences like ourselves. The apparent purposelessness and deadness of the greater part of that order we explained as intelligible on the supposition that the subjective purposes and interests of many of its members are too unlike our own for our recognition. We then saw that if nature consists of such sentient experiences, the apparent domination of it by absolute law and uniformity cannot be the final truth. Such uniformity as there is must be approximate, and must result from our having to deal in bulk with collections of facts which we cannot follow in their individual detail, and will thus be of the same type as the statistical uniformities established by the anthropological sciences in various departments of human conduct. Next, we saw that the uniformities we call the "laws" of nature are, in fact, of this type; that they represent average results computed from a comparison of large collections of instances with which we cannot, or cannot so long as we adhere to our scientific purpose, deal individually, are only absolute while they remain hypothetical, and never afford ground for absolute assertion as to the course of concrete events.

We further saw that the only uniformity science requires of the actual course of nature is uniformity sufficiently close to enable us, for our special purposes, to neglect the individual deviations, and that the principle of Uniformity itself is not a logical axiom but a practical postulate, expressing the condition necessary for the successful formulation of rules for practical intervention in the course of events. Finally, while we saw that we have no *a priori* logical warrant for the assumption that such rules can be formulated for all departments of the physical order, we are bound on methodological grounds to assume that they can, unless we have special positive reasons for believing the contrary. Thus the universality of a postulate of uniformity does not mean that it is universally *true*, but that it has universally to be made wherever we have an interest in attempting the formulation of general rules.

§ 5. (4) *The Conception of the Physical Order as a Mechanism.* The conception of nature as rigidly conformable to general laws, finds its completest expression in the view of the whole physical order as a complicated *mechanism.*

It is not easy to say just how much is always implied when we hear of a "purely mechanical" theory of the world or of physical processes. Sometimes all that is meant is that the theory in question treats the principle of rigid uniformity according to general laws as an ultimate axiom. Sometimes, again, a "mechanical view" of the world is taken to mean, in a narrower sense, one which regards all the chemical, electrical, and other processes of the physical order as merely complicated cases of change of configuration in a system of mass particles. In this narrower sense the "mechanical" theory of the physical world is another name for the somewhat crude form of realist Metaphysics according to which nothing exists but moving masses, everything in the form of secondary qualities being a subjective illusion. Both the wider and the narrower form of the mechanical view agree in treating the processes of physical nature as unintelligent and unconscious, and regarding them as completely determined by antecedent conditions, without reference to any end or purpose which they effect. The theory owes the epithet "mechanical" to the analogy which is then supposed to subsist between the physical order and the various machines of human construction, in which the various constituent parts similarly execute movements determined by relation to the remaining parts, and not by any consciousness of an end to be attained.[1]

It is of course manifest that, so understood, the mechanical view of physical processes is forced upon us by our practical needs wherever it is requisite to formulate rules for successful intervention in the course of nature. If we are to intervene with success in the course of events, that course must, as we have already seen, be capable of being regarded as approximately uniform, otherwise we can have no security that our intervention according to rule and precedent will have a uniform and unambiguous result. Hence, if we are to formulate general rules for practical intervention, we must be able to treat the course of things as—to all intents and purposes—mechanical. And, on the contrary, if there are processes which cannot be even approximately regarded as mechanical, our power of framing general rules for the practical manipulation of events cannot extend to those processes. The limits of the mechanical view of events are likewise the limits of empirical science and of the general precepts of the practical arts.

We see this admirably exemplified in the study of human natures. The behaviour of large aggregates of human beings, as we have already learned, exhibits approximate uniformity, at least in many respects, and may thus be treated as to all intents and purposes mechanical in those respects. Hence it is possible to have a number of empirical sciences of human nature, such as Ethnology and Sociology, in which those uniformities are collected and codified, and to base on these sciences a number of general prudential maxims for the regulation of our behaviour towards our fellow-men considered in the abstract. But when we come to deal with the actual conduct of concrete human individuals, the mechanical view, as we have seen, fails us. What a concrete individual

---

[1] For some comments upon the "mechanical view" in the narrower and more special sense, see Chapter VI. of the present Book. It may be convenient, for the sake of precision, to call this more special form of the mechanical view the "mechanistic" theory of nature.

will do can only be inferred with certainty from the knowledge of his interests and purposes; there can thus be no general science of individual character, and consequently no general rules of prudence for behaviour towards an individual fellow-man. It is not to the so-called sciences of human nature, but to personal experience of the individual himself, we have to go for the knowledge how to regulate our conduct towards the actual individuals with whom life brings us into direct and intimate personal relation. Philosophical reflection upon the nature and limits of scientific knowledge fully confirms the verdict passed by the practical sense of mankind on the doctrinaire pedantry which seeks to deduce rules for dealing with actual individuals from anything but concrete understanding of individual character and purpose.

The mechanical view of physical processes is thus an indispensable postulate of the various empirical sciences which seek to describe those processes by the aid of general formulæ. Hence the protests which are sometimes urged against the use of mechanical interpretations in descriptive science are really in spirit no more than the expression of a personal distaste for the whole business of scientific generalisation and description. If there are to be sciences of physical processes at all, these sciences must be mechanical, in the wider acceptation of the term. It does not, however, follow because the mechanical view of physical processes is a necessity for our empirical sciences, that this view is consequently ultimately true. As we have learned already, when we pass from the statement that the processes of the physical order may, for the purpose of description by general formulæ, and the invention of practical methods for their production, be treated as to all intents mechanical, to the very different assertion that the physical order really is rigidly mechanical, we have deserted empirical science for dogmatic Metaphysics, and our metaphysical dogma must stand or fall by its own ultimate coherency and intelligibility as a way of thinking about Reality. The usefulness of the mechanical interpretation for other purposes is no evidence whatever of its value for the special purpose of the metaphysician.[1]

§ 6. Our previous discussion has already satisfied us that, as Metaphysics, the postulate of Uniformity upon which the

[1] Psychology ought probably to be excluded from the sciences for which the mechanical view is fundamental. But Psychology does not deal with any part of the physical order. See the present writer's review of Münsterberg's "Grundzüge der Psychologie" in *Mind* for April 1902; and cf. *infra*, Bk. IV. chaps. 1, 2.

mechanical view of the physical order rests, is unintelligible and therefore indefensible. But we may supplement the discussion by one or two reflections which throw into striking relief the inadequacy of that concept of the physical order as a huge self-acting machine which is so often offered us to-day as the last word of scientific thought. In the mechanical metaphysical theories two points always receive special emphasis. The physical order, according to the thorough-going exponents of the doctrine, is a mechanism which is (*a*) self-contained and self-acting, and (*b*) entirely devoid of internal purpose.

Now, in both these respects the supposed world-machine differs absolutely from the real machines upon analogy with which the mechanical theory is in the last resort based. Every real machine is, to begin with, the incarnation of the internal purpose of a sentient being. It is something which has been fashioned for the express object of attaining a certain result, and the more perfect its structure the greater is the impossibility of understanding the principle of construction without comprehension of the result it is devised to effect. Why the various parts have precisely the shape, size, strength, and other qualities they have, you can only tell when you know what is the work the maker of the machine intended it to do. In so far as this is not the case, and the structure of the machine can be explained, *apart* from its specific purpose, by consideration of the properties of the material, the patterns of construction consecrated by tradition, and so forth, it must be regarded as an imperfect realisation of its type. In a perfect machine the character and behaviour of every part would be absolutely determined by the demands made on that part by the purpose to be fulfilled by the working of the whole; our inability ever to produce such a perfect mechanical structure causes all our actual machines to be imperfect and inadequate representations of the ideal we have before us in their construction.

Thus a true machine, so far from being purposeless, is a typical embodiment of conscious purpose. It is true that the machine, once set going, will continue to work according to the lines embodied in its construction irrespective of the adequacy with which they effect the realisation of the maker's purpose. A watch, once wound up, will continue to go, though the indication of the lapse of time may, under fresh circumstances, cease to meet the interests of its maker or owner; and again, if the construction of the watch was faulty, it will not properly execute the purpose for which it was made. The machine has in itself no power of fresh purposive adaptability by which to modify the purpose it reflects, or to remedy an initial defect in its execution. But this merely shows that the purpose exhibited in the machine's construction originated outside the machine itself, and that the originator had not the power to carry out his purpose with complete consistency. It does not in the least detract from the essentially teleological and purposive character of the machine *quà* machine.

This brings us to our second point. Just as no true machine is purposeless, so no true machine is self-acting. Not only are all machines in the end the product of designing intelligence, but all machines are dependent upon external purposive intelligence for control. They require intelligence to set them going, and they require it equally, in one form or another, to regulate and supervise their working. However complicated a piece of machinery may be, however intricate its provisions for self-regulation, self-adjustment, self-feeding, and so forth, there is always, if you look carefully enough, a man somewhere to work it. The obvious character of this reflection has unfortunately not prevented metaphysicians from drawing strange inferences from their own neglect of it.

Closer reflection upon the true character of machinery would thus suggest a very different interpretation of the analogy between the uniformities of the physical order and the regular working of our machines from that adopted by the "mechanical" view of nature, as elaborated into a metaphysical doctrine. It would lead us to conceive of the apparently mechanical as playing everywhere the same part which it fulfils in our own system of social life. We should think of the mechanical as filling an indispensable but subordinate place in processes which, in their complete character, are essentially teleological and purposive. Teleological action obviously depends for its success upon two fundamental conditions. It requires the establishment of types of reaction which remain uniform so long as their maintenance satisfies the attainment of the end towards which they are directed, and at the same time the power of modifying those types of reaction from time to time so as to meet fresh situations encountered or created in the progressive attainment of that end. In our own individual physical life these two conditions are found as the power to form habits, and the power to initiate spontaneously fresh response to variation in the environment. In so far as our dominant interests can be best followed by the uniform repetition of one type of reaction, attention is diverted from the execution of the reaction which becomes habitual, semi-conscious, and, as we correctly say, "mechanical," the attention being thus set free for the work of initiating the necessary fresh modifications of habitual action. Our various industrial and other machines are devices for facilitating this same division of labour. The machine, once properly constructed and set in action, executes the habitual reaction, leaving the attention of its supervisor free to introduce the requisite relatively novel variations of response according to new situations in the environment.

There is nothing to prevent our interpreting the mechanical uniformities exhibited by the physical order in terms of this analogy. We should then have to think of the "laws" or "uniformities" in physical nature as corresponding to the habitual modes of reaction of the sentient beings of whose inner life the physical order is phenomenal; these uniformities would thus be essentially teleological in their own nature, and would also stand in intimate interrelation with the spontaneous initiation of fresh responses to variations in the environment on the part of the same sentient beings. Habit and spontaneity would mutually imply each other in nature at large as they do in our own psychical life, and the "mechanical" would in both cases be simply the lower level to which teleological action approximates in proportion as attention ceases to be necessary to its execution.

This conception would harmonise admirably with the result of our previous inquiry into the kind of evidence by which the existence of uniform "laws of nature" is established. For it would be an inevitable consequence of those subjective limitations which compel us to deal in bulk with processes we are unable to follow in their individual detail, that our observation of the physical order should reveal the broad general types of habitual response to typical external conditions, while failing to detect the subtler modifications in those responses answering to special variations in those conditions. Just so the uniformities ascertained by the statistical study of human nature are simply the exhibition on a large scale of the leading habitual reactions of human beings upon typical external situations, as disentangled from the non-habitual spontaneous responses to fresh elements in the external situation with which they are inseparably united in any concrete life of individual intelligent purpose.

There seems no objection to this conception of "laws of nature" as being the formulæ descriptive of the habitual behaviour of a complex system of sentient beings, beyond that based on the allegation that these "laws" are absolute, exact, and without exception. We have seen already that physical science has no means of proving this allegation, and no need whatever to make it, the whole doctrine of "rigid," "unvarying" conformity to law being a mere practical postulate falsely taken by a certain school of thinkers for an axiom. We have also seen that the notion of rigid unvarying law is fundamentally irreconcilable with the only intelligible interpretation we were able to give to the conception of the real existence of the physical order. Thus we have no reason to accept it as true, and the fullest ground for dismissing it as false. But for the unintelligent superstition with which the "laws of nature" are worshipped in certain quarters, it would indeed have been unnecessary to deal at such length and with such reiteration with so simple a matter.

One suggestion, already made in slightly different words, may be once more emphasised in conclusion. Even among human beings the relative prominence of fresh spontaneous adaptations and habitual reactions in the life of the individual fluctuates greatly with the different individuals. The "intelligence" of different men, as gauged by their power of fresh adaptive modification of established habits of reaction, ranges over a great variety of different values. If we could acquire the same kind of insight into the individual purposes of non-human agents that we have into those of our immediate fellows, we should presumably find an even wider range of differences in this respect. In principle we have no means of setting any definite limits to the range in either direction. We can conceive a degree of attentive control of reaction so complete that every reaction represents a fresh stage in the realisation of an underlying idea, so that intelligence is everything and habit nothing; and again, we can conceive a state of things in which mere habit is everything and intelligent spontaneity nothing. Somewhere between these ideal limits all cases of finite purposive intelligence must be comprised, and it would be easy to show that neither limit can be actually reached by finite intelligence, though there may be indefinite approximation to either.[1]

---

[1] Compare with the argument of this chapter, Royce, "Nature, Consciousness, and Self-consciousness," in *Studies of Good and Evil;* and "Mind and Nature," by the present writer in *International Journal of Ethics*, October 1902. The invet-

Consult further:—H. Lotze, *Metaphysic*, bk. i. Introduction X. (Eng. trans., vol. i. p. 18), bk. ii. chaps. 7, 8 (Eng. trans., vol. ii. pp. 66–162); E. Mach, *The Science of Mechanics*, pp. 481–504 (Eng. trans.); K. Pearson, *Grammar of Science*, chaps. 3 (The Scientific Law), 9 (The Laws of Motion); J. Royce, " Nature, Consciousness, and Self-consciousness" (in *Studies of Good and Evil*); J. Stallo, *Concepts and Theories of Modern Physics*, chaps. 1, 10–12 (metaphysical standpoint, " Phenomenalist"); J. Ward, *Naturalism and Agnosticism*, part 1, lects. 2–5.

erate prejudice that " laws of nature," to be of scientific use, must be rigidly exact uniformities is so strong, that it may be worth while, even after the preceding discussion of general principles, to assist the reader by reminding him of the elementary fact that the most familiar quantities involved in our scientific formulæ (π, e, the vast majority of second and third roots, of logarithms of the natural numbers, of circular functions of angles, etc.) are incapable of exact evaluation. This of itself renders a scientific law, in the form in which it can be applied to the determination of actual occurrences, merely approximate, and thus shows that *exact* uniformity is unnecessary for the practical objects of the empirical sciences.

CHAPTER IV

SPACE AND TIME

§ 1. Are time and space ultimately real or only phenomenal? § 2. The space and time of *perception* are limited, sensibly continuous, and consist of a *quantitative* element together with a *qualitative* character dependent on relation to the *here* and *now* of immediate individual feeling. § 3. *Conceptual* space and time are created from the perceptual data by a combined process of synthesis, analysis, and abstraction. § 4. They are unlimited, infinitely divisible, and there is valid positive ground for regarding them as mathematically continuous. Thus they form infinite continuous series of positions. They involve abstraction from all reference to the *here* and *now* of immediate feeling, and are thus homogeneous, *i.e.* the positions in them are indistinguishable. They are also commonly taken to be unities. § 5. Perceptual space and time cannot be ultimately real, because they involve reference to the *here* and *now* of a finite experience; conceptual space and time cannot be ultimately real, because they contain no principle of internal distinction, and are thus not individual. § 6. The attempt to take space and time as real leads to the difficulty about qualities and relations, and so to the indefinite regress. § 7. Space and time contain no principle of unity; there may be many space and time orders in the Absolute which have no spatial or temporal connection with each other. § 8. The antinomies of the infinite divisibility and extent of space and time arise from the indefinite regress involved in the scheme of qualities and relations, and are insoluble so long as the space and time construction is taken for Reality. § 9. The space and time order is an imperfect phenomenal manifestation of the logical relation between the inner purposive lives of finite individuals. Time is an inevitable aspect of finite experience. *How* space and time are transcended in the Absolute experience we cannot say.

§ 1. THE problems which arise for the metaphysician from the fact that the physical order, as it is presented to our senses, consists of elements having position in space and time, are among the oldest and most perplexing of all the riddles suggested by the course of our experience. Adequate discussion of them would demand not only far more space than we are at liberty to bestow on the topic, but such a familiarity with the mathematical theory of order and series as is scarcely possible to any one but an original mathematician. All that we can do in the present chapter is to deal very superficially with one or two of the leading problems, more with a view to indicating the nature of the questions which Metaphysics has to face, than of providing definite answers to them.

The fundamental problem for Metaphysics is, of course, whether space and time are ultimate Realities or only appearances; that is, would the whole system of Reality, as directly apprehended by an absolute all-containing experience, wear the forms of extension and succession in time, or is it merely a consequence of the limitations of our own finite experience that things come to us in this guise? It may indeed be urged that the contents of the universe must form an order of some sort for the absolute experience, in virtue of their systematic unity, but even so it is not clear that order as such is necessarily spatial or temporal. Indeed, most of the forms of order with which we are acquainted, both in everyday life and in our mathematical studies, appear to be, properly speaking, both non-spatial and non-temporal. Thus, *e.g.*, it is seemingly by a mere metaphor that we speak of the "successive" integers of the natural number-series, the "successive" powers of an algebraical symbol, the "successive" approximations to the value of a continued fraction, in language borrowed from the temporal flow of events, the true relation involved being in the first two cases the non-temporal one of logical derivation, and in the third the equally non-temporal one of resemblance to an ideal standard. The full solution of the metaphysical problem of space and time would thus involve (1) the discrimination of spatial and temporal order from other allied forms of order, and (2) a decision as to the claim of this special form of order to be ultimately coherent and intelligible.

The problem thus presented for solution is often, and usually with special reference to the Kantian treatment of space and time in the *Transcendental Æsthetic*, put in the form of the question whether space and time are subjective or objective. This is, however, at best a misleading and unfortunate mode of expression which we shall do well to avoid. The whole distinction between a subjective and an objective factor in experience loses most of its significance with the abolition, now effected by Psychology, of the vicious Kantian distinction between the "given" in perception and the "work of the mind." When once we have recognised that the "given" itself is constituted by the movement of selective attention, it becomes impossible any longer to distinguish it as an objective factor in knowledge from the subjective structure subsequently raised upon it. Kant's adherence to this false psychological antithesis so completely distorts his whole treatment of the "forms of intuition," that it will be absolutely necessary in a brief discussion like our own to deal with the subject in entire independence of the doctrines of the *Æsthetic*, which unfortunately continue to exercise a disproportionate influence on the current metaphysical presentment of the problem.[1] It should scarcely be necessary to point out that the metaphysical questions have still less to do with the psychological problems, so prominent in recent science, of the precise way in which we come by our perception of extension and succession. For Metaphysics the sole question is one not of the origin but of the logical value of these ideas.

It is of fundamental importance for the whole metaphysical treatment of the subject, to begin by distinguishing clearly between space and time as forms of *perception*, and space and time as *conceptual* forms in which we construct our scientific notion of the physical order. One chief source of the confusions which beset the Kantian view is the neglect of Kant and most of his followers to make this distinction with sufficient clearness. We cannot insist too strongly upon the point that the space and the time of which we think in our science as containing the entire physical order, are not space and time as directly known to us in sense-perception, but are concepts elaborated out of the space and time of direct perception by a complicated process of synthesis and analysis, and involving abstraction from some of the most essential features of the space and time of actual experience. The following brief discussion may serve to illustrate the general nature of the relation between the two forms of space and time, and to exhibit the leading differences between them.

§ 2. *Perceptual Space and Time.* Both space and time, as we are aware of them in immediate perception, are (1) *limited*. The space we actually behold as we look out before us with a resting eye is always terminated by a horizon which has a more or less well-defined outline; the "specious present," or portion of duration of which we can be at any time aware at once as an immediately presented content, has been shown by elaborate psychological experimentation to have a fairly well-defined span. Whatever lies outside this "span of

[1] The student who desires to think out the problems for himself would probably do well to take the discussions of Locke (*Essay*, bk. ii. chaps. 13-15) and Hume (*Treatise of Human Nature*, bk. i. pt. 2) rather than that of Kant as his starting-point, as they are less vitiated by psychological superstitions. In recent metaphysical work the chapters on the subject in Mr. Bradley's *Appearance and Reality* will probably be found most useful. Much may be learned from Mr. Russell's work, *Foundations of Geometry*, with which should, however, be compared the largely discrepant results of his later article, "Is Position in Space and Time Relative or Absolute?" (*Mind*, July 1901).

attention" belongs either to the no longer presented past or to the not yet presented future, and stands to the sensible present much as the space behind my back to the actually beheld space before my eyes. Of course, in either case the limits of the actually presented space or time are not absolutely defined. To right and left of the line of vision the visible horizon gradually fades off into the indistinctly presented " margin of consciousness"; the "sensible present" shades away gradually at either end into the past and the future. Yet, though thus not absolutely defined, sensible space and time are never boundless.

(2) Perceptual space and time are both internally *sensibly continuous* or unbroken. Concentrate your attention on any lesser part of the actually seen expanse, and you at once find that it is itself an expanse with all the characteristics of the wider expanse in which it forms a part. Space as actually seen is not an aggregate of *minima visibilia* or perceptual points in which no lesser parts can be discriminated; so long as space is visually or tactually perceived at all, it is perceived as containing lesser parts which, on attending to them, are found to repeat the characteristics of the larger space. So any part of the "specious present" to which special attention can be directed, turns out itself to be a sensible duration. Perceived space is made of lesser spaces, perceived time of lesser times; the "parts" not being, of course, actually distinguished from each other in the original percept, but being *capable* of being so distinguished in consequence of varying movements of attention.

(3) On investigating the character of our actual perception of space and time, it appears to contain two aspects, which we may call the quantitative and the qualitative. On the one hand, whenever we perceive space we perceive a certain magnitude of extension, whenever we perceive time we perceive a longer or shorter lapse of duration. Different spaces and different times can be quantitatively compared in respect of the bigness of the extension or the duration comprised in them. On the other hand, the percept of space or time is not one of mere extension or duration. It has a very different *qualitative* aspect. We perceive along with the magnitude of the extension the *form* of its outline. This perception of spatial form depends in the last resort upon perception of the *direction* assumed by the bounding line or lines. Similarly, in dealing with only one dimension of perceived space, we never perceive *length* (a spatial magnitude) apart from the perception of *direction* (a spatial

quality). The same is true of the perception of time. The lapses of duration we immediately perceive have all their special direction-quality; the "specious present" is essentially a simultaneously presented *succession*, *i.e.* a transition from before to after. It must be added that, in perceptual space and time, the directions thus perceived have a unique relation to the perceiving subject, and are thus all qualitatively distinct and irreversible. Direction in space is estimated as right, left, up, down, etc., by reference to axes through the centre of the percipient's body at right angles to each other, and is thus for any given moment of experience uniquely and unambiguously determined. Direction in time is similarly estimated with reference to the actual content of the "focus of consciousness." What is actually focal is "now," what is ceasing to be focal is "past," what is just coming to be focal is "future" in its direction.[1]

This is perhaps the most fundamental and important peculiarity of the space and time of actual perception. All directions in them are unambiguously determined by reference to the *here* and *now* of the immediate experience of an individual subject. As a consequence, every individual subject has his own special perceptual space and time; Geometry and Mechanics depend, to be sure, on the possibility of the establishment of correspondences between these spatial and temporal systems, but it is essential to remember that, properly speaking, the space and time system of each individual's perception is composed of directions radiating out from his unique *here* and *now*, and is therefore individual to himself.[2]

§ 3. *The Construction of the Conceptual Space and Time Order of Science.* For the purposes of practical life, no less than for the subsequent object of scientific description of the physical order, it is indispensably necessary to establish equations or correspondences between the individual space and time systems of different percipients. Apart from such

---

[1] We are not called upon to enter into such specially psychological questions as, *e.g.*, whether both directions, past and future, can be detected within the "specious present" of direct perception, or whether the specious present only contains the elements "now" and "no longer," the "not yet" being a subsequent intellectual construction, as is held, *e.g.*, by Mr. Bradley and Mr. Shadworth Hodgson.

[2] We may indeed go still further, and say that every unique moment of experience has its own unique spatial and temporal system. The method by which I weave the perceived space-time systems of different experiences within my own mental life into a single conceptual system, is in principle the same by which the spaces and times of myself and other men are made into one system for the purpose of practical intercourse.

correspondences, it would be impossible for one subject to translate the spatial and temporal system of any other into terms of his own experience, and thus all practical intercourse for the purpose of communicating directions for action would come to an end. For the communication of such practical directions it is imperative that we should be able mentally to reconstruct the spatial and temporal aspects of our experience in a form independent of reference to the special *here* and *now* of this or that individual moment of experience. Thus, like the rest of our scientific constructions, the establishment of a single conceptual space and time system for the whole of the physical order is ultimately a postulate required by our practical needs, and we must therefore be prepared to face the possibility that, like other postulates of the same kind, it involves assumptions which are not logically defensible. The construction is valuable, so far as it does its work of rendering intercommunication between individuals possible; that it should correspond to the ultimate structure of Reality any further than the requirements of practical life demand is superfluous.

The main processes involved in the construction of the conceptual space and time of descriptive science are three,— synthesis, analysis, abstraction. (*a*) *Synthesis*. Psychologically speaking, it is ultimately by the active movements of individual percipients that the synthesis of the individual's various perceptual spaces into one is effected. As attention is successively directed, even while the body as a whole remains stationary, to different parts of the whole expanse before the eye, the visual space which was originally " focal " in presentation becomes " marginal," and the " marginal " focal by a sensibly gradual transition. When to the movements of head and eyes which accompany such changes in attention there are added movements of locomotion of the whole body, this process is carried further, and we have the gradual disappearance of originally presented spaces from presentation, accompanied by the gradual emergence of spaces previously not presented at all. This leads to the mental construction of a wider space containing *all* the individual's different presentation-spaces, the order in which it contains them being determined by the felt direction of the movements required for the transition from one to another.

As we learn, through intercommunication with our fellows, of the existence for their perception of perceptual extension never directly presented to our own senses, the process of synthesis is extended further, so as to comprise in a single spatial system all the presentation-spaces of all the individual percipients in an order once again determined by the direction of the movements of transition from each to the others. Finally, as there is nothing in the principle of such a synthesis to impose limits upon its repetition, we think of the process as capable of indefinite continuance, and thus arrive at the concept of a space stretching out in all directions without definite bounds. This unending repetition of the synthesis of perceived spaces seems to be the foundation of what appears in theory as the Infinity of Space.

Precisely similar is the synthesis by which we mentally construct a single time system for the events of the physical order. *Now* means for me the content which occupies the centre of attentive interest. As attention is concentrated on the different stages in the realisation of an interest, this centre shifts; what was central becomes first marginal and then evanescent, what was marginal becomes central. Hence arises the conception of the events of my own inner life as forming a succession of moments, with a determinate order, each of which has been a *now*, or point of departure for directions in perceptual time, in its turn. As with space so with time, the intrasubjective intercourse of man with man makes it possible for me mentally to extend this conceptual synthesis of moments of time so as to include *nows* belonging to the experience of others which were already past before the first *now* of their experiences which I can synchronise with a *now* of my own, and again *nows* of their experiences relatively to which the last *now* which synchronises with one of my own is past. The indefinite repetition of such a synthesis leads, as before with space, to the thought of a duration reaching out endlessly into past and future, and thus gives us the familiar concept of the Infinity of Time.[1]

(*b*) *Analysis*. Equally important is the part played by mental *analysis* in the formation of the conceptual space and time system. As we have already seen, successive attention to lesser parts of a presented extension, or a presented lapse, reveals within each lesser part the same structure which belongs to the whole, and thus establishes the *sensible continuity* of space and time. In actual fact, the process of attending successively to smaller and yet smaller portions of space and time cannot, of course, be carried on indefinitely, but we can conceptually frame to ourselves the thought of the indefinite repetition of the process beyond the limits arbitrarily imposed

---

[1] For an account of the psychological processes involved in all this, see, *e.g.*, Stout, *Manual of Psychology*,[3] bk. iii. pt. 2, chaps. 3-5; bk. iv. chap. 6.

on it by the span of our own attention. Thus, by an act of mental analysis, we arrive at the concept of space and time as *indefinitely divisible*, or possessed of no ultimately un-analysable last parts, which is an indispensable pre-requisite of Geometry and Dynamics.

This indefinite divisibility of conceptual space and time is not of itself enough, as is often supposed, to establish their *continuity* in the strict mathematical sense of the word; their continuity depends upon the further assumption that whatever divides a series of positions in space or events in time unambiguously into two mutually exclusive classes, is itself a position in the space or event in the time series. This assumption does not seem to be absolutely requisite for all scientific treatment of the problems of space and time,[1] but is demanded for the systematic establishment of the correspondence between the spatial and temporal series and the continuous series of the real numbers. Moreover, it seems impossible to assign any positive content to the notion of a something which should bisect the spatial or temporal order without occupying a position in that order. Hence we seem inevitably led by the same analytical process which conducts us to the conception of the spatial and temporal orders as infinite series to think of them also as continuous series in the strict sense of the term. The alternative conception of them as discontinuous, if not absolutely excluded, does not seem to be called for by any positive motive, and is incompatible with the complete execution of the purposes which demand application of the number-series to a spatial or temporal content.

(c) *Abstraction*. The part played by abstraction in the formation of the conceptual space and time order out of the data of perception is often overlooked by theorists, but is of fundamental importance, as we shall see immediately. We have already learned that the most significant fact about the time and space order of individual experience is that its directions are *unique*, because they radiate out from the unique *here* and *now* of immediate feeling. In the construction of the conceptual space and time order we make entire abstraction from this dependence on the immediate feeling of a subject. Conceptual space contains an infinity of positions, but none of them is a *here;* conceptual time an infinity of moments, but none of them is a *now*. As the time and space of the conceptual order are taken in abstraction from the differences

---

[1] Thus Dedekind (*Was sind und was sollen die Zahlen?* p. xii.) maintains that none of the constructions of Euclid involve the continuity of space.

between individual points of view, no one point in either can be regarded as having more claim than any other to be the natural "origin of co-ordinates" with reference to which directions are estimated. We shall have repeated opportunity in the remainder of this chapter to observe how important are the consequences of this abstraction.

Abstraction also enters in another way into the construction by which conceptual space and time are created. Actual perceived space and time are indeed never empty, but always filled with a content of " secondary " qualities. In other words, they are always one aspect of a larger whole of fact. Extension is never perceived apart from some further visual or tactual quality of the extended, temporal lapse never perceived without some change in presented content, however slight. But in constructing the conceptual space and time system, we abstract altogether from this qualitative aspect; we think solely of the variety of positions and directions in time and space without taking any account of the further qualitative differences with which they are accompanied in concrete experience. Thus we come by the notion of an *empty* space and an *empty* time as mere systems of positions into which various contents may subsequently be put.

Strictly speaking, the notion of an empty space or an empty time is unmeaning, as the simple experiment of thinking of their existence is sufficient to show. We cannot in thought successfully separate the spatial and temporal aspects of experience from the rest of the whole to which they belong and take them as subsisting by themselves, any more than we can take timbre as subsisting apart from musical pitch or colour-tone from saturation. We can, however, confine our attention to the spatial-temporal system of positions without taking into account the special secondary properties of the extended and successive. It is from this logical abstraction that the illusion arises when we imagine an empty set of spatial and temporal positions as having first to exist in order that they may be subsequently " filled " with a variety of contents.[1]

§ 4. *Characteristics of the Conceptual Time and Space*

[1] Of course, a physical *vacuum* is not the same thing as *empty space*. For the purposes of any special science a *vacuum* means a space not occupied by contents of the special kind in which that special science is interested. Thus, in the ordinary parlance of Physics, a *vacuum* means simply a space in which there is no *mass*. Whether it is desirable, for the purposes of physical science, to assume the existence of *vacuum*, is altogether a question for Physics itself, and to decide it in the affirmative is not to maintain the existence of that unmeaning abstraction, absolutely empty space. In any case, it may be observed that the widespread notion that motion is only possible in a physical *vacuum* is a mistake, motion being perfectly possible in a fluid *plenum*.

Order. The following characteristics of the conceptual space and time created by the construction we have just examined, call for special notice. Conceptual space and time are necessarily taken, for reasons already explained, to be *unlimited*, and *indefinitely divisible*. Though it does not seem inevitable that they should be *continuous*, we appear to be unable to attach any positive meaning to the notion of their discontinuity, and, in the practical need for the application to them of the complete number-series, we have a valid positive ground for taking them as continuous. But space and time are thus resolved, in the process of their conceptual construction, into *continuous infinite series* of which the terms are spatial and temporal positions or points. Unlike the *parts* of perceptual space and time, these conceptual terms are not themselves spaces or times, as they contain no internal multiplicity of structure. Conceptual space and time are thus not wholes or aggregates of parts, but systems of relations between terms which possess no quantitative character.

Between any two terms of the spatial, or again of the temporal, series there is one unique relation, which is completely determined by the assignment of the terms, their *distance*. In the temporal series, which has only one dimension, you can only pass from any one given term to any other through a series of intermediate terms which is once and for all determined when the initial and final terms are given, hence nothing is required beyond the terms themselves to fix their distance. The spatial series is multi-dimensional, *i.e.* you can pass from any one term in it to any second by an indefinite variety of routes through intermediate terms, but it is still true that there is one and only one such route which is completely determined when the terms in question are known, namely, the straight line passing through both. This straight line constitutes the unique *distance* of the two points from each other.[1] Thus the

---

[1] It must be carefully noted that *distance* as thus defined is not properly a *quantitative relation*, and involves no notion of magnitude, but only of relative place in a series. It should also be observed that in assuming the existence of such a unique relation between every pair of points, it is tacitly taken for granted that the number of dimensions of the spatial order is finite. In a space of an infinite number of dimensions, such unique relation would be impossible. (See Russell, *Foundations of Geometry*, p. 161 ff.) Our justification for making this assumption, as also for taking time to be of one dimension only, seems to be that it is indispensable for all those practical purposes which depend on our ability to create a science of Geometry, and that we have no positive ground for assuming the opposite. Thus ultimately the assumption appears to be of the nature of a postulate.

genuine concept of which those of space and time are species is not that of *magnitude* or *quantity*, but of *serial order*.

Further, and this is a point of fundamental difference between conceptual space and time, and the spaces and times of immediate perception, any one position in either order, taken by itself, is qualitatively indistinguishable from any other. All points of space, all moments of time, are alike, or, as it is also phrased, conceptual space and time are *homogeneous* throughout. It is not until you take at least two terms of the spatial or temporal series and consider the relation they determine, that distinction becomes possible. This homogeneity of conceptual space and time is an inevitable consequence of the abstraction from the immediate feelings of the individual subject of experience involved, as we saw, in the process of their construction. In our actual perception of spatial and temporal extension, that part of perceived space and time which stands in direct unity with immediate feeling is qualitatively distinguished as the *here* and *now* from all the rest, and thus does not depend upon the specification of a second spatial or temporal position for its recognisability. *Here* is where *I* am, *now* is *this* felt present. And similarly, every other part of the actually presented space and time gets a unique qualitative character from its special relation to this *here* and *now;* it is right or left, behind or in front, before or after. When we abstract altogether from the unique relation with individual experience which thus makes the *here* and *now* of perception, as we do in constructing our conceptual space and time order, every position alike becomes the mere possibility of a *here* or a *now*, and as such mere possibilities the various positions are indistinguishable. Practically, this homogeneity is important as the indispensable condition for the quantitative comparison of different portions of extension or duration.

An apparently inevitable consequence of the homogeneity of conceptual space and time is the *relativity* of spatial and temporal position. As we have seen, positions in conceptual space and time are not distinguishable until you take them in pairs. In other words, to fix one position in space or one date you have to give its relation to another position or date, and similarly to fix this you must specify a third, and so on indefinitely. To say *where* A is means to say how you get to it from B, and B again is only known by the way it is reached from C, and so on without end. Logically, this is a simple consequence of the nature of space and time as conceptually analysed into endless series To specify any term in the series you must give the unique relation it bears to some other term, its logical *distance*. And, in a series which has neither first nor last term, this second term cannot be defined except by its logical distance from a third. In actual perception this difficulty is avoided, owing to the fact that immediate feeling gives us the *here* and *now* from which all our directions are measured. But in conceptual space or time there is nothing to distinguish any one here which we may take as our " origin of co-ordinates," or any one now which we take as our present from any other, and hence the endless regress seems inevitable.

It follows, of course, that in conceptual space and time there is no principle by which to distinguish different directions. In perception they can be distinguished as right and left, up and down, and so forth. But since what is right to one percipient is left to another, in conceptual space, where complete abstraction is made from the presence of an individual percipient, there is neither right nor left, up nor down, nor any other qualitative difference between one direction and another, all such differences being *relative* to the individual percipient. When we wish to introduce into conceptual space distinctions between directions, we always have to begin by arbitrarily assigning some standard direction as our point of departure. Thus we take, *e.g.*, an arbitrarily selected line _____ as such a standard for a given plane,
       A   B
and proceed to distinguish all other directions by the angle they make with A B and the *sense* in which they are estimated (whether as from B to A or from A to B). But both the line A B and the difference of sense between A B and B A can only be defined by similar reference to some other standard direction, and so on through the endless regress.

Similarly with conceptual time. Here, as there is only one dimension, the difficulty is less obvious, but it is no less real. In conceptual time there is absolutely no means of distinguishing before from after, past from future. For the past means the direction of our memories, the direction qualified by the feeling of "no longer"; the future is the direction of anticipation and purposive adaptation, the direction of "not yet." And, apart from the reference given by immediate feeling to the purposive life of an individual subject, these directions cannot be discriminated. In short, conceptual time and space are essentially relative, because they are systems of relations which have no meaning apart from qualitative differences in the terms which they relate;

while yet again, for the purpose of the conceptual construction which yields them, the terms have to be taken as having no character but that which they possess in right of the relations.[1]

One other feature of the space and time construction is sufficiently important to call for special mention. Space and time are commonly thought of as *unities* of some kind. All spatial positions, it is usually assumed, fall within one system of space-relations; all dates have their place in one all-inclusive time. This character of unity completes the current conception of the spatial and temporal order. Each of those orders is a unity, including all possible spatial or temporal positions; each is an endless, infinite, continuous series of positions, which all are purely relative. There are other peculiarities, especially of the current concepts of space, with which it is not necessary to deal here, as they are of an accidental kind, not arising out of the essential nature of the process by which the conception is constructed. Thus it is probably a current assumption that the number of dimensions in space is three and no more, and again that the Euclidean postulate about parallels is verified by its constitution. As far as perceptual space is concerned, those assumptions depend, I presume, upon empirical verification; there seems to be no reason why they should be made for the conceptual space-order, since it is quite certain that a coherent science of spatial relations can be constructed without recourse to them.[2]

---

[1] The ablest detailed account of the relativity of spatial position readily accessible to the English reader, will be found in Mr. Russell's *Foundations of Geometry*, chaps. iiiA, iv. Mr. Russell has since, in *Mind* for July 1901, attempted to prove the opposite view, that positions in space and time are *inherently* distinct, but without discussing his own previous arguments for relativity. Into the purely mathematical part of Mr. Russell's later contentions I am not competent to enter. I may, however, suggest that the question of Metaphysics cannot be decided merely by urging, as Mr. Russell does, that fewer assumptions are required to construct a geometry on the hypothesis of absolute than on that of relative position. The superior convenience of an assumption for certain special purposes is no proof of its ultimate intelligibility. And when Mr. Russell goes on to admit that points in space are *indistinguishable for us*, he seems to me to give up his case. For is not this to admit that, after all, the space with which we deal in our geometrical science is relative from beginning to end? How differences of quality of which we, by hypothesis, can know nothing, can help or hinder our scientific constructions, it is indeed hard to see.

[2] This may be brought home even to those who, like myself, are not mathematicians, by the perusal of such a work as Lobatchevsky's *Untersuchungen zur Theorie der Parallel-Linien*, where a consistent geometry of triangles is constructed in entire independence of the postulate of parallelism. Of course, in the end it must be a mere question of nomenclature whether a form of serial order independent of these quasi-empirical restrictions is to be called "space" or not.

§ 5. The question now is, whether the whole of this spatial and temporal construction is more than imperfect, and therefore contradictory, appearance. I will first state in a general form the arguments for regarding it as appearance, and then proceed to reinforce this conclusion by dealing with some special difficulties. Finally, I propose to ask whether we can form some positive conception of the higher order of Reality of which the spatial and temporal series are phenomenal.

That the space and time order is phenomenal and not ultimate, can, I think, be conclusively shown by a general argument which I will first enunciate in principle and then develop somewhat more in detail. An all-comprehensive experience cannot apprehend the detail of existence under the forms of space and time for the following reason. Such an experience could be neither of space and time as we perceive them, nor of space and time as we conceptually reconstruct them. It would not be of perceptual space and time, because the whole character of our perceptual space and time depends upon the very imperfections and limitations which make our experience fragmentary and imperfect. Perceptual space and time are for me what they are, because I see them, so to say, in perspective from the special standpoint of my own particular *here* and *now*. If that standpoint were altered, so that what are actually for me *there* and *then* became my *here* and *now*, my whole outlook on the space and time order would suffer change. But the Absolute cannot look at the space and time order from the standpoint of my *here* and *now*. For it is the finitude of my interests and purposes which confine me in my outlook to this *here* and *now*. If my interests were not bound up in the special way in which they are with just this special part or aspect of the life of a wider whole, if they were co-extensive with the life of that whole, every place and every time would be my *here* and *now*. As it is, *here* is where my body is, *now* is this particular stage in the development of European social life, because these are the things in which I am primarily *interested*. And so with all the other finite experiences in which the detail of the absolute experience finds expression. Hence the absolute experience, being free from the limitations of interest which condition the finite experiences, cannot see the order of existence from the special standpoint of any of them, and therefore cannot apprehend it under the guise of the perceptual space and time system.

Again, it cannot apprehend existence under the forms of space and time as we conceptually reconstruct them. For Reality, for the absolute experience, must be a complete individual whole, with the ground of all its differentiations within itself. But conceptual space and time are constructed by deliberate abstraction from the relation to immediate experience implied in all individuality, and consequently, as we have just seen, they contain no real principle of internal distinction, their constituent terms being all exactly alike and indistinguishable. In short, if the perceptual time and space systems of our concrete experience represent individual but imperfect and finite points of view, the conceptual space and time of our scientific construction represents the mere abstract possibility of a finite point of view; neither gives a point of view both individual and infinite, and neither, therefore, can be the point of view of an absolute experience. An absolute experience must be out of time and out of space, in the sense that its contents are not apprehended in the form of the spatial and temporal series, but in some other way. Space and time, then, must be the phenomenal appearance of a higher reality which is spaceless and timeless.

§ 6. In principle, the foregoing argument appears to me to be complete, but, for the sake of readers who care to have its leading thought more fully developed, it may be re-stated thus. Perceptual space and time cannot be ultimately real as they stand. They are condemned already by the old difficulty which we found in the notion of reality as made up of qualities in relation. Perceptual space and time are aggregates of lesser parts, which are themselves spaces and times; thus they are relations between terms, each of which contains the same relation once more in itself, and so imply the now familiar indefinite regress.[1] Again, when we try in our conceptual space and time construction to remedy this defect by reducing space and time altogether to mere systems of relations, the difficulty turns out to have been merely evaded by such a process of abstraction. For, so long as we keep rigidly to our conceptual construction, the terms of our relations are indistinguishable. In purely conceptual space

---

[1] It must be carefully remembered that the essential defect of the indefinite regress is not its interminableness, but its monotony. We ourselves held that Reality is an individual composed of lesser individuals which *repeat* the structure of the whole, and that the number of these individuals need not be finite. But, in our view, the higher the order of individuality the more self-explanatory was its structure, whereas in the indefinite regress an incomprehensible construction is endlessly repeated *in the same form*.

and time, as we have seen, there is no possibility of distinguishing any one direction from any other, since all are qualitatively identical.

Indeed, it is obvious from first principles that when the sets of terms between which a number of relations of the same type holds are indistinguishable, the relations cannot be discriminated. To distinguish directions at all, we must, in the end, take at least our starting-point and one or more standard directions reckoned from it—according to the number of dimensions with which we are dealing—as independently given, that is, as having recognisable qualitative differences from other possible starting-points and standard directions. (Thus, to distinguish before and after in conceptual time, you must at least assume some moment of time, qualitatively recognisable from others, as the epoch from which you reckon, and must also have some recognisable qualitative distinction between the direction "past" and the direction "future.") And with this reference to qualitative differences we are at once thrown back, as in the case of perceptual time and space, on the insoluble old problem of Quality and Relation. The assumed starting-point and standard directions *must* have qualitative individuality, or they could not be independently recognised and made the basis for discrimination between the remaining directions and positions: yet, because of the necessary homogeneity of the space and time of conceptual construction, they *cannot* have any such qualitative individuality, but must be *arbitrarily* assumed. They will therefore themselves be capable of determination only by reference to some other equally arbitrary standard, and thus we are once more committed to the indefinite regress. The practical usefulness of these constructions thus depends on the very fact that we are not consistent in our use of them. In all practical applications we use them to map out the spatial and temporal order of events as seen in perspective from a standpoint which is, as regards the conceptual time and space order itself, arbitrary and indistinguishable from others.

§ 7. Instead of further elaborating this general argument, a task which would be superfluous if its principle is grasped, and unconvincing if it is missed, I will proceed to point out one or two special ways in which the essential arbitrariness of the spatial and temporal construction is strikingly exemplified. To begin with, a word may be said about the alleged *unity* of space and time. It is constantly taken for granted, by philosophers as well as by practical men, that there can be only *one* spatial and one temporal order, so that all spatial relations, and again all temporal relations, belong to the same system. Thus, if A has a spatial relation to B and C to D, it is assumed that there must be spatial relations between A and C, A and D, and B and C, B and D. Similarly if A is temporally related with B, and C with D. This view is manifestly presupposed in the current conception of Nature, the "physical universe," the "physical order," as the aggregate of all processes in space and time. But there seems to be no real logical warrant for it. In principle the alleged unity of all spatial and temporal relations might be dismissed, on the strength of the one consideration that space and time are not individual wholes, and therefore can contain no principle of internal structural unity. This is manifest from the method by which the space and time of our conceptual scheme have been constructed. They arose, as we saw, from the indefinite repetition of a single type of relation between terms in which we were unable to find any ultimately intelligible principle of internal structure. But unity of structure cannot be brought into that which does not already possess it by such mere endless repetition. The result of such a process will be as internally incoherent and devoid of structure as the original data. Hence space and time, being mere repetitions of the scheme of qualities in relation, cannot be true unities.

This becomes clearer if we reflect on the grounds which actually warrant us in assigning position in the *same* space and the *same* time to a number of events. For me A and B are ultimately in the same space when there is a way of travelling from A to B; they are in the same time when they belong to different stages in the accomplishment of the same systematic purposes. Thus in both cases it is ultimately from relation to an identical system of purposes and interests that different sets of positions or events belong to one space or one time. The unity of such a space or time is a pale reflection in abstract form of the unity of a life of systematic purpose, which is one because it has unique individual structure. It is in this way, from the individual unity of the purpose and interests of my ordinary waking life, that I derive the right to refer its experiences to a single space and time system. Similarly, it is in virtue of the inclusion of my own and my fellow-men's purposes in a wider whole of social systematic purpose that I can bring the space and time relations of their experience into one system with my own. And again, the sensible occurrences of the physical order belong to one space and time with the space and time relations of human experience, because of the varying ways in which they condition the development of our own inner purposive life. But there are cases, even within our own conscious life, where this condition appears to be absent, and in these cases we do not seem to be able to make intelligible use of the conception of a single time or a single space.

Take the case of our dreams. The events of my dreams stand in spatial and temporal relations within the dream itself, but there would be no sense in asking what are the spatial relations between the places seen in my dreams and the places marked on the map of England; or what are again the temporal relations between the events of last night's dream and those of this morning, or those of the dreams of last week. Precisely because there is usually no systematic identity of purpose connecting the dream with the waking life or with other dreams, the time and space of the dream have no position with respect to the time and space system of waking life, nor those of one dream with relation to those of another.[1] Of course, it may be said that the dream-space and dream-time are "imaginary," but the problem cannot be got rid of by the use of an epithet. To call them imaginary is merely to say that they are not systematically connected with the time and space of waking life, not to disprove their genuineness as actual space and time constructions.

Similarly, if there are intelligent purposes of which our human purposive life is debarred from taking account as such, as we urged that there must be behind the phenomenal physical order, the time and space within which those purposes are conceived and executed would have no place in *our* spatial and temporal system. The phenomenal events of the physical order would fall within our system, but not the life of inner purpose of which that order is the manifestation to our senses. Ultimately, in fact, all spaces and all times could only form one spatial and temporal system on condition that the infinite absolute experience views all its contents in spatial and temporal form; then the various space and time systems corresponding to the purposes of the various groups of finite individuals would finally, for the infinite individual, form one great system of time and space

---

[1] Normally, that is; for brevity's sake I omit to note the possible case of a coherent dream-life continued from night to night. In principle there would be no difference between the case of the space and time of *such* a dream-life and those of our waking hours.

relations. But we have already seen that the infinite experience cannot comprehend its contents in spatial or temporal forms.

We infer, then, that there may be—indeed, if our interpretation of the physical order is valid, there must be—a plurality of spaces and times within the Real. Within any one such space or time all its members are spatially and temporally interrelated, but the various spaces are not themselves related in space, nor the various times before or after one another in time. Their relation is the purely logical one of being varying modes of the expression in a finite detail of the underlying nature of the ultimate Reality.[1] For the absolute experience they must be all at once and together, not in the sense of being in " one space and time," but in the sense of forming together the systematic embodiment of one coherent ground or principle.

§ 8. Similar consequences, as to the phenomenal character of space and time, follow from the consideration of the familiar Kantian antinomies founded upon the concept of spatial and temporal infinity. Space and time must be externally boundless and internally indefinitely divisible, and yet again cannot be either. Freed from unessential accessories, the argument for either side of the antinomy may be stated thus. Space and time must be boundless because all spatial and temporal existence means spatial and temporal relation to a second term, itself similarly related to a third term. For precisely the same reason both must be indefinitely divisible. Yet again, they can be neither, since only the individual exists, and within such an interminable network of relations between terms which are nothing but the supporters of these relations there is no principle of individual structure.[2] Thus the Kantian antinomies are a

---

[1] So the events of my dreams, though not occupying any place in the temporal series of the events of waking life, are so far *logically* connected with that series as both sets of events stand in relation to certain identical elements of psychical temperament and disposition. Another interesting case is that of so-called " dual personality." The experience of both the two alternating personalities can be arranged in a single temporal series only because of the way in which both sets are inwoven with the systematic interests of other men, whose personality does not alternate, or alternates with a different rhythm. If all mankind were subject to simultaneous alternations of personality, the construction of a single time-series for all our experiences would be impossible. In this discussion I have throughout followed the full and thorough treatment of the problem by Mr. Bradley, *Appearance and Reality*, chap. 18.

[2] Otherwise, conceptual space and time are, as we have seen, derivatives of the number-series, and we have already learned that the number-series leads to the problem of summing an endless series, and is therefore not an adequate way of representing ultimate Reality. (Bk. II. chap. 4, § 10). Another form of

simple consequence of the old difficulty about quality and relation. Space and time must be mere relations, and the terms of those relations therefore qualitatively indistinguishable; again, since they are relations they cannot be relations between nothings or, what is the same thing, between terms with no individual character. As in all cases where the problem of relation and quality arises, it then conducts us to the indefinite regress.

So long as we continue to look upon space and time as real, we have therefore to choose between two equally illogical alternatives. We must either arbitrarily refuse to continue the indefinite regress beyond the point at which its difficulties become apparent, as is done by the assertion that space and time have finite bounds or indivisible parts, or we must hold that the absolute experience actually achieves the summation of an unending series. With the recognition that space and time are phenomenal, the result of a process of construction forced on us by our practical needs, but not adequately corresponding to the real nature of individual existence, the difficulty disappears. Both sides of the antinomy become relatively true, in the sense that for our practical purposes we must be content to adopt now the one and again the other; both become ultimately untrue in the sense that space and time, being constructions of our own, are *really* neither finite nor infinite series, but are the one or the other according to the purposes for which we use our construction.

§ 9. If spatial and temporal position and direction must thus in the end be appearance, phenomenal of some more individual reality, we have finally to ask, Of what are they the appearance? It is not enough to say "of ultimate Reality," or "of the Absolute." *Ultimately* this is, no doubt, true of space and time, as it is of everything else, but we desire further to know if they are not *proximately* the appearance of some special features of the inner physical life of the lesser individuals which compose the Absolute. We naturally look for some third term, in the nature of finite individuality, to mediate between the structureless abstract generality of space and time relation, and the perfect individual structure of the spaceless and timeless Absolute Individual. We want, in fact, to connect the spatial and temporal form which our

the same difficulty would be that conceptual space and time are applications of the numerical series,—but application to *what?* To a material which is already spatial and temporal. All these puzzles are only different ways of expressing the essential relativity of space and time. But see the anti-Kantian view in, *e.g.*, Couturat, *L'Infini Mathématique*, pt. 2.

experience wears, with some fundamental aspect of our nature, as beings at once individual and finite.

Nor is it particularly difficult to make the connection. When we remember that space and time, as they actually condition our perception and movement, are the space and time which radiate out from an unique *here* and *now* of immediate feeling, it is fairly evident that the spatial and temporal aspect of our experience is, as already suggested, a consequence of that limitation of our attentive interests which constitutes our finitude. It is the narrowness of my interests, or at least of those which are sufficiently explicit to rise into the "focus" of consciousness, that is reflected in the distinction of my *here* from all the *theres* which are around me. *Here* is where my body is, because of the specially intimate connection of the realisation of my interests and purposes with those events in the phenomenal physical order which I call the state of my body. Were my interests widened so as to embrace the whole scheme of the universe, I should no longer perceive the contents of that universe as dispersed through space, because I should no longer have as my special standpoint a *here* to which other existence would be *there*.

My special standpoint in space may thus be said to be phenomenal of my special and peculiar interests in life, the special *logical* standpoint from which my experience reflects the ultimate structure of the Absolute. And so, generally, though the conclusion can for various reasons not be pressed in respect of every detail of spatial appearance, the spatial grouping of intelligent purposive beings is phenomenal of their inner logical affinity of interest and purpose. Groups of such beings, closely associated together in space, are commonly also associated in their peculiar interests, their special purposes, their characteristic attitude towards the universe. The local contiguity of the members of the group is but an "outward and visible sign" of an "inward and spiritual" community of social aspiration. This is, of course, only approximately the case; the less the extent to which any section of mankind have succeeded in actively controlling the physical order for the realisation of their own purposes, the more nearly is it the truth that spatial remoteness and inner dissimilarity of social purposes coincide. In proportion as man's conquest over his non-human environment becomes complete, he devises for himself means to retain the inner unity of social aims and interests in spite of spatial separation. But this only shows once more how completely the spatial order is a mere imperfect appearance which only confusedly adumbrates the nature of the higher Reality behind it. Thus we may say that the "abolition of distance" effected by science and civilisation is, as it were, a practical vindication of our metaphysical doctrine of the comparative unreality of space.

Similarly with time, though the temporal series may, in a sense, be said to be less of an unreality than the spatial. For it does not seem possible to show that spatial appearance is an *inevitable* form of finite experience. We can at least conceive of a finite experience composed entirely of successive arrangements of secondary qualities, such as sounds or smells, and the accompanying feeling-tones, though we have no positive ground for affirming the existence of such a type of experience. But the temporal form seems inseparable from finite intelligence. For the limitation of my existence to a certain portion of time is clearly simply the abstract and external aspect of the fact that my interests and purposes, so far as I can apprehend the meaning of my own life, occupy just this special place in the logical development of the larger whole of social life and purpose of which my own life is a member. So the position of a particular purposive act in the temporal series of acts which I call the history of my own life, is the outward indication of the logical place filled by this particular act in the connected scheme of interests which form my life on its inner side. But it is an inevitable consequence of the want of complete internal harmony we call finitude, that the aims and interests of the finite subject cannot be in the same degree present to its apprehension all at once and together. In being aware of its own internal purpose or meaning, it must, because it is finite and therefore not ultimately a completely harmonious systematic whole, be aware of that purpose as only partially fulfilled. And in this sense of one's own purposes as only partially fulfilled, we have the foundation of the time-experience, with its contrast between the "now" of fulfilment and the "no longer" and "not yet" of dissatisfied aspiration.

For this reason, dissatisfaction, unfulfilled craving, and the time-experience seem to be bound up together, and time to be merely the abstract expression of the yearning of the finite individual for a systematic realisation of its own purpose which lies for ever beyond its reach as finite. If this is so, only the absolute and infinite individual whose experience is throughout that of perfectly harmonious systematic realisation of meaning, can be outside the time-process; to it, "vanished and present are the same," because its whole nature is once for all perfectly expressed in the detail of existence. But the finite, just because its very nature as finite is to aspire to a perfection which is out of reach, must have its experience marked with the distinction of *now* from *by and by*, of desire from performance. In this temporal character of all finite experience we may perhaps afterwards discern the ultimate ground of morality, as we can already discern in the unresting struggle of the finite to overcome its finitude, practical evidence that time is not a form which adequately expresses the nature of Reality, and must therefore be imperfect appearance.[1]

Thus we seem finally to have reached the conclusion that time and space are the imperfect phenomenal manifestation of the logical relations between the purposes of finite individuals standing in social relations to each other; the inner purposive life of each of these individuals being itself in its turn, as we have previously seen, the imperfect expression, from a special logical "point of view," of the structure and life of the ultimate infinite individual. For the infinite individual itself the whole of the purposes and interests of the finite individuals must form a single harmonious system. This system cannot itself be in the spatial and temporal form; space and time must thus in some way cease to exist, as space and time, for the absolute experience. They must, in that experience, be taken up, rearranged, and transcended, so as to lose their character of an endless chain of relations between other relations.

Precisely *how* this is effected, we, from our finite standpoint, cannot presume to say. It is natural to draw illustrations from the "specious present" of perception, in which we appear to have a succession that is also simultaneous; or again, from the timeless and purely logical character science seeks to ascribe to its "laws of nature." But in the "specious present" we seem obliged to attend to *one* aspect, succession or simultaneity, to the exclusion of the other; probably we never succeed in equally fixing both aspects at once. It thus presents us rather with the problem than with its solution. And again, after our discussion of the meaning of law, we cannot affirm that Nature is, for the absolute experience, a system of general laws. Hence it seems well not to take

---

[1] Compare Prof. Royce's remarks, *The World and the Individual*, Second Series, lect. 3, "The Temporal and the Eternal," p. 134. I should certainly have had to acknowledge considerable obligation to Prof. Royce's discussion had not the present chapter been written before I had an opportunity of studying it.

these illustrations for more than they are actually worth as indications of the merely phenomenal character of time. Metaphysics, like the old scholastic theology, needs sometimes to be reminded that God's thoughts are not as ours, and His ways, in a very real sense when Philosophy has done its best, still past finding out.[1]

Consult further:—F. H. Bradley, *Appearance and Reality*, chaps. 4 (Space and Time), 18 (Temporal and Spatial Appearance); L. Couturat, *L'Infini Mathématique*, pt. 2, bk. iv. chap. 4 (against the Kantian antinomies); H. Poincaré, *La Science et L'Hypothèse*, pp. 68–109; H. Lotze, *Metaphysic*, bk. ii. chaps. 1–3; W. Ostwald, *Vorlesungen über Naturphilosophie*, lects. 5, 8; J. Royce, *The World and the Individual*, Second Series, lect. 3; B. Russell, *Foundations of Geometry: Is Position in Space and Time Absolute or Relative* (*Mind*, July 1901), *Principles of Mathematics*, pt. 6, vol. i.; H. Spencer, *First Principles*, pt. 2, chap. 3.

---

[1] Against the plausible attempt to solve the problem by simply thinking of the whole physical order as forming a "specious present" to the Absolute Experience, we may urge that the "specious present" itself regularly consists for us of a multiplicity of detail, which we apprehend as simultaneous without insight into its inner unity as the embodiment of coherent system. Hence the direct insight of the Absolute Experience into its own internal meaning or structure cannot be adequately thought of as mere simultaneous awareness of the detail of existence. So long as a succession is merely apprehended as simultaneous, its meaning is not yet grasped.

CHAPTER V

SOME CONDITIONS OF EVOLUTION

§ 1. The concept of *evolution* an attempt to interpret natural processes in terms of individual growth. § 2. Evolution means change culminating in an end which is the result of the process and is qualitatively new. The concept is thus teleological. § 3. Evolution, being teleological, is essentially either progress or degeneration. If it is more than illusion, there must be real *ends* in the physical order. And ends can only be real as subjective interests of sentient beings which are actualised by the process of change. § 4. Thus all evolution must take place within an *individual* subject. § 5. Further, the subject of evolution must be a *finite* individual. All attempts to make "evolution" a property of the whole of Reality lead to the infinite regress. § 6. The distinction between progressive evolution and degeneration has an "objective" basis in the metaphysical distinction between higher and lower degrees of individuality. § 7. In the evolutionary process, old individuals disappear and fresh ones originate. Hence evolution is incompatible with the view that Reality consists of a plurality of ultimately independent finite individuals.

§ 1. WE saw, in the first chapter of the present Book, that evolution or orderly development is a fundamental characteristic of the processes which compose the physical order as apprehended by the various empirical sciences. For the purposes of Mechanics and Mechanical Physics, indeed, we have no need to look upon Nature as the scene of development; for these sciences it is enough to conceive of it as a vast complex of changes of configuration and transformations of energy, connected by regular uniformities of sequence. As soon, however, as we come to regard Nature from the standpoint of those sciences which explicitly recognise differences of *quality*, as well as differences in position and quantity, among the objects with which they deal, this narrowly mechanistic conception of natural processes becomes inadequate. With the notion of physical processes as productive of changes of quality we are inevitably led to think of the physical order as a world in which the qualitatively new is derived from, or developed out of, the previously familiar by fixed lines of deviation and under determinate conditions.

Naturally enough, it is from the biological sciences, in

which the study of organic *growth* plays so prominent a part, that the impulse to conceive of physical change as development originally comes. As long ago as the fourth century B.C., Aristotle had taken the concept of growth or development as the foundation of the most influential scheme of metaphysical construction yet produced in the whole history of speculation. In Aristotle's view, however, the process of development was regarded as strictly confined within the limits of the individual life. The individual organism, beginning its existence as an undeveloped germ or potentiality, gradually unfolds itself in a series of successive stages of growth, which culminates at the period of complete maturity. But the individual germ itself is a product or secretion derived from a pre-existing mature individual of the same type as that into which this germ will ultimately grow. The number of distinct typical processes of growth is thus strictly determined, and each such process implies the previous existence of its completed result. In other words, the boundaries between *species* are fixed and ultimate; there can be no beginning in time of the existence of a new species, and therefore no origination of new species by development from other types. As Aristotle epigrammatically puts it, " It takes a man to beget a man."

A further point of weakness in the Aristotelian theory is the absence of any definite account of the *machinery* by which the process of growth is effected. We learn, indeed, that the latent capacity of the organic germ to develop according to a certain specific type is stimulated into activity by influences contained in the environment, but the precise nature of this process of stimulation was necessarily left in obscurity, in consequence of the imperfect knowledge possessed by Aristotle of the minute character of natural processes in general.

In the evolutionary theories of modern biology, it is precisely the problems of the origination of new *species*, and of the special character of the relations between the species and its environment by which this process is conditioned, that have attracted almost exclusive attention. And, with the steadily increasing success of evolutionary hypotheses in dealing with biological problems, there has naturally arisen a tendency to extend the application of the general concept of evolution far beyond the sphere in which it first originated. We have now not only more or less well-accredited hypotheses of the production by evolution of our chemical elements, but even ambitious philosophical constructions which treat the concept of evolution as the one and only key to all the problems of existence. In the presence of these far-reaching applications of evolutionary ideas, it becomes all the more necessary to bear in mind, in our estimate of the worth of the evolution concept, that its logical character remains unaltered by the extension of its sphere of applicability; it is still, in spite of all minor modifications, essentially an attempt to interpret natural processes in general in terms of individual growth.

We are not, of course, in the present chapter in any way concerned with the details of any one particular theory as to the special conditions which determine the course of organic or other evolution. What those conditions in any special case are, is a question, in the first instance, for that particular branch of empirical science which deals with the description of the particular aspect of the processes of the physical order under investigation. And though it would be a proper question for a complete Philosophy of Nature how the details of a well-established scientific theory must be interpreted so as to harmonise with the general metaphysical implications of the physical order, it is for many reasons premature to raise such a question in the present state of our actual knowledge of the details of evolutionary processes. All that can be done here is to ask what in general are the logical implications involved in thinking of a process as an evolution at all, and how those implications are related to our general interpretation of the physical order.

§ 2. Evolution obviously involves the two concepts, already criticised at length, of change and the dependence of the order and direction of change upon determinate conditions. But an evolutionary process is never a mere orderly sequence of changes. For instance, the changes of configuration and exchanges of energy which take place when work is done in a material system, conceived as composed of moving masses without any element of secondary quality, are not properly to be called a process of evolution. They are not an evolution or development, because, so long as we keep to the strictly kinetic view of natural processes as consisting solely in the varying configuration of systems of mass-particles, the end of the process is qualitatively undistinguishable from its beginning; nothing qualitatively *new* has emerged as its result. Or rather, to speak with more accuracy, the process has really no *end* and no unity of its own. It is only by an entirely arbitrary limitation of view, due to purely subjective interests of our own, that we isolate just this collection of mass-particles from the larger aggregate of such particles which form the physical order as regarded from the strictly kinetic standpoint, and call it *one system;* and again, it is with equal arbitrariness that we determine the point of time beyond which we shall cease to follow the system's changes of configuration. In the indefinitely prolonged series of successive configurations there is no stage which can properly be called final. Hence from the rigidly mechanistic point of view of Kinetics and Kinematics there are no evolutions or developments in the universe, there is only continuous change.

Development or evolution, then, definitely implies the culmination of a process of change in the establishment of a state of things which is relatively *new*, and implies, further, that the relatively new state of things may truly be regarded as the end or completion of this special process of change. Thus the fundamental peculiarity of all evolutionary ideas is that they are essentially *teleological;* the changes which are evolutions are all changes thought of as throughout relative to an *end* or *result*. Except in so far as a process of change is thus essentially relative to the *result* in which it culminates, there is no sense in calling it a development. We may see this even by considering the way in which the concepts of evolution and devolopment are used in the various departments of Physics. We sometimes speak of a chemical process as marked by the "evolution" of heat, or again we say that, if the second law of Thermo-dynamics is rigidly and universally true, the physical universe must be in a process of evolution towards a stage in which none of its energy will be available for work. But we can only attach a meaning to such language so long as we allow ourselves to retain the common-sense point of view according to which there are real qualitative differences between what abstract Mechanics treats as equivalent forms of "energy."

We can speak of the evolution of heat, just because we, consciously or unconsciously, think of heat as being really, what it is for our senses, something qualitatively new and distinct from the other kinds of energy which are converted into it by the chemical process. So we can intelligibly talk of the gradual conversion of one form of energy into another as an evolution only so long as we regard the various forms of energy as qualitatively different, and are therefore entitled to look upon the complete conversion of the one into another as the qualitatively new result of a process which is therefore terminated by its complete establishment. From the standpoint of the physical theories which regard the distinction between the forms of energy as only "subjective," there would be no sense in regarding that particular stage in the course of events at which one form of energy disappeared as the *end* or result of a process which terminates in it, and thus such terms as evolution and development would lose their meaning. Only the establishment of the qualitatively new can form a real *end* or *result*, and so afford a logical basis for the recognition of the changes in the physical order as distinct processes of development.

§ 3. This essentially teleological character of development is emphasised in the language of the biological sciences by the constant use of the concepts of progress and degeneration. For biology an evolution is essentially a process either in the progressive or in the regressive direction. Every evolution is an advance to a "higher" or a decline to a "lower" state of development. Now progress and regress are only possible where the process of change is regarded as throughout relative to the *end* to be attained by the process. Exactly how we conceive this end, which serves us as a standard for distinguishing progress from degeneration, is a secondary question; the point of fundamental importance is that, except in reference to such an end, there can be no distinction at all between progressive and retrogressive change. Thus, unless there are really ends in the physical order which determine the processes of change that culminate in their actual establishment, evolution cannot be real. If the ends, by the establishment of which we estimate progress in devolopment, are merely arbitrary standards of our own to which nothing in external reality corresponds, then the physical order must really be a mere succession of changes which are in no true sense developments, and the whole concept of nature as marked by development will be a mere human delusion. And, on the contrary, if there is any truth in the great scientific conceptions of evolution, there must be real ends in the physical order.

Now, there is only one intelligible way in which we can think of a process of change as really relative to an *end*. The resultant state which we call the end of the process, as being the final stage which completes this special process, and enables us to mark off all that succeeds it as belonging to a fresh process of development, must also be its end in the sense of being the conscious attainment of an *interest* or purpose underlying the whole process. It is only in so far as any state of things is, for some sentient being, the realisation of a subjective interest previously manifested in an earlier stage of experience, that that state of things forms the real culmination of a process which is distinguished from all other processes, and stamped with an individuality of its own, by the fact that it does culminate in precisely this result. The conceptions of *end* or *result* and of subjective *interest* are logically inseparable. Hence we seem forced to infer that, since evolution is an unmeaning word, unless there are genuine, and not merely arbitrarily assigned, ends underlying the processes of physical nature, the concept of evolution as characteristic of the physical order involves the metaphysical interpretation of that order as consisting of the teleological acts of sentient beings, which we had previously accepted on more general grounds. It would be useless to attempt an escape from this conclusion by drawing a distinction between two meanings of "end"—"a *last* state" and "the achievement of a purpose." For the whole point of the preceding argument was that nothing can be an "end" in the former sense without also being an end in the latter. Unless processes have ends which are their subjective fulfilment, it is only by an arbitrary convention of our own that we assign to them ends which are their *last* states. And if it is only an arbitrary convention that physical processes have ends in this sense, evolution itself is just such a convention and nothing more.[1]

§ 4. What is in principle the same argument may be put in another form, and the equivalence of the two forms is itself very suggestive from the metaphysical point of view. Evolution or development, like all change, implies the presence throughout successive stages in a process of something which is permanent and unchanging. But it implies something more definite still. Whatever develops must

---

[1] It might be objected that, *e.g.*, death is the *end* of life in the sense of being its last stage, without being the attainment of the interests which compose our inner life. But the illustration will not bear examination. The processes of change within the organism, when viewed simply *as* connected changes, do not cease with death; in fact, they have *no* end or last state. To call a man's death his end only means that the purposes for which *we* are interested in the study of his behaviour get complete fulfilment when we have followed him from the cradle to the grave. He is "done with" at death, because *we* have done with him. Only teleological processes can have a *last* stage. Note as a consequence of the significance of the concept of "ends" for evolution, that whereas the purely mechanistic interpretation of the processes of Nature logically leads to the thought of them as a continuous series, the series of successive organic or social types is essentially discontinuous, a point well brought out by Professor Royce, *The World and the Individual*, Second Series, lects. 5, 7.

therefore have a permanent *individual* character of its own of which the successive stages in the development process are the gradual unfolding. Unless the earlier and the later stages in a connected series of changes belong alike to the gradual unfolding, under the influence of surroundings, of a single individual nature, there is no meaning in speaking of them as belonging to a process of development. Only the individual can develop, if we are to attribute precise meaning to our words. We speak of the evolution of a society or a species, but if our words are not to be empty we must mean by such phrases one of two things. Either we must mean that the species and the society which develop are themselves individuals of a higher order, no less real than the members which compose them, or our language must be merely a way of saying that the life of each member of the social or biological group exhibits development.

When we reflect on what is really involved in our ordinary loose expressions about the "inheritance" of this or the other physical or social trait, we shall see that the former alternative is far less removed from ordinary ways of thought than might at first seem to be the case. If any kind of reality corresponds to our current metaphor of the "inheritance" of qualities, the groups within which such "inheritance" takes place must be something much more than mere aggregates of mutually exclusive individuals. A group within which qualities can be thus inherited must, as a whole, possess a marked individual nature of its own. Now we have already seen that all individuality is in the end teleological. A group of processes forms an individual life in the degree to which it is the expression of a unique and coherent interest or aim, and no further. Hence, once more, only what is truly individual can develop or evolve. And we readily see that it is precisely in so far as a set of processes form the expression of individual interest, that the demarcation of the group as a connected whole from all previous and subsequent processes possesses more than a conventional significance. Hence only processes which are the expression of individual interest possess "ends" or "last states," and thus the two forms of our argument are in principle identical. Once more, then, the significance of evolutionary ideas, if they are to be more than a purely conventional scheme devised for the furtherance of our own practical purposes, and as an artificial aid to classification, is bound up with the doctrine that the events of the physical order are really the expression of the subjective interests of sentient subjects of experience.[1]

§ 5. To proceed to a further point of the utmost importance. Not only does evolution imply the presence of *individuality* in the subject of the evolutionary process; it implies its possession of *finite* individuality. An infinite individual cannot have development or evolution ascribed to it without contradiction. Hence the Absolute, the Universe, or whatever other name we prefer to give to the infinite individual whole of existence, cannot develop, cannot progress, cannot degenerate. This conclusion might be derived at once from reflecting upon the single consideration that temporal succession is involved in all evolution, whether progressive or retrogressive. For temporal succession is, as we have seen, an inseparable consequence of finite individuality. But it will be as well to reach our result in a different way, by considering certain further implications of the concept of evolution which are manifestly only present in the case of *finite* individuality.

In every process of development or evolution there are involved a pair of interrelated factors, the individual nature which develops, and the environment which contains the conditions under which and the stimuli in response to which it develops. The undeveloped germ is as yet a mere possibility, something which *will* yet exhibit qualities not as yet possessed by it. In its undeveloped state, what it possesses is not the qualities characteristic of its later stages, but only "tendencies" or "dispositions" to manifest those

---

[1] I need hardly remind the reader of the vast difference between the view inculcated above and the doctrine of "ends in nature" as it figures in the old-fashioned "argument from design." The old-fashioned teleology assumed (1) that the "subjective interests" manifested in the evolutionary process are fundamentally human. We, it held, can recognise what these ends are, and further, they are for the most part summed up in the "design" of furthering our human convenience. (2) That these interests exist as the reflective designs of an anthropomorphic Ruler of Nature. Our doctrine is consistent with neither assumption. It follows from our whole interpretation of the physical order, that we do not and cannot know what kind of subjective interest of finite individuals is realised by any portion of it beyond that constituted by our own bodies and those of our near congeners, and therefore are absolutely without any right to fancy ourselves the culminating end of all evolution. Again, a subjective interest need not exist in the form of a definitely preconceived design; most of our own interests exist as unreflective cravings and impulses. Whether any part of the evolutionary process is due to deliberate reflective design on the part of superhuman intelligences, Metaphysics, I take it, has no means of deciding. This would be a question for solution by the same empirical methods which we employ in detecting the presence of design in the products of human art. In any case, reflective design is bound up with the time-process, and cannot therefore be ascribed to the infinite individual.

qualities, provided that the environment provides the suitable stimulus. Hence, if either of the two interrelated factors of development, the individual or the environment, is missing, there can be no evolution. Now, the infinite individual whole of existence has no environment outside itself to supply conditions of development and incentives to change. Or, what is the same thing, since the "possible" means simply that which will follow *if* certain conditions are realised, there is no region of unrealised possibility outside the realised existence of the infinite whole. Hence in the infinite whole there can be no development: it cannot progressively adapt itself to *new* conditions of existence; it must once and for all be in its reality all that it is in "idea." The infinite whole therefore evolves neither forward nor backward.

This impossibility of ascribing development to the whole of Reality is strikingly illustrated by a consideration of the *impasse* into which we are led when we try in practice to think of the whole universe as in process of evolution. So long as you are still in the presence of the fundamental distinction between the developing subject and its environment, you are logically driven, if everything is to be taken as a product of evolution, to supplement every evolutionary theory by a fresh evolutionary problem. To account for this special evolution (*e.g.*, the evolution of the *vertebrata*) you have to assume an environment with determinate qualities of its own, influencing the evolution in question in a determinate way in consequence of these qualities. But if everything has been evolved, you have again to ask by what process of evolution this special environment came to be what it is. To solve this problem you have once more to postulate a second "environment" determining, by interaction, the course of the evolution of the former. And thus you are thrown back upon the indefinite regress.

Unless, indeed, you are prepared boldly to assert that, as all determinate character is the product of evolution, the universe as a whole must have evolved out of nothing. (You would not escape this dilemma by an appeal to the very ancient notion of a "cycle" or "periodic rhythm" of evolution, in virtue of which the product of a process of evolution serves in its turn as the environment for the reiterated evolution of its own antecedent conditions, A thus passing by evolution into B and B back again into A. For you would at least have to accept this tendency to periodic rhythm itself as an ultimate property of all existence, not itself resulting by evolution from something else.) The dilemma thus created by the attempt to apply the concept of evolution to the whole of Reality, is sufficient to show that evolution itself is only thinkable as a characteristic of processes which fall within the nature of a system which, as a whole, does not evolve.

We may restate the same contention in the following form:—All development means advance towards an *end*. But only that which is as yet in imperfect possession of its end can advance towards it. For that which already is all that it has it in its nature to be there can be no advance, and hence no progressive development. Neither can such a complete individual degenerate. For even in degenerating, that which degenerates is gradually realising some feature of its own nature which was previously only an unrealised potentiality. Thus even degeneration implies the realisation of an end or interest, and is itself a kind of advance. As the biologists tell us, the atrophy of an organ, which we call degeneration, is itself a step in the progressive adaptation of the organisation to new conditions of life, and, as the moralists remind us, in the ethical sphere a "fall" is, in its way, an upward step. Hence what cannot rise higher in the scale of existence also cannot sink lower.

§ 6. Evolution is thus an inseparable characteristic of the life of finite individuals, and of finite individuals only. And this consideration gives us the clue to the metaphysical interpretation of the distinction, so significant for all evolutionary theory, between the progressive and retrogressive directions of the evolution process. To a large extent it is, of course, a matter of convention what we shall regard as progress and what as degeneration. So long as *we* are specially interested in the attainment of any end or culminating result, we call the line of development which leads up to that result progressive, and the line which leads to its subsequent destruction degeneration. And thus the same development may be viewed as progress or as degeneration, according to the special character of the interests with which we study it. Thus, for instance, the successive modifications of the vertebrate structure which have resulted in the production of the human skeleton are naturally thought of as progressive, because our special interest in human intelligent life and character leads us to regard the human type as superior to its predecessors in the line of development. At the same time, many of these modifications consist in the gradual loss of characteristics previously evolved, and are therefore degenerative from the point of view of the anatomical student, who is specially interested in the production of organs of increasing complexity of structure, and therefore takes the complexity of those structures as *his* standard in distinguishing progress from retrogression.

But the distinction is not a *purely* conventional one. As we have seen, degrees of individuality are also degrees of reality; what is more completely individual is also a completer representative of the ultimate structure of the infinite individual whole, and therefore more completely real. Hence we may say that advance in individuality is really, and not in a merely conventional sense, progress in development; loss of individuality is real degeneration. Thus we get at least the possibility of a true "objective" basis for distinction between the directions of evolutionary progress. But we must remember that it is only where we are able to know something of the actual interests of finite experiencing beings that we have safe grounds for judging whether those interests receive more adequate embodiment in consequence of the changes of structure and habit produced by evolution or not. Hence, while our insight into the inner lives of ourselves and our animal congeners theoretically warrants us in pronouncing the various developments in human social life to be genuinely progressive or retrogressive, and again in regarding the series of organic types which leads directly up to man as a true "ascent," our ignorance of the special character of the individual experiences of which the inorganic physical order at large is the phenomenal manifestation, makes it impossible for us to determine whether an "evolution" outside these limits is really progressive or not. We have to treat "cosmic evolution" in general, outside the special line of animal development which leads up to man, as indifferently a "progress" or a "degeneration" according to our own arbitrary point of view, not because it is not "objectively" definitely the one or the other, but because *our* insight is not sufficient to discern which it is.

§ 7. One more point may be noted, which is of some importance in view of certain metaphysical problems connected with the nature of finite individuality. If evolution is more than an illusion, it seems necessary to hold that it is a process in the course of which finite individuals may disappear and new finite individuals originate. This point is metaphysically significant, because it means that the fact of evolution is irreconcilable with any of the philosophical theories of ancient and modern times, which regard Reality as composed of a plurality of ultimately independent finite individuals or "personalities."[1] If these philosophical theories are sound, the course of the world's history must be made up of the successive transformations of finite individuals, who somehow remain unaffected and unaltered in their character by the various external disguises they assume. The individuals of such a philosophy would, in fact, be as little modified by these changes as the actors on a stage by their changes of costume, or the souls of the "transmigration" hypothesis by the bodies into which they successively enter. And thus development would not be even a relatively genuine feature of the life of finite individuals; it would be a mere illusion, inevitable indeed in the present condition of our acquaintance with the detailed contents of existence, but corresponding to no actual fact of inner experience.

On the other hand, if evolution is not a pure illusion, these metaphysical constructions cannot be valid. For the whole essence of the modern doctrine of evolution is contained in the principle that radical differences in kind result from the accumulation of successive modifications of individual structure, and once established continue to be perpetuated as differences in kind. Now, such differences in kind can only be interpreted metaphysically as radical differences in the determining aims and interests of the experiencing subjects constituting the physical order, and we have already seen that it is precisely the character of these dominant unique interests which forms the individuality of the individual. Thus the metaphysical interpretation of the evolution process seems inevitably to resolve it into a process of the development of fresh and disappearance of old individual interests, and thus into a process of the origination and disappearance of finite individuals within the one infinite individual whole.

A conclusion of the same sort would be suggested by consideration of those facts of our own individual development from which the wider evolutionary theories have, in the last resort, borrowed their ideas and their terminology. The mental growth of the individual human being is essentially a process of the formation of interests in things.

---

[1] Compare, *e.g.*, the first of the arguments for immortality in Plato's *Phædo*, p. 70 ff., and the remark in the *Republic*, with obvious reference to this argument, that the "number of souls is always the same" (611A). In Plato the doctrine is pretty certainly of Orphic *provenance*. Compare also the cyclic alternation of death and life in Heracleitus, the (Orphic) cycle of births of Empedocles, that of the Stoics, and in the modern world, to take only one instance, the "eternal recurrence" of Nietzsche.

Both our formal education, and our informal intellectual and moral training effected by the influence of social tradition and mutual intercourse, are processes consisting of an accumulation of minor modifications which ultimately culminate in the establishment of more or less unique personal interests in different aspects of existence. And inasmuch as this process is never terminated, it is always possible for our previously acquired interests to undergo such modification as renders them obsolete, and substitutes novel interests in their places. So far as this is effected, we rightly say that we are no longer our "old selves." A new "self" or centre of unique individual interests has then developed within the former self.

Usually the process stops short of the point at which all sensible continuity seems suspended, but that this point can be actually reached, under exceptional conditions, is shown to superfluity by such facts as those of "conversion," to say nothing of the more pathological phenomena of "multiple personality." The same phenomena illustrate the fact that a new individuality, once evolved, may stand in various relations to the old individual interests it displaces. It may permanently replace them, or, as in so many cases of "conversion," may prove only temporary and pass back again into the old individuality, or the two may alternate periodically.[1] The one important point in which all these cases agree is simply the general one of the production in the course of development of a new individuality within the first individuality. It may perhaps be suggested that we have in these features of individual growth a hint as to the true nature of the process we call the origination of new species by evolution.[2]

To recapitulate: evolution implies change determined by reference to an end, and thus constituted into an individual process. Such "ends" have no meaning, except in so far as the processes of change are viewed as the progressive attainment of individual interests, and thus evolution is only possible where there is finite individuality. This is the philosophical justification for our previous assertion that

---

[1] The same phenomenon of the formation of a new individuality within the limits of an already existing one, is illustrated by the familiar facts of the moral conflict between the "higher" and "lower" self.

[2] Compare Royce, *The World and the Individual*, Second Series, p. 305 ff., where a view of this kind is worked out in some detail. Prof. Royce's second volume unfortunately came into my hands too late to enable me to make all the use of it I could have wished; the same is the case with Mr. Underhill's essay on "The Limits of Evolution" in *Personal Idealism*.

evidence of structural evolution, where it can be had, affords reasonable presumption that what appears to us *one thing* is really a true individual of some degree, and not a mere arbitrary grouping together on our part of states which possess no inner unity. Further, evolution is a process in which new individuals arise and old ones disappear. Hence its significance for Metaphysics as excluding all theories which make Reality consist of a mere plurality of unchanging finite individuals. It is significant also from another point of view. Implying, as it so manifestly does, the presence of individual subjects of experience throughout the physical order, the concept of Nature as a realm of evolutionary processes is infinitely nearer to the full truth for Metaphysics than the purely mechanistic view of it as a mere succession of connected changes.

Consult further:—F. H. Bradley, *Appearance and Reality*, chaps. 27, 28 (pp. 497, 499, 508 of ed. i. for criticism of concept of Progress); H. Lotze, *Metaphysic*, bk. ii. chap. 8 ("Forms of the Course of Nature," Eng. trans., vol. ii. pp. 109, 162); J. Royce, *The World and the Individual*, Second Series, lect. 5; H. Sidgwick, *Philosophy: its Scope and Relations*, lects. 6 and 7 (for some general consideration of the bearing of evolution on Metaphysics); G. E. Underhill, "The Limits of Evolution" (in *Personal Idealism*); J. Ward, *Naturalism and Agnosticism*, vol. i. lects. 7-9 (criticism of Spencer's evolutionary philosophy), 10 (on *biological* evolution).

CHAPTER VI

THE LOGICAL CHARACTER OF DESCRIPTIVE SCIENCE

§ 1. Scientific *description* may be contrasted with philosophical or teleological *interpretation*, but the contrast is not absolute. § 2. The primary end of all scientific description is intercommunication with a view to active co-operation. Hence all such description is necessarily restricted to objects capable of being experienced in the same way by a plurality of individuals. § 3. A second end of scientific description is the *economising* of intellectual labour by the creation of *general* rules for dealing with typical situations in the environment. In the course of evolution this object becomes partially independent of the former. § 4. From the interest in formulating *general* rules arise the three fundamental postulates of physical science, the postulates of *Uniformity*, *Mechanical Law*, and *Causal Determination*. § 5. The mechanical view of physical Nature determined by these three postulates is systematically carried out only in the abstract science of *Mechanics*; hence the logical completion of the descriptive process would mean the reduction of all descriptive science to Mechanics. That the chemical, biological, and psychological sciences contain elements which cannot be reduced to mechanical terms, is due to the fact that their descriptions are inspired by æsthetic and historical as well as by primarily "scientific" interests. § 6. The analysis of such leading concepts of mechanical Physics as the Conservation of Mass and of Energy shows them to have only *relative* validity.

§ 1. IN its general outlines our interpretation of the significance of the physical order is now complete. We have seen reason to hold that in that order we have the appearance to our human senses of a great system or complex of systems composed of purposive sentient beings, whose interests are for the most part so widely removed from our own as to preclude all direct intercourse, but who are nevertheless historically connected with ourselves by that unceasing process of the development of new forms of individual interest which we know empirically as the evolution of life and intelligence on our planet. As we have tried throughout the four preceding chapters to show in detail, there is no real inconsistency between this general interpretation of the meaning of the physical order and the working assumptions of our various empirical sciences. At the same time it is obvious that in executing the task of the detailed description and calculation of the phenomenal course of events, the empirical sciences, while not rejecting such a metaphysical interpretation, ignore it; and the more conscientiously they exclude from their programme all amateur excursions into extraneous metaphysical speculation, the more thoroughly is the work of description and mathematical formulation done. It seems advisable, therefore, to conclude our brief sketch of the principles of Cosmology with a short discussion of the nature of the limitations imposed on empirical science, by the special character of the objects it sets before it, and of the way in which the existence of these limitations is revealed by analysis of the most general concepts of the empirical sciences themselves.

It is important, in the first place, to be quite clear as to the sense in which we speak of *description* as the work of the empirical sciences, and as to the meaning of the contrast between such description and a philosophical *interpretation* of existence. In this connection there are two points which seem to call for special and repeated emphasis. (1) The contrast between interpretation and description is not an absolute one. *Complete* description would of itself be something more than mere description, and would pass into philosophical interpretation. Thus a significant purposive movement is not adequately described when, *e.g.*, its direction, velocity, momentum, and duration have been assigned. The complete description of such a movement would require the recognition of its meaning for the being executing it as a step in the realisation of a craving or a design, and would thus merge in what we have called philosophical interpretation. So generally, if all existence is ultimately experience and all experience essentially teleological, such description as can be distinguished from interpretation must always be incomplete from the logical standpoint, though adequate to fulfil certain special purposes.

(2) The descriptions of science, again, must be carefully distinguished from such descriptions as can be effected by the mere multiplication of unanalysed sensible detail. Scientific description, it must be remembered, is always description undertaken with a view to the *calculation* and prediction of the course of events. This implies that it must be description in general terms, and, wherever possible, by the aid of mathematical analysis. Natural processes are described by the empirical sciences which deal with them, not in their concrete individual detail, but only in so far as they exhibit certain uniform aspects permitting of reduction to formulæ

suitable for calculation. Such description is frequently spoken of as *explanation*, and is expressly contrasted by this difference in nomenclature with the mere accumulation of sensible detail. We must not, however, allow the difference in question to blind us to the essentially descriptive character of all scientific hypotheses. It is sometimes urged that scientific *explanation* must differ in its logical character from description, because the "substance," "agencies," and "media," in terms of which explanation is couched, are largely of a kind inaccessible to sense-perception. It must be remembered, however, that hypotheses as to such imperceptible objects are only valuable so far as they serve as connecting-links by which we may calculate sensible events from sensible data. Whatever intermediate links empirical science may find it useful to assume, it invariably takes the sensible occurrences of the phenomenal physical order as the starting-point, and again as the goal of its inferences.[1] All its hypothetical constructions are thus subservient to the main interest of the accurate description of the course of sensible events. The only kind of "explanation" which can be reasonably contrasted, in respect of its logical character, with description is teleological interpretation, and even here the contrast, as we have seen, is not final.

§ 2. We have to ask, then, what is the object at which scientific descriptions aim? What purpose do they seek to fulfil, and how does the essential character of this purpose determine the logical character of the descriptive process? Now, it is at once evident that all description has for its immediate object one or other of two practical ends, which are so closely connected as to be ultimately coincident. Historically, it is beyond a doubt that the original purpose of all description of physical events was intercommunication with a view to social co-operation. I have already referred to this function of description with special reference to the use of causal descriptions in science, but may conveniently deal with the same point rather more fully and in a more general way here.

In a society of finite individuals with interrelated aims and objects, each of the individuals can only attain satisfaction for his own subjective interests by some degree of

[1] And, again, the intermediate links themselves, however imperceptible, have always to be thought of as exhibiting properties identical in kind with those of objects given in direct presentation. As Mill said, a hypothesis which assumes at once an entirely unfamiliar agent and an equally unfamiliar mode or law of operation, would be useless. Thus the imperceptibles of scientific hypothesis belong essentially to the physical order.

concerted action along with the rest. And concerted action is only possible where the co-operating individuals can reduce their various views of their common external environment to common terms, equally intelligible to all, and similarly indicate to each other their respective special contributions to the common task. There must be a common understanding of the difficulty to be met, and of the precise part each is to play in meeting it. Thus intercommunication between individuals is an indispensable requisite of all effective practical co-operation.

But again, intercommunication is only possible by means of description in *general* terms. Only in so far as there are identical elements in the experiences of the various individuals can one communicate the contents of his experience to another. Immediate feeling, precisely because of its unique individual character, is essentially incommunicable. Thus in communicating information about my own body to another, I am of necessity forced to speak of my body in terms not of the immediate experience I have of it in organic sensation, but of those complexes of sense-presentations which he and I alike get through our organs of special perception. And so the whole physical order can only serve as a basis of co-operation between individuals so far as it is describable in the last resort as a complex of sense-presentations equally accessible to the observation of all the individuals. Any kind of experience of nature which is uniquely peculiar to myself, and therefore incapable of being got under assignable conditions by any other individual endowed with the same organs of perception, is necessarily incommunicable, and therefore useless as a basis for concerted action. Hence science is restricted by its very purpose to describe the physical order in such a way that its descriptions may be available for the objects of practical art, to the description of it in its phenomenal aspect as a mere complex of related presentations or possibilities of presentation. It is no accident, but a logical consequence of the conditions of intercommunication, that all scientific description must start from and end with occurrences of the phenomenal order which any individual may experience by conforming to the prescribed conditions of perception. Thus we see that it is an epistemological characteristic of the physical order as investigated by science, that it consists exclusively of those objects which are, in principle, perceptible by more than one individual. If there are objects in their own nature incapable of being experienced by more than one individual, such as, *e.g.*, my own inner life, those objects cannot belong to the physical order of science.[1]

§ 3. There is a second purpose of description which arises out of the first as human experiences become more reflective. Description not only enables me to communicate the particular situation of the moment to others, and devise in concert with them means for coping with it; it also enables me to formulate beforehand *general* rules for my own behaviour in recurrent situations of the same type. The need for the possession of such general views originates, of course, while description is still confined to its original function in assisting social co-operation. From the practical point of view of those industrial arts out of which our various physical sciences have arisen, it is an economical advantage of the first magnitude to be able once and for all to formulate a *general* rule for dealing with the indefinitely numerous occurrences of typical situations, instead of having to deal with each occurrence separately as it arises.

The advantages of such general rules speedily make themselves felt in the increased power and importance enjoyed by the section of society which is in possession of them, a consideration which may help us to understand why, in early stages of civilisation, such rules are commonly jealously guarded as the hereditary secrets of close corporations.[2] Thus it comes to be the special aim of scientific description to assist the formulation of general rules for the practical manipulation of the objects of the physical order. And, with the progress of reflection, this originally secondary object of the descriptive process becomes to a large extent independent of the primary object of intercommunication. Even where I have no need or no desire for intercommunication and co-operation with my fellows, it becomes my interest to seek generalised descriptions of typical situations in the physical order as the basis of practical rules for my own voluntary intervention in that order.

§ 4. The interest in the formulation of general rules for practical interference with nature, again, necessarily dictates the form which our scientific descriptions will take, and is thus the source of those practical postulates of empirical science with which we have already made some acquaintance.

---

[1] This is the characteristic selected by Prof. Münsterberg as the basis of his own distinction between "physical" or "superindividual" and "psychical" or "individual" objects. See *Grundzüge der Psychologie*, i. 15–77.

[2] Cf. Mach, *Science of Mechanics*, p. 4. Mach, however, erroneously as I think, makes the intercommunication a *secondary* consequence of the rise of specialised industrial classes.

It compels us to assume, in the first place, as an indispensable condition of success in our descriptions, that there are situations in the physical order which may be treated with sufficient accuracy for our practical purposes, as recurring identically; in the second place, that, so long as *we* abstain from intentional intervention in the course of events, they succeed one another in a fixed routine order, or, in other words, that there are no departures in nature from established routine of such a kind as to interfere with our calculations; in the third place, that every event in the physical order is, within the limits requisite for our successful devising of means to our ends, determined by antecedent events. It is thus our interest in obtaining general rules for the production of effects in the physical order by intentional interference with it which is the source of the three fundamental postulates of empirical physical science, the postulates of uniformity, of the omnipresence of routine or mechanical "law," and of the causal determination of subsequent by antecedent events.

The dependence of physical science upon these three fundamental postulates thus does not prove their ultimate truth, as we have already shown at length in preceding chapters: it proves only that where they cannot be treated as approximately true, within the limits in which their falsity could be detected by sensible experiment, our special interest in devising rules for the manipulation of events cannot be gratified. Conversely, wherever that interest can be successfully gratified, these postulates must be for all practical purposes equivalent to the truth. Hence, if we remember that the ultimate object of all physical science is the successful formulation of such practical rules for action, we can see that it is a logical consequence of the character of the interests which dominate our scientific descriptions, that the physical sciences should adopt a rigidly mechanical view of the physical order. Only, in proportion as any one branch of physical science succeeds in carrying out in detail this conception of the physical order as an interconnected mechanism of sequences rigidly determined by laws of sequence, does it succeed in effecting the purposes by which all physical science has been called into existence. We may thus call the mechanical conception of the physical order the most general postulate of physical science. Only, we must once more take care to recollect that a fundamental postulate of physical science need not in the least be an ultimate truth; such a postulate is in the end nothing more than a way of stating the nature of the interest which physical science subserves, and, as we have sufficiently seen, that interest is not the purely logical one of consistent thinking, but the practical one of successful interference with nature.

§ 5. It does not, of course, follow that all the sciences which deal in any way with the events of the physical order can as a matter of fact carry out this mechanical view of their objects with equal success. It is only in the various branches of abstract Mechanics that we get anything like complete systematic adherence to the postulates of the mechanical theory of physical nature as previously enumerated. For the physical, chemical, and still more for the biological sciences, it remains an unrealised ideal—and one we have no right to think ever completely realisable—that all the facts of electrical and chemical, and again of physiological process should be ultimately capable of reduction to routine uniformities upon which confident calculation and prediction can be based.

Thus, even in Chemistry, limits are set to the successful adoption of the purely mechanical point of view, by the fact that chemical combination is regularly productive of *new qualities* in the compound which could not have been predicted from a knowledge of the properties of its constituents, but have to be ascertained *a posteriori* by actual experiment. It is true, no doubt, that we seem to be increasingly able, as our chemical knowledge advances, to say in general what properties may be expected to result from the combination of given elements, but there is no logical ground for supposing that we shall ever be able to foretell *all* the properties of an as yet unexamined compound, and in any case such knowledge could only be of a general sort. However much we might know, in advance of the results of the combination of certain elements in certain proportions, it would still be impossible to predict with absolute certainty the precise result of trying the combination in a particular concrete case.

Still less realisable would be the ideal of the reduction of Biology to applied Mechanics. It is not merely that the isolated physiological process regularly exhibits *qualitative* aspects of a chemical or electrical kind, which we have no right to reduce to mere quantitative changes. Beyond this, as the very terminology of our evolutionary hypotheses is enough to show, it is impossible to state the facts of biological evolution without introducing, under such names as "sexual selection," continual reference to a subjective factor, in the form of the likes and dislikes, habits and cravings of sentient beings, and this selective factor, being in its own nature incapable of direct presentation in identical form to a plurality of experiences, is not even a member of the physical order. With the case of Psychology we shall be better able to deal in connection with the special discussions of the following Book. (See especially Bk. IV. chap. 1.)

Considerations of this kind seem to necessitate the following general view of the logical character of descriptive physical science. The only science in which the postulates of description are rigidly carried out to their logical consequences is the science of abstract Mechanics in its various branches (Statics, Kinetics, etc.). Mechanics owes its power to follow out these postulates to its abstract character. Precisely because it regards only those aspects of the actual physical order which are consistent with the fundamental postulate of describability by general formulæ, Mechanics is constrained to be a purely abstract and hypothetical science. For since every actual process involves the appearance of the qualitatively novel, and since all concrete *quality* is in its essence unique, no actual process can be merely mechanical.

Thus the only way of conceiving the physical order which is logically consistent with the postulates of descriptive science in their rigidity, is one which treats all natural changes as reducible to equations. And it is only in abstract Mechanics that this view is systematically carried out.[1] Consequently, it is only in so far as all physical science can be reduced to abstract Mechanics that we can attain the ultimate purpose of our scientific constructions, the calculation and prediction of the course of occurrences by means of general formulæ. This conclusion, derived in the first instance from reflection on the logical nature of scientific description, is fully borne out by our actual experience of the results of our scientific theories. Just because we cannot ultimately reduce all chemical and biological processes to mere quantitative changes in a material of uniform quality, we are unable to predict with absolute confidence the precise result of a concrete chemical experiment, and still more unable to foretell the precise behaviour of a living organism.

[1] *I.e.*, the *mechanical* view of Nature, to be thoroughly self-consistent, must be purely *mechanistic*.

Hence follow two very important results. (1) There is a real practical justification for the attempt, as far as possible, to treat the chemical and biological phenomena *as if* they were simply more complicated instances of the relations familiar to us in Mechanics. For though they are not really purely mechanical, it is only in so far as we can treat them without appreciable error as exactly measurable that they admit in principle of calculation.

(2) At the same time, there is also ample justification for the use of qualitative and teleological categories in Chemistry and Biology. For the interests which chemical and biological knowledge subserve are not limited by our need for practical rules for intervention in the course of nature. Over and above this original *scientific* interest, which can only be gratified by a mechanical treatment of the subject, we have an *æsthetic* interest in the serial grouping of processes according to their qualitative affinities, and an *historical* interest in tracing the successive modifications which have led to the establishment of a relatively stable form of human social existence. In so far as the chemical and biological sciences involve the recognition of qualitative distinctions and the consequent use of categories which are non-mechanical, it is these æsthetic and historical interests, and not the primary scientific interest in the control of natural phenomena, which are subserved by their elaboration.

Hence, while Chemistry and Biology, even apart from the possibility of their conversion into branches of applied Mechanics, are essentially descriptive sciences, the task fulfilled by them, so far as they use qualitative and teleological categories, is one of æsthetic and historical rather than of properly scientific description. And æsthetic and historical description, having another object than that of purely scientific description, are under no necessity to conform to the postulates imposed on the latter by the special character of the interests it aims at satisfying. Thus we can see how the right of Chemistry and Biology to be regarded as something more than mere applied Mechanics, can be reconciled with Kant's profoundly true assertion that any branch of knowledge contains just so much *science* as it contains of Mathematics. When we come, in connection with the special problems of the following Book, to discuss the aims and methods of Psychology, we shall find in that study a still more striking example of the way in which the narrowly "scientific" interest may play a markedly subordinate part in determining the procedure of a branch of knowledge which must, because of its systematic character, be called a " science " in the wider acceptation of the term.[1]

§ 6. Since it is only complete and all-embracing knowledge which can be in the last resort a completely self-contained and self-explaining system, we must expect to find that the concepts employed in the mechanical interpretation of the physical order lead us into contradiction the moment we try to treat them as a complete account of the concrete nature of the whole of Reality. This is shown more particularly in two ways. On the one hand, the application of the categories of Mechanics to the whole of Reality leads inevitably to the indefinite regress. On the other, in their legitimate application to a lesser part of existence they are all demonstrably *relative*, that is, they always appear as one aspect of a fact which has other aspects, and without these other aspects would have no meaning. It is worth our while to consider both these points in some detail.

For the successful application of the mechanical view to the physical order, we need to treat that order as consisting of the changing configurations of a whole of qualitatively homogeneous related parts. Any departure from this point of view would involve the recognition of differences which cannot be treated as merely quantitative, as mere subjects for calculation and prediction, and would thus necessitate the introduction of a non-mechanical factor into our interpretation of the universe. The mechanical view, fully carried out, thus involves the conception of the universe as a system extended and ordered in space and time, and capable of spatial and temporal change, but manifesting a quantitative identity throughout its changes. In the actual constructions of physical science this quantitative identity is represented principally by the principles of the Conservation of Mass and the Conservation of Energy. Both these latter principles are thus, in their general form, neither axioms of

---

[1] To put the matter more succinctly, as regards the position of Chemistry and Biology, we may say that while chemical and biological *facts* are never merely mechanical, chemical and biological *science*, so far as they subserve the strictly scientific interest of calculation and the formulation of general rules, must always be so. The *facts* only lend themselves to this special purpose in so far as they admit of being, without sensible error, treated *as if* they conformed to the postulates of universal Mechanism. The special and more difficult case of psychological facts I reserve for separate discussion in the following Book (*infra*, Bk. IV. chap. 1).

I am glad to be able to refer the reader, for a view of the logical worth of the mechanical postulates which appears in principle identical with my own, to the interesting discussion of Mr. W. R. B. Gibson in *Personal Idealism*, p. 144 ff.

CHARACTER OF DESCRIPTIVE SCIENCE

knowledge nor verifiable empirical facts, but a part of the general mechanical postulate. There is no ultimate logical principle in virtue of which we are constrained to think of the particular quantities we denote as mass and energy as incapable of increase or diminution, nor again have we any experimental means of proving that those quantities are more than approximately constant.[1] It is, however, a necessary condition of success in calculating the course of events, that there should be *some* quantitative identity which remains unaffected in the various processes of physical change, and it is chiefly in the special forms of the quantitative constancy of Mass and Energy that we seem at present able to give definite expression to this *a priori* postulate of mechanical construction.

Now, with regard to spatial and temporal direction and position, we have seen already both that they are always relative, position and direction being only definable with respect to other positions and directions arbitrarily selected to serve as standards of reference, and that, when taken as ultimate realities, they involve the indefinite regress. It only remains to show that the same is true of the other fundamental concepts of the mechanical scheme, mass and energy. Taking the two separately, we may deal first of all with the notion of *mass*. The mass of a material system is often loosely spoken of as its "quantity of matter," but requires, for the purposes of logical analysis, a more precise definition. Such a definition may be given in the following way. In order to explain what is meant by the constancy of the mass of a body, it is necessary to consider the mutual relations of at least three different bodies, which we will call A, B, and C. It is found that, at a given distance, in the presence of A, C receives an acceleration m, and in the presence of B a second acceleration n; then the mass of A is said to stand to that of B in the ratio m/n, which is the ratio of the accelerations which they respectively produce on C, and this ratio is constant, whatever body we choose for C. Hence, if we arbitrarily take B as our unit for the measurement of mass, the mass of A as determined by the foregoing experiment will be represented by the *number m*. By the principle of the *Conservation* of Mass is meant the doctrine that the ratio m/n as above determined does not

---

[1] Compare Bradley, *Appearance and Reality*, chap. 23, note 2 to p. 331 (1st ed.); Lotze, *Metaphysic*, bk. ii. chap. 7, pp. 209, 210 (Eng. trans., vol. ii. p. 89 ff.); Ward, *Naturalism and Agnosticism*, vol. i. pp. 84-91 (Conservation of Mass), 170-181 (Conservation of Energy).

alter with the lapse of time.[1] That is, the ratio between the accelerations produced by any pair of bodies or a third body is constant and independent of this third body itself. This proposition is verifiable approximately by direct experiment for a particular pair of bodies, but when affirmed as universally true becomes a part of the general mechanical postulate.

Now, it is obvious from the foregoing explanation of the meaning of mass (1) that mass is a relative term. It is a name for a certain constant ratio which requires no less than three distinct terms for its complete definition. Hence there would be no meaning in ascribing mass to the whole physical order or "universe." The "universe" could only have a mass as a whole if there were some body outside the universe, but capable of interaction with it, so that we could compare the relative accelerations, in the presence of this body, of the whole "physical universe," and of our arbitrarily selected unit of mass. But the "universe," by supposition, contains all physical existence, and there is therefore no such accelerating body outside it. Hence we cannot say, without an implicit contradiction, that the whole of existence possesses the property of mass, nor *a fortiori* that its mass is constant. It is only subordinate parts of the universe to which the principle of the Conservation of Mass can be intelligibly applied.

(2) It is also clear that the mass of a body is only one aspect of a whole of existence which possesses other aspects, not regarded in our mechanical constructions. The bodies which actually exhibit a constant ratio in their accelerations have other properties over and above the fact of this constant ratio. They have always, in actual fact, *qualitative* differences from one another and from other things, which we disregard in our mechanical treatment of them because they make no difference to this special property, in which for purposes of calculation we are peculiarly interested. It is by the barest and most palpable of abstractions that, in Mechanics, we treat bodies as if they were masses and nothing more. Thus the facts taken into account by the mechanical interpretation of nature are, so far as its reduction of bodies to masses is concerned, a mere aspect of a

---

[1] If we merely desired to fix the sense of the term *mass* without introducing the concept of *constant* mass, we might of course consider two bodies only, A and B. Then the ratio $\dfrac{\text{mass of B}}{\text{mass of A}} = \dfrac{\text{acceleration of A in presence of B}}{\text{acceleration of B in presence of A}}.$ See Mach, *Science of Mechanics*, p. 216 ff.; and Pearson, *Grammar of Science*, p. 302 (2nd ed.), on which the above account is based.

fuller reality which we treat as equivalent to the whole for no better reason than the practical one that it suits a special object of our own that it should be so equivalent, and that this object is empirically found to be attained by regarding it as equivalent.

Precisely the same is the case with the complementary concept of Energy. The kinetic energy, or capacity of a body for doing work against resistance, is found experimentally to be measured by half the square of its velocity multiplied by its mass. It is further found by experiment that, so far as we can measure, the energy of a material system not acted upon from without remains constant. That the constancy is absolute is, of course, once more not a matter for direct empirical proof, but a part of the postulate that the physical order shall be capable of a mechanical interpretation. Now we can see at once, from what has been previously said of the concept of Mass, that the physical order or "universe" as a whole cannot be intelligibly said to possess kinetic energy, whether constant or otherwise. What cannot be said to have mass clearly cannot have a property only explicable in terms of mass. We might indeed have inferred the same consequence directly from the definition of energy as capacity for doing "work" in overcoming resistance. The "universe," having nothing outside itself, can have no source of possible resistance to overcome, and therefore cannot be thought of as doing "work." Hence, once more, it is only the parts of the physical order, considered as parts, to which energy can be ascribed.

(3) Again, it is even more evident in the case of energy than in the case of mass, that we are dealing with one aspect singled out by abstraction from a whole possessed of other aspects not regarded in a purely mechanical construction. For (*a*) the capacity for work of an actual body does not always exist in the "kinetic" form of actual motion. There are various forms of non-kinetic energy, such as, *e.g.*, the energy of "position" of a resting body, the heat of a body of higher temperature than its surroundings, which Mechanics treats as equivalent to "kinetic" energy, because they are theoretically capable of being converted into it. And these forms of non-kinetic energy are *qualitatively* different both from energy of actual motion and from each other. It is by a mere abstraction that we treat them as identical because they are, for certain special purposes, equivalent. The qualitative differences may make no difference with respect

to a particular purpose of our own, but they are none the less really there.

Again, the mechanical scheme itself is quite insufficient to explain why or when these different forms of energy are replaced by one another. As has been well said by Professor Ward, the doctrine of the Conservation of Energy asserts no more than that a certain quantitative identity is maintained in all exchanges of energy. But when or in what direction these exchanges shall take place, the principle itself does not enable us to say. Thus, to take a simple example: if I know the mass of a stone lodged on a roof, the height of the roof from the ground, and the acceleration produced by gravity at the spot in question, I can determine the "potential energy" of the stone. But my data tell me nothing as to whether this potential energy will remain for ever in its potential form, or whether the stone will yet be dislodged and its energy converted into kinetic shape, and if so, when. The principles of the mechanical interpretation of nature are thus inadequate to describe the concrete course of events in so simple a case as that of the fall of a stone. *If* the stone falls, then by the aid of the mechanical postulate I can describe one aspect of the process, namely, the amount of kinetic energy which will be evolved; and again, *if* certain previous conditions are fulfilled, *e.g.*, *if* the support gives way, and *if* the descent of the stone is not previously arrested, the mechanical postulate enables me to infer that the stone *will* fall and will reach the ground with just this kinetic energy. But I can never escape, so long as I keep within the mechanical scheme, from this necessity of hypothetically assuming as given data which the mechanical scheme itself cannot fully determine.

All these considerations show how the very nature of the mechanical scheme itself justifies our previous conclusion, that it is in all its details simply the expression of a postulate created by our practical need that the course of nature shall admit of calculation with sufficient exactitude for the devising of successful rules for intervention in it, but logically incapable of being without contradiction regarded as the real truth about any concrete natural process. The internal evidence, derived from examination of the fundamental concepts of scientific Mechanism, thus confirms the view we have already adopted on different grounds, that the whole physical order is merely the appearance of a more ultimate reality of a kind akin to our own sentient and purposive life. At the same time, our examination of mechanism may serve to throw some useful light on the often misconceived antithesis between Reality and Appearance. We call the physical order, as conceived by mechanical science, "appearance," not because we regard it as illusory or deceptive in itself, or because it is not the manifestation of a true reality, but because it takes account only of those particular aspects of Reality which are important and significant for certain very special purposes. What appears to us as the physical order is, indeed, true Reality, and is, in fact, an integral part of the only Reality there is, but it appears to us in this special form and under these special restrictions because *we* have arbitrarily excluded every other aspect of the concrete facts from our purview by the choice of our initial postulates of descriptive science. By the nature of the special questions we put to our world, in our physical science, we determine in advance for ourselves the general character of the answer we are to receive.

Rigidly scientific investigation, for instance, finds mechanical determination everywhere in the world, and purposive spontaneity nowhere, just because it has previously resolved that it will accept "mechanical explanation" and nothing else as the answer to its questions. So far as we bear in mind the presence of these self-imposed logical limitations throughout our mechanical science, their existence need lead to no illusion or deception. The success of our mechanical postulates shows that, within the sphere of their logical applicability, the course of the world does really conform to them, and thus the results won by their application are genuine truth, so far as they go. It is only when we forget the limits set to the logical applicability of the mechanical postulates, by the special nature of the interests they subserve, and proceed to treat them as logically indispensable conditions of all existence and all knowledge, that the truths of mechanical science are perverted into the illusions and falsehoods of a mechanical philosophy.

Consult further :—F. H. Bradley, *Appearance and Reality*, chaps. 11 (Phenomenalism), 22 (Nature); H. Lotze, *Metaphysic*, bk. ii. chaps. 7, 8; E. Mach, *Science of Mechanics*, chap. 2, § 5, p. 216 ff.; K. Pearson, *Grammar of Science*, chaps. 7, 8; H. Poincaré, *La Science et L'Hypothèse*, parts 3 and 4, chaps. 6-10; J. B. Stallo, *Concepts and Theories of Modern Physics*, chaps. 2-6, 10-12; J. Ward, *Naturalism and Agnosticism*, vol. i. lects. 2-6.

BOOK IV

RATIONAL PSYCHOLOGY: THE INTERPRETATION OF LIFE

CHAPTER I

THE LOGICAL CHARACTER OF PSYCHOLOGICAL SCIENCE

§ 1. The various sciences which deal with the interpretation of human life all avail themselves of the fundamental categories of Psychology. Hence we must ask how the concepts of Psychology are related to actual experience. § 2. Psychology is a body of abstract descriptive formulæ, not a direct transcript of the individual processes of real life. It presupposes the previous construction of the physical order. § 3. The psychological conception of conscious life as a succession of " mental states " or " images " is a transformation of actual experience devised primarily to account for the experience of other subjects, and subsequently extended to my own. The transformation is effected by the hypothesis of " introjection." §§ 4, 5. The logical justification of the psychological transformation of facts is twofold. The psychological scheme serves partly to fill up the gaps in our theories of physiological Mechanism, and also, in respect of the teleological categories of Psychology, to describe the course of human conduct in a form capable of ethical and historical appreciation. Psychology may legitimately employ both mechanical and teleological categories. § 6. The objections sometimes brought against the possibility of (*a*) psychological, (*b*) teleological description are untenable.

§ 1. THE net result of our brief examination of some of the most important cosmological concepts has been to confirm us in the " idealistic " or " spiritualistic " interpretation of existence to which our first two books in principle committed us. The reader who has followed us so far with acquiescence will now be fully prepared to admit that we shall at least be nearer the truth in conceiving the universe as composed of sentient and purposive subjects of experience, akin in principle to the members of human society, than as constituted, entirely or in part, of mechanically interacting and interdependent elements. The acceptance of an idealist interpretation of the universe, however, still leaves us face to face with a number of problems of the gravest philosophical import. We have still to ask how in particular we can most truly conceive the systematic unity which is formed by the whole multiplicity of apparently more or less independent subjects of experience, what degree of permanence and individuality, so far as we can judge, belongs to ourselves as members of that system, and what light is thrown by our ethical, religious, and æsthetic aspirations and ideals on the concrete character of the whole system and on our own place in it. Again, before we can attack these momentous problems with any reasonable hope of success, we shall need to know which among the categories employed by the various sciences dealing with mental life are of fundamental significance, and what is the logical relation of those sciences to the concrete realities of immediate experience, and to the constructions of physical science. Only on the basis of a rational theory as to the purposes subserved by the various mental sciences, and the possible limitations imposed by those purposes on the use of the corresponding categories, can we decide how far the interpretation of existence as a whole in terms of Psychology, Sociology, or Ethics, is legitimate.

It is clear that the complete execution of the programme indicated in the previous paragraph would involve a systematic philosophical interpretation of the significance of human life for which some such name as the *Metaphysics of Society* or *Metaphysics of History* would be a more adequate designation than the traditional title of *Rational Psychology*. I have, however, retained the ancient name for this subdivision of our task, mainly on the ground that our own elementary discussion will be primarily concerned with those most simple and universal psychological concepts of which the various more concrete social and historical sciences make the same constant use as chemistry and the other physical sciences do of the mechanical concepts of mass, energy, velocity, etc. Whatever view we adopt of the precise degree of connection between Psychology on the one side and the various social and historical sciences on the other, it is at least manifest that Ethics, Sociology, History, and the rest all involve the constant use of such psychological categories as those of *self, will, thought, freedom*, and that thus any sound metaphysical interpretation of history and society must begin with investigation into the logical character of the science to which these concepts belong, just as a sound Metaphysic of nature had to start by an examination of the postulates of Mechanics. I suppose that there is no need to utter more than a passing word by way of reminder to the reader, that such an investigation presupposes the previous creation of a purely empirical science of Psychology. The business of Metaphysics with Psychology is not to dictate in advance how it *must* construct its view of the world, but to ascertain the logical character of the completed construction, and its relation to the general system of human knowledge.

§ 2. *The Place of Psychology among the Sciences.*—From the metaphysician's point of view, it is of the utmost importance to recognise clearly and constantly that Psychology, like the other sciences, deals throughout not with the actual experiences of real subjects, but with "data" obtained by the artificial manipulation and transformation of actual experience into a shape dictated by certain special interests and purposes. This is a point upon which the idealist metaphysician, in particular, is peculiarly liable to go wrong when left to himself. Starting with the conviction that the key to the nature of existence as a whole is to be found in our own direct experience of our sentient and purposive life, he almost inevitably tends, unless he has given particular attention to the methodology of psychological science, to take it for granted that the concepts and hypotheses of the psychologist afford a description of this experience in its concrete directness, and may therefore be treated without misgiving as a fruitful source of certain knowledge about the inmost structure of the absolute or infinite individual itself. And even the reiterated demonstration that one or another of the current categories of Psychology cannot be predicated of the absolute whole of reality without flagrant contradiction, frequently fails to produce conviction where it is not accompanied by direct proof of the artificiality and remoteness from concrete actuality of the psychologist's data. Hence it would be worse than useless to discuss such questions as, whether the infinite individual can properly be thought of as a "self" or an "ethical person," or again as a "society of ethical persons," or again whether finite "selves" are "eternal" or only transitory constituents of the world-system, without first arriving at some definite view as to the way in which these psychological concepts are derived from the concrete actualities of experience, the special interests which lead to their formulation, and the restrictions imposed by those interests on the sphere of their valid application.

That Psychology, like all descriptive science, deals throughout with data which are not concrete experience-realities, but artificial products of a process of abstraction and reconstruction, should be sufficiently clear from the very consideration that, like the other sciences, it is a body of *general* descriptions of typical situations. An actual process of knowing or acting, like every actual event, is always individual, and because of its individuality defies adequate description. It is only in so far as a situation admits of being generalised by the selection of certain of its aspects or qualities as representative of its whole reality, that it is capable of being described at all. Even History and Biography, in which the teleological interpretation of a series of events as internally united by the singleness of the purpose underlying them takes the place of external connection in accord with mechanical laws of sequence as the ideal of explanation, are only possible on the condition that such transformation of the concrete realities of life as is implied in such a degree of abstraction and reconstruction can be carried out without detriment to the special interests of the historian and the biographer. And Psychology is unreal and abstract even as compared with history. It provides us with general formulæ which are, or should be, valuable as affording a means of describing certain universal features of the processes of willing and knowing which it is desirable to study in isolation, but it is of itself as incapable of adequately tracing the actual course of a real process of willing or thinking, as Mechanics is of following the actual course of a real individual process in "external" nature. In this respect the concepts and formulæ of scientific Psychology stand on precisely the same footing, as regards their relation to the individual and actual, as do those of scientific Physics. Their truth and validity means simply that by substituting them for concrete actualities we can get answers to certain special questions which we have an interest in solving, not that they are unaltered transcripts of the actualities themselves.

This is perhaps most strikingly shown by observing that the very existence of Psychology as a distinct branch of science presupposes that artificial severance of the unity of direct experience into a physical order and a non-physical realm external to that order, of which we have already investigated the origin. Psychology has no subject-matter at all until we have first, for the practical reasons already discussed, constructed the physical order by the inclusion in it of all those experience-contents which are equally accessible under specified conditions to the observation of a plurality of subjects, and then gone on to assign to the realm of "psychical" or "mental" existence whatever experience-contents fall outside the system so defined. And this whole separation of the physical and the psychical or mental, as we have already seen, has no place in the direct experience of actual life. In actual life, until we come to reconstruct it in thought for the purposes of description and calculation, there are neither material bodies nor "immaterial minds" or "consciousnesses" which are "in" them or "animate" them; there are simply sentient and purposive beings and the environment of things to which they have to adjust themselves in the execution of their purposes. How and for what reasons this naïvely realistic view of existence comes to give place to the dualistic conception of a physical world and a plurality of non-physical beings in relation with it, we have already seen in our study of the methodology of the physical sciences. We have now to follow the development of the dualistic line of thought somewhat further, before we can see precisely what is the character of the logical reconstruction of actual experience presupposed by the existence of a science of Psychology.

§ 3. As we have already learned, our recognition of the actuality of our own and our fellow-men's life of unique and incommunicable feeling compelled us to admit the existence of much that, from its incommunicable nature, falls outside the sphere of physical reality. We have now to see how Psychology, in taking this non-physical existence as its subject-matter, conceives of its mode of existence and its relation to the subject-matter of the physical sciences. In recent years, much light has been thrown upon the methodological problem in question by the labours of Avenarius and his followers, from whom the substance of our account will be largely drawn. What Avenarius has for the first time made perfectly clear is, that the psychological interpretation of our own experience is throughout based upon reading into that experience a theory originally devised to meet a difficulty suggested by the existence of our fellow-men.

We have already seen, in dealing with the subjectivist's fallacy, what this difficulty is. So long as I am concerned only with the analysis of my own experience, there is nothing to suggest the distinction between a physical and a psychical aspect of existence. All that I require, or rather all that I should require had I any interest in analysing my own experience independent of the need for intercommunication, is the simpler and more primitive distinction between myself as one thing in the world and the other things which form my environment. But the case is altered when I come, after the creation of the concept of a physical order, to analyse the experience of my fellow-men. My fellow-men, on the one hand, belong to the physical order, and, as belonging to it, are known to me as objects cognisable through my senses. On the other hand, it is necessary for all the purposes of practical intercourse to credit them with the same kind of sentience and feeling which I directly know in myself. This sentience and feeling are, of course, inaccessible to the perception of my own senses; I can see my fellow's eye and can hear his voice, but I cannot see that he sees or hear that he hears. My fellow thus comes to be thought of as having a double existence; besides that aspect of him in which he is simply one among other things perceived, or in principle perceptible, by my senses, he has another aspect, not directly perceptible but necessarily presupposed in all social relation with him. On the side of his body he belongs entirely to the physical order; but there is, associated with this bodily existence, another side to him which I call his psychical aspect. Now, how must this "psychical aspect" be supposed to be constituted when once it has come to be thus artificially separated in thought from the physical side of my fellow's existence? It is here that the theory of "introjection," as worked out by Avenarius, comes to our aid.

When I perceive any object directly, without sophisticating myself by devising psychological hypotheses about the process, what I am aware of is, on the one side, the thing as a constituent of my environment, and, on the other, a variety of movements or impulses to movement in myself, marked by a peculiar tone of satisfied or dissatisfied feeling, and determined by the relation in which the thing in question stands to my various interests. But when I come to explain to myself what is meant by my fellow-man's assertion that he also perceives the same object, a difficulty seems to arise which renders this simple analysis inadequate. The perceived object, the sun for example, appears to belong to *my* world of sensible things, for I too see the sun. Not so my fellow-man's perception of it; as I cannot "see him seeing the sun," so to say, I find it hard to understand how the sun, which is a thing in my sensible world, can be an object for his perception, which is not in my sensible world. Hence I draw the inference that while I see the *actual sun*, the content of my fellow's perception is an *image* or *idea* of the sun (cf. p. 81).

By the extension of this process of inference I come to think of the non-physical aspect of my fellow's existence as consisting, as a whole, of a vast complex of successive ideas or images, attended with their characteristic tone of satisfied and dissatisfied feeling; as this series of "mental states" or "ideas" has now to be represented as in some way related to the sensible physical reality I call my fellow's body, I imagine it as going on "within" his skin somewhere, and thus arrive at the conception of my fellow as a dualistic compound of a physical factor, perceptible by my senses, his *body*, and a non-physical factor, composed of a stream of "mental images," and imperceptible to sense, his *mind*. One further step remains to be taken and the work of "introjection" is complete. That step is the artificial re-interpretation of my own experience in terms of the distinction I have been led to establish for the case of my fellow. I come to think of my own conscious life in terms of the distinction between body and mind, and to analyse what as originally experienced was the direct reaction of a unitary self upon the things which formed its environment into a succession of "mental states" or "images" going on "within" a body, their relation to which will yet form a prominent scientific problem.

Now, it is only when this process of "introjection" has reached its final issue, and the actual life of sentient purposive intercourse with the other actual things of our environment has been replaced in thought by the conception of a mental succession of "images" or "contents of consciousness," taken to "refer" to "things" which are themselves "outside consciousness," while the felt unity of experience has given way to the radical sundering of human existence into a physical and a psychical aspect, that we have reached the point of view from which psychological science takes its departure. Only when the actualities of experience have been artificially transformed into "mental states" or "images" of actualities by the hypothesis of "introjection," and thus definitely constituted into a non-physical order, have we the materials for the construction of a special science of the "psychical side" of our nature. Psychology, in fact, presupposes "psychical states" as the material of its studies, and "psychical states" are not data of immediate experience, but symbols derived from and substituted for the actual data of experience by an elaborately artificial method of transformation. Hence we should be committing a grave fallacy in Logic if we were to argue that since subjects of experience are the sole real things, the hypotheses of Psychology must be the final metaphysical truth about the world.

When we attempt to criticise the logical validity of the process of "introjection," and the scientific constructions of a

Psychology built up on an introjectionist foundation, we cannot fail to observe certain apparent gross breaches of logic which affect it. In the first place, the fundamental assumption that my fellow's "mental life" is composed of "images" of the actual things of my own experience, is clearly at variance with the principle previously implied in the construction, for purposes of co-operation, of the physical order as composed of things *equally* accessible to the perception of a plurality of individuals. This discrepancy is once more done away with, when the process of introjection has been completed, by the reduction of my own mental life to a succession of images or states of consciousness, but only at the cost of forgetting that the original motive to "introjection" was a supposed disparity between my own and my fellow's relation to the physical things of my environment.

Hence it is not strange that Avenarius should apparently hold the whole introjectionist transformation of the "naïvely realistic" standpoint to be essentially fallacious, and should close his discussion of the subject with the proposition that all attempts to vary the "natural view of the world" lead to superfluities or contradictions.[1] It does not, however, seem necessary to follow him in this unfavourable judgment. Indeed, if we reflect that such a thorough-going rejection of all the results of introjection must involve as a consequence the repudiation of the whole science of Psychology, a science which may fairly be said to be at present about as fully justified by its successful growth as most of the physical sciences, we shall probably be inclined to hold that a process so fruitful in results *must* have its logical justification, however artificial the assumptions upon which it rests.

§ 4. What, then, is the logical justification for that elaborate transformation of experience which is necessary to bring it into the form presupposed by psychological science? In principle the question is not hard to answer. The "ideas," "mental states," and so forth, of Psychology are, as we have seen, *symbols* which we substitute for certain concrete actualities, and, like all symbols,[2] they only partially correspond to the material they symbolise. But, like other symbols, they

---

[1] See Avenarius, *Der Menschliche Weltbegriff*, p. 115 *ad fin.*

[2] Or rather, like all symbols which are not identical with the things they represent. In the latter case, as when, *e.g.*, for any purpose I count the numbers of the natural number series themselves, beginning with 1, there may appear to be complete correspondence. But the usefulness of the process depends on the fact that the 1 which I count and the 1 by which I count it are at least *numerically* distinct—how much *more* distinction this implies I do not stay to discuss here—and hence, I take it, it is by an abuse of language that the process is called "representation of a thing by itself."

are admissible as substitutes for the things symbolised on two conditions: (1) that the individual symbol corresponds to that which it symbolises according to a definite and unambiguous scheme, and (2) that the substitution of the symbol for the thing symbolised is required in order to make the latter amenable to such manipulation as is necessary for the solution of some particular class of problem. Now, there can be no doubt that the first of these conditions is fulfilled by the translation of our actual experience into the introjectionist symbols of Psychology. For in the external or "physical" events which correspond to a "mental state," I possess an unambiguous means of recognising the actual experience for which the mental state in question stands in the symbolism of Psychology. If the various physical "conditions" and forms of "expression" of the mental state are indicated with sufficient fulness and accuracy, they enable me to identify the corresponding actual experience when it occurs in my own life, or even to produce it experimentally for the express purpose of interpreting the Psychologist's symbolism. The only question, then, that can reasonably be raised as to the legitimacy of psychological symbolism, is the question whether such a transformation of the actualities of immediate experience is demanded for the attainment of some specific purpose or interest.

It seems, I think, that the transformation is really required for more purposes than one. In the first place, one obvious use of psychological hypotheses is that, like the hypotheses of physical science, they assist us to calculate the course of events, in so far as it is independent of purposive interference of our own, and thus to form prudential rules for our own guidance in so interfering. This seems to be the principal use of those parts of Psychology which deal with the more mechanical aspects of mental life, *e.g.*, the laws of the formation of fixed habits and associations by repetition, the gradual passing of voluntary into involuntary attention, and so forth. We are interested in studying the laws of habit and association, just as we are in formulating mechanical laws of physical nature, because we require to guide ourselves by such knowledge whenever we directly and intentionally interfere in the life of our fellows for educational, punitive, or general social purposes. Unless we can forecast the way in which our fellow will continue to act, so far as his behaviour is not modified by fresh purposive initiative, we shall be helpless to decide how we must intervene in his life to produce a given desired effect. Similarly, the direct moulding of our own future in a desired direction would be impossible apart from such knowledge of what that future is likely to be without intentional direction.

It may be said, of course, with justice, that, so far as Psychology presents us with such routine uniformities of succession, it is a mere supplementary device for making good the defects in our anatomical and physiological knowledge. If our physiological science were only sufficiently extensive and minute, we might reasonably expect to be able to describe the whole course of human action, so far as it is amenable to mechanical law, and exhibits routine uniformity in purely physiological terms. Instead of talking about the "association" of "ideas" or the production of a "habit" by repetition, we should then, for instance, be able to describe in physiological terminology the changes effected in a cerebral tract by the simultaneous excitement of two nervous centres, and to write the complete history of the process by which a permanent "conduction-path" arises from the reiteration of the excitement. Such a definite substitution of physiological for psychological hypotheses is pretty evidently the goal which the modern "experimental Psychology" has set before itself, and which it is constantly trying to persuade itself it has reached, in respect of some parts at least of its subject.

Nor does there seem any reason to doubt that, since the physiological counterpart of a routine uniformity of mental sequence must itself clearly be a routine uniformity, all psychological laws of uniform mechanical sequence might be ultimately replaced by their physiological equivalents, if only our knowledge of the structure and functions of the nervous system were sufficiently advanced. Hence Professor Münsterberg is perfectly self-consistent in arguing from the premisses that the sole function of psychological science is to provide us with mechanical uniformities of sequence by the aid whereof to calculate the future behaviour of our fellows, in so far as it is not modified by fresh purposive initiative, to the conclusion that the whole of Psychology is a temporary stop-gap by which we eke out our defective Physiology, but which must sooner or later cease to be of use, and therefore cease to exist as Physiology advances.[1]

It would, of course, remain true, even if we were to accept this view of the case without reservation, that Psychology is, in the present state of our knowledge, an indispensable adjunct to Physiology. For, while our knowledge of the physiology of the nervous system is at present too frag-

[1] See *Grundzüge der Psychologie*, vol. i. chap. 11, pp. 415-436.

mentary and vague to be of much practical use in enabling us to forecast even the simplest sequences in the behaviour of our fellows, Psychology is, temporarily at least, in many respects in a more advanced condition. Thus, if it were necessary, before we could infer the probable effects of exposure to a particular stimulus on a man's behaviour, to frame a workable hypothesis as to the physiological occurrences in the nervous system between the first reception of the stimulus and the issuing of the ultimate bodily reaction, we should still be waiting helplessly for the means of framing the simplest general judgments as to the probable effects of our actions on our social circle. This is because the nervous changes intervening between the reception of the stimulus and the reaction can only be rendered accessible to observation by devices which postulate for their invention an extremely advanced condition of physical science in general and of Physiology in particular. There is no direct method of translating the actual processes which we experience into an unambiguous physiological symbolism, or, *vice versâ*, of testing a physiological hypothesis by retranslating it into facts of direct living experience. On the other hand, when we have given the assumed conditions of the occurrence of the stimulus, it is comparatively easy to observe what follows on them in actual life, and to translate it into the introjectionist Psychology, or, *vice versâ*, to test a theory couched in terms of that Psychology by comparison with the actualities of experience.

For this reason psychological hypotheses are, in the present state of knowledge, an indispensable mediating link between actual experience and physiological theory, and if ever they should come to be finally superseded by purely physiological descriptions of human conduct, we may be sure that the triumphant physiological theories will themselves first have been won by the process of establishing psychological formulæ and then seeking their physiological analogues. This is illustrated in the actual history of contemporary science by the extent to which the cerebral physiologists are dependent for their conception of the structure of the nervous system on the previous results of purely psychological investigation. We might present the mutual relations of concrete experience, Psychology and nervous Physiology, in an epigrammatic form, by saying that the connecting link between the subject of experience and the brain of Physiology is the "mind" or "consciousness" of Psychology.

§ 5. It is, I think, questionable whether such a view as Professor Münsterberg's does full justice to the interests which prompt us to the construction of the psychological symbolism. On his theory, Psychology, it will be seen, is essentially a science of routine or mechanical uniformities of sequence, just like the various branches of mechanical Physics. According to him, teleology must be ruthlessly banished from scientific Psychology. In other words, though all the actual processes of direct experience are pervaded by teleological unity of interest or purpose, yet in substituting our psychological symbols for the actualities we must deprive them of every vestige of this teleological character. Nor is this demand that Psychology shall translate experience into a series of non-purposive routine sequences an arbitrary one on Professor Münsterberg's part. If the sole function of Psychology is to facilitate calculation and prediction of the course of events, so far as it is *not* controlled by purposive interference, Psychology must, of course, either follow rigidly mechanical lines in its descriptions, or fail of its object. But I would suggest that over and above this function of facilitating calculation and prediction at present fulfilled by Psychology as *locum tenens* for a perfected Physiology, Psychology has another and an entirely distinct function, in which it would be impossible for it to be replaced by Physiology or by any other branch of study. This function is that of affording a set of symbols suitable for the description, in abstract general terms, of the teleological processes of real life, and thus providing Ethics and History and their kindred studies with an appropriate terminology.

It is manifest enough that neither the ethical appreciation of human conduct by comparison with an ideal standard, nor the historical interpretation of it in the light of the actual ends and ideals which pervade it and give it its individuality, would be possible unless we could first of all describe the events with which Ethics and History are conceived in teleological language. Apart from the presence throughout those events of more or less conscious striving towards an ideal end, there would be nothing in them for the moralist to applaud or blame, or for the historian to interpret. Thus, if Ethics and History are to have their subject-matter, there must be some science which describes the processes of human life and conduct in terms of teleological relation to an end. Now, to what science can we go for such descriptions? From our previous examination of the postulates of physical science, it is clear that the requisite material cannot be afforded by any branch of physical science which remains rigidly consistent with its own postulates. The nature of the interests in response to which the concept of the physical order was constucted, as we saw, required that the physical order should be thought of and described in terms of rigid mechanism. Hence no science which describes the processes of human life in purely physical terminology can indicate their purposive or teleological character in its descriptions. The purposive character of human conduct, if recognised at all in our descriptions, must find its recognition in that science which describes the aspect of human experience that is in principle excluded from the physical order. In other words, it is Psychology to which we have to go for such a general abstract conception of teleological unity as is necessary for the purposes of the more concrete sciences of Ethics and History.

This function of Psychology is indeed quite familiar to the student of the moral and historical sciences. In Ethics, as Professor Sidgwick has observed, the whole vocabulary used to characterise human conduct, apart from the specially ethical predicates of worth, is purely psychological. All the material which Ethics pronounces "good" or "bad," "right" or "wrong"—"acts," "feelings," "tempers," "desire," etc.,— it has taken over bodily from Psychology. And so, too, History would have nothing left to appreciate if a record of merely physical movements were substituted for accounts of events which imply at every turn the psychological categories of "desire," "purpose," "intention," "temptation," and the rest. Universally, we may say all the teleological categories of human thought on examination prove to be either avowedly the property of Psychology, or, as is the case with the concepts of biological evolutionism, thinly disguised borrowings from it.

If this is so, we seem to be justified in drawing certain important inferences. (1) It will follow that of the two distinct offices which Psychology at present fulfils, one belongs to it, so to say, in its own right and inalienably, while the other is exercised by it temporarily, pending the majority of Cerebral Physiology. While, as we have seen, those parts of psychological doctrine which are concerned with the more mechanical aspects of conduct may ultimately be replaced by Physiology, the parts which deal with the initiation of fresh purposive adjustments, such as the psychology of attention and of feeling, are in principle irreducible to Physiology, and must retain a permanent value so long as mankind continues to be interested in the ethical and historical appreciation of human life.[1]

(2) It will also follow that, at present and for long enough to come, Psychology is bound, *pace* Professor Münsterberg, to use both mechanical and teleological hypotheses and categories. Such a mixture of two different logical standpoints would no doubt be intolerable in a science which owed its existence to the need of satisfying a single interest of our nature. For the kind of interest which is met by mechanical hypotheses is baffled by the introduction of teleological modes of thought, and *vice versâ*. But, according to our view, the interest to which Psychology owes its creation is not single but double. We have an interest in the mechanical forecasting of human action, and an interest in its ethical and historical interpretation, and Psychology, as at present constituted, has to satisfy both these conflicting interests at once. Hence the impossibility of confining it either to purely mechanical or to purely teleological categories. If, indeed, our Physiology had reached the point of ideal completeness, so that every routine uniformity at present expressed in psychological terminology as the establishment of an "association" or "habit" could be translated into its physiological correlate, we should be able to dispense altogether with psychological hypotheses as aids to the calculation of the course of events, and to restore logical unity to Psychology by confining it entirely to the task of providing Ethics and History with the teleological categories they require for the description of their subject-matter. But such a reform of method would be most premature in the present condition of our physiological knowledge.[2]

---

[1] This is strikingly illustrated by the procedure of Professor Münsterberg himself. He expels selective interest from his psychological account of attention, in obedience to the principle that teleological ideas must be kept out of a descriptive science, and then, when confronted with the problem what it is that does decide what presentations shall actually be attended to, makes the selection a function of the sub-cortical motor-centres in the brain, thus reintroducing into biology the teleological categories previously declared inadmissible. See *Grundzüge der Psychologie*, vol. i. chap. 15, pp. 525–562. I may once more note, for the benefit of the reader who is interested in methodology, that whereas the processes of the mechanical sciences are essentially continuous, the teleological processes of finite life as conceived by ethical and historical science appear, as Professor Royce has insisted, to be of the nature of *discontinuous* series, *i.e.* to consist of terms *between* which intermediate links cannot be interpolated. Why I cannot accept what appears to be Professor Royce's view, that ultimate Reality itself is a discontinuous series, will perhaps be clear from Chap. 3 and the following chapters of the present Book. But see also the Supplementary Note at the end of the present chapter.

[2] Psychology is, of course, far from being the only branch of study which, in its present state, employs categories of both types. Compare the constant

§ 6. There are two points of difficulty which our discussion has so far failed to deal with, but must not leave entirely unnoticed. We have allowed ourselves to assume (*a*) that description in psychological terms, and (*b*) that description in teleological terms, are possible. Both these assumptions have been questioned, and it is clear that if the first is unsound there can be no science of Psychology at all, while, if the second is unsound, Psychology cannot use teleological conceptions. Hence it is absolutely necessary to attempt some justification of our position on both questions.

As to (*a*), it has been argued that since only that which is accessible on equal terms to the perception of a plurality of subjects can be described by one subject to another, and since all objects so accessible to the perception of a plurality of subjects were included in our construction of the physical order, description can only be of physical objects. A "mental state" must be in principle incapable of description, because it can only be experienced by *one* subject.

Now, if Psychology claimed to be the *direct* description of immediate experience, as it is experienced, this contention would certainly be fatal to its very existence. But, as we have seen, Psychology makes no such claim. Its data are not the actualities of immediate experience themselves, but symbols derived from those actualities by a certain process of transformation. And though what Psychology calls its "facts" cannot, of course, like physical facts, be directly exhibited to the sense-perception of a plurality of subjects, we have in the physical conditions and concomitants of a "mental state" assignable marks by which we may recognise when it occurs in our own life, the actual experience of which the psychologist's "mental state" is the symbol. Thus, though I cannot directly produce for inspection a sample

---

use made in biological evolutionary theories of the teleological ideas of, *e.g.*, the "*struggle* for existence," the "survival of the *fittest*," "sexual *selection*," etc., ideas bodily conveyed from Sociology and Psychology. As we have just seen, the precisians who object to this mixture of higher and lower categories in Psychology are in the awkward predicament of only being able to get rid of it there by accentuating its presence in Physiology and Biology. Where they go wrong is in exaggerating the amount of logical unity attributable to any body of inquiries which happens, in virtue of being pursued by the same men and with the same accessories, to be called by a common name. It would require only a slight further exaggeration to argue that since all branches of knowledge are alike knowledge, they must be all either exclusively mechanical or exclusively teleological. There is no reason in the nature of things why "Psychology" should not at a particular period in the growth of knowledge cover as wide a range of inquiries, with as much internal variety of aim and method, as, say "Mathematics."

of what in Psychology I call "the sensation of red," I can indirectly, by assigning the upper and lower limits of the wave-length corresponding to the sensation, make every one understand what actual experience I am thinking of when I use the term.

(*b*) The second difficulty need not detain us long. The view that *all* description must be exclusively mechanical, rests upon the assumption that no other kind of description will answer the purpose for the sake of which we set out to describe things. Now, so far as description is undertaken for the purpose of establishing practical rules for intervention in the course of occurrences, this assumption is perfectly justified. If we are to lay down general rules for meddling in the course of events, we must of course assume that, apart from our meddling, it goes on with routine regularity. And we have already seen that for this very reason the mechanical interpretation of Nature is a fundamental postulate of physical science, so long as it confines itself strictly to the work of formulating "laws of Nature," and does not attempt the task of historical appreciation. But, as we have also seen, the historical appreciation of a series of events as marked by the progressive execution of an underlying plan or purpose, is only possible when the events themselves have been described in essentially teleological terms as processes relative to ends.[1] Hence we have no right to contend that *all* scientific descriptions shall be of the mechanical type, unless we are also prepared to maintain that the *only* purpose they subserve is that of the formulation of general rules for practice.

If the historical appreciation of events is a legitimate human interest, the description of events in terms of end and purpose must also be a legitimate form of description. Now, in point of fact, even the "physical sciences" themselves, when they come to deal with the facts of organic life, largely desert the primary scientific ideal of the formation of general laws for the historical ideal of the detection of lines of individual development, and if our previous conclusions are correct, it is much more for the latter than for the former purpose that we are interested in the construction of a science of Psychology. What a human being wants

[1] And they cannot be so described without the introduction of psychological ideas. Thus, *e.g.*, in classifying a series of implements dating from different periods in the history of civilisation, so as to throw light on the evolution of some particular type of tool or machine, we have to take as our *fundamentum divisionis* the adequacy with which the different varieties accomplish the kind of *work* they were *designed* to perform, and are thus committed at once to the use of the psychological concepts of purpose and satisfaction.

Psychology for, in the main, is not so much to help him to forecast the behaviour of other men, as to assist him to understand how the successive stages of his own individual development and that of his "social environment" are knit into a unity by the presence of all-pervading permanent interests and ends. The contention that psychological description must, on grounds of logical method, be of the mechanical type, seems therefore to repose on misconception as to the uses of Psychology.

The preceding discussion may perhaps appear somewhat arid and wearisome, but it was indispensable that our subsequent examination of the metaphysical problems suggested by the recognition of the psychical realm of existence should be based upon a definite view as to the connection between psychological conceptions and the actualities of experience, and such a view, in its turn, presupposes a positive theory of the interests to which psychological construction ministers and the logical procedure by which it is affected. The general result of our investigation has gone to show negatively that Psychology is not a direct transcript of real experience, but an intellectual reconstruction involving systematic abstraction from and transformation of experience, and positively that the reconstruction depends for its legitimacy upon its serviceableness for the special purposes, partly of the practical anticipation of events, but principally of their historical and ethical appreciation. The significance of those conclusions will be more apparent in the course of the two following chapters.

Consult further:—R. Avenarius, *Der Menschliche Weltbegriff;* F. H. Bradley, "A Defence of Phenomenalism in Psychology" (*Mind,* January 1900); H. Münsterberg, *Grundzüge der Psychologie,* vol. i. chap. 2 (The Epistemological Basis of Psychology), 11 (Connection through the Body); J. Ward, Art. "Psychology" in *Encyclopædia Britannica, ad init.* ("The Standpoint of Psychology"); *Naturalism and Agnosticism,* vol. ii. lect. 16.

SUPPLEMENTARY NOTE TO CHAPTER I.

On the Discontinuity of the Teleological Series of Ethics and History.

We have previously seen that every continuous series is indefinitely divisible, and that consequently no two terms of such a series are *immediately* coadjacent. On the other hand, any series which consists of terms which are immediately coadjacent, and between which intermediate terms of the same series cannot be inserted, is not indefinitely divisible, and *a fortiori* not continuous. Applying this to the case of a series of psychical processes, we can see that where the sequence is of a mechanical routine type it is continuous, since it can be indefinitely divided into smaller fragments, each exhibiting the same law of sequence as the whole. (Strictly, it ought to be added that the other condition of continuity is also fulfilled, since whatever point of time thus divides the sequence falls within the series itself.) But where you have new teleological adaptation there is a manifest solution of this continuity. The new purpose emerges at a definite point in the sequence: what has gone before up to this point belongs to the working out of a different interest or purpose, what comes after to the working out of the now freshly emerged interest. Each may form a continuous process within itself, but the transition from the one to the other is not continuous. There is where the old purposive series ends and the new one begins, a genuine case of immediate coadjacency of terms between which intermediate members cannot be interposed.

In another connection, it would, I think, be easy to show how this consideration is of itself fatal to the reality of Time. My point here is simply to maintain that the facts just referred to do not warrant the inference that "ultimate Reality" or "the Absolute" is for itself a discontinuous series. My objection to this view is that the "emergence of new selective interest" is itself essentially a feature of the finite experience which, because finite, appears in a temporal form. The distinction between the "new" and the "habitual" has no meaning for a completed and infinite experience, which embraces all existence in a perfectly harmonious form. Or, to put it in another way, the serial form of arrangement itself has no significance except for an experience which has to advance progressively from one stage to another of partial insight and comprehension. This seems as true of "logical" order or ethical order of valuation according to moral worth as of merely numerical order. In fact, we said in Book II. chap. 4, § 10, that the serial arrangement is the simplest and most general expression of that relational mode of apprehension which we decided to be at once inevitable for finite knowledge and inadequate to express Reality. It is on this ground that I feel obliged, as I understand the problem at present, to hold that ultimate Reality is neither a continuous nor a discontinuous series, for the reason that it is not for itself a series at all.

CHAPTER II

THE PROBLEM OF SOUL AND BODY

§ 1. The problem of psychophysical connection has to do with the correlation of scientific abstractions, not of given facts of experience. § 2. The "consciousness" of Psychology is thus not the same thing as the finite individual subject of experience, and Reality must not be said to consist of "minds" in the psychologist's sense. Again, we must not assume *a priori* that there can be only *one* working hypothesis of psychophysical connection. § 3. The possible hypotheses may be reduced to three, Epiphenomenalism, Parallelism, and Interaction. § 4. *Epiphenomenalism* is legitimate as a methodological principle in Physiology; it is untenable as a basis for Psychology because it implies the reduction of psychical facts to mechanical law. § 5. *Parallelism*. The arguments for Parallelism as necessarily valid to Psychophysics because of its congruity with the postulates of mechanical Physics, are fallacious. We cannot assume that Psychology must necessarily conform to these postulates. § 6. As a working hypothesis Parallelism is available for many purposes, but breaks down when we attempt to apply it to the case of the initiation of fresh purposive reactions. A teleological and a mechanical series cannot ultimately be "parallel." § 7. We are thus thrown back on the hypothesis of *Interaction* as the only one which affords a consistent scheme for the correlation of Physiology and Psychology. We have, however, to remember that what the hypothesis correlates is scientific symbols, not actual facts. The actuality represented by both sets of symbols is the same thing, though the psychological symbolism affords a wider and more adequate representation of it than the physiological.

§ 1. FEW questions have more constantly attracted the attention of philosophers, especially perhaps of those philosophers who have lived since the establishment of Christianity as the religion of the Western world, than that of the relation between the soul or mind and the body; and perhaps no question has given rise to graver misconceptions for want of a correct insight into the true logical character of the problem under discussion. Both in the half-scientific speculations of ordinary persons and in the more systematic theories of metaphysicians and psychologists, the subject is constantly approached under the totally erroneous preconception that the dualistic separation of human life into a bodily and a mental part or aspect is a datum of immediate experience which we can directly verify in ourselves, and that the task of philosophy is by ingenious but unverifiable hypothesis to transcend this chasm between given realities. From the standpoint of our previous chapter we can easily see that such a view fundamentally misrepresents the real philosophical problem.

So long as we are concerned with human existence as we directly find it in our immediate experience, or assume it in our practical social relations with our fellows, no question of the relation between body and mind can arise, because neither term of the relation is as yet before us. For my own immediate experience I am neither a body nor a soul, nor yet a composite of the two, but simply an individual subject of experiences in direct intercommunion with other individuals. Under the influence of conscious or unconscious dualistic prepossessions, we often speak as if it were a directly experienced fact that I can communicate with my fellow-subjects only indirectly through the medium of an alien "material" body, and we sometimes contrast this supposed restriction with an imagined higher state of existence, in which "disembodied spirits" may conceivably have direct intercourse with each other. But the truth is, that this direct intercourse and influence of one intelligent and purposive individual on another is no privilege reserved for our enjoyment in "a better world than this"; it is, as we can see if we will only forget our dualistic prepossessions, the very truth about our actual life. In actual life, before we have contaminated our direct enjoyment of it with psychological prejudices, we know nothing of the interposition of an inert "material" organisation between ourselves and the members of our social environment. The severance of the original unity of experience into a physical and a psychical aspect is entirely a product of our own abstraction-making intellect. "Body" and "soul" are not given actualities of experience, but artificial mental constructions of our own derived from the actual "facts" of life by the elaborate processes which we have just been studying.

As we have seen in constructing our concept of a mechanical physical order, we abstract certain elements of our direct experience from the whole, and consider them under the name of our "bodies" as if they had a separate existence; we then, by the aid of the hypothesis of "introjection," represent those elements of direct self-experience which were omitted from the physical order as forming by themselves a second distinct whole or system called the "soul." When we have reached this point, we are, of course, compelled to raise the question how these two systems, the bodily and the mental, must be supposed to be connected. But the important fact to remember is that the two systems are not facts of experience, but products of abstraction. Our task in discussing their relation is not to transcend a *given* dualism, but to get rid of one which we have manufactured for ourselves by the manipulation of experience in the interests of certain special scientific problems. Hence, as Münsterberg well puts it, we have not to *find the* connection which subsists, as an actual fact, between body and soul, but to *invent a* connection in keeping with the general scheme of our artificial physical and psychological hypotheses.[1]

§ 2. As far as the interests of Metaphysics are concerned, this recognition that the problem of soul and body has to do solely with highly artificial products of scientific abstraction, and not with anything which can be called a "given" actuality, is the one principle of supreme importance which emerges from the discussion of the subject. Two very significant inferences may at once be drawn from it. (1) We clearly must not call the finite subjects of experience, of whom we saw reason to hold that ultimate Reality is exclusively constituted, "minds" or "souls" in the psychologist's sense.[2] To call them so would inevitably be to imply that exclusion from the physical order of "bodies" apart from which the psychological concept of the "soul" or "mind" has no significance. Or, in other words, it would identify them

---

[1] Compare the following striking passage from Avenarius, *Menschliche Weltbegriff*, p. 75: "Let an individual M denote a definite whole of 'perceived things' (trunk, arms and hands, legs and feet, speech, movements, etc.) and of 'presented thoughts' as I, ... then when M says 'I have a brain,' this means that a brain belongs as part to the whole of perceived things and presented thoughts denoted as I. And when M says 'I have thoughts,' this means that the thoughts themselves belong as a part to the whole of perceived things and presented thoughts denoted as I. But though thorough analysis of the denotation of I thus leads to the result that we *have* a brain and thought, it never leads to the result that the *brain has* the thoughts. The thought is, no doubt, a thought of 'my Ego,' but not a thought of 'my brain' any more than my brain is the brain of 'my thought.' *I.e.* the brain is no habitation, seat, generator, instrument or organ, no support or substratum of *thought*. Thought is no indweller or commander, no other half or side, and also no product, indeed not even a physiological function or so much as a state of the *brain*."

[2] As elsewhere in this work, I am using the terms "mind" and "soul" as virtually interchangeable names for the object studied by the psychologist. So far as there is any definite distinction of meaning between the terms as currently used by English writers, "soul" seems to carry with it more of the implication of substantiality and relative independence than "mind." It might not be amiss to adopt the term "soul" as a name for the finite subject of experience as he is for himself in actual social life, and to confine the name "mind" to the construction which symbolises this subject for psychological purposes. But the popular antithesis between soul and body is perhaps too strongly rooted to admit of this suggestion. In earlier passages, *e.g.*, Book II. chap. 2, § 6, I have used the term "spirit" in the sense here suggested for "soul."

not with what they are for their own direct experience, but with what they become for one another's theoretical reflection under the influence of "introjection." As we have seen, it is legitimate and necessary for special scientific purposes to treat ourselves and other individuals *as if* we were such series of "mental states," but it is never legitimate to forget that, when we do this, we are substituting a highly unreal symbolism for directly experienced facts.

One consequence of confusing the symbolism with the fact may be noted in passing: when we have substituted the series of mental states for the felt unity of actual conscious life, we go on to ask ourselves how the fact and its symbol—the symbolic nature of which we have forgotten—are related. And thus arise all the unanswerable, because fundamentally unmeaning, questions as to the way in which the "self" *has* or *owns* the succession of "states." Failing to see that the succession of states is simply the unitary subject itself, as it appears from the point of view of the "introjection" hypothesis, we then find ourselves confronted by the alternatives of foisting upon our Psychology the useless and unthinkable fiction of a changeless "substratum" of mental states—the soul-substance of the pre-Kantian psychologists—or resolving real life into a succession of discontinuous "mental images." With the recognition that Psychology never deals directly with experienced reality, but always with the hypothetical products of an abstraction which is only justified by its usefulness for the special purposes of the psychologist, all these difficulties disappear.

(2) Another important consequence of our principle is that we cannot dogmatically assert that there can be only *one* legitimate theory of the "connection between mind and body." If "mind" and "body" were really given as distinct but connected in direct experience, it might well be that there could only be one account of their connection answering to experienced fact. But since the separation is itself of our own intellectual manufacture, as we are dealing throughout with artificial creations of our own abstraction, any theory of their connection which is desirable for the solution of a special problem or class of problems will be legitimate *for that particular class of problems*. Thus the physiologist may legitimately, if it answers his special purposes, adopt a working hypothesis which the psychologist may find untenable, and again different types of psychological problem may legitimately assume different working

hypotheses.[1] I shall aim at showing in the immediately following paragraphs that there is one typical psychophysical hypothesis which, on the whole, lends itself better than its rivals to the general purposes of both Physiology and Psychology, but we shall see, as we proceed, that the hypotheses we reject are also legitimate for the solution of important special problems. In fact, our chief interest, as students of Metaphysics, in the further discussion of psychophysical connection will be to point out the fallaciousness of the metaphysical arguments which are commonly used to establish some one hypothesis as necessarily and exclusively true.

§ 3. Turning now to consider the chief types of hypothesis which have been, or are at present, actually put forward by metaphysicians and psychologists, we may perhaps group them under the five main heads of (1) Pre-established Harmony, (2) Occasionalism, (3) Epiphenomenalism, (4) Psychophysical Parallelism, (5) Interaction. For our purpose in the present chapter the number of alternatives may be further reduced by the omission of the first two. Neither the Pre-established Harmony of Leibnitz nor the Occasionalism advocated by Geulincx and Malebranche, and in a one-sided form by Berkeley, is likely to find much support from the philosophy of the present day. Both doctrines are, moreover, —that of Leibnitz avowedly and that of the Occasionalists by implication,—much more than special psychophysical hypotheses. They are in principle attempts to get rid of all transeunt causality, and have been discussed in their general bearings in our chapter on the Causal Postulate, where we satisfied ourselves that any science which recognises, as Psychology has to do, the existence of finite things must also admit the principle of transeunt causality, at any rate as a working hypothesis.

Each of the three remaining types of view has its supporters among contemporary students of science and philosophy. The epiphenomenalist theory is largely adopted by

[1] So, in dealing with astronomical problems, we are free to adopt either the Copernican or the Ptolemaic scheme, whichever happens to be the more *convenient* for our special purpose. The superior *truth* of the Copernican system seems to mean no more than that the range of its utility is the wider of the two. I may observe that I do not here employ the term "utility" in the narrowly practical sense of those philosophers who, *e.g.*, condemn all speculation about the "Absolute" on the ground of inutility. Whatever satisfies *any* human aspiration is for me, so far, "useful." It follows that there is, for me, no such thing as the "useless knowledge" which "Pragmatism" denounces. Thus, if a man's peace of mind depends upon speculation about the "Absolute" —on the habits of angels, or any other topic you like (and this is a matter in which every man must in the end decide for himself)—Pragmatism would appear to be false to its own principle in forbidding him to speculate.

the workers in the physical sciences, and though not much countenanced by psychologists and metaphysicians, has the explicit support of Dr. Shadworth Hodgson, while some versions of the parallelist doctrine, notably that of Münsterberg, approach it very closely. The parallelist hypothesis is perhaps at present the most popular among the psychological specialists, and is represented by writers of such eminence as Wundt, Münsterberg, Ebbinghaus, Höffding, and Stout. Finally, Interaction has powerful champions in Bradley, Ward, and James; to say nothing of its adoption by so sound a physiologist as Mr. McDougall. Both the latter doctrines, again, have historical connections with the great philosophical systems of the past, Parallelism with that of Spinoza, and Interaction with those, to mention no other names, of Descartes and Locke. In the philosophy of the ancient world the psychophysical issue can hardly be said to appear in a well-defined form, but we may perhaps state that Plato's psychological doctrine is decidedly one of Interaction, while the view of Aristotle, though too complex to admit of very precise formulation, inclines rather towards Parallelism.

§ 4. *Epiphenomenalism.* Of the three hypotheses which remain for discussion, the theory of Epiphenomenalism has the least to recommend it, and is open to the most serious objections. According to this view, all causal connections are exclusively between physical states. Bodily changes succeed one another in accord with uniform laws of sequence, which it is the province of the physiologist to discover, and every bodily change is completely determined by bodily antecedents. Certain bodily conditions are further attended by corresponding "states of consciousness," but those states stand in no causal connection with subsequent bodily states, nor yet with one another. They are thus consequences or effects, but are never causes. The whole series of physical changes, from birth to death, which makes up the history of the human body, goes on precisely as it would if "consciousness" were entirely absent. This is what is meant by the assertion that all mental states are *epi*phenomena, superfluous accessories, which arise in the course of the connected series of bodily changes, but are entirely without any determining influence upon it. The doctrine may be diagrammatically represented thus
$$\begin{matrix} \overset{\frown}{a\text{---}\alpha} \\ | \\ \overset{\frown}{b\text{---}\beta} \\ | \\ \overset{\frown}{c\text{---}\gamma} \end{matrix}$$
; where the italic letters symbolise

physical and the Greek letters psychical states, the vertical lines indicating the course of causal sequence.

If a psychophysical hypothesis were ever directly applicable to the actualities of experience, we might, of course, dismiss Epiphenomenalism at once as inherently absurd. For nothing is more certain than that in the actual life of direct experience our knowledge and our interests do determine the course of our actions. That what we believe and desire does make all the difference in the world to the way in which we behave, is one of those elementary verities out of which no scientific hypothesis can claim to reason us. Hence, when the defenders of the theory attempt to draw practical moral and juristic consequences from their doctrines, we are within our rights in simply declining to concern ourselves with so absurd a travesty of the simplest facts of experience. So long, however, as the hypothesis is put forward simply as a working hypothesis for the correlation of our physiological and psychological theories, the case is different. Its validity as a psychophysical theory must be estimated solely by the degree in which it renders this systematic correlation feasible, and is not necessarily impaired by the manifest absurdities which result from mistaking the doctrine for a description of actual life.

Now, if we look at the hypothesis from this point of view, we can at once see that it is really legitimate for some purposes. For the purpose of physiological science it is obviously to our interest that we should be able to deduce the later from the earlier stages of a physiological process. We have thus an interest in treating physiological changes, if we can, as unconditioned by any but physiological antecedents. And every actual success in establishing a uniformity or "law" of Cerebral Physiology is proof that the assumption that, for the process in question, the only determining conditions which count are physiological, is equivalent to the truth. The physiologist, then, is clearly justified in treating the psychical series as epiphenomenal, if he means no more by this than that he intends to deal, as a physiologist, only with processes which can be successfully resolved into uniform sequences on the assumption that they involve only physiological terms. Though whether any processes in the nervous system can be successfully treated as purely physiological sequences, nothing but the physiologist's actual success in obtaining results from his initial postulate can decide.

If, however, the physiologist should go on, as he sometimes does, to make the assertion that not only can some nervous processes be treated *as if* their psychical accompaniments made no difference, but that they really are what they would be without those accompaniments, or even that *all* nervous process is what it would be without "consciousness," he commits a gross logical fallacy. It is a mere blunder in logic to argue that because the presence of certain circumstances makes no difference to the special result which follows on a given antecedent, the result would equally follow in their absence. For it might be that in their removal the very antecedents in which we are interested would disappear. We are not at liberty to infer that, because the course of certain physiological processes can be computed without taking their mental correlates into account, they could occur apart from those correlates.

Even more serious are the consequences which follow when it is assumed that *all* mental processes without exception may be regarded as epiphenomenal, *i.e.* that all human action, if only our Physiology were sufficiently advanced, might be brought under laws of purely physiological sequence. Such an assumption would lead at once to the following dilemma: Either our Physiology must remain rigidly faithful to the fundamental postulates of mechanical science, or not. If it is faithful to them, its descriptions of human action must rigidly exclude all reference to teleological determination by reference to conceived and desired ends. *I.e.* we must treat human conduct as if it were fatally determined apart from any possible influence of human choice and intention, and thus stultify that whole work of historical and ethical appreciation which we have already seen to be the principal *raison d'être* of Psychology as a science. We must revert, in fact, to a theory of life which is identical with the extremest forms of Pagan or Mohammedan fatalism in everything except the name it gives to its *ineluctabile fatum* Or, if we are not prepared to do this, we must allow Physiology itself to use the psychological categories of desire, selection, and choice, and thus covertly admit that human action, after all, cannot be described without the introduction of factors not included in the physical order. It is no doubt due to their realisation of this dilemma that psychologists are all but universally agreed to reject the epiphenomenalist hypothesis, while its popularity with physiologists may be explained by observing that physiological uniformities can manifestly only be successfully established for those processes which can be treated *as if* they were only physiologically conditioned.

§ 5. *Parallelism.* The hypothesis of Parallelism attempts, while preserving some of the characteristic features of the cruder view just described, to avoid its unsatisfactory consequences. Agreeing with Epiphenomenalism in the doctrine that physiological changes must be treated as determined only by physiological antecedents, Parallelism denies that the events of the psychical series are mere "secondary" effects of their physiological correlates. According to it, the series of physical and that of psychical events are strictly "parallel," but not causally connected. Each event in either series has its precise counterpart in the other, but the physical events do not cause the psychical events, nor *vice versâ*. The successive members of the physical series form a connected causal sequence, independent of their psychical concomitants, while these latter, it is generally assumed,[1] form a similar chain of causally connected psychical states. Thus every nervous change is determined solely by precedent nervous changes, and the corresponding psychical change by the corresponding antecedent psychical changes. In diagrammatic shape our hypothesis now takes the form

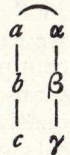

$$\overset{\frown}{\begin{matrix} a & \alpha \\ | & | \\ b & \beta \\ | & | \\ c & \gamma \end{matrix}}$$

Usually it is further added that the ultimate metaphysical explanation of this parallelism without mutual dependence must be found in the (Spinozistic) doctrine of *Identity*, *i.e.* the doctrine that the physical and psychical series are two different "sides" or "aspects" of a single reality. Some supporters of Parallelism (*e.g.*, Ebbinghaus) conceive this single reality as a *tertium quid*, equally adequately expressed by both the series, others (*e.g.*, Stout) hold that its real nature is more adequately revealed in the mental than in the physical series.

The grounds commonly adduced in favour of the parallelistic view as the most satisfactory psychophysical theory, are of two kinds. As a positive argument it is urged

[1] The assumption is not always made, however. Professor Münsterberg, who classes himself as a supporter of Parallelism, holds on metaphysical grounds that all causal connection must be between physical states. Hence he denies that psychical states can be causally connected with one another, except indirectly through the causal relations of their physical correlates. His doctrine is thus hardly to be distinguished from Epiphenomenalism, except in terminology, though he avoids the consequence of practical Fatalism by his insistence upon the purely artificial nature of both the physical and the psychical series. (His reason for refusing to admit causal relation between psychical states is that causal connection can only be established between universals, whereas every psychical state is *unique*. Does not this argument imply a confusion between the actual experience and its psychological symbol?)

that cerebral anatomy has already to some extent confirmed the doctrine of correspondence between definite physical and psychical processes by its successful "localisation" of specific sensory and motor processes in various cortical "centres," and may reasonably be expected to accomplish further such "localisations" in the future. Stress is also laid upon the formal analogy between the psychological laws of retentiveness, association, and habit, and the physiological theories of the formation of "conduction-paths" in the brain. These positive contentions do not, however, take us far. The correspondences upon which they rest, so far as they are ascertained experimentally and are not mere deductions from the principle of Parallelism itself, would be equally natural on a theory of Interaction, or of one-sided dependence of either series on the other. The real strength of the case for Parallelism rests upon certain negative assumptions which are widely believed to exclude the hypothesis of causal dependence of either series on the other. These negative assumptions appear to be in the main three.

(1) It is said that, while we can without difficulty conceive how the later stages of a continuous physical or psychical process can be connected by causal law with its earlier stages, we are entirely unable to conceive how psychical events can arise from physical antecedents, or *vice versâ*, because of the utter disparateness of the physical and the psychical. The physical process, it is urged, is continuous, and so, on the other side, is the psychical, but when we attempt to think of a cerebral change conditioning a mental change, or *vice versâ*, there is a complete solution of continuity which we cannot bridge by any causal formula.

(2) The doctrine of Conservation of Energy is sometimes supposed to be incompatible with the admission of psychical states among the antecedents or consequents of physical states. It is said that if psychical states can influence the course of nervous change, there will be "work" done in the organism without the expenditure of energy, and if the total effect of nervous change is not exclusively physical there will be loss of energy without "work" being done by the organism, and in either case the principle of Conservation will be contravened.

(3) Finally, it is maintained that it is a fundamental postulate of the physical sciences, that every change of configuration in a material system such as the living organism is assumed to be, is due to exclusively physical antecedents, and that this postulate must therefore be respected in

Psychophysics. These are, so far as I can gather them from the works of the psychologists who adopt the parallelist view, the principal arguments by which their case is supported.

It is clear that if all—or any—of these contentions are valid, it must follow that Parallelism is not only a legitimate but the only legitimate hypothesis for the co-ordination of physical and psychical science. I believe, however, that every one of them is fallacious, and that for the following reasons:—

(1) The argument from the inconceivability of causal relation between the physical and the psychical is perhaps the most effective of the alleged grounds for denying inter- action between the psychical and the physical. Yet its force is not really so great as it might appear. It is not denied that we can, in simple cases, assign the conditions under which a mental state follows on a physical state (*e.g.*, we can assign the physical conditions of the emergence of a given sensation). But, it is argued, we cannot show why those conditions (*e.g.*, the stimulation of the retina, and indirectly of the "optical centres" in the brain by light of a given wave length) should be followed by this particular sensation (*e.g.*, green, and not some other colour). This means that we cannot construct a mathematical equation connecting the character of the sensation with that of the stimulus, as we can to connect the earlier with the later stages of a purely physical process. This is, of course, obvious enough. It is only by making complete abstraction from the appearance of new *qualities* in the course of a process, and by treating it as a purely geometrical and quantitative transformation, that we can render it amenable to our equations.

As we saw in our discussion of Causality, mathematical Physics only succeeds in its constructions on the condition of excluding all *qualitative* change, as "subjective," from its purview. But we also saw there that the origination of the qualitatively new is an essential part of the idea of Causality, and that in reducing all change in the physical world to quantitative transformation, mathematical Physics really does away with the causal concept. We are, in fact, in precisely the same logical position if we speak of physiological changes as *causing* sensation, as when we speak of a quantitative change in the proportions of a chemical compound as the *cause* of alteration in its qualities. The objection that the psychical effect cannot be connected by an equation with its alleged cause, would hold equally in any case of the production of the qualitatively new, *i.e.* in every case where we use the category of causality at all. And for that very reason it has no force when urged as an objection to psychophysical causality in particular.[1]

(2) The argument from the Conservation of Energy may be more briefly dismissed, as its fallacious character has been fully recognised by the ablest recent exponents of the parallelistic view, such as Dr. Stout and Professor Münsterberg. As Dr. Stout points out, the argument involves a formal *petitio principii*. The principle of Conservation of Energy has only been established for what are technically known as conservative material systems, and no absolute proof has been given, or seems likely to be given, that the human organism is such a conservative system. Further, as has been urged by many critics, and notably by Professor Ward, the principle of conservation, taken by itself, is simply a law of exchanges. It asserts that the *quantity* of the energy of a conservative system remains constant under all the transformations through which it passes, but, apart from the rest of the postulates of mechanical science, it affords no means of deciding *what* transformations of energy shall occur in the system, or *when* they shall occur. Hence there would be no breach with the special principle of Conservation of Energy if we were to assume that psychical conditions can determine the moment at which energy in the organism is transformed *e.g.*, from the kinetic to the potential state, without affecting its quantity.

(3) It is, however, true that it is inconsistent with the postulates of mechanical Physics, taken as a whole, to admit the determination of physical sequences by non-physical conditions. To admit such determination would be to stultify the whole procedure of the mechanical sciences. For, as we have seen in our Third Book, the primary object of mechanical science is to reduce the course of events to rigid laws of uniform sequence, and thus to facilitate the formulation of practical rules for our own interference with it. It is therefore a legitimate postulate of mechanical science that—for its special object—desire and will shall be excluded from our conception of the conditions which determine events, and the whole course of nature treated *as if* conditioned only by physical antecedents. If there is any department of experienced reality which cannot be successfully dealt with

---

[1] Most supporters of Parallelism, it may be noted, stultify their own case, so far as it rests on this special contention, by admitting the causal determination of psychical states by one another, though, as psychical states are essentially qualitative, the reduction of causation to quantitative identity is particularly inadmissible here. Professor Münsterberg is quite consistent, therefore, in denying psychical causality and reducing Parallelism to Epiphenomenalism.

according to these postulates, then the formulation of rigid laws of uniform sequence is, in principle, impossible for that department, and it must be excluded from the "world" which mechanical science investigates.

But the fact that mechanical science can only attain its end by treating all physical events as independent of non-physical conditions, does not afford the slightest presumption that they must be treated in the same way for all purposes and by every branch of inquiry. Whether Psychology, in particular, is under the logical necessity of conforming to the mechanical postulates, will depend upon our view as to whether the object subserved by Psychology is the same as that of the mechanical sciences, or different. If our purpose in psychological investigation is not identical with the purposes of mechanical science, there is no sense in demanding that we shall hamper our procedure as psychologists by adherence to postulates based upon the special nature of the interests to which mechanical science has to minister.

Now, we have already contended that the aims of Psychology only partially and temporarily coincide with those of the mechanical sciences. If we were right in holding that the principal object of Psychology is to provide a general terminology of which History and Ethics can avail themselves in their appreciations of life, it follows at once that Psychology imperatively needs the recognition of that very teleological aspect of human action which is excluded on principle, and rightly so for the special purpose of mechanical Physics, by the fundamental mechanical postulates. Thus the argument that the parallelistic hypothesis must be the most suitable for the psychologist, because it conforms to the mechanical postulates of sciences which deal with experience from a different standpoint and in a different interest, loses all its cogency.[1]

Now that we have, as I trust, sufficiently disposed of the *a priori* arguments for the parallelistic view, we are in a position to estimate it, as a psychological hypothesis, purely on its merits as evinced by its actual success. But first we must point out once more that the whole question is not one as to actualities, but purely as to the most satisfactory way of bringing two sets of abstractions, originally devised for divergent purposes, into touch with one another; and further,

---

[1] The reader who has followed the argument of our Third Book will not need to be reminded that the world of purely mechanical processes is simply an ideal construction based on postulates which we make for their practical convenience, and in no sense a direct transcript of the world of actual experience.

that *if* the hypothesis were put forward as a final metaphysical truth about the constitution of the real world, it would be manifestly self-contradictory.

In the first place, Parallelism, taken for anything more than a convenient working hypothesis, would involve a flagrant breach of logic. It is obvious that, as Mr. Bradley has urged, you cannot infer from the premisses that one total state, containing both a physical and a psychical element, causes another complex state of the same kind, the conclusion that the physical aspect of the first, by itself, has caused the physical, and the psychical the psychical aspect of the second. To get this conclusion you need a "negative instance," in which either the physical or the psychical state is found apart from its correlate, but followed by the same consequent as before, and Parallelism itself denies the possibility of such an instance. From the premisses that $a\,\alpha$ is always followed by $b\,\beta$, it attempts to infer, without any "dissection of nature," that a by itself was the necessary and sufficient condition of b, and α of β. And this is, of course, logically fallacious. Dr. Ward expresses the same point differently when he urges that unvarying and precise concomitance *without* causal connection is a logical absurdity.

That the supporters of the hypothesis themselves are conscious of the difficulty, is shown by their unanimous assertion that the psychical and physical series are ultimately manifestations of one and the same reality. What they do not explain is how, if this is so, the two series can be phenomenally so utterly disparate as to exclude mutual influence on one another. The difficulty becomes insuperable when we reflect that on the parallelistic view the physical series must be rigidly mechanical, as otherwise we shall have a breach with those mechanical postulates which are supposed to require the exclusion of psychical states from the determining conditions of physical occurrences. Thus, if teleology is to be recognised anywhere in our scientific constructions, it must be in our conception of the psychical series. And on the whole the supporters of Parallelism admit this in practice by the free use of teleological categories in their Psychology. But it ought by now to be clear to us that the nature of the identical reality cannot be expressed with equal adequacy in a teleological series, and in one which is, by the principles of its construction, purely mechanical. Here, again, most of the parallelists are really in agreement with us, for they usually in the end call themselves "Idealists," and assert that the "mental" series is a more faithful representation of Reality than the physical. But if the two series are not on the same level in respect of their nearness to Reality, it is hard to see how there can be exact correspondence between them. This is a point to which we shall immediately have to return.[1]

§ 6. When we ask, however, whether Parallelism, apart from these questions of ultimate philosophy, is legitimate *as a working hypothesis in Psychology*, the answer must be that, in certain departments of psychological investigation, it certainly is so. In practice, the doctrine of the parallel but independent series amounts, for the most part, to little more than a methodological device for the division of labour between the physiologist and the psychologist, the physiologist restricting himself to the formulation of such uniformities as can be established between nervous processes, considered as if independent of external influence, and the psychologist doing the same for their psychical accompaniments. As a principle of methodical procedure, therefore, in those parts of Psychology which deal with the more passive and, as we may say, routine-like aspects of mental life, Parallelism is a useful and therefore a legitimate working hypothesis.

The question by which its claim to be the *best* hypothesis must be decided is, to my mind, that of its applicability to the case of the fresh initiation of new purposive adaptations to changes in the organism's environment.[2] For it is just in dealing with these cases that Psychology, if it is to fulfil the purpose we have ascribed to it, must most obviously discard mechanical for teleological categories. Hence it is here, if anywhere, that a difficulty of principle must make itself felt when we attempt to treat the psychical and the physical series as exactly parallel and corresponding. It seems to follow necessarily from the conception of physical science as based upon the mechanical postulate, that a teleological and a mechanical series cannot possibly run "parallel" in all their details in the fashion presupposed by the hypothesis under consideration.

If Psychology is to be of any use in supplying Ethics and History with the subject-matter of their appreciations, it is

[1] The "neutral Monism" to which the doctrine of rigid Parallelism logically leads, when put forward as more than a working hypothesis, will, one may hope, in England at least, fail to survive the exposure of its illogicalities in the second volume of Professor Ward's *Naturalism and Agnosticism*.

[2] This case includes, as will be apparent on a little reflection, not only the initiation of new motor reactions upon a sensation or percept, but also that of sensation itself as a qualitatively novel reaction upon physiological stimulation, and thus includes both the processes in which supporters of Interaction have always recognised the causal interconnection of the physical and the psychical.

manifest that it must make the assumption that desire and choice are operative in determining the course of human action, and thus must—at certain points at least—explicitly employ the categories of teleology. These categories, again, cannot possibly be translated into the rigidly non-teleological symbolism of a physical science, based upon the mechanical postulates, as every science of "general laws" must be. It follows that "exact parallelism *without* mutual interference" cannot, consistently with the purpose which Psychology subserves, be employed, even as a working hypothesis throughout the whole field of psychological investigation itself. When the attempt to extend its employment to the whole sphere of psychical processes is seriously made, it leads inevitably to the crude fatalism of the doctrine that there is no such thing as choice or action (free or otherwise) in the universe. In actual practice, the supporters of Parallelism, who reject this doctrine when it is explicitly avowed under the name of Epiphenomenalism, only succeed in doing so because they do not really insist on carrying out the parallelistic hypothesis in their Psychology. They commonly make their hypothesis prominent, while they are dealing with the comparatively passive and routine-like aspects of mental life, association, habituation, etc., but allow themselves to lose sight of it as soon as they come to treat of such explicitly teleological concepts as attention and choice. Their procedure is also rendered easier for them by the liberal use which evolutionary biologists, even while professing with their lips fidelity to the mechanical postulates, allow themselves to make of teleological categories which are really purely psychological.

It would be an easy task, if space permitted, to show in detail how the fundamentally different principles underlying the construction of the mechanical and the teleological series involve the presence, in the individual members of each series, of characters to which nothing corresponds in those of the other. Thus we might ask, with Dr. Ward, what corresponds in the psychical scheme to the composition of the units of the physiological scheme out of their various chemical components, and of these, again, out of more elementary physical "prime atoms"?[1] or, from the opposite side, we might ask, what is the cerebral equivalent, in terms of a rigidly mechanical Physiology, of the psychological character of "meaning" or "significance"? But the multiplication of

---

[1] It is with great pleasure that I note the coincidence of my own view on the impossibility of reconciling Parallelism with the recognition of the psychological

these problems becomes superfluous if the reader has once grasped our principle, that exact correspondence is only possible between series which are either both mechanical or both—and both in the same degree—teleological. Between a genuinely teleological and an honestly mechanical series such correspondence is logically impossible, because of the fundamental difference between their types of construction.

§ 7. For the reasons just produced, it is, I think, necessary to hold that the oldest and simplest hypothesis of the connection between body and mind, that of *Interaction*, is after all the most satisfactory. According to this view, the two series cannot be thought of as presenting an exact correspondence, and must be thought of as causally influencing each other at different points, precisely as any two sets of physical events do. If we adopt it we shall recognise in sensation a psychical state which has physical processes among its immediate antecedents, and in motor reaction similarly a physical process with psychical antecedents. It is scarcely to be denied that this conception of body and mind, as two things which stand in causal relation, is the hypothesis which most naturally presents itself, when once we have artificially broken up the unity of immediate experience into a physical and a psychical side, and so created the problem of psychophysical connection. So natural is it, that even psychologists who accept one of the other hypotheses are to be found constantly speaking of voluntary movement in terms which, if they mean anything, imply causal determination of bodily by mental process, while no psychologist of any school has ever succeeded in expressing the relation of sensation to stimulus in any other phraseology than that of Interaction. Probably the hypothesis would never have been exposed to hostile criticism at all, but for the metaphysical objections, already dismissed by us as fallacious, founded upon the notion that the mechanical postulates with which Interaction conflicts are ascertained truths about the actual structure of the reality with which we are in touch in immediate experience.

It is clear that, from the nature of the problem to

importance of "meaning" with that of Mr. Gibson (essay on "The Problem of Freedom," in *Personal Idealism*, p. 150 ff.). Professor Münsterberg's declaration, that the consciousness investigated by Psychology "knows nothing by its knowledge and wills nothing by its will," seems to me a confession of the bankruptcy of Parallelism as a basal psychological hypothesis. Still more so his elaborate and brilliant demonstration that the "brain" with which my "mind" may be regarded as "parallel" is not the brain as studied and charted by the anatomist, *i.e.* not the brain as a physical object at all. See *Psychologie*, i. 415-428.

be solved, we cannot be called upon to *prove* the actual occurrence of psychophysical interaction. As a working hypothesis for the interrelation of two sets of scientific abstractions, the theory is in principle incapable of direct establishment by the "appeal to facts." All that is requisite for its justification is to show that it is (*a*) not in principle at variance with any fundamental axiom of scientific procedure, and (*b*) enables us to co-ordinate our scientific results in the manner most suitable for the uses to which we propose to put them. Both these conditions are fulfilled by the hypothesis of Interaction, if our foregoing arguments are sound. We have seen the fallacious nature of the objections brought against it on *a priori* grounds of logical method, and have also seen that it is positively demanded if we are at once to be faithful to the mechanical postulates upon which physical science depends for its successes, and to recognise in our psychological constructions that teleological character of human action which is all-essential for History and Ethics. In substance this is the whole case for the Interaction hypothesis, and no further accession of strength would result from its elaboration in detail.

It may be added that it is one great recommendation of the hypothesis of Interaction, that it is quite consistent with the full recognition of the relative usefulness of the alternative theories, though they, as we have seen, are unable to do justice to those aspects of fact which can only be expressed in terms of Interaction. Thus the hypothesis of Interaction can readily afford to admit that, for certain purposes and up to a certain point, it is possible to treat physical or psychical processes *as if* they were determined solely by physical or psychical conditions respectively, and even to treat some physical processes *as if* the presence of their psychical concomitants made no difference at all to their occurrence. The reason of this is, that whereas a mechanical hypothesis can give no intelligible account of a purposive process at all, a teleological hypothesis can quite easily account for the apparently mechanical character of some of the processes which fall under it. As we have seen (Book III. chap. 3, § 6), a purposive reaction, once established, approximates to mechanical uniformity in the regularity with which it continues to be repeated, while the conditions are unchanged, and the end of the reaction is therefore still secured by its repetition.

Thus we can readily see that, even if we contented ourselves with the attempt to translate into the language of psychological science the processes which make up the life of an individual subject, many of them would appear to be going on with routine uniformity. And when we deliberately set ourselves to obtain uniformities by taking an average result, derived from comparison of a multitude of subjects, our results are, of course, always mechanical in appearance, because the element of individual purpose and initiative has been excluded by ourselves from our data in the very process of taking the average. Hence we can understand how, on the hypothesis of Interaction itself, all those mental processes which consist in the repetition of an already established type of reaction should come to appear mechanical, and thus to suggest that mechanical conception of psychical processes which is common to the epiphenomenalist and the parallelist view. Interaction, and Interaction alone, is thus a hypothesis capable of being applied to the *whole* field of psychological investigation.

I will conclude this chapter with some considerations on the bearing of our result upon the special problems of Metaphysics. We have explicitly defended Interaction as being no statement of actual experienced fact, but a working hypothesis for the convenient correlation of two scientific constructions, neither of which directly corresponds to the actualities of experience. This means, of course, that Interaction cannot possibly be the final truth for Metaphysics. It cannot ultimately be the "fact" that "mind" and "body" are things which react upon each other, because, as we have seen, neither "mind" nor "body" is an actual datum of experience; for direct experience and its social relations, the duality subsequently created by the construction of a physical order simply has no existence. Nor can it be maintained that this duality, though not directly given as a datum, is a concept which has to be assumed in order to make experience consistent with itself, and is therefore the truth. For the concept of Interaction manifestly reposes upon the logically prior conception of the physical as a rigidly mechanical system. It is because we have first constructed the notion of the "body" on rigidly mechanical lines that we have subsequently to devise the concept of "mind" or "soul" as a means of recognising and symbolising in our science the non-mechanical character of actual human life. And since we have already seen that the mechanical, as such, cannot be real, this whole scheme of a mechanical and a non-mechanical system in causal relation with one another can only be an imperfect substitute for the Reality it is intended to symbolise.

In fact, we might have drawn the same conclusion from the very fact that the psychophysical hypothesis we have adopted is couched in terms of Transeunt Causality, since we have already satisfied ourselves that all forms of the causal postulate are more or less defective appearance.

The proposition that the psychophysical theory of the "connection" of "body" and "mind" is an artificial transformation, due to the needs of empirical science, of the actual teleological unity of human experience, is sometimes expressed by the statement that mind and body are really one and the same thing. In its insistence upon the absence of the psychophysical duality from actual experience, this saying is correct enough, but it perhaps fails to express the truth with sufficient precision. For, as it stands, the saying conveys no hint of the very different levels on which the two concepts stand in respect to the degree of truth with which they reproduce the purposive teleological character of real human experience. It would perhaps be nearer the mark to say that, while the physiologist's object, the "body," and the psychologist's object, the "mind," are alike conceptual symbols, substituted, from special causes, for the single subject of actual life, and may both be therefore said to "mean" or "stand for" the same thing, their actual content is different. For what in the language of physiology I call my "body" includes only those processes of actual life which approximate to the mechanical ideal sufficiently closely to be capable of being successfully treated as merely mechanical, and therefore brought under a scheme of general "laws" of nature. Whereas what, as a psychologist, I call my "mind" or "soul," though it includes processes of an approximately mechanical type, includes them only as subordinate to the initiation of fresh individual reactions against environment which can only be adequately expressed by teleological categories. Thus, though "mind" and "body" in a sense mean the same actual thing, the one stands for a fuller and clearer view of its true nature than the other. In Dr. Stout's terminology their *intent* may be the same, but their content is different.[1]

Consult further :—R. Avenarius, *Der Menschliche Weltbegriff;* B. Bosanquet, *Psychology of the Moral Self*, lect. 10; F. H. Bradley, *Appearance and Reality*, chap. 23; Shadworth Hodgson, *Metaphysic of Experience*, vol. ii. pp. 276–403; William James, *Principles of Psychology*, vol. i. chaps. 5

[1] See his essay on "Error" in *Personal Idealism*.

and 6; H. Lotze, *Metaphysic*, bk. iii. chaps. 1 and 5 (Eng. trans., vol. ii. pp. 163-198, 283-517); H. Münsterberg, *Grundzüge der Psychologie*, i. chaps. 11. (pp. 402-436), 15 (pp. 525-562); G. F. Stout, *Manual of Psychology*,[3] Introduction, chap. 3; James Ward, *Naturalism and Agnosticism*, vol. ii. lects. 11 and 12 (art. "Psychology" in Supplement to *Encyclopædia Britannica*, p. 66 ff.).

CHAPTER III

THE PLACE OF THE "SELF" IN REALITY

§ 1. The "self" is (1) a teleological concept, (2) implies a contrasted not-self (where this contrast is absent from an experience there is no genuine sense of self); (3) but the limits which divide self and not-self are not fixed but fluctuating. The not-self is not a merely external limit, but consists of discordant elements within the individual, which are extruded from it by a mental construction. (4) The self is a product of development, and has its being in the time-series. (5) The self is never given complete in a moment of actual experience, but is an ideal construction; probably selfhood implies some degree of *intellectual* development. § 2. The Absolute or Infinite Individual, being free from all internal discord, can have no not-self, and therefore cannot properly be called a self. § 3. Still less can it be a person. § 4. In a *society* of selves we have a more genuinely self-determined individual than in the single self. Hence it would be nearer the truth to think of the Absolute as a Society, though no finite whole adequately expresses the Absolute's full nature. We must remember, however, (*a*) that probably the individuals in the Absolute are not all in *direct* relation, and (*b*) that in thinking of it as a Society we are not denying its real individuality. § 5. The self is not in its own nature imperishable; as to the particular problem of its continuance after death, no decision can be arrived at on grounds of Metaphysics. Neither the negative presumption drawn from our inability to understand the conditions of continuance, nor the lack of empirical evidence, is conclusive; on the other hand, there is not sufficient metaphysical reason for taking immortality as certain.

§ 1. WE have already, in Book II. chap. I, § 5, incidentally raised the question whether the whole spiritual system which we found ground to regard as the reality of the universe, can properly be spoken of as a "self." We decided that to apply such a predicate to it was at least misleading, and might prepare the way for serious intellectual sophistication. Our discussion of the general character of psychological conceptions has now made it possible for us to return to the problem with reasonable hopes of being able to treat it more fully, and to arrive at some definite conclusion as to the amount of truth embodied by the notion of "self."

First of all, then, let us attempt to fix the general meaning of the concept, and to single out some of its more prominent characteristics. It would clearly require much more space than we can spare to enumerate all the senses in which the notion of "self" has been used in Psychology, and the work,

THE PLACE OF THE "SELF" IN REALITY

when done, would not be entirely germane to our metaphysical purpose. What I propose to attempt here will be simply to consider certain aspects of the concept of "self" which are manifestly indispensable for the purpose of ethical and historical appreciation, and to ask what their value is for the metaphysical interpretation of existence.

(1) It is manifest, to begin with, that "self" is a teleological concept. The self whose quality is revealed in Biography and History, and judged in Ethics, has for its exclusive material our emotional interests and purposive attitudes towards the various constituents of our surroundings; of these, and of nothing else, our self is made. And the self, again, is one and individual, just in so far as these interests and purposes can be thought of as forming the expression, in the detail of succession, of a central coherent interest or purpose. Where this central interest appears not to exist at all, we have no logical right to speak of a succession of purposive acts as the expression of a single self. Thus, though it may be necessary for some of the practical purposes of police administration to take bodily identity as evidence of identity of self, we all recognise that what a man does in a state of mental alienation complete enough to abolish continuity of purpose, is not material for his biographer except in so far as the knowledge of it may modify his interests and purposes on his return to sanity. And even in cases where we may acquiesce in the necessity for assuming responsibility before the law for "deeds done in the body," conscience acquits us of moral guilt if we honestly feel we can say, "I was not myself when it was done."[1] The teleological character of the unity we ascribe to the self is further illustrated by the puzzles suggested by the "alternate"

[1] "Bodily identity" itself, of course, might give rise to difficult problems if we had space to go into them. Here I can merely suggest certain points for the reader's reflection. (1) All identity appears in the end to be teleological and therefore psychical. I believe this to be the *same* human body which I have seen before, because I believe that the interests expressed in its actions will be continuous, experience having taught me that a certain amount of physical resemblance is a rough-and-ready criterion of psychical continuity. (2) As to the ethical problem of responsibility referred to in the text, it is obviously entirely one of less and more. Our moral verdicts upon our own acts and those of others are in practice habitually influenced by the conviction that there are degrees of moral responsibility within what the immediate necessities of administration compel us to treat as absolute. We do not, *e.g.*, think a man free from all moral blame for what he does when drunk, or undeserving of all credit for what he performs when "taken out of himself," *i.e.* out of the rut of his habitual interests by excitement, but we certainly do, when not under the influence of a theory, regard him as deserving of *less* blame or credit, as the case may be, for his behaviour than if he had performed the acts when he was "more himself." On all these topics see Mr. Bradley's article in *Mind* for July 1902.

and "multiple" personalities occasionally brought to light in the study of hypnotism and of mental pathology. Finally, in the fairly numerous cases of "conversion," where a man, as we say, becomes a "new being" or parts with his "old self," we only recognise him as identical with his past self in so far as we succeed in thinking of his "new life" as being the expression of aims and interests which were, at least implicitly and as "tendencies," already present, though concealed, in the "old."

(2) The self implies, and has no existence apart from, a not-self, and it is only in the contrast with the not-self that it is aware of itself as a self. This seems to me clear, as a matter of principle, though the consequences of the principle are in much current speculation partly misconceived, partly neglected. The most important among them, for our purposes, are the following. The feeling of self is certainly not an inseparable concomitant of all our experience. For it only arises—and here nothing but direct experimentation can be appealed to as evidence—as a contrast-effect in connection with our awareness of a not-self, whether as imposing restraints upon the expression of the self, or as undergoing modification by the self. Hence experiences from which this contrast is absent seem to exhibit no trace of genuine "self-consciousness."[1] Feeling, where you can get it in its simple form, seems to be universally allowed to be an instance in point. Much of our perception appears to me, though I know the view is not widely current among psychologists, to be in the same position. *E.g.*, normally when I am looking at an object, say for instance, a white-washed wall, I do not find that I am in any real sense "conscious of self." The content of my awareness seems, to me at least, to be just the wall in a setting of a mass of unanalysed feeling, organic and other, which you may, if you please, from your standpoint as an external observer, call my perceiving self, but of which I am only aware *as* the setting of the perceived wall.

It is only when attention to the content of the perception becomes difficult (as, *e.g.*, through fatigue of the organs of sense, or conflict with some incompatible purpose) that I am normally aware of the perceived object as a not-self opposed to and restricting my self. The same is, I think, true of much of our life of conscious purposive action. I do not find that in my intellectual pursuit of a chosen study, or again in my social relations to the other members of my community, I

[1] So "self-consciousness," in the bad sense, always arises from a sense of an incongruity between the self and some contrasted object or environment.

have explicit awareness of the "facts" of science, or the interests and purposes of others as a not-self with which my own interests are contrasted as those of the self, except in so far as I either find these facts and interests in actual collision with some aim of my own, or experience the removal of such a collision. In ordinary social life, for instance, I have a strong feeling of self as opposed to not-self when the plans of some member of my immediate circle clash with my own, and again when I succeed in winning such a recalcitrant over to my own side; my self in the one case feels repression, in the other expansion. But I do not think it can be said that the self-feeling arises in actual life where there is temporarily no consciousness of opposition or its removal. For instance, while we are harmoniously working with other men for a previously concerted end, the consciousness of self and its contrasted not-self scarcely appears to enter into our experience.[1] This is, I presume, why practical worldly wisdom has always regarded "self-consciousness" as a source of weakness and moral failure. While we are steadily engaged in the progressive execution of a purpose, we "lose ourselves" in the work; it is only upon a check that we become "self-conscious."

(3) The next point to be noted is that there is no definite line of demarcation between self and not-self. In particular, we must not fall into the error of supposing that the whole *content* of the relation between self and not-self is *social*,—the self on its side consisting of *me*, and the not-self of other men. It is true, no doubt, that the *origin* of the distinction is mainly social, since it is in the main through experience of what it is to have my execution of a desired act repressed by others, and again to have the stumbling-blocks which have previously restricted my action removed by their co-operation, that I come to be definitely aware of what I want, and of the fact that it is I who want it. But it would be hard to show that the distinction between the self and the not-self could not originate at all except in a social medium, and it is clear that the range of its applicability, when originated, is not limited to the social relation. There seems, on the one hand, to be no feature in our experience whatever which is entirely excluded from entering into the constitution of what is felt as the self. My social intimates,

---

[1] Though, of course, it does appear in the process of framing and initiating the scheme of concerted action; the other self is here contrasted with my own, precisely because the removal of the collision between my purpose and my environment is felt as coming from without.

my professional colleagues, my regular occupations, even my clothes or articles of furniture, to which I have grown accustomed, may be so essential to the continuity of my characteristic interests in life that their removal would make my character unrecognisable, or possibly even lead to insanity or death. And as thus indispensable to the teleological unity of my existence, all these "external" objects seem to be capable of passing into and becoming part of the self.

We see an extreme instance of this in the case of the savage transplanted into civilised surroundings, who fails in body and mind and finally dies, without recognisable disease, simply from the disappearance of the interests connected with his old surroundings; or that of the clinging affectionate persons who, in the same way, fade away upon the loss of a beloved relative or friend. In a minor degree we see the same thing in those changes of character which common speech happily describe by such phrases as "he has never been himself since—his wife died, since he lost that money," and so forth. In principle there seems to be no factor of what we should currently call the self's environment which may not in this way come to be part of the content of the self.[1]

On the other side, it seems difficult to say whether there is anything which ordinarily forms part of the "self" which may not, under special conditions, become a part of what we recognise as the "not-self." Thus our bodily feelings and sensations, our thoughts and desires, and in particular our virtuous and vicious habits, are usually reckoned as definitely belonging to our self. Yet in so far as we can think of any desire or habit as an element which is discordant with the rest of our self, and ought not to be there,—and the whole business of moral progress depends on our being able to take up this attitude,—we, so far, relegate that element to the not-self. To will the habit or desire to be otherwise is already, in principle, to expel it from the teleological unity which makes up our inner life. So again with our thoughts: in so far as we can suspend our assent to a judgment, and balance reasons for or against accepting it into the general system of our beliefs, the judgment clearly belongs to the external not-self.

Yet it is at least conceivable that there may be in-

---

[1] It might be said that it is not these features of the environment themselves, but my "ideas" of them, which thus belong to the self. This sounds plausible at first, but only because we are habitually accustomed to the "introjectionist" substitution of psychological symbols for the actualities of life. On the question of fact, see Bradley, *Appearance and Reality*, chap. 8, p. 88 ff. (1st ed.).

tellectual as well as moral habits so deeply engrained in our constitution that we cannot thus set them over-against the self for judgment and sentence. We must not deny that there are cases in which we could not will or think differently, or even mentally entertain the possibility of thinking or willing differently, without the destruction of our life's continuity of purpose. Again, our bodily sensations seem to belong in a very special way to our self. Yet in so far as we can acquire the power of voluntarily observing them, or again of withdrawing attention from them, they are in principle reduced to the position of elements in the not-self.

Even pleasure and pain do not seem to belong inalienably to the self's side of the contrast. *E.g.*, to adapt a Platonic illustration, if I feel pleasure in contemplating the vulgar or obscene, and at the same time feel disgusted with myself for being so pleased, the pleasure seems in the act of condemnation to be recognised as no part of my "true" self, but an alien element obtruded on the self against its nature. Pain, by reason of that urgency and insistency which give it its biological importance, is much harder to banish from the self; but experience, I think, will convince any one who cares to make the experiment, that bodily pains, when not too intense (*e.g.*, a moderately severe toothache), can, by directing attention to their sensational quality, be sometimes made to appear as definitely foreign to the experiencing self. And the history of asceticism, ancient and modern, as well as the practice of "mind-curers," suggests that this process of extrusion can be carried further than we commonly suspect.

Organic or "common" sensations of general bodily condition probably form the element in experience which most obstinately resists all attempts to sever it from the whole self and treat it as a foreign object, though in some cases we certainly seem able to extrude the organic sensation from the felt self by analysis of its quality and "localisation." Still, it must be admitted that if there are any elements in experience which are absolutely incapable of transference to the not-self, they are probably in the main masses of unanalysed and unanalysable organic sensation.[1]

---

[1] A colleague of my own tells me that in his case movements of the eyes appear to be inseparable from the consciousness of self, and are incapable of being extruded into the not-self in the sense above described. I do not doubt that there are, in each of us, bodily feelings of this kind which refuse to be relegated to the not-self, and that it would be well worth while to institute systematic inquiries over as wide an area as possible about their precise character in individual cases. It appears to me, however, as I have stated above, that in ordinary perception these bodily feelings often are apprehended simply as qualifying the perceived content without any opposition of self and not-self.

All these considerations make two points very clear. (*a*) The self in which we are interested in Ethics and History is not anything with definitely fixed boundaries. The line dividing it from its complement, the not-self, is one which we cannot draw according to any precise logical rule; and again, what is at one time on one side of the boundary is at another on the other. If there is any part of our experience at all which must be regarded as always and essentially belonging to the self's side of the dividing line, it will in all probability be merely masses of bodily feeling which are manifestly *not* the whole of what Ethics and History contemplate when they appraise the worth of a self.[1]

Further, a conclusion follows as to the nature of the opposition of self to not-self. The not-self, as the readiness with which most of the contents of experience can pass from one side of the antithesis to the other shows, is in a sense included in at the very time that it is excluded from the self. The various factors of which the not-self can, at different times, be composed, our fellows, the physical world, thoughts, habits, feelings, all agree in possessing one common characteristic; when referred to the self, they are all elements of discord within the whole of present experience, and it is on account of this discordancy that we treat them as foreign to our real nature, and therefore as belonging to the not-self. We may thus say with accuracy that what is ascribed to the not-self is so ascribed because previously found to be discrepant, and therefore excluded from the self; in other words, the not-self is not an external limit which we somehow *find* in experience side by side with the self, but is *constructed* out of experience-data by the extrusion of those data which, if admitted into the self, would destroy its harmony. Thus we finite beings are confronted by a not-self ultimately because in our very finitude, as we have seen in earlier chapters, we contain in ourselves a principle of strife and disharmony. The not-self is no merely external environment, but an inevitable consequence of the imperfection of internal structure which belongs to all finitude.

(4) The self is essentially a thing of development, and as

At any rate, the problem is one of those fundamental questions in the theory of cognition which are too readily passed over in current Psychology.

[1] Of course, you can frame the concept of a "self" from which even these bodily feelings have been extruded, and which is thus a mere "cognitive subject" without concrete psychical quality. But as such a mere logical subject is certainly not the self of which we are aware in any concrete experience, and still more emphatically not the self in which the historical and ethical sciences are interested, I have not thought it necessary to deal with it in the text.

such has its being in the time-process. This is a point upon which it seems for many reasons necessary to insist. Its truth seems manifest from our previous consideration of the nature of the experiences upon which the concept of the self is based. As we have seen, it is primarily to our experience of internal disharmony and the collision of purpose that we owe our distinction between self and not-self. And such experience seems only possible to beings who can oppose an ideal of what ought to be, however dimly that ideal may be apprehended, to what is. A being who either was already all that it was its nature to become, or was incapable of in some way apprehending the fact that it was not so, would thus not have in its experience any material for the distinction between the self and the foreign and hostile elements in experience. And, as we have already seen in our Third Book, time is the expression in abstract form of the fundamental nature of an experience which has as yet attained only the partial fulfilment of its purpose and aspirations, and is therefore internally subject to that want of perfect harmony in which we have now sought the origin of the distinction between self and not-self. Hence we may, I think, take it as certain, at least for us who accept this account of the origin of the self concept, that selves are necessarily in time and as such are necessarily products of development.

This conclusion seems in accord with positive facts which are too well established to permit of question. It is probable that there is not a single element in what I call my present self which is not demonstrably the product of my past development, physical and mental. Nor does it appear reasonable to contend that though the material of my existing self is a result of development, its form of selfhood is underived. It is not merely that my present self is not as my past self, but we cannot avoid the admission that my mental life is the result of a process of development by which it is continuously connected with that of the embryo and even the spermatozoon. And thus it seems to have its beginnings in experiences which are probably so little removed from simple feeling as to afford no opportunity for the sense of self as contrasted with not-self. Or if we maintain that the contrast cannot be altogether absent from even the crudest forms of experience, we still have to reckon with the fact that, one stage further back in my personal history, I had no existence even as an animalcule. An embryonic self is at least not positively inconceivable, but where was Levi's selfhood while he was yet in the loins of his father? If we will consider what we mean when we say we have all had parents, it will, I think, be confessed that our self must be admitted to have been actually originated in the course of development, impossible as we find it to imagine the stage of such a process.[1]

(5) Finally, we must deal briefly with one more point of some importance. The self, as we can now see, is never identical with anything that could be found completely existing at any one moment in my mental life. For one thing, it is thought of as having a temporal continuity which goes far beyond anything that can be immediately experienced at any given moment. It stretches out both into the past and the future beyond the narrow limits of the "sensible present." Again, this temporal continuity is only an abstract expression of the inner sameness and continuity of aims and interests we ascribe to the self. My experiences are, as we have seen, thought of as being the life of one self ultimately because I look on them as the harmonious expression of a consistent attitude of interest in the world. And any elements in experience which will not coalesce in such a harmony are, by one device or another, extruded from the true self and declared to be alien intruders from elsewhere. Now, in real life we never find this complete and absolute harmony of the contents of experience; there are always, if we look for them, elements in our actual experience which are discordant, and conflict with the system of interests which, on the whole, dominates it. Hence self, in the last resort, is seen to be an *ideal* which actual experience only imperfectly realises,—the ideal of a system of purposes and interests absolutely in harmony with itself. And there must be, at least, grave doubt as to the logical self-consistency of this ideal, doubts which we must shortly face.

For the present the point to which I want to call attention is this. Must we say that any degree of felt continuity of existence is enough to constitute rudimentary selfhood, or ought we to hold that there is no true self where there is not at least as much *intellectual* development as is implied in the power to *remember* the past and *anticipate* the future, as one's own? In other words, are we to make

---

[1] That we cannot imagine it does not appear to be any ground for denying its actuality. It is never a valid argument against a conclusion required to bring our knowledge into harmony with itself, that we do not happen to possess the means of envisaging it in sensuous imagery.

selfhood as wide in its range as sentient life, or to limit it to life sufficiently rational to involve some distinct and explicit *recognition* of the contrast between self and not-self? This is perhaps, in the main, a question as to terminology; for my own part, I confess I find the second alternative the more satisfactory. I do not see that such a degree of teleological continuity as is implied in the mere feeling of pain, for instance, deserves to be recognised as genuine selfhood; and there is, I think, in the unrestricted use of the term self, selfhood, as applied to merely feeling consciousness, a danger of ambiguity. When we have once applied the terms in such a case, we are inevitably tempted to over-interpret the facts of such simple mental life in order to bring them into fuller accord with what we know of selfhood in our own life.[1] At the same time, it is clear that we have no right dogmatically to deny the presence of the intellectual processes involved in the recognition of self where our methods of observation fail to detect them.

§ 2. We may now approach the problem of the degree of reality which belongs to the self. We have to ask, how far is the conception of self applicable to the individual experiences which in our Second Book we identified as the contents of the system of real existence? Is the infinite individual experience properly to be called a self? Again, is every finite experience a self? And how must we take finite selves, if they are real, to be related to each other? Lastly, perhaps, we might be called on in this connection to face the question how far an individual finite self is more than a *temporary* feature in the system of existence. Our conclusions on all these points were no doubt in principle decided by the discussions of our Second Book, but it is desirable to make some of them more explicit than was possible there.

First, then, I think it is clear that the infinite experience or "Absolute" cannot properly be called a self. This is immediately apparent if our view as to the essential implications of self-feeling be accepted. We have urged that self is only apprehended as such in contrast to a simultaneously apprehended not-self. And the not-self, we have seen, is composed of all the discordant elements of experience, so far as their discord has not been overcome. It was for this

---

[1] I venture to think that some of the rather gratuitous hypotheses as to the rational selfhood of animal species *quâ* species put forward by Professor Royce in the second volume of *The World and the Individual*, are illustrations of this tendency to unnecessary over-interpretation.

reason that we held the self to be indissolubly bound up with that experience of the world as a process in time, with a "no longer" and "not yet," which is the universal characteristic of finitude. It must follow that an experience which contains no discordant elements, in their character as unresolved discords, is not characterised by the contrast-effect which is the foundation of selfhood. An experience which contains the whole of Reality as a perfectly harmonious whole can apprehend nothing as outside or opposed to itself, and for that very reason cannot be qualified by what we know as the sense of self.

To put the same thing in another way, "self," as we have seen, is essentially an ideal, and an ideal which is apprehended as contrasted with the present actuality. Hence only beings who are aware of themselves as in process of becoming more fully harmonious in their life of feeling and purpose than they at present are, can be aware of themselves as selves. Self and imperfection are inseparable, and any being which knows nothing of the opposition between the ideal and the actual, the *ought* and the *is*, must also know nothing of the feeling of self. Or in yet a third form of words, only creatures whose life is in time—and therefore only finite creatures—can be selves, since the time-experience is an integral constituent of selfhood.

One objection which might be brought against this inference is sufficiently ingenious to deserve special examination. It may be urged that though the experience of imperfection and thwarted purpose are conditions without which we in particular could not come to the apprehension of self, they do not remain as ingredients in the experience of selfhood when once it has been developed. Hence, it might be said, the "Absolute" may conceivably have the experience without having to acquire it through these conditions. In general principle, no doubt this line of argument is sound enough. It is perfectly true that the special conditions through which we come to have experience of a certain quality cannot, without investigation, be taken as everywhere indispensable for that experience. *E.g.*, even if it were proved that the pessimists are right in saying that *we* never experience pleasure except as a contrast with previous pain, it would still not follow that the pleasure, as felt, *is* the mere rebound from the pain, and has no further positive quality of its own, and it would then still be an open question whether other beings might not experience the pleasure without the antecedent pain. But the principle does not seem applicable to the case now under consideration, since it is our contention that the contrast of the discordant factor with the rest of the experience to which it belongs is not simply an antecedent condition, but is in fact the central core of the actual apprehension of self. It is not simply that we do not, if our previous analysis has been correct, have the feeling of self except in cases where such a contrast is present, but that the feeling of self *is* the feeling of the contrast. Hence our result seems untouched by the undoubtedly sound general principle to which we have referred.

That our conclusion is so frequently opposed by philosophers who adopt a generally idealistic position, is, I believe, to be accounted for by the prevalence of the belief that experience, as such, is essentially characterised by consciousness of self. To experience at all, it is commonly thought, is to be aware of one's *self* as in relation to an environment of the not-self. Hence to deny that the absolute Reality is a self is often thought to be equivalent to denying that it is an experience at all and this, from the idealistic point of view, would mean to deny that it is real. But if our previous analysis was sound, it is not even true of human experience as such that it is everywhere conditioned by the felt contrast of self with not-self. From the point of view of that analysis, the contrast only exists where there is felt discord between experience as a whole and some of its constituents. The conception of our experience as essentially marked by a sense of self, must therefore rest upon our intellectual reconstruction effected by the transparent fiction of ascribing to every experience features which analysis detects only in special cases and under special conditions. Hence it is quite possible for us to unite the affirmation that all real existence ultimately forms a single experience-system, with the denial that that system is qualified by the contrast-effect we know as the sense of self. How, indeed, should that outside which there is nothing to afford the contrast, so distinguish itself from a purely imaginary other?[1]

§ 3. If the Absolute is not a self, *a fortiori* it is manifest

---

[1] Is it necessary to refer in particular to the suggestion that for the Absolute the contrast-effect in question may be between itself and its component manifestations or appearances? This would only be possible if the finite appearances were contained in the whole in some way which allowed them to remain at discord with one another, *i.e.* in some way incompatible with the systematic character which is the fundamental quality of the Absolute. I am glad to find myself in accord, on the general principle at least, with Dr. McTaggart. See the Third Essay in his recent *Studies in Hegelian Cosmology.*

that it cannot be a "Person." Exactly how much is intended when the "personality" of the Absolute, or indeed of anything else, is affirmed, it would not be easy to determine. A "self" does not seem to be necessarily a "person," since those philosophers who hold that there is no reality but that of selves, while admitting that the lower animals are selves, do not usually call them persons. But it is hard to say how much more is included in personality than in selfhood. If we bear in mind that personality is, in its origin, a *legal* conception, and that it is usually ascribed only to human beings, or to such superhuman intelligences as are held capable of associating on terms of mutual obligation with human beings, we may perhaps suggest the following definition. A person is a being capable of being the subject of the specific obligations attaching to a specific position in human society. And it becomes manifest that, if this is so, personality is, as Mr. Bradley has said, finite or meaningless.

For a society of persons is essentially one of ἴσοι καὶ ὅμοιοι, social peers, with purposes mutally complementary though not identical, and standing in need of each other's aid for the realisation of those purposes. Only those beings are personal for me whose aims and purposes are included along with mine in some wider and more harmonious system, and to whom I therefore am bound by ties of reciprocal obligation. But it is clear that, to ask whether the wider system which is thus the foundation of our mutual rights and duties as persons, is itself a person, would be ridiculous. Thus, *e.g.*, there would be no sense in asking whether "human society"—the foundation of our moral personality—is itself a person. You might, in fact, as reasonably ask whether it can be sued for trespass or assessed under schedule D for Income Tax.

Still more manifestly is this true of the Absolute which includes within it all the (conceivably infinitely numerous) groups of mutually recognising persons, and all those other forms of experience which we cannot properly call personal. Between the whole system and its component elements there can be no such relation of mutual supplementation and completion as is the essence of genuine personality. If the system, as a whole, may be said to supplement and correct our defects and shortcomings, we cannot be said, in any way, to supplement it; the Absolute and I are emphatically not, in any true sense, ἴσοι καὶ ὅμοιοι, and the relation between us cannot therefore be thought of as personal. All this is so obvious, that, as I take it, the personality of the Absolute or whole of existence would find no defenders but for the gratuitous assumption that whatever is an individual experience or spiritual unity must be personal. This, as far as I can see, is to assume that such an individual *must* have an external environment of other experience-subjects of the same degree of harmonious and comprehensive individuality. And for this assumption I can, speaking for myself, see no ground whatever.[1]

§ 4. If we cannot, then, properly say that the Absolute, or the Universe,—or whatever may be our chosen name for the infinite individual which is the whole of existence,—is a self or person, can we say that the finite individuals which compose it are one and all selves, and that the Absolute is therefore a society of selves? Our answer to this question must depend, I think, upon two considerations,—(*a*) the amount of continuity we regard as essential to a self, and (*b*) the kind of unity we attribute to a society.

(*a*) If we regard *any* and every degree of felt teleological continuity as sufficient to constitute a self, it is clear that we shall be compelled to say that selves, and selves only, are the material of which reality is composed. For we have already agreed that Reality is exclusively composed of psychical fact, and that all psychical facts are satisfactions of some form of subjective interest or craving, and consequently that every psychical fact comprised in the whole system of existence must form part of the experience of a finite individual subject. Hence, if every such subject,

---

[1] It would be fruitless to object that "societies" can, in fact, have a legal corporate personality, and so can—to revert to the illustration used above—be sued and taxed. What can be thus dealt with is always a mere *association* of definite individual human beings, who may or may not form a genuine spiritual unity. *E.g.*, you might proceed against the Commissioners of Income Tax, but this does not prove that the Commissioners of Income Tax are a genuine society. On the other hand, the Liberal-Unionist Party probably possesses enough community of purpose to enable it to be regarded as a true society, but has no legal personality, and consequently no legal rights or obligations, *as a party*. Similarly, the corporation known as the Simeon Trustees has a legal personality with corresponding rights and duties, and it also stands in close relation with the evangelical party in the Established Church. And this party is no doubt a true ethical society. But the corporation is not the evangelical party, and the latter, in the sense in which it is a true society, is not a legal person.

I may just observe that the question whether the Absolute is a self or a person must not be confounded with the question of the "personality of God." We must not assume off-hand that "God" and the Absolute are identical. Only special examination of the phenomena of the religious life can decide for us whether "God" is necessarily the whole of Reality. If He is not, it would clearly be possible to unite a belief in "God's" personality with a denial of the personality of the Absolute, as is done, *e.g.*, by Mr. Rashdall in his essay in *Personal Idealism*. For some further remarks on the problem, see below, Chapter V.

whatever its degree of individuality, is to be called a self, there will be no facts which are not included somewhere in the life of one or more selves. On the other hand, if we prefer, as I have done myself, to regard some degree of intellectual development, sufficient for the *recognition* of certain permanent interests as those of the self, as essential to selfhood, we shall probably conclude that the self is an individual of a relatively high type, and that there are consequently experiences of so imperfect a degree of teleological continuity as not to merit the title of selves.

And this conclusion seems borne out by all the empirically ascertained facts of, *e.g.*, the life of the lower animals, of human infants, and again of adults of abnormally defective intellectual and moral development. Few persons, unless committed to the defence of a theory through thick and thin, would be prepared to call a worm a self, and most of us would probably feel some hesitation about a new-born baby or a congenital idiot. Again, finite societies are clearly components of Reality, yet, as we have seen, it is probably an error to speak of a society as a self, though every true society is clearly an individual with a community and continuity of purpose which enable us rightly to regard it as a unity capable of development, and to appreciate its ethical worth. Hence it is, perhaps, less likely to lead to misunderstandings if we say simply that the constituents of reality are finite individual experiences, than if we say that they are selves. The self, as we have seen, is a psychological category which only imperfectly represents the facts of experience it is employed to correlate.

(*b*) Again, if we speak of the Absolute as a society of finite individuals, we ought at least to be careful in guarding ourselves against misunderstanding. Such an expression has certainly some manifest advantages. It brings out both the spiritual character of the system of existence and the fact that, though it contains a plurality of finite selves and contains them without discord, it is not properly thought of as a self, but as a community of many selves.

At the same time, such language is open to misconstructions, some of which it may be well to enumerate. We must not, for instance, assume that all the individuals in the Absolute are necessarily in *direct* social interrelation. For social relation, properly speaking, is only possible between beings who are ἴσοι καὶ ὅμοιοι, at least in the sense of having interests of a sufficiently identical kind to permit of intercommunication and concerted cooperation for the realisation of a common interest. And our own experience teaches us that the range of existence with which we ourselves stand in this kind of relation is limited. Even within the bounds of the human race the social relations of each of us with the majority of our fellows are of an indirect kind, and though with the advance of civilisation the range of those relations is constantly being enlarged, it still remains to be seen whether a " cosmopolitan " society is a realisable ideal or not. With the non-human animal world our social relations, in consequence of the greater divergence of subjective interest, are only of a rudimentary kind, and with what appears to us as inanimate nature, as we have already seen, direct social relation seems to be all but absolutely precluded.

Among the non-human animals, again, we certainly find traces of relations of a rudimentarily social kind, but once more only within relatively narrow limits; the different species and groups seem in the main to be indifferent to one another. And we have no means of disproving the possibility that there may be in the universe an indefinite plurality of social groups, of an organisation equal or superior to that of our human communities, but of a type so alien to our own that no direct communication, not even of the elementary kind which would suffice to establish their existence, is possible. We must be prepared to entertain the possibility, then, that the individuals composing the Absolute fall into a number of groups, each consisting of members which have direct social relations of some kind with each other, but not with the members of other groups.

And also, of course, we must remember that there may very well be varieties of degree of structural complexity in the social groups themselves. In some the amount of intelligent recognition on the part of the individuals of their own and their fellows' common scheme of interests and purposes is probably less articulate, in others, again, it may be more articulate than is the case in those groups of co-operating human beings which form the only societies of which we know anything by direct experience.

On the other hand, we must, if we speak of the Absolute as a society, be careful to avoid the implication, which may readily arise from a false conception of human societies, that the unity of the Absolute is a mere conceptual fiction or " point of view " of our own, from which to regard what is really a mere plurality of separate units. In spite of the now fairly complete abandonment in words of the old atomistic theories, which treated society as if it were a mere collective name for a multitude of really independent "individuals," it may be doubted whether we always realise what the rejection of this view implies. We still tend too much to treat the selves which compose a society, at least in our Metaphysics, as if they were given to us in direct experience as *merely* exclusive of one another, rather than as complementary to one another. In other words, of the two typical forms of experience from which the concept of self appears to be derived, the experience of conflict between our subjective interests and our environment, and that of the removal of the discord, we too often pay attention in our Metaphysics to the former to the neglect of the latter. But in actual life it is oftener the latter that is prominent in our relations with our fellow-men. *We*—the category of co-operation—is at least as fundamental in all human thought and language as *I* and *thou*, the categories of mutual exclusion. That you and I are mutually complementary factors in a wider whole of common interests, is at least as early a discovery of mankind as that our private interests and standpoints collide.

If we speak of existence as a society, then we must be careful to remember that the individual unity of a society is just as real a fact of experience as the individual unity of the members which compose it, and that, when we call the Absolute a society rather than a self, we do not do so with any intention of casting doubt upon its complete spiritual unity as an individual experience. With these restrictions, it would, I think, be fair to say that if the Absolute cannot be called a society without qualification, at any rate human society affords the best analogy by which we can attempt to represent its systematic unity in a concrete conceptual form. To put it otherwise, a genuine human society is an individual of a higher type of structure than any one of the selves which compose it, and therefore more adequately represents the structure of the one ultimately complete system of the Absolute.

We see this more particularly in the superior independence of Society as compared with one of its own members. It is true, of course, that no human society could exist apart from an external environment, but it does not appear to be as necessary to the existence of society as to that of a single self, that it should be sensible of the contrast between itself and its rivals. As we have already sufficiently seen, it is in the main from the experience of contrast with other human selves that I come by the sense of my own selfhood. Though the contents of my concept of self are not purely social, it does at least seem clear that I could neither acquire it, nor retain it long, except for the presence of other like selves which form the complement to it. But though history teaches how closely similar is the part played by war and other relations between different societies in developing the sense of a common national heritage and purpose, yet a society, once started on its course of development, does appear to be able to a large extent to flourish without the constant stimulus afforded by rivalry or co-operation with other societies. One man on a desert land, if left long enough to himself, would probably become insane or brutish; there seems no sufficient reason to hold that a single civilised community, devoid of relations with others, could not, if its internal organisation were sufficiently rich, flourish in a purely "natural" environment. On the strength of this higher self-sufficiency, itself a consequence of superior internal wealth and harmony, a true society may reasonably be held to be a finite individual of a higher type than a single human self.

The general result of this discussion, then, seems to be, that neither in the self nor in society—at any rate in the only forms of it we know to exist—do we find the complete harmony of structure and independence of external conditions which are characteristic of ultimate reality. Both the self and society must therefore be pronounced to be finite appearance, but of the two, society exhibits the fuller and higher individuality, and is therefore the more truly real. We found it quite impossible to regard the universe as a single self; but, with certain important qualifications, we said that it might be thought of as a society without very serious error.[1]

---

[1] I suppose that any doctrine which denies the ultimate reality of the finite self must expect to be confronted by the appeal to the alleged revelation of immediate experience. *Cogito, ergo sum*, is often taken as an immediately certain truth in the sense that the existence of myself is something of which I am directly aware in every moment of consciousness. This is, however, an entire perversion of the facts. Undoubtedly the fact of there being experience is one which can be verified by the very experiment of trying to deny it. Denial itself is a felt experience. But it is (*a*) probably not true that we cannot have experience at all without an accompanying perception of self, and (*b*) certainly not true that the mere feeling of self as in contrast with a not-self, when we do get it, is what is meant by the self of Ethics and History. The self of these sciences always embraces more than can be given in any single moment of experience, it is an ideal construction by which we connect moments of experience according to a general scheme. The value of that scheme for any science can only be tested by the success with which it does its work, and its truth is certainly not established by the mere consideration that the facts it aims at connecting are actual. Metaphysics would be the easiest of sciences if you could thus take it for granted that any construction which is based upon some aspect of experienced fact must be valid.

It will, of course, follow from what has been said, that we cannot frame any finally adequate conception of the way in which all the finite individual experiences form the unity of the infinite experiences. That they must form such a perfect unity we have seen in our Second Book; that the unity of a society is, perhaps, the nearest analogy by which we can represent it, has been shown in the present paragraph. That we have no higher categories which can adequately indicate the precise way in which all existence ultimately forms an even more perfect unity, is an inevitable consequence of the fact of our own finitude. We cannot frame the categories, because we, as finite beings, have not the corresponding experience. To this extent, at least, it seems to me that any sound philosophy must end with a modest confession of ignorance.

> "There is in God, men say,
> A deep but dazzling darkness,"

is a truth which the metaphysician's natural desire to know as much as possible of the final truth, should not lead him to forget.

§ 5. This is probably the place to make some reference to the question whether the self is a permanent or only a temporary form in which Reality appears. In popular thought this question commonly appears as that of the immortality (sometimes, too, of the pre-existence) of the soul. The real issue is, however, a wider one, and the problem of immortality only one of its subsidiary aspects. I propose to say something briefly on the general question, and also on the special one, though in this latter case rather with a view to indicating the line along which discussion ought to proceed, than with the aim of suggesting a result.

It would not, I think, be possible to deny the temporary character of the self after the investigations of the earlier part of this chapter. A self, we said, is one and the same only in virtue of teleological continuity of interest and purpose. But exactly how much variation is enough to destroy this continuity, and how much again may exist without abolishing it, we found it impossible to determine by any general principle. Yet the facts of individual development seemed to make it clear that new selves—*i.e.* new unique forms of interest in the world—come into being in the time-process, and that old ones disappear.

And again, both from mental Pathology and from normal Psychology, we found it easy to cite examples of the formation

THE PLACE OF THE "SELF" IN REALITY

and disappearance, within the life-history of a single man, of selves which it seemed impossible to regard as connected by any felt continuity of interest with the rest of life. In the case of multiple personality, and alternating personality, we seemed to find evidence that a plurality of such selves might alternate regularly, or even co-exist in connection with the same body. The less striking, but more familiar, cases of the passing selves of our dreams, and of temporary periods in waking life where our interest and characters are modified, but not in a permanent way by exceptional excitements, belong in principle to the same category. In short, unless you are to be content with a beggarly modicum of continuity of purpose too meagre to be more than an empty name, you seem forced to conclude that the origination and again the disappearance of selves in the course of psychical events is a fact of constant occurrence. No doubt, the higher the internal organisation of our interests and purposes, the more fixed and the less liable to serious modification in the flux of circumstance our self becomes; but a self absolutely fixed and unalterable was, as we saw, an unrealised and, on the strength of our metaphysical certainty that only the absolute whole is entirely self-determined, we may add, an unrealisable ideal. We seem driven, then, to conclude that the permanent identity of the self is a matter of degree, and that we are not entitled to assert that the self corresponding to a single organism need be either single or persistent. It is possible for me, even in the period between birth and death, to lose my old self and acquire a new one, and even to have more selves than one, and those of different degrees of individual structure, at the same time. Nor can we assign any certain criterion by which to decide in all cases whether the self has been one and identical through a series of psychical events. Beyond the general assertion that the more completely occupied our various interests and purposes are, the more permanent is our selfhood, we are unable to go.[1]

[1] This is why Plato seems justified in laying stress upon the dreams of the wise man as evidence of his superiority (*Republic*, bk. ix. p. 571). His ideal wise man is one whose inner life is so completely unified that there is genuine continuity of purpose between his waking and sleeping state. Plato might perhaps have replied to Locke's query, that *Socrates* waking and *Socrates* asleep *are* the same person, and their identity is testimony to the exceptional wisdom and virtue of Socrates.

If it be thought that at least the *simultaneous* co-existence within one of two selves is inconceivable, I would ask the reader to bear in mind that the *self* always includes more than is at any moment given as actual matter of psychical fact. At any moment the self must be taken to consist for the most part of unrealised *tendencies*, and in so far as such ultimately incompatible tendencies are part of my whole nature, at the same time it seems reasonable to

These considerations have an important bearing on the vexed question of a future life. If they are justified, we clearly cannot have any positive demonstration from the nature of the self of its indestructibility, and it would therefore be in vain to demand that philosophy shall prove the permanence of all selves. On the other hand, if the permanence of a self is ultimately a function of its inner unity of aim and purpose, there is no *a priori* ground for holding that the physical event of death *must* necessarily destroy this unity, and so that the self *must* be perishable at death. For Metaphysics, the problem thus seems to resolve itself into a balancing of probabilities, and, as an illustration of the kind of consideration which has to be taken into account, it may be worth while to inquire what probable arguments may fairly be allowed to count on either side.

On the negative side, if we dismiss, as we fairly may, the unproved assertions of dogmatic Materialism, we have to take account of the possibility that a body may, for all we know, be a necessary condition for the existence of an individual experience continuous in interest and purpose with that of our present life, and also of the alleged absence of any positive empirical evidence for existence after death. These considerations, however, scarcely seem decisive. As to the first, I do not see how it can be shown that a body is indispensable, at least in the sense of the term "body" required by the argument. It is no doubt true that in the experience of any individual there must be the two aspects of fresh teleological initiative and of already systematised habitual and quasi-mechanical repetition of useful reactions already established, and further, that intercourse between different individuals is only possible through the medium of such a system of established habits. As we have already seen, what we call our body is simply a name for such a set of habitual reactions through which intercommunication between members of human societies is rendered possible. Hence, if we generalise the term "body" to stand for any system of habitual reactions discharging this function of serving as a medium of communication between individuals forming a society, we may fairly say that a body is indispensable to the existence of a self. But it seems impossible to show that the possibility of such a medium of communication is removed by the dissolution of the particular system

say that I have simultaneously more than one self. Ultimately, no doubt, this line of thought would lead to the conclusion that "my whole nature" itself is only relatively a whole.

of reactions which constitutes our *present* medium of intercourse. The dissolution of the present body *might* mean no more than the individual acquisition of changed types of habitual reaction, types which no longer serve the purpose of communication with the members of *our* society, but yet may be an initial condition of communication with other groups of intelligent beings.

As to the absence of empirical evidence, it is, of course, notorious that some persons at least claim to possess such evidence of the continued existence of the departed. Until the alleged facts have been made the subject of serious and unbiassed collection and examination, it is, I think, premature to pronounce an opinion as to their evidential value. I will therefore make only one observation with respect to some of the alleged evidence from "necromancy." It is manifest that the only kind of continuance which could fairly be called a survival of the self, and certainly the only kind in which we need feel any interest, would be the persistence after death of our characteristic interests and purposes. Unless the "soul" continued to live for aims and interests teleologically continuous with those of its earthly life, there would be no genuine extension of our selfhood beyond the grave. Hence any kind of evidence for continued existence which is not at the same time evidence for continuity of interests and purposes, is really worthless when offered as testimony to "immortality." The reader will be able to apply this reflection for himself if he knows anything of the "phenomena" of the vulgar Spiritualism.[1]

When we turn to the positive side of the question, it seems necessary to remark that though the negative considerations we have just referred to are not of themselves enough to disprove "immortality," provided there is any strong ground for taking it as a fact, they would be quite sufficient to decide against it, unless there is positive reason for accepting it. That we have no direct evidence of such a state of things, and cannot see precisely *how* in detail it could come about, would not be good logical ground for denying its existence if it were demanded by sound philosophical principles. On the other hand, if there were no reasons for believing in it, and good, though not conclusive, probable reasons against it, we should be bound to come provisionally to a negative conclusion.

Have we then any positive grounds at all to set against

---

[1] Compare the valuable essay by Mr. Bradley on the "Evidence of Spiritualism" in *Fortnightly Review* for December 1885.

the negative considerations just discussed? Pending the result of inquiries which have recently been set on foot, it is hard to speak with absolute confidence; still, the study of literature does, I think, warrant us in provisionally saying that there seems to be a strong and widely diffused feeling, at least in the Western world, that life without any hope of continuance after death would be an unsatisfactory thing. This feeling expresses itself in many forms, but I think they can all be traced to one root. Normally, as we know, the extinction of a particular teleological interest is effected by its realisation; our purposes die out, and our self so far suffers change, when their result has been achieved. (And incidentally this may help us to see once more that dissatisfaction and imperfection are of the essence of the finite self. The finite self lives on the division of idea from reality, of intent from execution. If the two could become identical, the self would have lost the atmosphere from which it draws its life-breath.) Hence, if death, in our experience, always took the form of the dissolution of a self which had already seen its purposes fulfilled and its aims achieved, there would probably be no incentive to desire or believe in future continuance. But it is a familiar fact that death is constantly coming as a violent and irrational interrupter of unrealised plans and inchoate work. The self seems to disappear not because it has played its part and finished its work, but as the victim of external accident. I think that analysis would show, under the various special forms which the desire for immortality takes, such as the yearning to renew interrupted friendships or the longing to continue unfinished work, as their common principle, the feeling of resentment against this apparent defeat of intelligent purpose by brute external accident.[1]

Now, what is the logical value of this feeling as a basis for argument? We may fairly say, on the one hand, that it rests on a sound principle. For it embodies the conviction, of which all Philosophy is the elaboration, that the real world is a harmonious system in which irrational accident plays no part, and that, if we could only see the whole truth, we should realise that there is no final and irremediable defeat for any of our aspirations, but all are somehow made good. On the other side, we must remember that the argument from the desire for continuance to its reality also goes on

---

[1] Death, however, though the most striking, is not the only illustration of this apparently irrational interference of accident with intelligent purpose. Mental and bodily disablement, or even adverse external fortune, may have the same effect upon the self. This must be taken into account in any attempt to deal with the general problem.

to assert not only that our aspirations are somehow fulfilled and our unfinished work somehow perfected, but that this fulfilment takes place in the particular way which we, with our present lights, would wish. And in maintaining this, the argument goes beyond the conclusion which philosophical first principles warrant.

For it might be that, if our insight into the scheme of the world were less defective, we should cease to desire this special form of fulfilment, just as in growing into manhood we cease to desire the kind of life which appeared to us as children the ideal of happiness. The man's life-work may be the realisation of the child's dreams, but it does not realise them in the form imagined by childhood. And conceivably it might be so with our desire for a future life. Further, of course, the logical value of the argument from feeling must to some extent depend upon the universality and persistence of the feeling itself. We must not mistake for a fundamental aspiration of humanity what may be largely the effect of special traditions and training. Hence we cannot truly estimate the worth of the inference from feeling until we know both how far the feeling itself is really permanent in our own society, and how far, again, it exists in societies with different beliefs and traditions. In itself the sentiment, *e.g.*, of Christian civilisation, cannot be taken as evidence of the universal feeling of mankind, in the face of the apparently opposite feelings, *e.g.*, of Brahmins and Buddhists.

I should conclude, then, that the question of a future life must remain an open one for Metaphysics. We seem unable to give any valid metaphysical arguments for a future life, but then, on the other hand, the negative presumptions seem to be equally devoid of cogency. Philosophy, in this matter, to use the fine phrase of Dr. McTaggart, "gives us hope,"[1] and I cannot, for my own part, see that it can do more. Possibly, as Browning suggests in *La Saisiaz*, it is not desirable, in the interests of practical life, that it should do more. And here I must leave the question with the reader, only throwing out one tentative suggestion for his approval or rejection as he pleases. Since we have seen that the permanence of the self depends upon its degree of internal harmony of structure, it is at least conceivable that its

[1] Dr. McTaggart's phrase is more exactly adequate to describe my view than his own, according to which "immortality" is capable of philosophical proof. (See the second chapter of his *Studies in Hegelian Cosmology*.) I have already explained why I cannot accept this position. I believe Dr. McTaggart's satisfaction with it must be partly due to failure to raise the question *what it is* that he declares to be a "fundamental differentiation" of the Absolute.

continuance as a self, beyond the limits of earthly life, may depend on the same condition. Conceivably the self may survive death, as it survives lesser changes in the course of physical events, *if* its unity and harmony of purpose are strong enough, and not otherwise. If so, a future existence would not be a heritage into which we are safe to step when the time comes, but a conquest to be won by the strenuous devotion of life to the acquisition of a rich, and at the same time orderly and harmonious, moral selfhood. And thus the belief in a future life, in so far as it acts in any given case as a spur to such strenuous living, might be itself a factor in bringing about its own fulfilment. It is impossible to affirm with certainty that this is so, but, again, we cannot deny that it may be the case. And here, as I say, I must be content to leave the problem.[1]

Consult further :—B. Bosanquet, *Psychology of the Moral Self*, lect. 5 ; F. H. Bradley, *Appearance and Reality*, chaps. 9 (The Meanings of Self), 10 (The Reality of Self), 26 (The Absolute and its Appearances,—especially the end of the chapter, pp. 499–511 of 1st ed.), 27 (Ultimate Doubts); L. T. Hobhouse, *Theory of Knowledge*, part 3, chap. 5 ; S. Hodgson, *Metaphysic of Experience*, bk. iv. chap. 4 ; Hume, *Treatise of Human Nature*, bk. i. part 4, §§ 5, 6; W. James, *Principles of Psychology*, vol. i. chap. 10 ; H. Lotze, *Metaphysic*, bk. iii chaps. 1 (especially § 245), 5 ; *Microcosmus*, bk. iii. c. 5 ; J. M. E. McTaggart, *Studies in Hegelian Cosmology*, chap. 2 (for a detailed hostile examination of Dr. McTaggart's argument, which I would not be understood to endorse except on special points, see G. E. Moore in *Proceedings of Aristotelian Society*, N.S. vol. ii. pp. 188–211); J. Royce, *The World and the Individual*, Second Series, lects. 6, 7.

---

[1] I ought perhaps to say a word—more I do not think necessary—upon the doctrine that immortality is a fundamental "moral postulate." If this statement means no more than that it would be inconsistent with the rationality of the universe that our work as moral agents should be simply wasted, and that therefore it must somehow have its accomplishment whether we see it in our human society or not, I should certainly agree with the general proposition. But I cannot see that we know enough of the structure of the universe to assert that this accomplishment is only possible in the special form of immortality. To revert to the illustration of the text, (1) our judgment that the world must be a worthless place without immortality *might* be on a level with the child's notion that "grown-up" life, to be worth having, must be a life of continual play and no work. (2) If it is meant, however, that it is not "worth while" to be virtuous unless you can look forward to remuneration—what Hegel, according to Heine, called a *Trinkgeld*—hereafter for not having lived like a beast, the proposition appears to me a piece of immoral nonsense which it would be waste of time to discuss.

CHAPTER IV

THE PROBLEM OF MORAL FREEDOM

§ 1. The metaphysical problem of free will has been historically created by extra-ethical difficulties, especially by theological considerations in the early Christian era, and by the influence of mechanical scientific conceptions in the modern world. § 2-3. The analysis of our moral experience shows that true "freedom" means teleological determination. Hence to be "free" and to "will" are ultimately the same thing. Freedom or "self-determination" is genuine but limited, and is capable of variations of degree. § 4. *Determinism* and *Indeterminism* both arise from the false assumption that the mechanical postulate of *causal* determination by antecedents is an ultimate fact. The question then arises whether mental events are an exception to the supposed principle. § 5. *Determinism*. The determinist arguments stated. § 6. They rest partly upon the false assumption that mechanical determination is the one and only principle of rational connection between facts. § 7. Partly upon fallacious theories of the actual procedure of the mental sciences. Fallacious nature of the argument that complete knowledge of character and circumstances would enable us to predict human conduct. The assumed data are such as, from their own nature, could not be known *before the event*. § 8. *Indeterminism*. The psychical facts to which the indeterminist appeals do not warrant his conclusion, which is, moreover, metaphysically absurd, as involving the denial of rational connection. § 9. Both doctrines agree in the initial error of confounding teleological unity with causal determination.

§ 1. THE problem of the meaning and reality of moral freedom is popularly supposed to be one of the principal issues, if not *the* principal issue, of Metaphysics as applied to the facts of human life. Kant, as the reader will no doubt know, included freedom with immortality and the existence of God in his list of unprovable but indispensable "postulates" of Ethics, and the conviction is still widespread among students of moral philosophy that ethical science cannot begin its work without some preliminary metaphysical justification of freedom, as a postulate at least, if not as a proved truth. For my own part, I own I cannot rate the practical importance of the metaphysical inquiry into human freedom so high, and am rather of Professor Sidgwick's opinion as to its superfluousness in strictly ethical investigations.[1] At the same time, it is impossible to pass over the subject without discussion, if only for the excellent illustra-

---
[1] See *Methods of Ethics*, bk. i. chap. 4, § 6 (pp. 72-76 of 5th ed.).

tions it affords of the mischief which results from the forcing of false metaphysical theories upon Ethics, and for the confirmation it yields of our view as to the postulatory character of the mechanico-causal scheme of the natural sciences. In discussing freedom from this point of view as a metaphysical issue, I would have it clearly understood that there are two important inquiries into which I do not intend to enter, except perhaps incidentally.

One is the *psychological* question as to the precise elements into which a voluntary act may be analysed for the purpose of psychological description; the other the ethical and juridical problem as to the limits of moral responsibility. For our present purpose both these questions may be left on one side. We need neither ask how a voluntary act is performed—in other words, by what set of symbols it is best represented in Psychology—nor where in a complicated case the conditions requisite for accountability, and therefore for freedom of action, may be pronounced wanting. Our task is the simpler one of deciding, in the first place, what we mean by the freedom which we all regard as morally desirable, and next, what general view as to the nature of existence is implied in the assertion or denial of its actuality.

That the examination of the *metaphysical* implications of freedom is not an indispensable preliminary to ethical study, is fortunately sufficiently established by the actual history of the moral sciences. The greatest achievements of Ethics, up to the present time, are undoubtedly contained in the systems of the great Greek moralists, Plato and Aristotle. It would not be too much to say that subsequent ethical speculation has accomplished, in the department of Ethics proper as distinguished from metaphysical reflection upon the ontological problems suggested by ethical results, little more than the development in detail of general principles already recognised and formulated by these great observers and critics of human life. Yet the metaphysical problem of freedom, as is well known, is entirely absent from the Platonic-Aristotelian philosophy. With Plato, as the reader of the *Gorgias* and the eighth and ninth books of the *Republic* will be aware, freedom means just what it does to the ordinary plain man, the power to " do what one wills," and the only speculative interest taken by the philosopher in the subject is that of showing that the chief practical obstacle to the attainment of freedom arises from infirmity and inconsistency in the will itself; that, in fact, the unfree man is just the criminal or "tyrant" who wills the incompatible, and, in a less degree, the "democratic" creature of moods and impulses, who, in popular phrase, "doesn't know what he wants" of life.

Similarly, Aristotle, with less of spiritual insight but more attention to matters of practical detail, discusses the ἑκούσιον, in the third book of his *Ethics*, purely from the standpoint of an ideally perfect jurisprudence. With him the problem is to know for what acts an ideally perfect system of law could hold a man non-responsible, and his answer may be said to be that a man is not responsible in case of (1) physical compulsion, in the strict sense, where his limits are actually set in motion by some external agent or cause; and (2) of ignorance of the material circumstances. In both these cases there is no responsibility, because there has been no real act, the outward movements of the man's limbs not corresponding to any purpose of his own. An act which does translate into physical movement a purpose of the agent, Aristotle, like practical morality and jurisprudence, recognises as *ipso facto* free, without raising any metaphysical question as to the ontological implications of the recognition.

Historically, it appears that the metaphysical problem has been created for us by purely non-ethical considerations "Freedom of indifference" was maintained in the ancient world by the Epicureans, but not on ethical grounds. As readers of the second book of Lucretius know, they denied the validity of the postulate of rigidly mechanical causality simply to extricate themselves from the position into which their arbitrary physical hypotheses had led them. If mechanical causality were recognised as absolute in the physical world, and if, again, as Epicurus held, the physical world was composed of atoms all falling with constant velocities in the same direction, the system of things, as we know it, could never have arisen. Hence, rather than give up their initial hypothesis about the atoms, the Epicureans credited the individual atom with a power of occasional uncaused and arbitrary deviation from its path, as a means of bringing atoms into collision and combination. Thus with them "freedom of indifference" was the result of *physical* difficulties.

In the Christian Church the doctrine seems to have owed its wide—though not universal—acceptance to equally non-ethical difficulties of a *theological* kind. If God "foreknew from all eternity" the transgression of Adam and all its consequences, how could it be compatible with His justice to punish Adam and all his posterity for faults foreseen by Adam's Creator?[1] The difficulty of reconciling the divine omniscience with the divine justice was supposed to be avoided—in truth, it was only evaded[2]—by assuming that man was created with a "free will of indifference," so that obedience would have been just as easy as transgression if man had chosen to obey. In our own time the problem has assumed a rather different complexion, owing to the enormous developments of mechanical physical science, which began with Galileo and Descartes. Rigid causal determination being assumed as a first principle of physical science, the question arose whether the assumption should not also be extended to the psychical sphere. If so extended, it seemed to strike at the roots of moral responsibility, by making all human acts the inevitable "consequences of circumstances over which we have no control"; if not admitted, the rejection of the principle of rigid causal determination has often been thought to amount to the denial that there is any principle of rational connection in the psychical sphere. Hence, while persons specially interested in the facts of the moral life have frequently inclined to the more or less radical denial of rational connection between the events of the psychical series, others, whose special interests have lain in the direction of the unification of knowledge, have still more commonly thought

---

[1] So Omar Khayyám—

"Oh Thou, who didst with pitfall and with gin
Beset the Road I was to wander in,
Thou wilt not with Predestined Evil round
Emmesh, and then impute my Fall to Sin."
(FITZGERALD, ed. 4, stanza 80.)

And our own poet—

"Thou madest man in the garden; thou temptedst man, and he fell," etc.

(For the original of the stanzas on Predestination in Fitzgerald's Omar, see, *e.g.*, the Persian text of Whinfield, quatrains 100, 126, 197.)

[2] Evaded, because, even granting the satisfactoriness of the solution for the special case of Adam, there would still be the problem of reconciling the alleged "free will" of his descendants with their inheritance of "original sin." The more rigid Calvinism, with its insistence on the natural corruption of man's heart and the absoluteness of predestination, seems to secure logical consistency at the expense of outraging our moral convictions. Like so many popular theological problems, this of the conflict between God's omniscience and justice arises from a misconception of the issue. It is only when the category of time is illogically applied to the *ex hypothesi* perfect, and therefore timeless, nature of God that God's knowledge comes to be thought by as *fore* knowledge *before the event*, and thus occasions the difficulty which the "free-will" theory was intended to remove. See on this point, Royce, *The World and the Individual*, vol. ii. lect. 8, and compare Bradley, *Ethical Studies*, p. 19. Of course, the case would be altered if we thought of God as finite and imperfect, and therefore in time. But there would then be no longer any reason for believing either in His omniscience or His omnipotence, and so no problem would arise.

it necessary to hold that human action is determined by antecedents in the same sense and to the same degree as the occurrences of the purely physical order.

It will be our object to show that these rival doctrines of Indeterminism and Determinism, or Necessitarianism, are alike irrational, alike incompatible with what in practice we understand as moral freedom of action, and alike based upon the false assumption that rigid mechanical determination is itself an actual fact, and not a mere postulate of the special physical sciences, valid only so far as it is useful. But before we enter upon our task, it is necessary to begin with a statement as to the real meaning of ethical freedom itself. Until we know what we mean by the kind of freedom we, as moral beings, desire and think we ought to have, it will be useless to ask whether we are or are not free.

§ 2. "Free" and "freedom" are manifestly what are called by the logicians "privative" terms; they denote the absence of certain restrictions. To be "free," in whatever special sense you may use the word, means to be free *from* something. What, then, are the typical limitations which, in practice, we resent as making us unfree? They seem to be, in the main, the following:—(1) We are not free when our limbs are actually set in motion by an external physical agency, human or non-human. And the reason why we are then unfree is that the resulting movements of our bodies do not express a purpose of our own. They either express the purpose of some other being who moves our limbs as seems good to him, or, as in the case where we are set in motion by the "forces" of the inanimate world, express no purpose at all that is recognisable to us as such. And in either case *we* have expressed no purpose of our own by our movements; they do not truly belong to *us* at all, and there is therefore no freedom. It is not necessary that the result of the movement should be one which, if it had been suggested, we should have declined to entertain as a purpose of our own. We *might* perhaps, if left to ourselves, have done just what another man or the system of physical forces has done for us. Still, so long as the deed, whatever it was, was done for us and not by us, so long as it corresponded to no actual purpose of ours, it was not a free act.

(2) Again, we are not truly free when we act in ignorance (not due to previous free action of our own)[1] of the special

[1] Remember that abstention from acting is itself action, just as in Logic every significant denial is really an assertion. Hence our proviso meets the case of wilful neglect to inform myself of the material circumstances.

circumstances. Here there is, as there was not in the former case, a genuine act. We actually purpose to do something, but what we purpose to do is not the deed which results from our movements. *E.g.*, if I shoot a comrade by mistake for one of the enemy, it is true that *I* purpose to shoot, and so far the shooting is an act, and a free act, of my own. But I did not purpose to shoot my comrade, and so the result, in its concreteness, is not the expression of my purpose, and I consequently regard myself as not fully free in doing it, and therefore not morally accountable for it. So far our analysis coincides with that of Aristotle, previously referred to.

(3) Again, I am not acting freely where the circumstances are not such as to admit of the formation of purpose at all. For this reason, merely automatic action—if there is such a thing—is not genuine action, and therefore not free.[1] Impulsive action without reflection, again, comes under this category. It is, of course, accompanied by feelings of satisfaction, and if impeded gives rise to craving, and so cannot be called simply non-purposive. But in genuinely impulsive reaction, where the possibility of reflection is excluded, there can be little clear awareness of the concrete character of the purpose that is being put into execution, and hence such action is not truly free. And in practical life, though we are certainly held morally responsible for impulsive action, in so far as it is thought we might have modified it by previous habitual practice of reflection or by avoiding a situation which we had reason to think would deprive us of the power to reflect, we are never held as fully accountable for the deed of impulse as for the reflectively thought out and deliberately adopted purpose.[2]

Further, we feel ourselves unfree when we fail to execute our purposes, either from sheer inability to attend to a consistent scheme of action, or because we attend equally to purposes which are internally incompatible. This is why the "democratic" man, whose interests are an incoherent medley without logical unity, and the "tyrannical man," or, as we

---

[1] The only automatic acts of which we really *know* the psychical character are our own "secondarily automatic" or "habitual" acts. It is, of course, a problem for the casuist how far any particular reaction has become so completely automatic as to be no longer an occasion for the imputation of merit or guilt.

[2] For purposes of law it may often be impossible to draw the distinction, and we may have to acquiesce in the rough-and-ready alternative between entire accountability and complete non-accountability. But in passing moral judgment on ourselves or others *in foro conscientiæ*, we always recognise that accountability is a thing of degrees. On this point see Mr. Bradley's previously quoted article in *Mind* for July 1902.

should now say, the "criminal type," whose passions are constantly at war with one another and with his judgment, are regarded by Plato as the typically unfree beings. To be really free, in the last resort, we must have purposes which are coherent and abiding. And it is thus no paradox to say that unfreedom in the end means, in the main, not knowing your own mind, while to be free is to know what you mean.

§ 3. We may now draw some important consequences from this review of the facts upon which every valid interpretation of freedom has to be based. (1) Freedom, as Locke said in that famous chapter "On Power" which is still the classic discussion of the whole subject as far as English philosophy is concerned, "belongs to the man, not to the will." The proper question to ask is, "Am I free?" not "Is my will free?" or "Have I a free will?" For "freedom" and "will," as the facts enumerated above show, are but the negative and the positive name for the same property, the property of acting so as to put what we first possessed as our private purpose into execution in the world of sensible fact. I "will" when my outward deed is thus the expression of my purpose; in the same case, and in no other, I am "free." Thus to "will" and to be "free" are one and the same thing; a will which was not free would be a will which was not the translation into sensible fact of any one's purpose, and thus no will at all. Thus the question, "Are we free?" might be also put in the equivalent form, "Can we ever will anything?" and to the question, as thus put, experience gives a ready answer. For we certainly do conceive purposes, and we certainly, in some of our movements, do translate those purposes in act. And therefore we may say that freedom is undoubtedly, in the only sense in which it is desired, a fact of immediate experience.[1]

(2) If we retain the expression "freedom to *will*" by the side of the phrase "freedom to *act*," it can only be in a very special sense. It is clear that not only may my outward deed be a translation into fact of my present purpose, but my present purpose itself, as a psychical event, may also be a

---

[1] It must, however, be carefully noted that will in the sense in which it is equivalent to freedom must be taken to include what some writers, *e.g.*, Bradley, call a "standing" will—*i.e.* any series of acts originally initiated by an idea of the resultant changes, which is approved of by us unconditionally. In the actual execution of such a series of acts many of the stages are habitual reactions which, as such, are not accompanied by the "idea" of their specific result as a determining condition of their occurrence. The sphere of moral freedom is arbitrarily restricted when it is assumed that an *actual* volition is indispensable for every stage of the "free" action.

translation into fact of a former purpose. This is largely the case with all results of deliberate self-training and discipline, and to a less degree with all acquired habits. Thus, *e.g.*, the movements by which I write these lines are the expression of my preconceived purpose to write the present paragraph, but that purpose itself, as an event in my history, is similarly the expression of a former purpose to compose a work on Metaphysics. Thus there is a real sense in which we can agree with Leibnitz in criticising Locke's dictum that we are free to act, but not free to will. For the mental conception of a purpose is itself an act, and in so far as it translates into existing thoughts and feelings a previous purpose it may be said itself to be "freely willed."[1]

(3) Freedom, in actual experience, is always limited, and, moreover, admits of the most various degrees. As to the first point, it follows immediately from our consideration of the circumstances which make us unfree. If to be fully free means that your outward deed is the full expression of an inward consistent purpose, then we can see at once that complete freedom is, for all finite beings, an infinitely distant *ideal*. For it means (*a*) that I am not hampered in the execution of my purpose by vacillation of interest or conflict of incompatible interests within myself; (*b*) nor by the establishment of "habitual" reactions so nearly mechanical as to repeat themselves out of season unless checked by special reflection; (*c*) nor by the limits set to my power to "act or to forbear" in the physical world by the action of my fellows and of "brute" nature.[2] Hence

---

[1] The reader should study for himself Locke's famous chapter (*Essay*, bk. ii. chap. 21). Locke's treatment, hampered as it is by his unfortunate retention of the discussion of his first edition side by side with a somewhat modified re-statement, compares favourably for clearness and sound sense with that of most subsequent philosophers, notably with Kant's unintelligible attempt to reconcile the absolute freedom of man as "noumenon" (a fictitious quality of a fictitious being) with his equally absolute unfreedom as "phenomenon" (another equally palpable fiction).

For Leibnitz's criticism of Locke, see *Nouveaux Essais*, II. xxi., particularly §§ 8–25. (The English translation by Langley can only be used with extreme caution.) On the whole question the reader should also consult Green, *Prolegomena to Ethics*, bk. ii. chap. 1; Bradley, *Ethical Studies*, Essay 1, and article in *Mind* for July 1902; W. R. B. Gibson, "The Problem of Freedom" (in *Personal Idealism*).

[2] Then, are "animals" free? I see no reason to deny that, since their life, in its degree, must have teleological continuity to be a life at all, they too must possess a rudimentary degree of freedom, though a degree not sufficient to fit them for a place as ἴσοι καὶ ὅμοιοι in human society, and therefore, for the special purposes of human ethical systems, negligible. Similarly, a human imbecile may possess a degree of freedom which is important for the educator who is interested in the "care of the feeble minded," and yet may rightly be treated for the different purposes of a penal code as simply unfree.

only an experience which is absolutely devoid of internal conflict and external, partly discrepant environment, in other words, only the experience which is the infinite whole, can be in all its detail entirely and absolutely free. From the possibilities of internal lack of unity of purpose and external collision with rival purpose which are inseparable from our position as finite beings, it must follow that we are never more than partially or relatively free.

And that the degree to which we are free varies with the nature of our purposes and their relation to the environment, is also manifest. There is an indefinite plurality of such degrees, ranging up from the total or all but total absence of freedom in the case of directly constrained motion up to the case of cordial co-operation with the other members of a relatively self-supporting social group in the conscious and systematic execution of an elaborate and coherent scheme of action. To indicate the principal distinctions among such grades of freedom which are of practical importance for law and morality is the task of systematic Ethics, and need not be attempted by us here. We may add that our investigation has made it apparent that true moral freedom, of whatever degree, is no inalienable heritage into which men step by the "accident of birth," but—in the main and as an actual possession— a prize which has to be won by the double discipline of self-knowledge and self-mastery, and of social comradeship, and may be, and is, forfeited by the neglect of the arts by which it was first gained. No doubt one man's inherited disposition may make the practice of self-control, or again of social fellowship, easier to him than to another, and to this extent we may say that we are born with a greater or lesser "capacity for freedom," but of its actual possession we have all to say, "with a great price purchased I this freedom."

(4) Finally, our examination of the facts of morality enables us to *define* true freedom. We are free, as we have seen, just so far as our experience is the embodiment of coherent and permanent interest or purpose, and freedom is, like "will," simply an abstract expression for the teleological unity which, in varying degrees, is an essential feature of all experience. Hence we can at once see that freedom does not mean "absence of rational connection" or "absence of determination," but does mean, as so many recent philosophers have told us, for us finite beings, *self-determination*. I am most free when acting for the realisa-

tion of a coherent rational purpose, not because my conduct is "undetermined"; in other words, because there is "no telling" what I shall do next, but because it is, at such times, most fully determined teleologically by the character of my inner purposes or interests,—in other words, by the constitution of my *self*. The more abiding and logically coherent my various purposes in action, the freer I am, because it is my *whole* self or system of rationally connected interests, and not the insistence of others, or some passing whim or impulse which I may forthwith disown as no part of my "true self," which is getting expression in my outward deeds. And if it were possible for a finite being to become absolutely free, as we have seen that it is not, such a being would, in the very moment of its entire deliverance, become also absolutely determined from within; its whole life, as manifested to the outsider in the series of its deeds, would become the perfect and systematic expression of a single scheme of coherent purposes.

§ 4. We see, then, that such a genuine but limited freedom as is really implied in the existence of morality is not only compatible with, but actually demanded by, the principles of a sound Metaphysics. From the side of morality we meet with the demand that human beings shall be, in part at least, creatures whose outward acts shall be the genuine expression of individual purpose; from the side of Metaphysics we have already learned that just this teleological unity, genuine though imperfect, is the essential nature of every finite experience. We are now to see how a problem in itself quite simple leads to insoluble difficulties and to the rival absurdities of Indeterminism and Determinism when it is perverted by an initial metaphysical blunder. The initial mistake of both the rival theories consists simply in taking rigid mechanical determination of events by their antecedents in accord with the principle of Causality as an actual fact, the divergence between them only concerning the extent of the sphere of existence for which such determination prevails. According to the indeterminist, the action of conscious beings forms a solitary exception to a principle of determination which is absolutely valid for all purely physical processes. According to the determinist, there are no exceptions to the principle, and our confessed inability to predict the course of an individual life or a period of history from general laws in the same way in which we predict an eclipse or a display of leonids, is due merely to the greater complexity of the necessary data, and the temporary imperfections of our mathematical methods.

It should be noted that there is no substantial disagreement between the more sober representatives of the two views as to the actual facts of life. The indeterminist usually admits that in practice, when you know enough of a man's character and of the influences brought to bear upon him, you can tell with some confidence how he will conduct himself, and that social intercourse, education, and penal legislation would be impossible if you could not. Similarly, the determinist admits that it would be very rash to treat your predictions of human behaviour in practice with absolute confidence, and that the unexpected does frequently happen in human life. The dispute is solely about the philosophical interpretation of facts as to which there is virtually universal agreement. According to the determinist interpretation, *if* you were put in possession of the knowledge of a man's "character" and of his "circumstances" (and it is assumed that it is theoretically possible to have this knowledge), and had sufficient skill to grapple with the mathematical problems involved, you could calculate his whole behaviour in advance, from the cradle to the grave, with infallible precision. According to the indeterminist, you could not do so, and your failure would arise not from any theoretical impossibility of obtaining the supposed data, but from their insufficiency. Our behaviour, he alleges, is not exclusively determined by the interaction of "character" and circumstances; even with the complete knowledge of both these elements, human action is incalculable, because of our possession of a "free will of indifference" or power to act indifferently according to or in violation of our "character." You can never say beforehand what a man will do, because of this capacity for acting, under any conditions, with equal facility in either of two alternative ways.

I propose to show briefly that the determinist is right in saying that conduct is completely determined by "character" —if the term be understood widely enough—and circumstances, but wrong in holding that this makes infallible prediction possible; on the other hand, that the indeterminist is right in denying the possibility of such prediction, but wrong in the reason he gives for his denial. Infallible prediction is impossible, not because of the existence of "free will of indifference," but because the assumed data of the prediction are such that you could not possibly have them until *after the event*. Finally, it will be pointed out that the two errors both arise from the same false metaphysical theory that the causal principle is a statement of real fact.[1]

§ 5. *Determinism.* To begin with the view of the determinist. Human conduct, he says, must be, like other processes, unequivocally determined by antecedents, and these antecedents must consist of (*a*) character and (*b*) external circumstance. For (1) to deny the causal determination of our acts by antecedents is to deny the presence of rational connection in the psychical sphere, and thus to pronounce not only Psychology, but all the sciences which take psychical events as their material and attempt to discover rational connections between them, in principle impossible. Thus the very existence of Psychology, Ethics, and History proves the applicability of the principle of causal determinism to "mental states."

(2) This is still more evident if we reflect that all science consists in the formulation of "laws" or "uniformities," and that the formulation of "laws" rests upon the principle that "same result follows under same conditions"—*i.e.* upon the principle of causal determination.

(3) Further, if psychical events are not so determined, then Psychology and the mental sciences generally are inconsistent with the general principles of the mechanical physical sciences.

(4) And, as a matter of fact, we do all assume that psychical events are causally determined by their antecedents. In Psychology we assume that our choices are determined by the strength of the *motives* between which we choose. Hence, if you know what are the "motives" present to a man's choice, and the relative strength of each, the determinist thinks the prediction of his conduct is reduced to the purely mathematical problem of the solution of an equation or set of equations. That our present mathematical resources will not avail for the unequivocal solution of such equations is, on this view, a mere temporary

---

[1] Compare with what follows, Bradley, *Ethical Studies*, Essay I, and the notes appended to it. For a typical statement of the determinist case in its more sober form, see Mill, *System of Logic*, bk. vi. chap. 2. It is harder to find a reasonable statement of the opposite view, as most capable moral philosophers have adopted the doctrine of self-determination. For a defence of thoroughgoing Indeterminism, see James, *The Will to Believe* (Essay on *The Dilemma of Determinism*). In Professor Sidgwick's statement of the indeterminist view (see, *e.g.*, his posthumous lecture on T. H. Green's doctrine of freedom in *Lectures on the Ethics of Green, Spencer, and Martineau*, pp. 15-28), Indeterminism seems to me to be qualified to the point of being in principle surrendered.

defect incidental to the present condition of mathematical science. In principle the equations must be soluble, or "there is no science of human action."

(5) And in practical life we do all assume that it is possible to predict with considerable confidence the effect of typical conditions upon the aggregate of mankind, and also, when you have the requisite data, the effect of a definite set of conditions upon an individual man. Thus we count upon the deterrent effects of punishment, the persuasive influence of advertisement, etc.; and again, in proportion as we really know our friends, we believe ourselves able to answer for their conduct in situations which have not as yet arisen. Why, then, should we suppose it theoretically impossible, if adequate data were furnished, to calculate the whole career of a man or a society in advance, as the astronomer calculates the path of a planet from its elements? These are, I think, the chief of the stock arguments by which Determinism has been defended. (With the purely theological argument from the absoluteness of the divine foreknowledge I have already dealt in passing, and do not propose to refer to it again.)

§ 6. It is not difficult to see that the logical value of all these arguments is nothing at all. They fall of themselves into two groups, one based upon the general view that all rational connection, or at least all such rational connection as is significant for our knowledge, is mechanical causal sequence, the other upon an appeal to the supposed actual practice of the mental sciences. We may deal with the first group (arguments 1 to 3) first. It is certainly not true that causal determination by antecedents is the only form of rational connection. For there is manifestly another type of connection, which we have already seen to be fundamental for the mental sciences, namely, teleological coherence. And we have learned in our preceding books that no truly teleological or purposive series can really be mechanically determined by uniform causal laws of sequence, though it is often convenient for special purposes, as in the physical sciences, to treat such a series *as if* it were mechanically determined. Whether this type of procedure will be valid in the mental sciences, depends upon the further question whether our interest in the study of mental processes is of the kind which would be satisfied by the formulation of a number of abstract uniformities or laws of sequence, and the neglect of all those features of real mental life of which such laws take no account.

In the physical sciences, as we saw, this mechanical scheme was valid only because we have an interest—that of devising general rules for dealing with typical physical situations—which is met by neglecting all those aspects of concrete fact which the mechanical scheme excludes. But we also saw that the nature of our interest in psychological investigation was predominantly (and, in the case of the study of voluntary action, exclusively) of a different kind. Our interest in these investigations was to obtain such a teleological representation of psychical processes as might be made available for the appreciative judgments of Ethics and History and their kindred studies. Thus, even admitting the possibility of treating psychical life for some purposes, by abstraction from its teleological character, as if it were a mechanical sequence, the abstraction would be fatal for the purposes of the concrete mental sciences, and is therefore inadmissible in them. A teleological unity in which we are interested *as* a teleological unity cannot, without the stultification of our whole scientific procedure, be treated in abstraction from its teleological character.

This rejoinder to the first of the determinist's arguments is at the same time a refutation of the second. It is true that any science which aims exclusively at the discovery of "laws" or "uniformities" must adopt the causal principle, and must resolutely shut its eyes to all aspects of concrete fact which cannot be resolved into mechanical sequence of "same result" on "same conditions." But, as we saw in the first chapter of this book, the characteristic task of Psychology, except in those parts of it which appear to be mere temporary substitutes for the Physiology of the future, is not the discovery of "*laws* of mental process," but the representation in abstract and general form of the teleological unity of processes which are the expression of subjective interests. Psychology, then, in its most characteristic parts, is not based upon the causal postulate of mechanical science, but on the conception of teleological continuity.

Our answer to the determinist's third argument is therefore that we admit the truth of the allegation that Psychology and all the more concrete mental sciences which make use of the symbolism of Psychology, because essentially teleological in their view of mental process, would be inconsistent with the mechanical postulates, if those postulates had any claim to admission into mental science as its ruling principles. We deny, however, that they have any such claim to recognition. Being, as we now know that they are, mere methodological rules for the elimination from our data of everything which is teleological, the mechanical postulates are only legitimate in Psychology so far as Psychology desires mechanical results. How far that is, we have learned in the first two chapters of the present Book, and we have found that the initiation of purposive action is not a process which Psychology can fruitfully treat as mechanical.

§ 7. Turning now to the determinist's allegations as to the factual procedure of the mental sciences, we may make the following observations :—(1) As to the argument from the psychological treatment of "motives" as the determining antecedents of choice, we say that it is either an empty tautology or a fallacy, according to the sense you please to put on the much-abused term "motive." Choice is causally determined by the "strongest motive"; what does this mean? If the "strongest motive" simply means the line of action we do in fact choose, the argument amounts to the true but irrelevant observation that we choose what we do choose, and not something else. But if "motives" are to be regarded as antecedents causally determining choice in proportion to their strength, as mechanical "forces" determine the path of a particle in abstract Mechanics, we must suppose the "strength" of the various "motives," like the mass of an attracting body, to be previously fixed, independent of the choice they determine. In other words, the determinist argument requires us to hold that alternative possibilities of action are already "motives" apart from their relation to the purpose of the agent who has to choose between them, and moreover have, also in independence of the purpose or "character" of the chooser, a "strength" which is in some unintelligible way a function of—it would not be easy to say of *what*, though it is incumbent on the determinist to know. And this seems no better than rank nonsense. An alternative is not a "motive" at all, except in relation to the already existing, but not fully defined, purpose of some agent, and whether it is a "strong" or a "weak" motive depends likewise on the character of the agent's purpose. The attempt to conceive of "motives" as somehow acting on a mind with an inherent "strength" of their own, as material particles attract other material particles proportionately to their masses, is so palpable an absurdity, that nothing more than the candid statement of it is needed for its complete exposure.

And (2) there is an equal absurdity inherent in the

determinist view as to the kind of prediction of conduct which is possible in concrete cases. We have seen already in our Third Book that no infallible prediction of the course of events in an individual case is ever possible. Mechanical calculation and prediction we found to be possible in the physical sciences simply because they deal with the average character of a vast aggregate of processes which they never attempt to follow in their concrete individual detail. And trustworthy prediction of human conduct by the aid of "causal laws" was seen to be of the same kind. Your uniformities might hold good, so long as they professed to be nothing more than statistical averages got by neglecting the individual peculiarities of the special cases composing them, but nothing but acquaintance with individual character and purpose would justify you in making confident predictions as to the behaviour of an individual man.

Now, when the determinist says, "if you knew a man's character and his circumstances you could predict his conduct with certainty," it is not this kind of individual acquaintance which he has in view. He means that the "character" of an individual man could be reduced to a number of general formulæ or "laws of mental action," and that from these "laws," by simply putting them together, you could logically deduce the man's behaviour. To see how irrational this assumption is, we need only ask what is meant exactly by the "character" which we suppose given as one of the elements for our supposed calculation. If it means the sum-total of the congenital "dispositions" with which we are born, then—apart from the difficulty of saying precisely what you mean by such a "disposition"—the determinist statement is not even approximately true. For (*a*) though it may be true that a man's behaviour in a given situation is an expression of his "character," yet the "character" is not the same thing as "congenital disposition." Disposition is the mere raw material of the "character," which is formed out of it by the influence of circumstance, the educational activity of our social circle, and deliberate self-discipline on our own part. And the "character" thus formed is not a fixed and unvarying quantity, given once and for all at some period in the individual's development, and thenceforward constant; it is itself, theoretically at least, "in the making" throughout life, and though you may, from personal intimate acquaintance with an individual man, feel strongly convinced that his "character" is not likely to undergo serious changes after a certain time of life, this conviction can never amount to more than what we properly call "moral" certainty, and is never justified *except* on the strength of individual familiarity.

(*b*) This leads us to our second point. If—to suppose the practically impossible—you did know a man's "character" with the knowledge of omniscience, you would clearly also know every act of his life. For his "character" is nothing but the system of purposes and interests to which his outward deeds give expression, and thus to know it completely would be to know them completely too. But—and this is what the determinist regularly overlooks—you could not possibly have this knowledge of the man's "character" until you were already acquainted with the whole of his life. You could not possibly thus know "character" as a datum given in advance, from which to calculate, with mathematical precision, the as yet unknown future acts of the man in question, because, as we have seen, the "character" is, in fact, not there as a given fact *before* the acts through which it is formed. Your data could at best be no more than a number of "dispositions" or "tendencies," and from such data there can be no infallible prediction, because, in the first place, "dispositions" are not always developed into actual fixed habits; and, in the second, your data, such as they are, are incomplete, seeing that "dispositions" may, and often do, remain latent and escape detection until the emergence of a situation adapted to call them out. So that, even if it were true that complete knowledge of a man's original stock of "dispositions" would enable you to calculate his career from its elements, it would still be impossible to be sure that your knowledge of his "dispositions" *was* complete.

Thus, if a "science of human nature" really means a power to calculate human conduct in advance from its elements, we must admit that there is not and can be no such science. As a fact, however, what we really mean by a "science of human nature," when we speak of it as possible or as partly existent already, is something quite different. We mean either Psychology, individual and social, which is simply an abstract symbolism for the representation of teleological process in its general nature, or History, which is the detection of coherent purpose in human action, *after the event;* or, again, Ethics and Politics, which are appreciations of such purpose by an ideal standard of *worth*. Not one of these sciences has ever attempted the calculation of human action in advance by general laws; such forecasts of the future as we do make, with rational confidence, are palpably based, wherever they are of value, on concrete experience, our own or that of others, and not upon the principles of an imaginary mechanics of the human mind.

§ 8. *Indeterminism.* With the fallacies of the indeterminist we must now deal more briefly. This is the more possible as Indeterminism, though common enough in popular moralising, has never won anything like the position of the rival doctrine as the professed creed of scientific investigators. The essence of the indeterminist position is the denial of the principle affirmed alike by the doctrine of self-determination and, in an unintelligent travesty, by the determinist theory that conduct results from the reaction of "character" upon circumstances. Seeing that, if all human action is mechanically determined in advance by its "antecedents," and is thus theoretically capable of being deduced from its "elements," there can be no true moral freedom, and, not seeing that the essence of true freedom is teleological as opposed to mechanical determination, the indeterminist thinks himself compelled to assert that human action is, in the last resort, not "determined" even by human character. There is a "free will of indifference" inherent in human nature, in virtue of which a man's acts, or at least those of them in respect of which he is morally "accountable," are free, in the sense of being independent of his character.

Freedom, according to this view, consists in the ability indifferently to adopt either of two alternative courses; so long as one alternative is closed to you (whether by your "character" or by external circumstances makes no difference according to the indeterminist), you are not "free" and not acting as a moral and accountable being. You are only acting freely in following your purpose when you could equally well follow its direct opposite. The arguments by which this doctrine is supported, over and above the general contention that determination by antecedents is incompatible with moral responsibility, are chiefly of the nature of appeals to immediate feeling. Thus we are told (1) that when we act from choice and not under compulsion we always have the immediate feeling that we could equally well act in the opposite sense; and (2) that it is a matter of direct experience that, in resisting temptation, we can and do act "in the line of *greatest* resistance," and that the "will" is therefore independent of determination by "motives."

The detailed discussion of the actuality of the alleged

facts belongs, of course, to Psychology, and I do not propose to enter into it here. But it should be manifest that, even admitting the facts to be as the indeterminist states them, they do not warrant the inference he bases on them. Thus (1) it is no doubt true that I often am aware, in resolving on a certain course of action, that I could, *if I pleased*, act differently. But the conditional clause by its presence makes all the difference between teleological determination and no determination at all. It is, *e.g.*, no genuine fact of experience that I am aware that I could violate all the habits of a lifetime, practise all the crimes I most abhor, and neglect all the interests to which I am most devoted. I could do all this " if I pleased," but before I could " please " I should have to become a different man ; while I am the man I am, it is a manifest absurdity to hold that I can indifferently express in my behaviour the purposes which constitute my individuality or their opposites.

(2) The argument from the successful resistance of temptations is equally fallacious. We have seen already that the determinist assumption against which it is directed, namely, that conduct is mechanically determined by the inherent " strength " of " motives," is itself unmeaning. "Motives" are, if they are anything, another name for the interests which constitute our character, not external influences which " work upon " that character, and thus their relative " strength " is nothing independent of character, but a new expression for the structure of the individual character itself. But the counter-argument of Indeterminism is just as unmeaning. To talk of the " conquest " of temptation as the " line of greatest resistance " is to use the very same unintelligible mechanical analogy as the determinist uses in talking of the antecedent " strength " of a " motive." There are, in fact, only two possible interpretations of the indeterminist's contention, and neither of them supports his conclusion. Either the " resistance " of which he speaks must be measured by our actual success in resisting the suggestion to act, and in that case the very fact that we do not yield to the temptation shows that for us yielding would have been the " line of greatest resistance " ; or else " resistance " must be measured by the extent to which the rejected alternative still persists as a psychical fact after its rejection. Then the alleged experience simply amounts to this, that we can and sometimes do, in obedience to training or conviction, refuse to act upon suggestions which as psychical facts have sufficient intensity to remain before the mind even after our refusal.

And this, interesting and suggestive as it is, seems no particular reason for denying the teleological determination of our conduct.[1]

The real metaphysical objection to Indeterminism however, is not that it is an unprovable and unnecessary hypothesis, but that it involves the denial of rational connection between human actions. By declaring that conduct is not determined by character, it virtually asserts that it is chance which ultimately decides how we shall actually behave in a concrete case. And chance is simply another name for the absence of rational connection. This is illustrated, *e.g.*, by the use we make of the conception of chance in the various empirical sciences. Thus, when I say that it is a matter of chance what card I shall draw from the pack, what I mean is that the result depends in part upon conditions which I do not know, and therefore cannot use as data for a conclusion in favour of one result rather than another. I do not, of course, mean that the result is not conditioned at all, or that, with a sufficient knowledge of the conditions it might not have been calculated in advance, but merely that I in particular have not this sufficient knowledge. Hence the admission of chance in the relative sense of "conditions not at present accurately known" does not conflict with the fundamental axiom of all thinking, the principle that all existence is a rational unity or scheme of some sort. In fact, since we never can know the "totality of the conditions" of anything, it would be true to say that there is an element of chance, in this relative sense, in all concrete actualities.

But absolute chance, such as the doctrine of an indeterminate free will maintains, would amount to the simple absence of any rational connection whatever between the facts which are alleged to issue from such a will. This is why the indeterminist view leads in the end, if consistently carried out, to the same metaphysical absurdity as the determinist. From failure to see that rational connection, such as is presupposed when we impute praise or blame to an agent on the score of his conduct, means teleological determination, both the rival theories in the end deny the rational interconnection of human acts, the one replacing it by the fiction of a purposeless mechanical "necessity," the other by the equal fiction of a "blind chance." And the two fictions are really the same thing under different names.

---

[1] See the admirable discussion of this experience in Dr. Stout's *Manual of Psychology*,[3] bk. iv. chap. 10, § 7.

For the only piece of definite information that could be extracted either from the assertion that human conduct is mechanically determined, or that it is the result of chance, is the conclusion that in either case it is *not* the expression of coherent purpose.

§ 9. It is thus obvious that Indeterminism fails, in precisely the same way as the opposing theory, to afford any theoretical basis for moral responsibility. True, I cannot be "responsible" for deeds which are the outcome of a purely mechanical system of antecedents, because such deeds, not issuing from the purposes of my self, are in no true sense mine; but the same would be equally true of the results of an indeterminate free will. As not owing their existence to my purpose, those results are in no real sense "my" acts, and the choice of the name "free will" for their unknown source only serves to disguise this consequence without removing it. Only as issuing from my character, and as the expression of my individual interests, can acts be ascribed to me as "mine" and made the basis of moral approbation in censure of my "self."

Thus we see that the determinist and the indeterminist are led alike to impossible results because of the common error involved in their point of departure. Both start with the false assumption that the causal determination of an event by its "antecedents"—which we have in our earlier books seen to be a postulate ultimately not in accord with reality, but permissible in so far as it permits us to obtain useful results by treating events as if they were thus determined—is ultimately real as a feature of concrete existence. Having thus at the outset excluded genuine teleological determination from their conception of the world of change, both theorists are alike debarred from the correct understanding of those psychical processes for the comprehension of which teleological categories are indispensable.

In the terms of theories which treat determination as purely mechanical, the factors which manifestly are the determining conditions of conduct, namely, character and the alternative possibilities of action, inevitably come to be conceived of as the temporal "antecedents" of the act which issues from them. And when once this notion of character as a sort of pre-existing material upon which "motives" from without operate has been framed, it matters little in principle whether you take "character" and "motive" by themselves as the complete antecedents by which action is determined, or add a third "antecedent" in the form of an inexplicable arbitrary "free will." In either case all possibility of a truthful representation of the freedom actually implied in moral accountability was surrendered when the "character" which expresses itself through an act, and the "motive" which is another name for that character as particularised by reference to circumstances, were falsely separated in thought from each other, and then further treated as the temporal antecedents of the act in which they are expressed. In our own treatment of the problem of freedom we were able to escape both sides of the dilemma, because we recognised from the first that the categories of mechanical determination are not the expression of real fact, but limitations artificially imposed upon facts for special purposes of a kind which have nothing in common with the ethical and historical appreciation of human conduct, and therefore irrelevant and misleading when applied out of their rightful sphere.

Consult further:—H. Bergson, *Sur les données immédiates de la conscience;* F. H. Bradley, *Ethical Studies*, Essay 1; W. R. B. Gibson, "The Problem of Freedom" (in *Personal Idealism*); T. H. Green, *Prolegomena to Ethics*, bk. i. chap. 3, bk. ii. chap. 1; W. James, *Principles of Psychology*, vol. ii. chap. 26; *Will to Believe* (*The Dilemma of Determinism*); J. Locke, *Essay concerning Human Understanding*, bk. ii. chap. 21 (on *Power*); J. Martineau, *Types of Ethical Theory*, vol. ii. bk. i. chap. 1; J. S. Mill, *Logic*, bk. vi. chap. 2 ff.; J. Royce, *The World and the Individual*, Second Series, lect. 8; H. Sidgwick, *Methods of Ethics*, bk. i. chap. 5; *Lectures on the Ethics of Green*, etc., pp. 15–29.

CHAPTER V

SOME METAPHYSICAL IMPLICATIONS OF ETHICS AND RELIGION

§ 1. If Reality is a harmonious system, it must somehow make provision for the gratification of our ethical, religious, and æsthetic interests. § 2. But we cannot assume that ethical and religious postulates are necessarily *true* in the forms in which our practical interests lead us to make them. § 3. Thus, while morality would become impossible unless on the whole there is coincidence between virtue and happiness, and unless social progress is a genuine fact, " perfect virtue," " perfect happiness," " infinite progress " are logically self-contradictory concepts. § 4. But this does not impair the practical usefulness of our ethical ideals. § 5. In religion we conceive of the ideal of perfection as already existing in individual form. Hence ultimately no part of the temporal order can be an adequate object of religious devotion. § 6. This leads to the *Problem of Evil*. " God " cannot be a finite being within the Absolute, because, if so, God must contain evil and imperfection as part of His nature, and is thus *not* the already existing realisation of the ideal. § 7. This difficulty disappears when we identify " God " with the Absolute, because in the Absolute evil can be seen to be mere illusory appearance. It may, however, be true that religious feeling, to be practically efficient, may need to imagine its object in an ultimately incorrect anthropomorphic form. § 8. The existence, within the Absolute, of finite " divine " personalities, can neither be affirmed nor denied on grounds of general Metaphysics. § 9. Proofs of the " being of God." The principle of the " ontological " and " cosmological " proofs can be defended against the criticism of Hume and Kant only if we identify God with the Absolute. The " physicotheological proof " could only establish the reality of finite superhuman intelligences, and its force depends purely upon empirical considerations of evidence.

§ 1. THE metaphysician is perhaps at times too ready to treat experience as though it were constituted solely by intellectual interests; as though our one concern in dealing with its deliverances, as they come to us, were to construct out of them a system of knowledge satisfactory to our demand for coherent thinking. This is, of course, a one-sided, and therefore, from the standpoint of Metaphysics itself, an imperfect expression of the nature of our attitude as intelligences towards the world of our experience. Our moral, religious, and artistic, no less than our logical, ideals represent typical forms of our general interest as intelligent beings in bringing harmony and order into the apparently discordant material of experience. Hence no study of metaphysical principles, however elementary, would be complete without some discussion of the light thrown by these various ideals upon the ultimate structure of the system of Reality in which we and our manifold interests form a part. If it is the fundamental principle of a sound philosophy that all existence forms a harmonious unity, then, if we can discover what are the essential and permanent features in the demands made by art, morality, and religion upon the world, we may be sure that these demands are somehow met and made good in the scheme of things.

For a world which met our ethical, religious, and æsthetic demands upon life with a *mere* negative would inevitably contain aspects of violent and irreconcilable discord, and would thus be no true world or systematic unity at all. In what follows I propose to discuss the double question, What appears to be the "irreducible minimum" of the demands which morality and religion make of the world, and how far the general conception of existence defended in our earlier chapters provides for their liquidation. The consideration of our æsthetic ideals and their metaphysical significance I propose to decline, on the ground both of its inferior practical interest for mankind at large, and of the very special and thorough training in the psychological analysis of æsthetic feeling which is, in my own judgment at least, essential for the satisfactory treatment of the question.

§ 2. In dealing with the subject thus marked out, it will be necessary to begin with a word, partly of caution, partly of recapitulation of previous results, as to the attitude towards the practical ideals of morality and religion imposed upon the metaphysician by the special character of his interests as a metaphysician. It will thus be apparent why I have spoken in the last paragraph of an "irreducible *minimum*" of ethical and religious postulation. There is a marked tendency among recent writers on philosophical topics, encouraged more specially by Professor James and his followers, to urge that any and every ideal which we think valuable for the purposes of morality and religion has no less claim to be accepted in Metaphysics as of value for our conception of Reality than the fundamental principles of logical thought themselves. Logical thinking, it is contended, is after all only one of the functions of our nature, by the side of others such as moral endeavour towards the harmonising of practice with an ideal of the right or the good, æsthetic creation of the beautiful, and religious co-operation with a "power not ourselves that makes for righteousness." Why, then, should the metaphysician assume that the universe is more specially bound to satisfy the demands of the logical intellect than those of the "practical reason" of morality and religion or the "creative reason" of art? Must we not say that the demand of the logician that the world shall be intelligible stands precisely on the same footing as the moralist's demand that it shall be righteous, or the artist's that it shall be beautiful, and that all three are no more than "postulates" which we make, in the last resort, simply because it satisfies our deepest feelings to make them? Must we not, in fact, say alike to the followers of Logic, of Ethics, of Religion, and of Art, "Your claims on the world are ultimately all of the same kind; they are made with equal right, and so long as any one of you is content to advance his postulate as a postulate, and at his own personal risk, no one of you has any pretension to criticise or reject the postulates of the others"?

The doctrine I have attempted to summarise thus briefly, I believe to be partly irrelevant in Metaphysics, partly mistaken, and therefore, so far as mistaken, mischievous. I pass lightly over the curious mental reservation suggested by the claim to believe as you list "at your own risk." As George Eliot has reminded us in *Adam Bede*, it is a fundamental fact of our position as members of a social order, that nothing in the world can be done exclusively at the risk of the doer. Your beliefs, so far as they receive expression at all, like all the rest of your conduct, inevitably affect the lives of others as well as your own, and hence it is useless to urge in extenuation of a false and mischievous belief to which expression has been given—and a belief which gets no kind of expression is no genuine belief at all —that it was entertained at your "personal risk." That no man liveth to himself is just as true of the metaphysician as of any other man, and he has no more claim than another to disregard the truth in practice.

To pass to a more important point. It is no doubt true that the attainment of satisfaction for our intellectual need for a coherent way of thinking about existence is only one of a number of human interests. And thus we may readily grant that morality, religion, and art have a right to existence no less than Logic. Further, the question whether any one of the four has a *better* right to existence than the others seems to be really unmeaning. There seems to be no sense in asking whether any typical and essential human aspiration has a superior claim to recognition and fulfilment rather than another. But it does not seem to follow that *for all purposes* our divergent interests and attitudes are of equal value, and that therefore they may not legitimately be used as bases for mutual criticism. In particular, it does not seem to follow that because Logic and morality, say, have an equal right to exist, there must be an equal amount of *truth* in the principles of Logic and the postulates of Ethics. Truth, after all, is perhaps not the "one thing needful" for human life, and it is not self-evident even that truth is the supreme interest of morality and religion.

On the face of things, indeed, it seems not to be so. *Primâ facie*, it looks as if the logician's ideal of truth and the moralist's ideal of goodness were, in part at any rate, divergent. For it is by no means clear that the widest possible diffusion of true thinking and the general attainment of the highest standard of moral goodness must necessarily go together. It may even be conducive to the moral goodness of a community that many members of it should not think on certain topics at all, or even should think erroneously about them.[1] And the ideals of goodness and beauty, we may remind ourselves, seem to be similarly divergent. It is by no means self-evident, and might even be said to be, so far as history enables us to judge, probably untrue, that the society in which the appreciation of beauty is most highly developed is also the society with the highest standard of goodness.

Now, if truth and goodness are not simply identical, we cannot conclude that the ultimate truth of a belief is proportionate to its moral usefulness in promoting practical goodness. And therefore the metaphysician, who takes ultimate truth as *his* standard of worth, would appear to be quite within his right in refusing to admit moral usefulness as sufficient justification for a belief, just as the moralist, from the point of view of his special standard of worth, may rightly decline to take the æsthetic harmoniousness of a life

---

[1] To take a couple of concrete illustrations. It may be—I do not say it is—conducive to moral goodness that there should be a general conviction that in the long run our individual happiness is strictly proportionate to our degree of virtue. But there is no means whatever of showing that this belief is true, and, as Mr. Bradley once pertinently argued against Professor Sidgwick, no philosopher is entitled to assert its truth on moral grounds unless he is prepared to maintain that he could produce more goodness and less badness by such an exact proportioning of happiness to merit than without it. Again, most of us would probably admit that ordinary moral rules, such as that against wilful lying, have exceptions. But we are not bound to hold it conducive to moral goodness that every one should be aware of this.

as sufficient evidence of its moral excellence. Until you have shown, what the view I am here opposing appears tacitly to assume, that truth, moral goodness, and beauty are one thing, you cannot rationally refuse the metaphysician's claim to criticise, and if necessary to condemn as not finally true, the "postulates" of which Ethics is entitled to assent, not that they are "true," but that they are practically useful.

And, of course, the same liberty must be granted to Ethics itself. The moralist, I would not only admit but insist, has a perfect right to criticise, from his special standpoint, the doctrines of the metaphysician. It may perfectly well be that certain "truths" are better not generally known, in the interests of practical goodness, and the moralist is fully justified in dwelling upon the fact. But when the metaphysician asserts the truth of a proposition solely on the strength of its value for the promotion of morality, he is deserting the criterion of value which he is bound in his capacity of metaphysician to respect. It is quite true that logic is not the only game at which it interests mankind to play, and that no one need play this special game unless he prefers it; but when you have once sat down to the game you must play it according to its own rules, and not those of some other. If you neglect this caution, you will most likely produce something which is neither good Metaphysics nor sound Ethics. There is every reason for Metaphysics to beware of a "will to believe" which in practice must mean that licence to indulge in uncriticised assertion which Socrates in the *Phædo* calls by the appropriate name of "misology," and identifies as the psychological source of the worst forms of practical "disillusionment with life."[1]

It follows, if these reflections are sound, that we must not, as metaphysicians, allow ourselves to assume the truth of any and every conviction about the nature of the world which we find personally inspiring and attractive, or even which we believe to have an invigorating effect upon the moral practice of mankind in general. We cannot, on *a*

[1] I have not taken into account the argument from origins, because it does not appear relevant. That our intellectual interest in "truth" is historically a derivative from an interest in the "useful," "science" an offshoot of the arts, is, as we have seen for ourselves, true enough, but it does not follow that the truth which is the ideal of the developed intellect is the same thing as the "useful" from which it has arisen. We rejected the claims of the mechanical postulate to be final truth, not because of their origin in the needs of industrial science, but because, as tested by the standard of final self-consistency, they were unsatisfactory to the intellect.

priori grounds, dismiss the suggestion that it may make for practical goodness that all of us to some extent, and many of us to a very great extent, should be dwellers in the imperfectly illuminated regions on the "mid way boundary of light and dark."[1] On the other hand, it would manifestly be incompatible with the presence of any rational unity of structure in the experience-world that there should be a final and absolute lack of harmony between that world, as it must be conceived by true thinking, and as it must be if our ethical aspirations are to be satisfied. Somehow and somewhere, if the world is a teleological unity at all, these aspirations must be provided for and made good by its real structure, though possibly not in the form in which, with our present limited insight, we desire that they should be met, and though, again, we may be unable ever to say precisely in *what* form they are met. What is simply inconceivable in a rational world is that our abiding aspirations should meet with blank defeat.

§ 3. What, then, appears to be the "indispensable minimum" of accord between known truth and our "ethical postulates," without which the moral life itself would become irrational? On the whole, I think we may say that morality cannot maintain itself except upon two suppositions—(1) that in the main and on the whole the world is so ordered that our moral struggle for fuller and stronger individuality of life is successful; that by living the moral life our individual character does become richer in coherent interest and more completely unified; and (2) that the gain thus won by our private struggles does not perish with our disappearance from this mortal scene, but is handed on to the successors who replace us in the life of the social order to which we belong. Speaking roughly, this means that unless morality is a delusion, the moral life is, on the whole, the happy life, and that there is such a thing as social progress. Now, both these conditions, I would contend, are shown by the actual experience of mankind to be met by the constitution of the real world. It was by the analysis of actual social life, and not by an appeal to postulates of a transcendental kind, that Plato and Aristotle showed that the good man is, in the main, even in the present state of society, the "happy" man. And it is by a similar analysis that the modern thinker must convince himself, if he convinces himself at all, that human societies are progressive.

So far, then, no question of ultimate metaphysical issues

---

[1] ἐν μεταιχμίῳ σκότου, to use the poet's phrase.

seems to be involved in the practical demand of the moral life. The case would, of course, be different if we were with Kant to regard it as a necessary demand of Ethics that the world shall be so constituted that, in the end, and for every individual agent, happiness shall be exactly proportioned to virtue. Still more so if we went on to assert that morality is a delusion unless every individual is predestined, by the nature of things, to the ultimate attainment of complete virtue and complete happiness. Views of this kind would manifestly have to be defended by an appeal to metaphysical principles which do not find their complete justification in the empirically known structure of human society. So too the demand that human society itself shall be progressive beyond all limits, cannot be shown to be justified by what is empirically known of the structure and the non-human environment of our society. And if Ethics really does postulate either the complete coincidence of virtue with happiness for the individual, or the infinite progress of society, it is clearly committed to the postulation of very far-reaching metaphysical doctrines.

Further, it must be frankly owned that these postulates, as they stand, are inconsistent with the scheme of metaphysical doctrine expounded and defended in the present work. For both moral goodness and moral progress are bound up with finite individuality and its characteristic form of existence, the time-process. Of "progress" this is manifest: all progress is advance in time, and is advance from a relatively worse to a relatively better. And with "virtue" it stands no otherwise. For to be virtuous is not simply to *have* an individuality which is at once harmonious and rich in contents, but to *make* such an individuality for ourselves out of the raw material of disposition and environment. Only in the progress towards fuller individuality are we moral agents, and, just because we are finite, the complete attainment of an absolutely harmonious individuality is for ever beyond us. Hence absolutely perfect virtue—and consequently absolutely perfect happiness—are incompatible with our nature as genuine but finite individuals. In all finite individuality there is inevitably some aspect of imperfection and consequently of sadness, though sin and sadness ought to fill, and can be empirically seen to fill, an increasingly subordinate place in proportion to the degree of individuality attained. The same reasoning is equally applicable to the case of any finite society.

Nor does this seem any ground for regarding the constitution of the universe as ethically unsatisfactory. To repeat the previously quoted remark of Mr. Bradley, no one has a right to call the universe morally unsatisfactory on the ground that it does not precisely apportion happiness to virtue, unless he is prepared to show that more goodness would be produced by making the correspondence exact, and to show this is impossible. Still more absurd would it be to censure the universe because neither *perfect* virtue nor *perfect* happiness is attainable. For morality itself has no existence except as the creation of finite individuals, and hence we cannot without absurdity censure the universe on *moral* grounds for containing finite individuals, and so providing for the existence of morality.

§ 4. Would the case be altered if we had, or thought we had, grounds for holding that the progress of human society has fixed and knowable bounds set to it by the nature of things? If we could know, for instance, that the physical environment of humanity is so constituted that human life *must* ultimately disappear from the earth? I cannot see that it would. No doubt the widespread acceptance of a belief that the end of things was at hand within a calculable period, might tend to lessen our moral earnestness, and if the period were taken to be sufficiently short, might lead to downright licence and wickedness. But so does a belief in the approaching dissolution of any historic and wide-reaching social order; and yet the fact that societies suffer dissolution is not commonly regarded as reasonable ground for an indictment against the universe. Nor is there any logical connection between such beliefs and their consequences. We cannot say that because human society is perishable, if it is perishable, its achievements must have been wasted and therefore its progress useless. The result of our achievements might, in some way unknown to us, survive our extinction as a race, even as we can partly see that the results of the individual life are preserved after our death.

And, in any case, it is beyond the power of Metaphysics to set any fixed limits to the existence and progress of human society. As we have seen, Metaphysics gives us no reason to deny, though it does not enable us to affirm, that the social life begun under present conditions may be continued under unknown conditions beyond the grave. And even the disappearance of physical human life within a calculable period cannot be shown to follow from any principle of Metaphysics. At most we can say that *if* certain assumed physical laws, especially that of the dissipation of energy, are valid for all physical processes, and if again, the psychical factor in living organisms is incapable of reversing the "down-grade" tendency of energy to pass into forms unavailable for work, then the human society we know must come to an end within a calculable time. But whether the assumptions upon which this conclusion is based are or are not true, Metaphysics by itself cannot determine.

We are thus left in the following position. That on the whole the virtuous life is also the happy life, and that there is genuine social progress,[1] seem to be empirically known certainties. "Absolute perfection" of the finite as finite, and "infinite progress" seem alike excluded as metaphysical impossibilities. But no definite limits can be set by Metaphysics to the possibilities of individual and social advance towards greater virtue and greater happiness. As for the theories in Physics which appear to threaten humanity with extinction within a measurable time, their truth is, to say the least of it, not assured, and we have, in our metaphysical conception of Reality as an individual whole, the certainty that, whatever becomes of the human species, nothing of all our aspirations and achievements can be finally lost to the universe, though we may be quite unable to imagine the manner of their preservation. And for the purposes of the moral struggle from a worse to a better, this seems to be quite as much conformity to our aspirations as we need ask of the world. For the suggestion that our ideals are not worth living for unless *we* enjoy the fruit of our labours in the form we in particular should like, seems nothing better than an appeal to the baser Egoism.

§ 5. When we consider the specially *religious* attitude of mind, we shall find that its demands upon the world go further than those of mere Ethics, and are, in part, of a rather different character. It would be impossible in a work like this to discuss at length the nature of the religious attitude, but this much at least would probably be admitted as beyond doubt. The religious attitude towards the world of experience

[1] Not, of course, *pure* progress. It does not require profound insight to discover that moral progress, like everything else, has its price, and that all "progressive evolution" implies "degeneration" as one of its aspects. But the moral progress of society will be genuine if, on the whole, our gain is—from the moralist's special standpoint—more than our loss. We have no reason to despair of our kind if the impartial historian, comparing the facts—not the self-complacent fictions of popular optimism—about our current social life with the facts—not the fancies of Apologetics—about social life, say, in the first century of the Roman Empire, can pronounce that there has been advance on the whole.

is distinguished from all others partly by the specific character of the emotions in which it finds its expression, partly by the intellectual beliefs to which those emotions give rise. Specifically religious emotion, as we can detect it both in our own experience, if we happen to possess the religious "temperament,[1] and in the devotional literature of the world, appears to be essentially a mingled condition of exaltation and humility arising from an immediate sense of communion and co-operation with a power greater and better than ourselves in which our ideals of good find completer realisation than they ever obtain in the empirically known time-order. In the various religious creeds of the world we have a number of attempts to express the nature of such a power and of our relation to it in more or less logically satisfactory conceptual terms. But it is important to remember that, though a theological belief when sincerely held may react powerfully upon religious feeling, the beliefs are in the last resort based upon immediate feeling, and not immediate feeling upon beliefs. In this sense, at any rate, it is true that all genuine religious life implies the practical influencing of feeling and action by convictions which go beyond proved and known truth, and may therefore be said to be matters of faith.

What the convictions to which we thus surrender the practical guidance of life are, in any individual case, seems to be largely a question of individual constitution and social tradition. Not only are the convictions as to the nature of the higher power represented by the great typical historical religions very various, but what we may call the individual religion of different persons exhibits even greater variety. There is hardly any important object of human interest which may not acquire for some man the significance which belongs to the completed realisation of his highest ideals. It is no more than the truth to say that a mother, a mistress, a country,

[1] The "religious" temperament is apparently shown by experience to be, in its intenser manifestations, quite as much an idiosyncrasy of congenital endowment as the "æsthetic." There are persons, not otherwise mentally defective, who seem to be almost devoid of it, just as there are others who have little or no sense of humour or feeling for beauty. As many of these persons are ethically excellent, some of them exceptionally so, and as again the religious temperament is often found strongly developed in persons of quite inferior ethical development, there seems to be no *direct* connection between religious sensibility and moral excellence, though, of course, religious feeling is the most powerful of moral influences when it is conjoined in the same person with ethical fervour. For a masterly description of some typical forms of religious feeling and belief the reader should consult Professor James's *Varieties of Religious Experience*. He will find my own views as to the philosophical interpretation of religion, if he cares to know them, in the final chapter of my *Problem of Conduct*.

or a movement, social or political, may be, as we often phrase it, a man's "religion."

Amid all this variety two general principles may be detected which are of primary importance to the metaphysical critic of religious experience. (1) It is essential to the religious experience that its object should be accepted as the really existing embodiment of an ideal. This is the point in which the religious attitude of mind differs most strikingly from that of mere morality. In the ethical experience the ideal is apprehended as something which does not yet exist, but has to be brought into existence by human exertion. Hence for the purely ethical attitude of mind the world has to be thought of as essentially imperfect, essentially out of accord with what it ought to be in order to correspond to our demands on it. Thus there is not for morality, as we shall directly see there must be for religion, such a thing as the "Problem of Evil." That the world, as it comes to us in the temporal order, contains imperfection and evil which must be done away with, is a practical presupposition without which morality itself would have no *raison d'être*.

But in religion the case is otherwise. It is only in so far as the object of our adoration, whatever it may be, is taken to be the really existing embodiment of our highest ideals, that it can produce, in our spiritual communion with it, that combined emotion of exaltation and abasement, that feeling of being at once ourselves already perfect so far as our will is one in its contact with our ideal, and absolutely condemned and "subject to wrath" so far as it is not, which distinguishes the religious from all other states of mind. But all real existence, as we saw in our Second Book, is essentially individual. Hence it is of the essence of religion that it looks upon the ideal as already existing *in individual form*. This is why devotion to an abstract principle, such as nationality, socialism, democracy, humanity, proves so much inferior as a permanent expression of religious life, to devotion to a person, however imperfect.[1]

(2) It follows that mere appearance in the time-order cannot be the ultimate object of religious devotion. For the time-order itself, as we have seen, is essentially unfinished

---

[1] So Hegel insisted that the fundamental significance of the Christian religion lies neither in the historical career nor in the moral teaching of Jesus (which indeed contained little that had not already been uttered in the form of precept or principle), but in the recognition by the Christian community of the union of God and Man as a fact already realised in individual form in the person of Christ. See Dr. McTaggart's essay on "Hegelianism and Christianity" in *Studies in Hegelian Cosmology*.

and incomplete, and no part of it, therefore, can be perfectly individual. The completely individual, if it exists at all, must have an existence which is not temporal. Hence no part of the temporal order of events, as such, can be finally satisfactory as an object of religious adoration. So far as it is possible to succeed in worshipping anything which forms part of that order, such as a man or a cause, this can only be done by regarding the temporal facts as an imperfect appearance of a reality which, because completely and perfectly individual, is in its true nature timeless. And it further follows that, since all finite individuality is, as we have already seen, only imperfectly individual, and because imperfect is temporal, the only finally adequate object of religious devotion must be the infinite individual or timeless Absolute itself.

That the great philosophical religions of the world have felt the force of this, is shown in history by the way in which they have inevitably tended to credit their various "gods" with omnipotence. Thus the god of the Hebrew religion, as at first presented to us in its earlier records, is represented as limited in power by the existence of other divine beings, and temporally changeable and mutable. But in the later Old Testament writings, the New Testament, and the subsequent constructions of ecclesiastical theology, we see the gradual development from these Hebrew beginnings of an idea of a God who is "all in all," and limited neither by the existence of other divine beings with opposing aims and interests, nor by the inherent resistance of "matter," to His purposes. So the Zoroastrian religion, in which the limitation of the power of the good being Ahura Mazda by the existence of a coordinate bad being, Angro Mainyus, was originally a fundamental tenet, is said to have become among the modern Parsis a pure monotheism.

§ 6. Now, it should be noted that this inevitable tendency of Religion itself to identify its object with ultimate Reality, conceived in its timeless perfection as a complete and infinite individual whole, leads to the difficult metaphysical "problem of evil." For if God is the same thing as the Absolute, it would appear that evil itself must be, like everything else, a manifestation of His nature. And if so, can we say that God is strictly speaking "good," or is the complete realisation of our ideals? It is this difficulty about evil, more than anything else, which has led many philosophers in both ancient and modern times to distinguish between the Absolute and God, and to regard God as simply one, though the highest and most perfect, among the finite individuals contained in the Absolute.[1] In the following paragraphs I propose not so much to offer a solution of this time-honoured puzzle, as to make some suggestions which may help to put the issue at stake clearly before the reader's mind.

The doctrine of the finitude of God does not appear in any way to remove the difficulty about evil; in fact, it renders it, if anything, more acute. For evil must now appear in the universe in a double form. On the one hand, it admittedly is taken to exist outside God, as a hostile factor limiting His power of shaping the world to His purpose. But again, as we have seen, every finite individual, because finite, falls short of complete internal harmony of structure, and thus contains an element of defect and evil within itself. Thus evil will be inherent in the nature of a finite God, as well as in that of the existence supposed to be outside Him. We have, in fact, one more illustration of the principle that all limitation involves self-limitation from within. It is only by forgetting this fundamental truth that we can conceive the possibility of a being who is "perfectly good" and yet is less than the Absolute.

And even when we overlook this, our difficulties are not removed. For a "finite" God with a further reality outside and in some way opposed to His own nature, even when illogically thought of as perfectly good, must be at best only such another being as ourselves, though on a larger scale. He, like us, must be simply a partly successful, partly unsuccessful, actor in a universe of which the constitution and ultimate upshot are either unknown or known not to satisfy our religious demand for the complete individual reality of our ideal.[2] This is the view which has in history been

[1] So Plato suggested in the second book of the *Republic*, that God is not the cause of all that happens to us, but only of the good things that befall us. Perhaps, however, Plato is here consciously adapting his expression to current theological doctrine of which he did not fully approve. For a modern defence of the same conception of a finite God, see Dr. Rashdall's essay in *Personal Idealism*. Other reasons which have often led to the same view, such as the desire to think of God as a mutable being like ourselves, capable of being influenced in His attitude toward us by our attitude towards Him, seem to rest too much upon idiosyncrasies of private feeling to be of serious philosophical weight. If private feeling is to count at all, one does not see why that of those who would feel outraged by such a conception of a finite changeable God should not be allowed an equal significance with that of their opponents. It is a palpable mistake to treat private feeling, whatever its worth may be, as all on one side in this matter.

[2] For if we once suppose that we know the universe, in which "God" is only one finite being among others, to be so constituted as to correspond to this demand, it will be the whole of which "God" is one factor, and not "God" by Himself, which will become the supreme object of religious emotion. Thus we may say, until God is thought of as the individual whole, He is not fully God.

actually adopted by religions like those of the Hellenes and the Norsemen, in which the gods are regarded as ultimately subject to an inscrutable and unethical Fate. But a finite being struggling, however successfully, against such an alien Fate is, after all, a fit object only for moral respect and sympathy, not for religious adoration. Such a being, however exalted, is still not that complete and harmonious individual realisation of all human aspiration for which Religion yearns, and is therefore not, in the full and true sense, God.

If, then, a finite ethical individual, however exalted, cannot be an adequate object of religious devotion, how does the case stand with the infinite individual whole of Reality? Can we worship the Absolute?[1] This is a question which needs some careful examination before we can venture on a positive answer.

§ 7. The problem, let it be observed, is not strictly psychological. Experience shows that individual men can derive religious support from belief in the most varied and most defective conceptions of the nature of the Deity. Beliefs which bring one man "peace in believing" might, if seriously entertained, blight another man's life; one man's God may be another's devil. This is, however, not the point. The real question is, whether the Absolute can be made into an object of religious worship, as we have seen that finite individuals cannot, without a breach of logic. Has it the character which, as we have seen, anything which is to correspond to our ideal of "God" must logically possess?

At first sight it certainly would seem that it has. For, as we have seen, the Absolute contains all finite existence, and contains it as a perfectly harmonious system. And therefore all finite aspiration must somehow be realised in the structure of the Absolute whole, though not necessarily in the way in which we, as beings of limited knowledge and goodness, actually wish it to be realised. The Absolute whole is thus, as nothing else can be, the concrete individual reality in which our ideals have actual existence. As all our ideals themselves are but so many expressions of our place in the system and our relation to the rest of it, so the system itself is their concrete harmonious embodiment.

[1] It should be scarcely necessary to point out that the Absolute, if it can be worshipped at all, can be worshipped only as conceived as fully individual. When it is falsely thought of as a "collection" or "aggregate" or "totality" of independent things, it is no more divine than any other collection. This is the fatal objection to vulgar "Pantheism." How far any of the serious thinkers who are popularly charged with "Pantheism" have countenanced this view of the Absolute as a mere collection, is another matter.

It is true, as we have already seen, that our ideals may not be realised in the whole just in the form in which we conceive them, but it must be remembered that in so far as we set up our private judgment and wishes as standards to which the whole is bound to conform on pain of condemnation, we are adopting an attitude which is at once illogical and irreligious. It is illogical, because it implies the assumption that with fuller knowledge of the system of Reality as a whole we should still desire the fulfilment of our aspirations in the special way which at present recommends itself to our imperfect insight. It is irreligious, because the demand that human desires shall be fulfilled in our way and not in " God's way " involves the setting up of human wisdom against God's, and is thus irreconcilable with genuine union of heart and will with the divine order.[1]

What then becomes, from this point of view, of the problem of evil? How can the presence of moral evil in the temporal order be reconciled with the thought of the Absolute whole as the complete and harmonious realisation of human ideals? I need not say that the *detailed* solution of the problem is out of the question. As beings whose insight is necessarily limited by our own finitude, we cannot hope to see how in detail everything that appears to us as evil might, with larger knowledge, be known as an integral constituent of a whole which, as a whole, is the realisation of human aspiration, and therefore free from evil. But it is at least possible to make suggestions which may show that the problem is a mere consequence of the inevitable defects of our insight, and that it would disappear with fuller knowledge. It is not hard to see that there are two main reasons why the structure of the universe seems to finite insight partly evil. Our insight into the nature and connection of our purposes themselves is never complete ; we are all, in part, ignorant of exactly what it is to which we aspire. Hence our purposes in part appear to be met by existence with a negative just because we are only imperfectly aware of what they mean and whither they tend. There is no more familiar fact than this, that even within the limits of our

---

[1] I am afraid that this essentially irreligious feeling has a great deal to do with the complaints sometimes urged against the Absolute as a poor substitute for a " living God." Partly these complaints spring, no doubt, from the mistaken notion that the Absolute is not a concrete individual but a mere " collective concept." But they seem also to be motived by a suspicion that a finite Deity might be more amenable than the Absolute to our wish to have our ideals gratified in our own fashion. And so far as this is the motive of them, such complaints are essentially impious.

human life growing experience is constantly teaching us how confused and defective our judgment at any moment as to what we really want, can be. Largely, then, our ideals seem to be at variance with actual existence, because we never fully know what they are.

Again, our knowledge of the effects of our acts is always imperfect in the extreme. We seem to fail because we cannot see far enough to understand fully what it is we have effected. And both these causes of the apparent discrepancy between the real and the ideal may be traced to a single root. Existence appears to be in part evil, because we cannot take it in at once and as a whole in its individual structure. We have to make acquaintance with it by piecemeal, and as a succession of fragmentary events in the time-series. And imperfection, we have seen, belongs to the time-series. Hence we can see that evil is at once a mere appearance, and an appearance which is inevitable to the finite experience conditioned by the temporal form. The so-called "problem" is thus in principle insoluble only so long as we falsely think of the time-order itself as a characteristic of the Absolute whole in its real individuality.[1]

May we say, then, that the Absolute or whole is known in Metaphysics to be "good"? The answer depends upon the precise meaning we attach to the statement. In the sense that it is the really existing embodiment of the ideals we are trying amid our ignorance and confusion to realise, we clearly must say "yes." But if we use the word "good" in a narrower sense, to mean "*ethically* good," we can hardly say without qualification that the whole is good. For "ethical goodness" belongs essentially to the time-order, and means the process of the gradual assertion of the ideal against apparent evil. To be morally good is to have an ideal that is not realised in the events of the time-order as they come to us in our finite experience, and to mould those events into conformity with the ideal. The moral life is from first to last a struggle, and where the struggle is absent it is misleading to speak of morality. Hence it is better not to call the Absolute " moral."

But we must remember that the Absolute is only not moral, because it is something very much more than moral,

---

[1] The reader will naturally think of the famous Socratic paradox, that "wrong doing is error," "vice is ignorance." If we interpret this to mean that the fundamental advantage of the good man over the bad lies in his truer insight into what he seriously wants, it seems to be true.

only not ethical because there is in it no divorce of ideal from actuality, as there is in the imperfect experience of its finite members. Or, as we might say, it is something more than "good" precisely because it is already good. In morality, let it be remembered, we have, as in all the experience of finite beings, a process which is throughout directed upon a result that, once attained, would transcend the process itself. Morality would not be content with anything less than the total abolition of the evil in the world ; and with the disappearance of evil, the struggle against it would itself disappear in some higher form of experience. Similarly, knowledge is constantly striving to exhaust the object of knowledge. So long as the object is in any respect unknown, the task of knowing is incomplete ; yet if once we could so know any object that nothing further remained to be known about it, there would be no aspect of not-self in the object which could distinguish it from the subject by which it is known, and knowledge itself would thus be done away. Thus we may see from the side alike of cognition and of will how the whole life of the finite being forms a constant endeavour to widen experience into the complete apprehension of a content which, because infinite, could not be apprehended without the disappearance of finitude itself. Thus does experience witness to the truth of our fundamental doctrine, that the finite individual repeats in itself, in an imperfect and inadequate form, the structure of the infinite individual of which it is an appearance.

I do not know whether it is necessary to say more than a word with reference to the thoughtless objection so often urged against all philosophical and religious doctrines which deny the ultimate reality of evil, or, what is the same thing, the existence of an independent devil. If existence is already perfect, it is said, why should we seek to make it better at great trouble and inconvenience to ourselves by moral and political endeavour? Ought we not rather to sit with folded hands acquiescing lazily in "things as they are"? The doubt might even be carried further than this. For to "take things as they are" is just as much a course of self-chosen action as any other line of conduct, and it might hence be argued that abstention and moral effort are alike out of place and absurd in a world where everything is "perfect."

The objection, of course, turns upon a mere confusion of existence as it is in its individual reality, and existence as it appears to us in the time-series. The argument for Quietism is based purely upon attributing to the essentially imperfect and incomplete series of temporal events the perfection which only belongs to the timeless whole. In that perfect whole our moral ideals and moral effort, as finite beings belonging to the temporal order, are of course included along with everything else, and its perfection is therefore no ground for treating them as nugatory. Our own moral struggle with the apparent evil of the time-series is itself an integral part of the Reality which, in its complete individual character, is already perfect, if we could but win to a point of view from which to behold it as it is. As Plotinus expresses it, "our striving is after good and our turning away is from evil, and thought with a purpose is of good and evil, and this is a good."[1]

If we may not say without qualification that the Absolute is good, and certainly must not say that it is in the proper sense "ethical," still less may we say that the Absolute is "morally indifferent." For the Absolute is only not ethical because it is already all that ethical life consists in striving to become. Hence the higher a finite being stands in the ethical scale, as judged by the double criterion of the wealth of its interests in the world and the degree of harmony between them, the more adequately does its structure repeat that of the whole, and the higher is its degree of reality. And this means that the good man's ideals are realised in the world-order with less of modification and reconstruction than the bad man's. In a sense, as Professor Royce maintains, even the bad man's confused and warring ideals get their fulfilment, since he too is aiming, however blindly, at a complete individuality as the goal of all his striving. But he is seeking it where it is not to be found, in the gratification of desires which cannot be allowed the supreme place in the direction of life without leading to the distraction and mutilation of the self. As Plato puts it, the bad man "does as he pleases," and for that very reason never "does what he wills." Hence the place of the good man in the economy of the universe is very different from that of the bad, and the

---

[1] *Enneads*, I. 8, 15 (quoted and translated in Whittaker, the *Neoplatonists*, p. 83). Plotinus had just previously made the correct observation that to deny the existence of evil in any and every sense means to deny the existence of good. (κακόν γε εἴ τις λέγοι τὸ παράπαν ἐν τοῖς οὖσι μὴ εἶναι, ἀνάγκη αὐτῷ καὶ τὸ ἀγαθὸν ἀναιρεῖν καὶ μηδὲ ὀρεκτὸν μηδὲν εἶναι.) We might thus say, if good is to be at all, evil must have some kind of relative or phenomenal existence as its antecedent condition. But, as thus serving as a condition for the realisation of good, evil is itself, from a more universal point of view, good, and therefore its existence *as* evil only apparent. On the whole question of the position of evil in the world-order, see the admirable essay on "Sin" in Dr. McTaggart's *Studies in Hegelian Cosmology*.

world-order itself is the very reverse of "indifferent" to the distinction between them.[1]

My own conclusion, then, which I offer to the reader simply as my own, is that anything less than the Absolute is an inadequate object of religious devotion, and that the Absolute itself has the structure which such an object requires. If it should be further suggested that at any rate, when we come to actual experience, we find that we cannot represent the object of our worship to ourselves in an individual form of sufficient concreteness to stir effectual emotion and prompt to genuine action without clothing it in imagination with anthropomorphic qualities which metaphysical criticism proves inapplicable to the infinite individual, I should be inclined to reply that I admit the fact. And I do not think we need shrink from the conclusion that practical religion involves a certain element of intellectual contradiction. Thus, though God is not truly God until we deny the existence of any independent "evil" by which His nature is limited, it seems probable that the thought of ourselves as "fellow-workers with God" would hardly lead to practical good works unless we also inconsistently allowed ourselves to imagine God as struggling against a hostile power and standing in need of our assistance. But this only shows that the practical value of religion in guiding action is not necessarily dependent upon its scientific truth.

§ 8. Of course, it would be quite open to us to hold that there may be, within the Absolute, finite beings of superhuman power and goodness with whom humanity is capable of co-operating for ethical ends. Only such beings, if they exist, would not be God in the same sense in which the Absolute may be called God. They might deserve and win our reverence and our co-operation, but because themselves finite and therefore only imperfectly real and individual, they could not logically take the place which belongs only to the completely and perfectly individual realisation of the ideal. That would still fall partly outside them in the nature, as a whole, of the system which harmoniously includes both

---

[1] When it is said that the Absolute, if it exists, must be morally indifferent, there is often a conscious or unconscious confusion of thought. The Absolute must certainly be "indifferent" in the sense that it does not feel the internal discord of hatred and animosity against any of its constituents. Deus, as Spinoza says, neminem potest odio habere. For the Absolute is not one of the two combatants; it is at once both combatants and the field of combat. But to infer that the Absolute, because devoid of the feelings of hatred and private partisanship, must be indifferent in the sense that our goodness and badness make no difference to our place in it, is a fallacy of equivocation for which unconsciousness and *bona fides* are scarcely sufficient excuse.

ourselves and them. Thus such beings would be "gods" in the sense of polytheism rather than God in that of monotheism.

Further, I can see no means of deciding *a priori* that there could be only one such being in the universe. Even supposing the series of finite beings to be itself finite, it is not evident that it could contain only one "best" member. And supposing it infinite, could there be a "best" member at all?[1] Also it appears quite beyond the power of Metaphysics to find either proof or disproof of the existence and agency of such finite but exalted beings. We cannot say that our general conception of Reality is such as to negative the suggestion, and yet again that general conception gives us no positive evidence in favour of taking it as true. It would certainly be the grossest presumption to maintain that the Absolute can contain no higher types of finite individuality than those presented by human society; on the other hand, it would be equally presumptuous to assert that we have reasoned knowledge of their existence and their direct social relation with ourselves. Hence we must, I think, be content to say that the hypothesis, so far as it seems to be suggested to any one of us by the concrete facts of his own individual experience, is a matter for the legitimate exercise of Faith.

§ 9. These reflections may naturally lead to some remarks, which shall be made as brief as possible, about the so-called philosophical "arguments for the existence of God," which played a prominent part in Metaphysics before their discrediting at the hands of Kant and Hume.[2] Kant's great achievement lies in having demonstrated that the whole force of the "proofs" depends upon the famous ontological argument, best known in modern Philosophy in the form adopted by Descartes in the fifth *Meditation.* Descartes there argues thus:—By "God" I mean a completely perfect being. Now, existence is a perfection, and non-existence an imperfection. Hence I cannot think of a non-existing perfect being without self-contradiction. Hence God, because by hypothesis

---

[1] Thus I do not understand why, apart from respect for the traditions of Christianity, Dr. Rashdall should hold that God, in his sense of the word, is one and not many. His argument appears to me to identify God with the Absolute, where it is required to maintain God's unity, and to distinguish them as soon as it becomes a question of proving God's "Personality" (see his essay in *Personal Idealism*). Professor James appears more logical in his obvious readiness to reckon with polytheism as a possible consequence of his denial of God's infinity (*Varieties of Religious Experience*, p. 524 ff.).

[2] Kant's famous onslaught will be found in the *Kritik der Reinen Vernunft*, Transcendental Dialectic, bk. ii. div. 3 ("The Ideal of Pure Reason"), §§ 3–7. Hume's criticisms are contained in his posthumous *Dialogues concerning Natural Religion.*

perfect, must exist, and is the *only* being whose existence logically follows from its definition.

Kant's even more famous criticism of this famous inference turns upon the principle which he had learned from his study of Hume, that logical necessity is "subjective." If I think of a logical subject as defined by certain properties, he argues in effect, I am *necessitated* to ascribe to it all the predicates implied in that definition. That is, I must affirm them or contradict myself. Hence, if "existence" is originally included among the perfections by which the subject "God" is defined, the proposition *God exists* is certainly necessary, but is also tautological, and amounts, in fact, to the mere assertion that "an existing perfect being is an existing perfect being." But if the "existence" spoken of in the predicate is something not included in the definition of the subject, then you cannot infer it from that definition. Now "real existence" is not a predicate which can be included in the definition of a concept. The predicates by which an imaginary hundred dollars are defined are the same as those of a real hundred dollars. It is not by the possession of a new predicate, but by being actually given in a concrete experience, that the real coins differ from the imaginary. Hence all propositions asserting real existence are *synthetic*, (*i.e.* assert of their subject something which is not contained in the concept of it), and the real existence of God or any other object can never be deduced from its definition.[1]

This Kantian criticism has itself been subjected to much criticism, principally at the hands of Hegel and those subsequent philosophers who have been specially affected by the Hegelian influence. What appears to be the general principle of the Hegelian criticism has been most clearly expressed in English philosophy by Mr. Bradley,[2] upon whose discussion the following remarks are chiefly founded.

---

[1] Kant's criticism had been in part anticipated on the first circulation of the *Meditations* by both Mersenne and Gassendi. See particularly Gassendi's strictures on Descartes' confusion of existence with properties in the "Fifth Objections," with Descartes' unsatisfactory reply. Leibnitz repeated the same objection, and proposed to amend the Cartesian proof by a formal demonstration that God's existence is *possible*, *i.e.* does not imply a formal contradiction. He then argues—If God's existence is possible, He exists (by the Cartesian proof). But God's existence is possible, therefore God exists. See, *e.g.*, Leibnitz, Works, ed. Erdmann, p. 177; and Latta, *Monadology of Leibniz*, p. 274. Hume's comments are even more akin to Kant's. "Whatever we conceive as existent we can also conceive as non-existent. There is no being, therefore, whose non-existence implies a contradiction. Consequently there is no being whose existence is demonstrable." (*Dialogues concerning Natural Religion*, part 9.)

[2] *Appearance and Reality*, chap. 24.

In estimating the worth of the ontological proof, we must distinguish between the general principle implied in it and the particular form in which it presents that principle. It is manifest that Kant is perfectly right when he contends that, taking existence to mean presence in the space and time-order, you cannot reason from my possession of any idea to the existence of a corresponding object. You cannot say whatever I conceive must exist as I conceive it. But the principle of the ontological proof is perhaps not necessarily condemned by its failure to be thus universally applicable. The principle involved appears to be simply this. The idea and the reality outside its own existence as a fact in the time-order which it "means" or "stands for" are mutually complementary aspects of a whole Reality which include them both. For there is, on the one side, no "idea" so poor and untrue as not to have some meaning or objective reference beyond its own present existence.[1] And, on the other, what has no significance for any subject of experience is nothing. Hence in its most general form the ontological argument is simply a statement that reality and meaning for a subject mutually imply one another. But it does not follow that all thoughts are equally true and significant. In other words, though every thought *means* something beyond its own existence, different thoughts may represent the structure of that which they mean with very different grades of adequacy. That which my thought means may be far from being real in the form in which I think it.

Now, we may surely say that the more internally harmonious and systematic my thought is, the more adequately it represents the true nature of that which it means. If thoroughly systematic coherent thought may be mere misrepresentation, our whole criterion of scientific truth is worthless. How freely we use this ontological argument in practice will be readily seen by considering the way in which, *e.g.*, in the interpretation and reconstruction of historical facts, the internal coherency of a systematic and comprehensive interpretation is taken as itself the evidence of its truth.[2] Hence it may be argued that if there is a systematic way

[1] No thought can be merely and absolutely false, any more than any act can be merely and without qualification bad. Though *words* may be entirely meaningless, thoughts cannot be.

[2] The appeal to experiment is no objection to the principle. For in making the experiment we do not, of course, get out of the circle of our thoughts, and the experiment only affords a criterion of truth in so far as it leaves us with a new thought which can only be brought into systematic harmony with our old ideas in one determinate way. Except as interpreted by thought, the experiment has no bearing on our knowledge.

...ng about Reality which is absolutely and entirely ...y coherent, and from its own nature must remain so, ...the detailed content of our ideas should grow in ...ity, we may confidently say that such a scheme of ...faithfully represents the Reality for which it stands, ...any thought can represent Reality. That is, while ...ght would not *be* the Reality because it still remains ...which *means* something beyond its own existence, ...require no modification of structure but only sup-...ation in detail to make it the truth.

...f we have anywhere thought which is thus internally ..., and from its own nature must remain so, however ...ge may extend, we have it surely in our metaphysical ...on of the real as the absolutely individual. Thus the ...cal proof appears, in any sense in which it is not ...s, to amount merely to the principle that significant ...gives us genuine knowledge; and therefore, since the ...hgoing individuality of structure of its object is pre-...d in all significant thought, Reality must be a perfect ...al. That this perfect individual must further be ...*i.e.* must have the special character ascribed to it by ...based upon specifically religious emotions, does not follow. How far the "God" of religion is a correct conception of the metaphysical Absolute, we can only learn from the analysis of typical expressions of the religious experience itself. And it is obvious that if by "God" we mean anything less than the Absolute whole, the ontological proof ceases to have any cogency. It is impossible to show that the possibility of significant thought implies the presence of a special finite being, not empirically known to us, within the Absolute.

The "cosmological" proof, or "argument from the contingency of the world," unlike the ontological, has the appearance, at first sight, of starting with given empirical fact. As summarised by Kant for purposes of criticism, it runs thus:—" If anything at all exists, there must be also an absolutely necessary being. Now, I exist myself; *ergo*, the absolutely necessary being exists." To make the proof quite complete, it would be necessary to show that the being whose existence is affirmed in the minor premisses, to wit, myself, is not itself the "absolutely necessary being," and the argument thus completed would become in principle identical with the second of the "proofs" given by Descartes in the third *Meditation*, where it is inferred that if I, a dependent being, exist, there must be a God on whom I and all things depend.[1] As Kant has pointed out, the whole force of this inference rests upon the previous admission of the ontological argument. By itself the cosmological proof only establishes the conclusion that if any dependent existence is real, independent existence of some kind must be real also. To convert this into a "proof of the existence of *God*," you must further go on to identify the "independent existence" thus reached with the "most real" or "most perfect" being of the ontological proof. For otherwise it might be suggested, as is done by one of the speakers in Hume's dialogue, that the series of phenomenal events itself, taken as an aggregate, is the "necessary existence" upon which the "contingent existence" of each several event depends. "Did I show you the particular causes of each individual in a collection of twenty particles of matter, I should think it very unreasonable should you afterwards ask me what was the cause of the whole twenty. This is sufficiently explained in explaining the cause of the parts."

To avoid this objection, we must go on to maintain that only the "most perfect being" can be an ultimately necessary being, and that its "necessary existence" is a consequence of its character. This, as we have seen, is the very assertion made in the ontological proof. Hence our criticisms of the ontological proof will be equally applicable to the cosmological. If we combine the two, restating them in accord with our previous remodelling of the former, the argument will take the following form. All propositions directly or indirectly refer to real existence. Hence it would be self-contradictory to assert that nothing exists. But existence itself is only conceivable as individual. Hence the absolutely individual must be really existent. And this is identical with the general principle of our own reasoning in Book II. of the present work. Clearly, if valid, it is valid simply as an argument for a metaphysical Absolute; it neither proves that Absolute itself to be what we mean in religion by God, nor affords any ground for asserting the existence of God as a finite individual within the Absolute.[2]

---

[1] This was also a favourite argument with Leibnitz, as Kant notes. For an acute examination of Leibnitz's use of it and the other "proofs," see B. Russell's *Philosophy of Leibniz*, chap. 15. For Hume's objections to it, see the already quoted part 9 of the *Dialogue concerning Natural Religion*. The other "proof" of the *Third Meditation*, namely, that my possession of an idea of God, which I could not have derived from empirical sources, proves the reality of the idea's object, is only a special form of the ontological argument from idea to existence.

[2] As thus remodelled, the double ontologico-cosmological argument might be attacked on two grounds—(1) That it only proves, once more, that *if* we admit

The *physico-theological* argument, also known as the argument from *design*, or the *teleological* proof, differs from the preceding two in being in its current forms honestly empirical. In the shape of an inference from the apparent presence of order and a regard for human good in the structure of nature to the existence of a wise and benevolent being or beings as the author or authors of nature, it has been the most popular of all theistic arguments both in the ancient world, where, according to Xenophon, it was specially insisted upon by Socrates, and in the modern defences of theological beliefs against rationalistic criticism. It must, however, be observed that the criticisms of Hume and Kant are absolutely fatal to the "argument from design," when it is put forward as a proof of the existence of a God of *infinite* goodness and wisdom. At best, as Kant says, the observed order and harmony of Nature would enable us to infer a finite degree of wisdom and goodness in its author. The assertion of the absolute harmoniousness and goodness of Nature, which we require to justify the inference to infinite wisdom and goodness in its author, goes far beyond the limits of the empirically verifiable, and can itself only be upheld by some form of the "ontological proof." Hence the "argument from design" could at best prove a God whose wisdom and goodness are, so far as knowable, limited. As Hume forcibly puts the same point, if the empirically known facts of the partial adaptation of Nature to human purposes are valid, as they stand, to prove a wise and good intelligence, are not the equally well-ascertained facts of the partial want of adaptation equally valid to prove defective goodness or defective wisdom?[1]

There is a deeper metaphysical reason for this difference between the results of the physico-theological and of the other "proofs," which may be briefly pointed out. The

that all propositions are concerned with real existence, either directly or remotely, we must admit the existence of the Absolute, but does not demonstrate that all propositions *are* so concerned. (2) That in saying that existence is only *conceivable* as individual we fall back into the Cartesian misconception of existence as a predicate. I should reply, (1) that the validity of the premiss in question cannot be denied without being confirmed in the act of denial. *I.e.* unless the suggested proposition that "some propositions at least have no reference to a reality beyond their own presence as psychical facts in my mind," itself has the very objective reference in question, it has no meaning, and is therefore no genuine proposition; (2) that we must distinguish between the *what* and the *that* of existence. The "that" of existence is not conceivable at all, but our position is that this inconceivable *that* is only logically, not really, separable from a *what*, and that it is precisely this inseparability of the *that* and the *what* which we mean by "individuality."

[1] *Dialogues concerning Natural Religion*, part 11.

whole conception of the order and systematic unity of the world as due to preconceived " design " is only intelligible if we suppose the author of that " design " to be finite, and subject, like ourselves, to temporal mutability. For in the notion of design itself are implied the severance of the mentally conceived ideal from the actuality which waits to be brought into accord with it, and consequently also the time-process, which we have already found to be characteristic of all finitude. Hence the physico-theological proof, by itself, can at best be used to establish the reality of finite " gods," not of " God," because it works throughout with the categories of finitude.

Upon the logical force of the argument, as thus limited by its initial assumptions, only one observation need be made. What the reasoning asserts is not merely that " Nature " is in reality a system exhibiting individuality and purposive interest, or even " design," but that it reveals the particular design of assisting and fostering human progress. Now, whether this is so or not would appear to be a question of empirical fact only capable of determination by the methods applicable to other problems of the same empirical kind. Probably the lines along which it will have to be decided in the future are of the following general kind. Evolutionary science seems clearly to have shown that in the influences it knows, *e.g.*, as " natural " and again as " sexual selection," we have processes which lead to beneficial results without being, so far as we can see, in the least directed by the conscious " design " of establishing those results.[1] We should have to ask, then, whether there is actual ground for holding that such influences are not of themselves sufficient to account for the development of human civilisation, so far as it is due to factors belonging to the " environment." If they are so sufficient, the " physico-theological " argument for benevolent super-human agency in moulding the course of human development, becomes superfluous; if they are not, their failure is, so far, good ground for the recognition of finite " designing " intelligences of a non-human kind as forming a factor in our environ-

[1] This is quite consistent with our own view, that all real processes are teleological in the sense of being marked by subjective interest. For (*a*) not by any means all teleological process is actual " design " or " volition " (impulse, organic craving, habit, etc., are all cases in point) ; and (*b*) actual volition need not always be volition for the result it actually produces. Sexual selection in man would be an instance of a process which may take the form of actual volition, but in that case is rarely, if ever, volition for that improvement of the stock which *de facto* issues from it.

ment. In either case the question appears to be one of empirical fact, and to be incapable of determination in advance on general metaphysical grounds.[1] Nor are we justified in assuming that "design in nature," supposing it to exist, must always be directed to securing ends which are either intelligible to us, or, if intelligible, "benevolent," in the sense of furthering our own special human interests. And here I must be content to leave the subject.

Consult further :—F. H. Bradley, *Appearance and Reality*, chaps. 25, 26; J. E. McTaggart, *Studies in Hegelian Cosmology*, chaps. 6, 8; J. Royce, *The World and the Individual*, Second Series, lects. 9, 10.

[1] Cf. Bradley, *Appearance and Reality*, pp. 200, 496-497 (1st ed.). Professor Flint's attempted reply to the Humian and Kantian criticism of the theistic "proofs" (*Agnosticism*, chap. 4) has not induced me to modify any of the opinions expressed in this chapter.

CHAPTER VI

CONCLUSION

§ 1. Can our Absolute Experience be properly called the "union of Thought and Will"? The Absolute is certainly the final realisation of our intellectual and our practical ideals. But (1) it includes aspects, such as, *e.g.*, æsthetic feeling, pleasure, and pain, which are neither Thought nor Will. (2) And it cannot possess either Thought or Will *as such*. Both Thought and Will, in their own nature, presuppose a Reality which transcends *mere* Thought and *mere* Will. § 2. Our conclusion may in a sense be said to involve an element of Agnosticism, and again of Mysticism. But it is only agnostic in holding that we do not know the precise nature of the Absolute Experience. It implies no distrust of the validity of knowledge, so far as it goes, and bases its apparently agnostic result on the witness of knowledge itself. Similarly, it is mystical in transcending, not in refusing to recognise, the constructions of understanding and will. § 3. Metaphysics adds nothing to our information, and yields no fresh springs of action. It is finally only justified by the persistency of the impulse to speculate on the nature of things as a whole.

§ 1. It seems advisable, in bringing this work to a conclusion, to bring together by way of recapitulation a few important consequences of our general principle which could not receive all the notice they deserve in the course of our previous exposition. Our main contention, which it may be hoped our discussion of special problems has now confirmed, was that the whole of Reality ultimately forms a single infinite individual system, of which the material is psychical matter of fact, and that the individuality of this system lies ultimately in a teleological unity of subjective interest. Further, we saw that all subordinate reality is again in its degree individual, and that the contents of the Absolute thus form a hierarchy of ascending orders of reality and individuality, and that in this way, while all finite individual existence is, as finite, appearance and not ultimate Reality, appearances, themselves are of varied degrees of worth, and that, apart from the appearances, there is no reality at all. And finally, we learned that all the aspirations of finite individuals must be somehow met and made good in the ultimate Reality, though not necessarily in the form in which they are consciously entertained by the finite aspirant.

This last conclusion naturally suggests the question, whether it would be a correct description of the ultimate Reality to call it the "union of Thought and Will." I will briefly indicate the reasons why such a description appears to be misleading. (1) The Absolute may no doubt be called the "union of Thought and Will," in the sense that its complete individual structure corresponds at once to our logical ideal of systematic interconnection, and our ethico-religious ideal of realised individual purpose. But it must be added that the Absolute appears to possess aspects which cannot fairly be brought under either of these heads. Æsthetic feeling, for instance, and the æsthetic judgments based upon it, must somehow be included as an integral aspect in the absolute whole of experience; yet æsthetic feeling cannot properly be regarded either as thought or as will. And the same objection might be raised in the case of pleasure. However closely pleasure may be connected with conative efforts towards the retention or renewal of the pleasant experience, it seems quite clear that the "pure" pleasures[1] are not forms of conscious "conation," and that even in those "mixed" pleasures, which depend in part for their pleasantness upon relief from the tension of precedent craving or desire, analysis enables us to distinguish two elements, that of direct pleasure in the new experience, and that of the feeling of relief from the craving. Hence, if it be admitted that the Absolute contains pleasure, it must also be admitted that it contains something which is neither thought nor will. The same argument would hold good, I think, even if we held with the pessimists, that the Absolute contains a balance of pain over pleasure. For, intimate as the connection is between pain and thwarted conation, it seems a psychological monstrosity to maintain that felt pain is always and everywhere an experience of the frustration of actual conscious effort; and unless this monstrosity can be maintained, we must recognise in pain too a fundamental experience-quality irreducible to thought or will. Thus, at best, the description of the Absolute, as the union of thought and will, would be incomplete.

(2) But, further, the description, if taken to mean that

[1] I use the epithet in its familiar Platonic sense. The "pure" pleasure is that which is not dependent, in whole or in part, for its pleasantness upon a previous ἔνδεια, or actual experience of craving or desire. I do not mean, as Plato possibly did, that a "mixed" pleasure, preceded by such ἔνδεια, is a *mere* contrast-effect without positive quality of its own.

the Absolute itself has thought and will, *as such*, would be not only incomplete but false. For actual thought and actual will can easily be shown to be essentially finite functions, neither of which could ever reach its goal and become finally self-consistent, without ceasing to be mere thought or mere will. Thus actual thought always involves an aspect of discrepancy between its content and reference. It is always thought *about* a reality which falls, in part, outside the thought itself, is only imperfectly represented by the thought's content, and for that very reason is a not-self to the thought for which it is an object. And the whole process of thinking may be described as a series of attempts on the part of thought to transcend this limitation. So long as the content of the thought is not adequate to the reality which it thinks, so long, that is, as there is anything left to know about the reality, thought restlessly presses forward towards an unreached consummation. But if the correspondence *ideae cum ideato* ever became perfect, thought's object would cease to contain anything which went beyond thought's own content. It would no longer be an "other" or "not-self" to the thought which knew it, and thus thought and its object would have become a single thing. But in this consummation thought would have lost its special character as an actual process, just as the object would have lost its character of a something, partly at least, "given" from without. Both mere thought and mere existence, in becoming one, would cease to have the character which belongs to them in finite experience precisely in virtue of our failure completely to transcend the chasm between them.

The same is the case with will. If, indeed, by will we mean a genuine actual process of volition, this result is already included in our criticism of the claim of thought as such to persist unchanged in the Absolute. For all genuine will implies possession of and actuation by an idea which is entertained explicitly as an unrealised idea, and is thus inseparable from thought. (This, I may incidentally observe once more, is why we carefully avoided speaking of the "subjective interest" we found in all experience-processes as "will.") But even if we improperly widen the interpretation of the term "will" to include all conative process, the general conclusion will remain the same. For all such processes imply the contrast between existence as it comes to us in the here and now of actual feeling, and existence as it should be, and as we seek to make it, for the satisfaction of our various impulses, cravings, and desires. It is the felt, even when not explicitly understood, discrepancy between these two aspects of a reality, which is ultimately one and harmonious under the discrepancy, that supplies all actual conative process with its motive force. And hence we seem driven to hold that conation as such, *i.e.* as actual striving or effort, can find no place in an experience in which the aspects of ideality and real existence are once for all finally united.

If we cannot avoid speaking of such an experience in terms of our own intellectual, and again of our own volitional processes, we must at least remember that while such language is true in the sense that the all-embracing harmonious experience of the Absolute is the unattainable goal towards which finite intellect and finite volition are alike striving, yet each in attaining its consummation, if it ever could attain it, would cease to be itself as we know it, and pass into a higher and directer form of apprehension, in which it could no longer be distinguished from the other. In the old mediæval terminology, the Absolute must be said to contain actual intellect and actual volition, not *formaliter* but *eminenter*.[1]

§ 2. It follows from all this that, just because the absolute whole is neither mere thought nor mere will, nor an artificial synthesis of the two, mere truth for the intellect can never be quite the same thing as ultimate Reality. For in mere truth we get Reality only in its intellectual aspect as that which affords the highest satisfaction to thought's demand for consistency and systematic unity in its object. And, as we have seen, this demand can never be quite satisfied by thought itself. For thought, to remain thought, must always be something less than the whole reality which it knows. The reality must always contain a further aspect which is not itself thought, and is not capable of being apprehended in the form of a thought-content. Or, what is the same thing, while all reality is individual, all the thought-constructions through which we know its character must remain general. We are always trying in our thought to grasp the individual as such, and always failing. As individual, the reality never becomes the actual content of our thought, but remains a "transcendent" object to which thought *refers*, or which it *means*. And hence our truest thought can at best give us but an imperfect satisfaction for

---

[1] Compare the argument of *Appearance and Reality*, chap. 26, pp. 469-485 (1st ed.), and the famous scholium to Prop. 17 of part 1 of Spinoza's *Ethics*, where it is contended that "if intellect and volition belong to the eternal essence of God, each of these attributes must at least be understood in a different sense from the current."

its own demand of congruence, between thought's content and its object. The reality can never be ultimately *merely* what it is for our thought. And this conclusion obviously lends a certain justification both to the agnostic and to the mystic. It is important to understand how far that justification extends.

First, then, a word as to the limits of justifiable Agnosticism. Our conclusion warranted us in asserting that Reality must contain aspects which are not thought, and again must combine thought with these other aspects in a unity which is not itself merely intellectual. In other words, we had to confess that we cannot understand the concrete character of the Infinite Experience, or, to put it in a more homely way, we do not know how it would feel to be "God." And if this is Agnosticism, we clearly shall have to own that we too are agnostics. But our result gave us no ground for doubting our own general conviction as to the place which intellect and truth hold in the Absolute. On the other hand, it left us with every reason for trusting that conviction. For our conclusion that mere truth cannot be the same thing as ultimate Reality was itself based upon the principle that only harmonious individuality is finally real, and this is the very principle employed by the intellect itself whenever it judges one thought-construction relatively higher and truer than another.

Thus *our* Agnosticism, if it is to be called so, neither discredits our human estimate of the relative truth of different theories about the real, nor lends any support to the notion that "Knowledge is relative" in the sense that there may conceivably be no correspondence between Reality and the scheme of human knowledge as a whole. It is based not on the distrust of human reason, but upon the determination to trust that reason implicitly, and it claims, in declaring mere truth to fall short of Reality, to be expressing reason's own verdict upon itself. Hence it does not, like vulgar Agnosticism, leave us in the end in pure uncertainty as to the ultimate structure and upshot, so to say, of the world, but definitely holds that we have genuine and trustworthy knowledge of the type of that structure and the nature of its materials. And it is upon this positive knowledge, and not upon an uncritical appeal to unknown possibilities, that it rests its denial of the simple identity of Reality with thought itself. For all we know, says the common Agnosticism, our thought is sheer illusion, and therefore we must confess that we have in the end no notion what the reality of the world may be. Thought is not illusory, says our systematic

Idealism, and therefore its own witness that Reality is an individual whole of experience which is more than thought is a positive contribution to our knowledge. Between these two positions there may be a superficial resemblance, but there is an essential difference in principle.

So again with the mystical element in our result. In holding that all genuine individuality, finite or infinite,[1] involves a type of immediate felt unity which transcends reduction to the relational categories of thought and will, we may fairly be said to have reached a conclusion which, in a sense, is mystical. But our result is not Mysticism, if by Mysticism is meant a doctrine which seeks ultimate Reality in mere unanalysed immediate feeling as such. The results of intellectual and volitional construction have not been treated by us as illusory and as a sort of intellectual and moral mistake. On the other hand, we urged that the ultimate unity of the real must transcend, and not merely fall short of, the rational scheme of thought and will. And we consequently insisted that our result, so far as it is a mystical one, can only be justified by following out the constructions of the logical intellect and the ethical will to their final consequence, and showing that each of them itself demands completion in an individual Reality which includes and transcends both. To quote the admirable words of Dr. McTaggart: "A Mysticism which ignored the claims of the understanding would no doubt be doomed. None ever went about to break logic, but in the end logic broke him. But there is a Mysticism which starts from the standpoint of the understanding, and only departs from it in so far as that standpoint shows itself not to be ultimate, but to postulate something beyond itself. To transcend the lower is not to ignore it." And it is only in this sense that philosophy is justified in asserting "above all knowledge and volition one all-embracing unity, which is only not true, only not good, because all truth and all goodness are but shadows of its absolute perfection."[2]

---

[1] I say "finite or infinite" advisedly. The mystic's condemnation of the relational scheme as inadequate to express the full nature of the real, holds good just as much in application to actual finite experience as in application to the ultimate whole. We may say not only of "God," but of human persons, that they are much more than the "union of thought and will" as such. And in personal human love, no less than in the saint's "beatific vision" or the philosopher's "intellectual love of God," we have a type of experience which may for some psychological purposes be analysed into a combination of ideational and volitional processes, but emphatically does not, in its concrete existence, consist of a synthesis of actual ideas and actual volitions. See *ante*, p. 152.

[2] *Studies in Hegelian Cosmology*, p. 292.

§ 3. The reader who has persevered to the conclusion of this volume may perhaps, on laying it down, experience a certain feeling of dissatisfaction. Our investigations, it might be complained, have added nothing to our stock of scientific information about the contents of the world, and have supplied no fresh practical incentives towards the strenuous pursuit of an elevated moral or religious ideal. I must at once admit the justice of this hypothetical criticism, and dispute its relevancy. Quite apart from the defects due to personal shortcomings and confusions, it is inherent in the nature of metaphysical study that it can make no positive addition to our information, and can of itself supply no motives for practical endeavour. And the student who turns to our science as a substitute for empirical Physics or Psychology, or for practical morality, is bound to go away disappointed. The reason of this we have already had occasion to see. Metaphysics has to presuppose the general principles of the various sciences and the general forms of practical experience as the materials upon which it works. Its object as a study is not to add to or to modify these materials, but to afford some coherent and systematic satisfaction for the intellectual curiosity which we all feel at times as to the general nature of the whole to which these various materials belong, and the relative truth and clearness with which that general nature is expressed in the different departments of experience. Its aim is the organisation, not the enlargement of knowledge. Hence for the student whose interests lie more in the enlargement of human knowledge by the discovery of new facts and laws, than in its organisation into a coherent whole, Metaphysics is probably undesirable, or desirable only as a protection against the intrusion of unrecognised and uncriticised metaphysical assumptions into the domain of empirical service. And similarly for the practical man whose interests in life are predominantly ethical, the main, if not the sole, value of metaphysical study lies in its critical function of exposing false metaphysical assumptions, which, if acted upon, might impair the vigour of spontaneous moral effort.

But for those in whom the speculative desire to form some coherent conception of the scheme of things to which we belong as a whole is strong, Metaphysics has a higher importance. In such minds the impulse to reflect on the nature of existence as a whole, if debarred from systematic and thorough gratification, is certain to find its outlet in unsystematic and uncriticised imaginative construction. Metaphysics they will certainly have, and if not conscious and coherent, then unconscious and incoherent Metaphysics. The soul that is not at rest in itself without some "sight of that immortal sea which brought it hither," if hindered from beholding the object of its quest through the clear glass of rational reflection, will none the less seek to discern it amid the distorting hazes and mists of superstition. It is in such seekers after the Infinite that Metaphysics has its natural and proper followers, and for them the study is its own justification and its own reward. If a work like the present should prove of any help to such students, whether by offering positive suggestions which they can accept, or by assisting them to know definitely why they reject its conclusions, it will perhaps have achieved as much as its writer could reasonably expect.

Consult further :—F. H. Bradley, *Appearance and Reality*, chap. 27 ; J. E. McTaggart, *Studies in Hegelian Cosmology*, chap. 9.

INDEX

Absolute, meaning of, 53 ff.; general character of, 60 ff.; not unknowable, 71 ff.; not a "self," 343 ff.; is it a society? 100, 347 ff.; a spiritual individual, 98 ff.; not necessarily the same as "God," 399 ff.; not "union of thought and will," 409 ff.

Activity not identical with conation, 55; and causation, 169; empirical nature of, 189.

Agnosticism, 68, 69, 71, 72; how far justifiable, 412.

Appearance and Reality, connection between, 105 ff.

Aristotle, 6, 42, 97, 266, 361, 386.

Attention, selective, 55, 66, 80; "span" of, 226, 244.

Avenarius, 35, 45, 80, 121, 174, 298 ff. 315.

Baldwin, J. M., 206.

Berkeley, 26, 64 ff., 75, 184, 185, 201 ff.

Body, my own, as describable object, 282.

Body, my own, and others, 203 ff.

Body and Soul, theories of, 313 ff.; in what sense the same, 332.

Bosanquet, B., 19, 26, 164.

Bradley, F. H., 9, 11, 23, 26, 55, 67, 88, 90, 131, 146, 199, 227, 243, 259, 289, 318, 326, 335, 338, 355, 364, 370, 384, 411.

Causation, 165 ff.; cause not identical with ground, 166; causation a postulate, 167 ff.; popular as distinguished from scientific sense, 169; causation and the indefinite regress, 177 ff.; continuity of causation, 171 ff.; Immanent and Transeunt Causality, 183 ff.; psychophysical causation, 322 ff.

Causes, Plurality of, 180 ff.

Chance, "pure," meaning of, 231, 232; chance and "free-will," 378.

Change, 158–164.

Character and freedom, 374.

Choice and motives, 373.

Consciousness, a misleading term, 79.

Consequence (see Ground).

Continuity, nature of, 171 (see Causation); continuity of space and time, 244, 250.

Contradiction, principle of, 19 ff.

Cosmology Rational, nature of, 43-49, 192–197.

Couturat, L., 149, 260.

Dedekind, 116, 149, 171.

Degrees of Reality, 108 ff.

Descartes, 128, 185, 318, 400 ff.

Description, as scientific ideal, 174; in physical Science, 280 ff.; in Psychology, 308 ff.

Determinism, 370–376.

Discontinuity of teleological series, 311.

Distance in space and time, 250.

Ends in Nature, 272, 405, 406.

Energy, conservation of, 292; kinetic and non-kinetic, 291; doctrine of, and psychophysical interaction, 322 ff.

Epiphenomenalism, 317, 318–320.

Epistemology and Metaphysics, 16.

Evil, problem of, 391 ff., 395 ff.

Evolution, not identical with mere change, 267; implies real ends, 268 ff.; is of finite beings only, 274 ff.; implies real progress and degeneration, 275; originates new individuals, 276.

Experience, what, 23 ff., 33 ff.; "pure," 35, 54.

Feeling, 23 ff., 55; in the Absolute, 467 ff.

Freedom, meaning of, 359 ff.

Free-will, origins of belief in, 361 ff.

Geulincx, 184, 185, 186, 317.

Gibson, W. R. B., 288, 329, 366.

God, proofs of being of, 400 ff.

Ground and Consequence, meaning of principle of, 164, 165.

INDEX

Harmony, Pre-established, 187, 317.
Hegel, 40 ff., 42 ff., 391, 401.
Herbart, 39, 42, 68.
Hobhouse, L. T., 74, 137, 138, 199.
Hume, 29, 75, 133, 169, 172, 183, 400 ff.

Identity, Psychophysical, doctrine of, 102, 321, 331, 332.
Identity, a teleological concept, 335. (*See also* Unity of Thing).
Imitation, significance of, for personality, 206.
Immanent Causality, 183 ff.
Immediacy, 32.
"Immortality," 354 ff.
Indeterminism, 376-379.
Individuality, nature of, 57, 98 ff.; degrees of, 109 ff.; infinite and finite, 115 ff.
Infinite Regress, 148 ff., 156 ; in space and time, 255 ff., 259 ; in causal relation, 177.
Infinity, meaning of, 116.
Interaction, Psychophysical, 317, 329-331.
Introjection, meaning of, 81 ; origin of, 81, 299 ff. ; justification of, 301 ff.

James, W., 53, 91, 318, 370, 382, 390, 400.

Kant, 11, 24, 39, 43, 69, 134, 188, 242 ff., 259, 359, 366, 387, 400 ff.

Law, meaning of, 218 ff.
Laws in Nature, 196, 229.
Leibnitz, 68, 82, 86, 91 ff., 117, 187 ff., 317, 366, 401, 404.
Locke, 128, 136, 200, 318, 353, 365, 366.
Lotze, 41, 42, 133, 224, 289.

Mach, E., 174, 175, 192, 223, 228, 283, 290.
Machine, nature of a, 236, 237.
McTaggart, J. E., 345, 357, 391, 398, 413.
Malebranche, 184, 185, 317.
Mass, definition of, 289 ; conservation of, 290 ; a relative concept, 290, 291.
Matter, meaning of, 198 ff.
Mechanical view of Nature, 233 ff., 237 ff., 283 ff.; postulates of, 284, 292 ff.
Mechanism, meaning of, 196, 237 ff.
Method of Metaphysics, 38 ff.
Mill, J. S., 24, 180 ff., 370.

Monadism, 86, 91, 94.
Monism, 85.
Münsterberg, H., 45, 67, 198, 283, 303 ff., 315, 318, 321, 324, 329.
Mysticism, 14, 33, 153 ; in what sense justifiable, 413.

Necessity and causal relation, 183.
Newton, 128, 200.
Nietzsche, 276.
Number-series, 151 ff., 248-250, 259.

Occasionalism, 184, 317.
Ontology, character of, 42.
Order, a teleological concept, 118 ; order in space and time, 251.
Organism, nature of a, 96.

Parallelism, Psychophysical, 317, 320-329.
Pearson, K., 75, 290.
Phenomenalism, 10, 136.
Physical order, nature of the, 194 ff., 198, 208, 282.
Plato, 3, 55, 77, 95, 276, 366, 386, 393, 398, 409.
Pleasure-pain, 55, 344.
Plotinus, 398.
Pluralism, 86 ff.
Position not a principle of individuation, 58 ; relativity of, 253.
Pragmatism, 317.
Prediction in science, 219 ff.
Progress not infinite, 387-389.
Psychical order, nature of the, 298 ff.
Psychology, character of, as a science, 296 ff.
Psychology and Physiology, 303 ff.
Psychology, Rational, nature of, 43 ff.
Purpose, nature of, 55 ff.

Qualities, primary and secondary, 128 ff.
Quality and relation, 140 ff.
Quality and substance, 128 ff.
Quality, spatial and temporal, 244.

Rashdall, H., 347, 393, 400.
Realism, Agnostic, 68, 71, 72 ; Dogmatic, 69, 72-75.
Relation and quality, 140 ff.
Relations and relatedness, 155.
Religion, metaphysical presuppositions of, 389 ff.
Responsibility and the self, 335.
Royce, J., 13, 33, 51, 56, 76, 116, 145, 148 ff., 206, 226, 239, 263, 270, 277, 307, 398.
Russell, B., 36, 58, 91, 142, 189, 243, 250, 253, 404.

INDEX

Self, 98, 107; nature of, 334-340; a teleological concept, 335; temporal character of, 341, 342.
Self-consciousness, genuine and fictitious, 79.
Sidgwick, H., 130, 359, 370.
Space, perceptual, 243-245; conceptual genesis of, 245-249; infinity of, 247; divisibility of, 248; continuity of, 248, 250; homogeneity of, 251; relativity of, 251; is it one or many? 253, 257; is not ultimate, 254-257; antinomies of, 259 ff.; of what is it phenomenal? 260.
Spencer, H., 40, 68.
Spinoza, 62, 101 ff., 318, 399, 411.
Stout, G. F., 33, 67, 135, 154 ff., 208, 247, 318, 324, 332, 378.
Subjectivism, what, 75; fallacy of, 76-81, 204 ff.
Substance, concept of, 128 ff.; and quality, 128-140.
Sufficient Reason, principle of, 164.

Teleological description not impossible, 309.
Teleological series, discontinuity of, 311.

Teleology, nature of, 55, 99, 125, 287, 371 ff.; in Psychology, 305 ff.; in Biology, 308; and Psychophysical Parallelism, 326 ff.
Thought and the Absolute, 61; not ultimate, 409.
Time, perceptual, 243-245; conceptual, genesis of, 245-249; infinity of, 247; divisibility of, 248; continuity of, 248, 250; homogeneity of, 251; relativity of, 251; is it one or many? 253, 257; not ultimate, 254-257; antinomies of, 259 ff.; of what is it phenomenal? 262; time and the self, 341, 344.
Truth, degrees of, 214.

Uniformities, statistical, 220 ff.
Uniformity in physical nature, 222, 227.
Unity of things teleological, 123-128.

Ward, J., 45, 64, 174, 225, 228, 289 318, 324, 326-328.
Whole and Part, category of, 96.
Will, nature of, 61, 118; not ultimate, 410.